Britain, Kenya and the Cold War

BRITAIN, KENYA AND THE COLD WAR:

Imperial Defence, Colonial Security and Decolonisation

David A. Percox

TAURIS ACADEMIC STUDIES
LONDON • NEW YORK

Published in 2004 by Tauris Academic Studies, an imprint of

I.B. Tauris & Co Ltd
6 Salem Road, London W2 4BU

175 Fifth Avenue, New York NY 10010
www.ibtauris.com

In the United States of America and in Canada distributed by Palgrave Macmillan, a division of St Martins Press, 175 Fifth Avenue, New York NY 10010

International Library of African Studies 13

ISBN 1 85043 460 3
EAN 978 1 85043 460 3

A full CIP record for this book is available from the British Library

A full CIP record for this book is available from the Library of Congress

Library of Congress catalog card: available

Printed and bound in Great Britain by TJ International Ltd, Padstow, Cornwall from camera-ready copy supplied by the author

Contents

Acknowledgements

I am grateful to the Research Committee of the Department of History in the University of Nottingham for providing the opportunity and funding to undertake this study. The most important of my debts of gratitude is to my erstwhile research supervisor, Prof Chris Wrigley, whose friendly advice, encouragement, and patience have made this project less arduous than it might have been. It has been a privilege to conduct most of this study under the stewardship of Professor Dick Geary, then Head of Department. Dr Stuart Thompstone provided valued friendship and frequent, refreshing reminders of the human face of academia. This was augmented by my friends and colleagues in the postgraduate office: Dr Jeannie Alderdice, Dr Paul Bracken, Dr Simon Constantine, Paul Evans, Peter Graham, Dr David Green, Chan Young Park, Dr Dave Pomphret, Kevin Sorrentino, Dr Claire Taylor, and Dr Matt Worley. Also, I should like to thank all at Nottingham who provided friendly ears and advice and who, although perhaps omitted nominally here, are never far from my thoughts.

I must thank Dr David Throup and Professor Charles Townshend who, as my special subject teachers during my undergraduate days at Keele, inspired me to begin to 'follow in the footsteps' which led to this book. Also, I should like to thank Professor John MacKenzie who, as my MA dissertation supervisor at Lancaster, provided all the advice and encouragement necessary to prepare me for what followed. I am equally grateful to Dr David Anderson, in the University of Oxford and Dr John Lonsdale, Fellow of Trinity College, Cambridge, for advice and encouragement while I 'ploughed the lonely furrow'.

I acknowledge Crown Copyright for materials consulted at the Public Record Office, Kew, and am grateful to the staff there for their efficient and friendly fulfilment of my requests. I am also grateful to the Trustees and staff of the Bodleian and Rhodes House Libraries, Oxford, the Imperial War Museum, and the National Army Museum, London.

Special thanks to and fond memories of the late Clive and Thelma Bousfield, not only for providing me with a 'home from home' during the research stint in London, but also for introducing me to the delights of ballet and opera. I also enjoyed the hospitality of Ewan Bingham, whose friendship and humanity were a perfect complement to the delightful suburbs of South East London. My research in Oxford was made all the more pleasurable by the convivial company of Debi Mauger and Terry McCabe, who opened their doors to me on more than one occasion.

I should also like to thank Paul Wilson, of Oriental and African Books, Shrewsbury and Peter Devitt in the RAF Museum, London, for invaluable bibliographical assistance and for friendship and kind words of encouragement. I am also grateful to Atul Bali, Dr Pete Cain, Mike Cassidy,

Tim Farrow, Rob and Violetta Halliday, Glyn and Emma Harris, Barry and Louise Hudson, Charlie Hughes, Julie Lea, Dr Spencer Mawby, Dave and Sally McCann, Matt Price, Sabhita Raju, Mark and Cari Regan, Mandy Robbins, Stuart and Linda Robertson, Shalini Sharma, and Dr Ben Williams and, of course, my two brothers, Derek and John, sister-in-law Eira and my parents, Dave and Gill.

Nick Benefield, David Morgan, Susie Rose and Kevin Rizak deserve special mention for reasons only they can know.

Thanks, of course, to Clare and all at IB Tauris for help, patience and understanding, and special thanks to Chris Fritsch for timely assistance with indexing.

Finally, in the hope that our future will be as fulfilling, interesting and loving as our past, I dedicate this book to Lina.

The greatest problem of all was Kenya. I inherited from Iain Macleod a strong emotional involvement in this country, which was, and I think still remains, the outstanding example of British influence in Africa.
Reginald Maudling, *Memoirs* (1978).

We should seek to achieve the orderly transfer of power to an African-dominated Government commanding the widest possible support in the country and having as its objective the development of Kenya as a modern democratic state; our tactics ... should be directed towards this end and we should take every opportunity to bring about any new political alignment which offers a sound prospect of our attaining our ultimate objective.
Reginald Maudling, 'Kenya Constitutional Conference', 30 January 1962.

ABBREVIATIONS AND ACRONYMS

ADC	Aide-de-Camp
A/DMO	Adjutant to the Director of Military Operations
AEM	African Elected Member (of Legislative Council)
ANF	Atlantic Nuclear Force
ANZAM	Australia, New Zealand and Malaya
A(O)C	Africa (Official) Committee
BATT	British Army Training Team
BFAP	British Forces Arabian Peninsula
BLFK	British Land Forces Kenya
BTK	British Troops Kenya
CDS	Chief(s) of the Defence Staff
CEC	Colony Emergency Committee
CID	Criminal Investigation Department
CIGS	Chief of the Imperial General Staff
C-in-C	Commander-in-Chief
CNC	Chief Native Commissioner
CO	Colonial Office
COMCAN	Commonwealth Communications Army Network (Signals Squadron)
COS	Chief(s) of Staff
CPC	Colonial Policy Committee
CRO	Commonwealth Relations Office
DC	District Commissioner
DCIGS	Deputy Chief of the Imperial General Staff
DDO	Deputy Director of Operations
DDSD	Deputy Director of Staff Duties (War Office)
DFP	Director(ate) of Forward Planning (MoD)
DIS	Director of Intelligence and Security
DMI	Director of Military Intelligence
DMO	Director of Military Operations
DOPC	Defence and Oversea Policy Committee
DSC	District Security Committee
DSD	Director of Staff Duties
EAC	East Africa Command
EADC	East Africa Defence Committee
EADWC	East Africa Defence Working Committee
EAF	East African Forces
EAHC	East Africa High Commission
EALF	East African Land Forces
EALFO	East African Land Forces Organisation
ECAC	Executive Committee of the Army Council

ABBREVIATIONS

ECS	Estimates Customer Status
EEMO	European Elected Members' Organisation
ERE	Extra-Regimental Engagement
GHQ	General Headquarters
GOC	General Officer Commanding
GSO	General Staff Officer
GSU	General Service Unit
HAA	Heavy Anti-Aircraft (Battery)
HCD	House of Commons Debates
HMG	Her/His Majesty's Government
HQ	Headquarters
INT	Intelligence
IWM	Imperial War Museum, Lambeth, London
ISWC	Internal Security Working Committee
JIC	Joint Intelligence Committee
JOC	Joint Operations Committee
JPS	Joint Planning Staff
KAR	King's/Kenya African Rifles
KADU	Kenya African Democratic Union
KANU	Kenya African National Union
KAU	Kenya African Union
KEM	Kikuyu, Embu, Meru
KIC	Kenya Intelligence Committee
KISA	Kikuyu Independent Schools Association
KKEA	Kikuyu Karinga Education Association
KKM	Kiama Kia Muingi (Council/Society of the People)
KLFA	Kenya Land Freedom Army
KNA	Kenya National Archives, Nairobi
KPR	Kenya Police Reserve
KR	Kenya Regiment/Kenya Rifles
KSLI	King's Shropshire Light Infantry
LCCPLO	Legislative Council Committee for the Preservation of Law and Order
LF	Lancashire Fusiliers
LFA	Land Freedom Army
LTSG	Long Term Study Group (of the DOPC)
MD	Minister for Defence (Kenya)
MEC	Middle East Command
MELF	Middle East Land Forces
MGA	Major-General in charge of Administration
MLC	Member of Legislative Council
MLF	Multi-Lateral Force
MLO	Member for Law and Order

MoD	Ministry of Defence
NAM	National Army Museum, Chelsea, London
NKG	New Kenya Group
NKP	New Kenya Party
OAG	Officer Administering the Government (of ...)
PC	Provincial Commissioner
PPS	Parliamentary Private Secretary/Preservation of Public Security
PREM	Prime Minister's Office
PRO	Public Record Office, Kew, London
QMG	Quartermaster-General
RAF	Royal Air Force
REAN	Royal East African Navy
RF	Royal Fusiliers
RHL	Rhodes House Library, Oxford
RM	Royal Marines
SC	Security Council (previously the War Council)
SLO	Security Liaison Officer (MI5)
T	Treasury
TANU	Tanganyika African National Union
UAR	United Arab Republic
VCDS	Vice Chief of the Defence Staff
VCIGS	Vice Chief of the Imperial General Staff
VQMG	Vice-Quartermaster-General
WC	War Council
WD	War Department (War Office)
WO	War Office

INTRODUCTION

British Defence, Colonial Internal Security and Decolonisation in Kenya, 1945–65

This book has two main aims. First, it seeks to bridge a significant gap in the current literature on post-war British defence and internal security policy in Kenya. The research that underpins this study was motivated by the key question: why does existing scholarship fail to consider in detail Kenya's place in British overseas defence policy, and is this neglect justified? The same can be asked of the relative lack of attention paid to internal security in Kenya prior to the declaration of the State of Emergency in October 1952 and, equally, following Britain's apparent military victory over Mau Mau in late 1956.[1] In surveying the defence and internal security aspects of British colonial policy in Kenya in the broad context of the 1945-65 period, the narrative account therefore attempts not only to fill a gap in the current historiography, but also provides the basis for considering whether or not the subject in fact warrants this earlier neglect.

In addressing this first aim, the book also demonstrates that political decolonisation in Kenya and British defence priorities and internal security policy were far more intricately connected than previous studies suggest, and were not confined simply to the Emergency years (1952-60). This study therefore provides a hitherto largely neglected, but important, backdrop to British political decision-making on Kenya during the post-war period, and in doing so contributes to a more complete understanding of British decolonisation.

The decision was taken to examine the evolution of defence and internal security policy between 1945 and 1965 in order to assess the various political developments in Kenya and responses to them in their post-war, thus Cold War, context. In taking this broad chronological approach, this study argues that British decolonisation in Kenya did not follow a pre-planned pattern; nor did it amount to a radical and rapid policy reversal, as such. Rather, when viewed from the defence and internal security perspectives, it can be seen that in responding to nationalist pressures and fears of a post-Mau Mau Kenyan civil war, and ultimately transferring power to an African majority government, Britain reacted in a calculated and pragmatic manner. The former suzerain was thereby able to enjoy a large degree of continuity in its aims and 'vital' interests even beyond Kenya's independence.

Historiography

Given that a principal aim of this study is to consider a hitherto largely neglected aspect of British decolonisation, it is pointless to simply catalogue all of the current works which might conceivably include more detail on post-war British defence and colonial internal security in Kenya. Suffice it to say that previous studies comprise of several categories which, for simplicity, will be surveyed selectively, implying neither any ranking nor any relative importance of each particular genre.

Understandably, Autobiographies (or memoirs) and Biographies of British decision-makers and key participants, that cover varying careers which spanned many years, tend to focus on 'public' political events rather than the necessarily covert defence and internal security deliberations which frequently underpinned them. Of course, the contentious issue of 'national security' (or 'public interest') dictates that some degree of government censorship is often imposed on such publications.[2] Nevertheless, autobiographies tend to be less informative than they could be and, for the most part, those consulted for this study provided few, if any, clues as to what might be gleaned about British defence and internal security policy in Kenya beyond the confines of 1952-6.[3] The same can be said of the handful of auto/biographies by/about key African nationalists.[4] In both cases, where accounts by participants or biographies have a bearing on this book, relevant citations can be found in the main text. For the purposes of this study, however, it should be stressed from the outset that most autobiographies and biographies of key participants tend to concentrate on the Mau Mau Emergency and surrounding political developments, if at all.[5]

For example, Lord Butler, the former Foreign Secretary (Oct. 1963-64), refers in his memoirs to his erstwhile Colonial Office colleagues Oliver Lyttelton and Reginald Maudling (although not Alan Lennox-Boyd) in the British political context, yet provides not even a mention of Kenya.[6] Maudling himself, while giving a fair indication of the political tensions in Kenya during his time in office, suggests in a rather self-laudatory manner that a great deal more was achieved in the February 1962 constitutional conference than detailed consideration of subsequent events and British concerns suggests.[7]

Studies of Imperialism and Decolonisation suffer even more than autobiographies and biographies from the necessity to convey information in as accessible and concise a manner as possible, and focus on political events and their socio-economic background.[8] Again, references to Mau Mau excepted, defence and internal security is largely ignored.[9] This is especially the case with introductory surveys.[10] The same is true of the multitude of specialist studies of Mau Mau and Political Development in Kenya which again, where relevant, are cited in the main book text.[11]

The few exceptions to this rule, including studies of British Defence Policy which refer to Kenya's strategic significance only in passing, rely almost exclusively upon Phillip Darby's pioneering, if largely non-primary source-based, study of Britain's 'east of Suez role' (1947-68).[12] Even the most recent primary source-based study of the transfer of power in Kenya largely dismisses strategic issues.[13] This general failure to take seriously Kenya's strategic significance becomes all the more apparent upon reading Clayton's essay on British military relations with the African members of the post-independence Commonwealth.[14]

Naturally, previous studies of British defence policy, if they consider Kenya at all, do so in the broader context of post-war Middle East Strategy, but only in passing, and only until 1956.[15] These important works do, however, provide invaluable background as well as a clear indication as to the early stage at which British defence planners began to think of Kenya in post-war geo-strategic terms. Kent's impressive documentary reader is particularly useful in this regard, as are the extensive collections edited by Goldsworthy and Hyam, respectively, under the auspices of the *British Documents on the End of Empire* project (BDEEP).[16] Yet, all such studies still fail to consider the effects of broader British defence priorities in Kenya, and largely ignore events from 1957 onwards.

Military and Regimental Histories, by definition, also concentrate on the operational phase of the Mau Mau Emergency, while the dozen-plus so-called Mau Mau Memoirs, again by definition, tell us little about British defence and internal security beyond the confines of 1952-6.[17]

With regard to Kenya, current studies of British Intelligence and Covert Operations, and those which deal with what might arguably be called Internal Security, including studies of Policing, tend either to be far too generalised, or to share the general fascination with the Mau Mau Emergency and subsequent political developments.[18] As a result, such studies can be loosely defined under the rubric of British Counter-Insurgency, and also demonstrate the common misconception that, following military victory over Mau Mau, the transfer of power in Kenya amounted simply to a more or less complicated series of administrative and constitutional negotiations. Newsinger and Paget go slightly further than most in revealing that after the Mau Mau Emergency Kikuyu militants continued to stockpile weapons and gather in the forests, and that the threat of further violence strengthened the nationalists' hands.[19] References to post-Mau Mau subversive movements, particularly *Kiama Kia Muingi* (KKM) and the Kenya Land Freedom Army (KLFA), but not much, if any, detail on the response to either, can be found in Füredi, Kanogo, and Rosberg and Nottingham.[20]

Three important works on British intelligence, by Aldrich, Bloch and Fitzgerald, and Heather, respectively, share many of the above failings with regard to Kenya.[21] In four pages devoted to British Cold War intelligence operations in Africa, Aldrich's impressive study makes no mention of Kenya, except to tell us that ex-Kenya Special Branch head, John Prendergast, moved on to Cyprus, Hong Kong, and Aden.[22] As with most studies of British counter-insurgency and intelligence in Kenya, Heather's thesis lacks any detailed consideration beyond 1956. While Bloch and Fitzgerald's study goes much further than most in outlining the span of British covert operations in Kenya from 1945 to beyond independence, and provides potentially useful background information, it lacks reference to primary sources other than newspapers and confidential interviews, and is written in 'journalese', perhaps explaining its absence from the bibliographies of many works on related subjects.

Sources

As well as referring to current secondary literature and several unpublished scholarly works, this study has relied mainly on British government documents in the Public Record Office, Kew (PRO). The perspective gained from the PRO documents has been supplemented by the private papers of participants 'on the ground', held at Rhodes House Library, Oxford (RHL), particularly the Oxford Development Records Project (ODRP) collection. Some of the papers of General Sir George Erskine (GOC, EAC, June 1953-May 1955), in the Imperial War Museum, London, were also useful. Unfortunately, the same cannot be said of the Lord Harding of Petherton (CIGS, Nov. 1952-Sept. 1955) and Field Marshal Sir Gerald Templer (CIGS, Sept. 1955-Sept. 1958) papers in the National Army Museum, London, because they relate mainly to personal or regimental matters and the experience of each in Cyprus and Malaya, respectively.

While all of the key military and political figures for the bulk of the period under investigation have long since passed away, it had been hoped that useful information could have been gleaned from interviews with surviving ex-Colonial Servants.[23] However, undertakings provided by two such individuals, who both had involvement in the intelligence side of the work of the Kenya administration during the latter stages of decolonisation, were never honoured, in one case because of ill health.[24] Subsequent enquiries, including an attempt to cast the net more widely among the Corona Club, received no reply. Given this reticence, anonymity must be respected.

With regard to the PRO, it hardly needs reiterating that time restrictions and the shear volume of potentially useful material available precluded consultation of all such documents in their entirety. Rather, a selective process was necessary, and involved mainly examination of documents relating to defence and internal security in Kenya which had clearly been ignored by previous studies, as well as revisiting 'political' documents consulted by others in order to assess the relative importance of defence and security issues during everyday political discourse. For example, the extensive

Cabinet (CAB) and Prime Minister's Office (PREM) papers provide a general overview of policy-making in a particular subject area, thus useful pointers for detailed scrutiny of specialised departmental files, and reveal far more about the defence and security aspects of decolonisation in Kenya than previous studies suggest. It must be stated, however, that the obvious choice for consultation, the records of the Colonial Office Intelligence and Security Department (CO 1035), are not only still closed to the public and scholars alike, but at the last time of inspection appeared to have had all trace of their existence removed from the PRO. This suggests that some of the evidence for Britain's often pragmatic, and occasionally cynical, approach to its colonies with regard to defence and security matters in this book cuts closer to the bone of the projected image of a magnanimously decolonising, nation-building former suzerain than some in Whitehall might care to admit. Equally, this could also demonstrate that some British colonial security decisions taken and implemented between the 1940s and 1960s, which would be open to inspection ordinarily, might still have a bearing on current policy in the 'post-imperial age'. It is hard to believe, however, that either current national security, or the unlikely survival of the majority of Britain's colonial intelligence and security officials from the 1940s onwards, warrants this continued closure.

Naturally, this study has benefited from the voluminous records of the Colonial Office East Africa Department (CO 822), as well as those of the Colonial Office Defence Department (CO 968), the Ministry of Defence (DEFE), and the War Office (WO). Given the inexorable link between government policy and finances, it remains a surprise that current historical scholarship still largely ignores the records of the Treasury. During the course of research for this book, at least one document (in T 225/2211), while unavailable elsewhere, was located in this way. One notable omission from this book is any reference to the records of the Colonial Office Police Department (CO 1037). Perusal of this series revealed quickly that, for the purposes of this study, little of substance could be gleaned that was not already in the East Africa Department files (CO 822) related to internal security matters. Besides, post-war colonial policing in Anglophone Africa generally has already been the subject of detailed scholarly analysis,[25] and policing in Kenya still warrants a comprehensive primary source-based study in its own right.[26]

Lastly, except for the occasional pertinent reference, government publications, such as Command Papers, have been largely ignored. This decision was taken, quite deliberately, because such publications tend, by there very nature, to perform as much a multi-faceted propaganda and public relations function as fulfilling any quasi-legal requirements. Clearly, given the nature of this study, what is of most interest is the secretive decision-making process, rather than what is presented for public consumption. Besides, any such documents, like defence white papers, for example, are more than adequately discussed in the existing secondary literature, and cited in the book as necessary.

Structure

In order to illustrate the post-war evolution of British defence and internal security policy in Kenya in relation to changing economic and political circumstances in Africa and elsewhere, this book is presented in a straightforward narrative form. The study makes no pretence of detailed analysis of economic and political issues, which are extensively surveyed by existing scholarship. Rather, it relates British defence and internal security planning and practice to key stages in, and concerns over, Kenya's rapidly changing socio-economic and political circumstances, and the developments intended to address them, or the lack thereof.

Chapter One ('Defence and Internal Security, 1945-52') places British defence and internal security planning in Kenya in its immediate post-war context. As was the case elsewhere in the Empire, between 1945 and 1950, Britain steadily altered its defensive focus in East Africa from a war footing towards contingency plans to cater for the escalating Cold War. While Kenya's strategic significance could be said to have been minimal, it was by no means non-existent. Given the apparent potential for East Africa's natural and manpower resources to be employed in aid of the severely hamstrung post-war British economy, Britain's main concern during this period was to maintain the region's internal security, and to ensure that communism did not take root. In addition to their internal security role, locally recruited African troops constituted a potential reserve for Egypt in the event of global war. While financial stringency ensured that socio-economic and political advances in Kenya were never quite adequate to keep abreast of nationalist aspirations and generally held African grievances, the largely unrepresentative colonial government also found it increasingly difficult to deal with the consequent widespread increases in crime and anti-colonial militancy. It is telling that, from late 1949 onwards, the Kenya government redoubled its efforts to plan for a possible State of Emergency.

Given the extensive literature on the military and so-called 'hearts and minds' aspects of the Mau Mau Emergency, Chapter Two ('British Counter-Insurgency in Kenya, 1952-6') provides neither an encyclopaedic nor an exhaustive account. Rather, it seeks to demonstrate the reactionary nature of British Counter-Insurgency as opposed to the common, and erroneous, view that the campaign constituted a progressive precursor to eventual decolonisation. Clearly, British efforts to repress Mau Mau were aimed at retaining, rather than relinquishing control.

Chapter Three ('East Africa, East of Suez, 1956-7') confirms that, in planning to station elements of the UK Strategic Reserve 'permanently' in

Kenya, Britain was less concerned with African political sensibilities than with addressing broader overseas interests following the evacuation from Suez in late 1956. With militant anti-colonial nationalism apparently brought to heel by superior firepower, force of numbers, and ever-sophisticated tactics, Kenya's enhanced strategic significance ensured that Britain had no intention of abandoning the colony. Political concessions to African nationalism during this period were presented as demonstrating Britain's commitment to developing Kenya in an orderly and rational manner. The aim, however, was to delay rather than to accelerate the transfer of power.

The intricate connection between Britain's fitful approach to political development and its strategic interests is considered in Chapter Four ('East Africa, East of Suez II, 1957-9'). Clearly, defence interests, and the administrative and financial minutiae involved in their realisation, had a considerable bearing on Britain's decision to avoid making any meaningful statements about Kenya's ultimate future. Indeed, the presence of a permanent garrison of British troops, it was thought, would in itself act as a 'stabilising influence in the background to the colony's political life'. In this light, all of the political concessions made to African nationalism until 1959, if not later, can be seen as a holding operation, intended to demonstrate the spirit, if not the substance, of British *bona fides*.

However, in restricting concessions to African nationalism to a slow, if reasonably steady trickle, in the hope of maintaining control under the guise of progress, Britain's position in Kenya became increasingly precarious. Chapter Five ('Internal Security and Decolonisation, 1956-9') assesses the apparent return to 'normality' following the military defeat of Mau Mau and the, albeit temporary, withdrawal of most British troops. Far from enjoying the newfound stability theoretically engendered by the apparently successful counter-insurgency campaign, Britain now had to deal with the contradictions inherent in its divisive and piecemeal political and socio-economic reforms. While a return to the scale of violence encompassed by Mau Mau was always thought to be unlikely, the resurgence of subversive activity, combined with nationalist agitation and threats of, if not actual, civil disobedience and constant industrial disputes, to stretch colonial Kenya's chronically undermanned security forces to the limit. Only when the veil of constitutional progress was shredded by the Africans' boycott of Legislative Council from November 1958, were the colonial authorities compelled to accede to African demands for a constitutional conference. Yet, the ethnically, and to some extent ideologically, fragmented nature of African politics in Kenya, which at one time must certainly have suited the British, now threatened to undermine the general policy of promoting the stable and 'moderate' polity deemed so essential to Britain's 'vital interests'. Britain therefore had no choice other than to tighten its control over Kenya's security forces while at the same time performing a slight of hand to ensure that adequate security legislation existed to effect maximum control after the withdrawal of Emergency Regulations. Indeed, the ultimate ending of the State of Emergency, in January 1960, depended as much on the completion of this replacement legislation as it did on meeting the timetable for the first (Kenya) Lancaster House conference.

Chapter Six ('Internal Security and Decolonisation II, 1959-65') shows how increasingly desperate the British became as they tried to guide the pace and nature of political developments in Kenya towards a moderate, pro-Western outcome. As ethnic, socio-economic, and personal political rivalries, and continued subversion threatened increasingly to draw Kenya into a civil war, Britain juggled with political compromise after political compromise, and hoped that there would be no recourse to the use of the troops that were frequently placed on standby to deal with such an eventuality. When, at last, the British felt assured that in Jomo Kenyatta's Kenya African National Union (KANU) they had finally found a 'moderate' and benevolently neutral successor government, they pulled out all of the stops to bolster Kenya's internal security and secure that regime in power. As ever, Britain's magnanimity came at a price.

In Chapter Seven ('Defence and Decolonisation, 1959-65') it is shown how, when the political and security situation in Kenya dictated that the best means of safeguarding 'vital interests' were, in the end, to grant independence, Britain ensured that in exchange for its assistance in maintaining the rehabilitated Kenyatta in office, it would continue to enjoy albeit minimal, if by no means insignificant, defence facilities. More importantly, the chapter demonstrates that achieving these ends was as much a priority as acquiescing to nationalist demands in order to bring about the kind of moderate government upon which Britain's strategic requirements depended. Indeed, Britain even tailored these requirements so that they would be politically acceptable to African ministers, thus less likely to jeopardise Kenyatta's position and, especially important from the British perspective, more likely to prolong the longevity of the post-independence defence agreement. With over flying and staging rights, and access to army training and recreation and naval dockyard facilities secured, the Wilson administration continued its predecessor's policy. Plans existed to intervene militarily to maintain Kenyatta in office, if necessary, while Britain trained his bodyguard, and maintained significant influence by training and equipping the Kenya armed forces. This continuity in policy persisted up to and beyond the date when this study closes, in 1965, before the onset of the financial crises which bought about Britain's withdrawal from east of Suez. Nevertheless, as a result of this shrewd approach to post-independence defence and internal security policy, Britain retained some military presence in Kenya until at least 1976, some ten years after ejection from Aden and four to five years after the large scale, if by no means complete, withdrawal from the Middle and Far East.

Notes

1. The only exceptions are my 'British Counter-Insurgency in Kenya, 1952-56: Extension of Internal Security Policy or Prelude to Decolonisation?', *Small Wars and Insurgencies*, 9/3 (Winter 1998), pp. 46-101, derived largely from Chapter Two of this book and the earlier 'The British Campaign in Kenya, 1952-1956: The Development of Counter-Insurgency Policy', MA dissertation, University of Lancaster, 1996, and 'Internal Security and Decolonization in Kenya, 1956-63', *Journal of Imperial and Commonwealth History*, 29/1 (Jan. 2001), pp. 92-116, derived from Chapters Five and Six.

2. For example, see the cabinet discussion on the publication of Lord Hankey's memoirs in: CAB 128/34, CC (60) 64th Meeting, Item 10, 'Lord Hankey's Memoirs', 15 Dec. 1960. More recently, of course, there was the farcical episode of the Thatcher government's banning the publication of the autobiography of the former Assistant Director of MI5, Peter Wright, which then became widely available after publication in Australia: Peter Wright, *Spy Catcher: The Candid Autobiography of a Senior Intelligence Officer* (Richmond, Victoria: William Heinemann Australia, 1987). See also: John D. Baxter, *State Security, Privacy and Information* (Hemel Hempstead: Harvester Wheatsheaf, 1990), pp. 17, 29, 36, 57, 58, 74, 82, 85-91, 145; Laurence Lustgarten and Ian Leigh, *In from the Cold: National Security and Parliamentary Democracy* (Oxford: Clarendon Press, 1994), pp. 237, 258-9, 279-85.

3. Two exceptions, which allude to the importance of defence and internal security issues to Lennox-Boyd's decision to hold the January 1959 Chequers conference on future policy in East Africa, are: Sir Michael Blundell, *So Rough a Wind: The Kenya Memoirs of Sir Michael Blundell* (London: Weidenfeld & Nicolson, 1964), pp. 261-2; Charles Douglas-Home, *Evelyn Baring: The Last Proconsul* (London: Collins, 1978), pp. 282-4.

4. J.M. Kariuki, *Mau Mau Detainee* (Harmondsworth: Penguin, 1964 [1963]); Malcolm MacDonald, *Titans and Others* (London: Collins, 1972), pp. 239-80; Tom Mboya, *Freedom and After* (London: Andre Deutsch, 1963); Jeremy Murray-Brown, *Kenyatta* (London: Fontana, 1974 [1972]); Oginga Odinga, *Not Yet Uhuru: an Autobiography* (London: Heinemann, 1969 [1967]).

5. Martin Gilbert, *'Never Despair': Winston S. Churchill 1945-1965* (London: Heinemann, 1988), pp. 803-4.

6. Lord Butler, *The Art of the Possible: the Memoirs of Lord Butler* (London: Hamish Hamilton, 1971), pp. 125, 127, 135, 140, 143, 145, 148, 156, 159, 160, 223, 233, 236, 239, 240, 241, 246, 248, 249.

7. Reginald Maudling, *Memoirs* (London: Sidgwick & Jackson, 1978), pp. 90, 92-6.

8. See, for example: John Hatch, *A History of Postwar Africa* (New York: Praeger, 1970 [1965]), passim.; Denis Judd, *Empire: The British Imperial Experience from 1765 to the Present* (London: Harper Collins, 1996), passim.; and Bernard Porter, *The Lion's Share: A Short History of British Imperialism, 1850-1970* (London, New York: Longman, 1975), passim.

9. Again, for example: A.N. Porter and A.J. Stockwell (eds.), *British Imperial Policy and Decolonization, 1938-64* Two Volumes (London: Macmillan, 1989, 1987), passim.

10. For example: Franz Ansprenger, *The Dissolution of the Colonial Empires* (London, New York: Routledge, 1989), pp. 69, 135, 173, 177, 197-201, 204; Raymond F. Betts, *Decolonization* (London: Routledge, 1998), pp. 2, 3, 8, 32, 33-5, 44, 49, 50, 56, 59; David Birmingham, *The Decolonization of Africa* (London: UCL Press, 1995), pp. 5, 6, 21, 39, 43-6, 47, 50, 52, 55, 79, 95; J.D. Hargreaves, *Decolonization in Africa* (London, New York: Longman, 1988), pp. 10, 18, 22, 38, 51, 53, 62, 71, 74, 89, 129-30, 160, 163, 164-5, 167, 186, 193-6, 210; R.F. Holland, *European Decolonization 1918-1981: an Introductory Survey* (London: Macmillan, 1985), pp. 144-9, 237-9, 240-8; Miles Kahler, *Decolonization in Britain and France: the Domestic Consequences of International Relations* (Guildford: Princeton University Press, 1984), pp. 4, 144-5, 246, 256, 298-9, 303-5, 313, 345-7, 353, 359.

11. For example: Wunyabari O. Maloba, *Mau Mau and Kenya: An Analysis of a Peasant Revolt* (London: James Currey, 1998 [1993]), passim.

12. Michael Carver, *Tightrope Walking: British Defence Policy since 1945* (London: Hutchinson, 1992) pp. 54, 55, 66; Phillip Darby, *British Defence Policy East of Suez 1947-1968* (London: Oxford University Press, 1973), pp. 10, 14, 21, 27, 36-8, 49, 51, 84-5, 124, 133, 146, 175, 185-6, 203-8, 238, 279-80; John Darwin, *Britain and Decolonisation: the Retreat from Empire in the Post-War World* (London: Macmillan, 1988), pp. 184-5 n.35, 262 n. 114; Robert Holland, *The Pursuit of Greatness: Britain and the World Role, 1900-1970* (London: Fontana, 1991), p. 293 n. 33; Jeffrey Pickering, *Britain's Withdrawal from East of Suez: the Politics of Retrenchment* (London: Macmillan, 1998), pp. 4, 68, 117 nn. 108-9, 121 n. 6, 122.

13. Keith Kyle, *The Politics of the Independence of Kenya* (London: Macmillan, 1999), pp. 122-3, 183-4.

14. Anthony Clayton, 'The Military Relations between Great Britain and Commonwealth Countries, with particular reference to the African Commonwealth Nations', in W.H. Morris-Jones and Georges Fischer (eds.), *Decolonisation and After: The British and French Experience* (London: Frank Cass, 1980), pp. 196, 201, 204-5, 207. See also: Chester A. Crocker, 'Military

Dependence: the Colonial Legacy in Africa', *Journal of Modern African Studies*, 12/2 (1974), pp. 265-86.

15. David R. Devereux, 'The Middle East and Africa in British Global Strategy, 1952-56', in Richard J. Aldrich and Michael F. Hopkins (eds.), *Intelligence, Defence and Diplomacy: British Policy in the Post-War World* (Ilford: Frank Cass, 1994), p. 173, *The Formulation of British Defence Policy Towards the Middle East, 1948-56* (New York: St. Martin's Press, 1990), pp. 18-9, 22, 25, 28, 42, 81-7, 94, 98, 100, 190; John Kent (ed.), *Egypt and the Defence of the Middle East* Three Volumes (London: The Stationary Office, 1998), passim., *British Imperial Strategy and the Origins of the Cold War 1944-49* (Leicester, London, New York: Leicester University Press, 1993), pp. 98, 100f, 129f, 148f, 205, 'Bevin's Imperialism and the Idea of Euro-Africa, 1945-49', in Michael Dockrill and John W. Young (eds.), *British Foreign Policy, 1945-56* (London: Macmillan, 1989), pp. 53f, 61f; Ritchie Ovendale (ed.), *British Defence Policy since 1945* (Manchester: Manchester University Press, 1994), pp. 7, 111-3.

16. David Goldsworthy (ed.), *The Conservative Government and the End of Empire 1951-1957* Three Volumes (London: HMSO, 1994), passim.; Ronald Hyam (ed.), *The Labour Government and the End of Empire 1945-1951* Four Volumes (London: HMSO, 1992), passim.

17. For an overview of the 'military history' of the Mau Mau Emergency, which is superfluous to the current remit, see: David Percox, 'Kenya: Mau Mau Revolt, 1952-1960', in Charles Messenger (ed.), *Reader's Guide to Military History* (Chicago, London: Fitzroy Dearborn, 2001), pp. 289-91. The British military units involved against Mau Mau can be traced in: Gregory Blaxland, *The Regiments Depart: A History of the British Army, 1945-1970* (London: William Kimber, 1971). Each unit's regimental history can then be found listed in: Ian S. Hallows, *Regiments and Corps of the British Army* (London: Cassell, 1994 [1991]). Mau Mau memoirs are analysed in: Marshall S. Clough, *Mau Mau Memoirs: History Memory and Politics* (Boulder, CO, London: Lynne Rienner, 1998).

18. Anthony Clayton, *Counter-Insurgency in Kenya: A Study of Military Operations Against Mau Mau* (Nairobi: Transafrica, 1976); Anthony Clayton and David Killingray, *Khaki and Blue: Military and Police in British Colonial Africa* (Athens, Ohio: Ohio University Centre for International Studies, 1989); W. Robert Foran, *The Kenya Police, 1887-1960* (London: Robert Hale, 1962); William F. Gutteridge, 'Military and Police Forces in Colonial Africa', in L.H. Gann and P. Duignan (eds.), *Colonialism in Africa, 1870-1960*, Vol.2: *The History and Politics of Colonialism, 1914-1960* (Cambridge: Cambridge University Press, 1970), pp. 286-319; Jock Haswell, *British Military Intelligence* (London: Weidenfeld & Nicolson, 1973), pp. 223-4; Heather, R.W., 'Counterinsurgency and intelligence in Kenya: 1952-6', PhD thesis,

University of Cambridge, 1994, 'Intelligence and Counter-Insurgency in Kenya, 1952-56', *Intelligence and National Security*, 5/3 (July 1990), pp. 57-83; Keith Jeffery, 'Intelligence and Counter-Insurgency Operations: Some Reflections on the British Experience', *Intelligence and National Security*, 2/1 (1987), pp. 125, 128-9, 140; David Killingray, 'The Maintenance of Law and Order in British Colonial Africa', *African Affairs*, 85 (1986), pp. 411-37; Frank Kitson, *Bunch of Five* (London: Faber & Faber, 1977), pp. 3-65, *Low Intensity Operations: Subversion, Insurgency and Peacekeeping* (London: Faber & Faber, 1971), pp. 31, 33, 42, 100, 123, 135-6, *Gangs and Counter-Gangs* (London: Barrie & Rockliff, 1960); Thomas R. Mockaitis, *British Counterinsurgency, 1919-1960* (London: Macmillan, 1990), pp. 5, 9, 25, 36, 38, 44-51, 124, 125-32, 135-8, 142, 148, 156, 167-71, 188-9; Hamish Morrison, '"Quis Custodiet Ipsos Custodes?" The Problems of Policing in Anglophone Africa during the Transfer of Power', PhD thesis, University of Aberdeen, 1995, pp. 8-12; John S. Pustay, *Counter-Insurgency Warfare* (New York: Free Press, 1965), pp. 78, 108, 114, 122-3; David Throup, 'Crime, politics and the police in colonial Kenya, 1939-63', in David M. Anderson and David Killingray (eds.), *Policing and Decolonisation: Nationalism, Politics and the Police, 1917-65* (Manchester: Manchester University Press, 1992), pp. 127-57; Charles Townshend, *Britain's Civil Wars: Counterinsurgency in the Twentieth Century* (London: Faber, 1986), pp. 198-207.

19. John Newsinger, 'Revolt and Repression in Kenya: The Mau Mau Rebellion, 1952-1960', *Science and Society*, 45/2 (Summer 1981), p. 184; Julian Paget, *Counter-Insurgency Operations: Techniques of Guerrilla Warfare* (New York: Walker & Co., 1967), p. 103.

20. Frank Füredi, *The Mau Mau War in Perspective* (London: James Currey, 1989), pp. 161, 175-7, 179-80, 185-93, 203-4; Tabitha Kanogo, *Squatters and the Roots of Mau Mau 1905-63* (London: James Currey, 1987), pp. 6, 148-9, 165-9, 171-3, 174, 176; Carl G. Rosberg, and John Nottingham, *The Myth of "Mau Mau": Nationalism in Kenya* (New York: Praeger, 1966). pp. 306-7.

21. Richard J. Aldrich, *The Hidden Hand: Britain, America and Cold War Secret Intelligence* (London: John Murray, 2001); Jonathan Bloch and Patrick Fitzgerald, *British Intelligence and Covert Action: Africa, Middle East and Europe since 1945* (Dingle, London: Brandon, Junction, 1983); Heather, 'Counterinsurgency and intelligence'.

22. Aldrich, *The Hidden Hand*, pp. 578, 600-4. Prof. Aldrich disclosed to this author that he had considered extending his study to include Kenya, but felt that Heather's coverage was definitive: personal communication, University of Nottingham, 11 Sept. 2001.

23. For this purpose I attended the 'Administering Empire' conference, held jointly by the University of London and the Corona Club, Senate House, University of London, 27-8 May 1999.

24. I considered an approach to the former head of Kenya's Special Branch, special security adviser to Rhodesian Prime Minister, Ian Smith, and head of security for the King of Bahrain, Ian Henderson. However, the idea was abandoned when it became clear that he was already involved, with Dr Randall Heather, in drafting his as yet unpublished (auto) biography.

25. Morrison, "'Quis Custodiet Ipsos Custodes?'", passim.

26. At the time of writing, I understand that comparative doctoral research into policing in Kenya and Uganda is being undertaken under the supervision of Dr Philip Murphy in the University of Reading.

CHAPTER ONE

Defence and Internal Security, 1945-52

Introduction

The so-called 'scramble for Africa' (c. 1879-1914) was essentially a function of competition between European states, if not necessarily always based upon any tangible future economic gains. For example, while the 'Belgian Congo' was in fact rich in natural resources, as was southern Africa, Britain's annexation of a large area of eastern Africa was motivated by a desire to secure pre-existing economic and strategic advantages elsewhere, particularly in Egypt, India, and the Far East.[1] In a sense, therefore, colonial state formation was about survival in the wider world; where practicable, decolonisation was too.

While any state may or may not adapt by becoming more 'inclusive', it must nevertheless protect itself and its citizens or subjects. Essentially, the state relies upon its monopoly of the use of force, underpinned by its legal and legislative processes, and in many cases legitimised by the democratic process, to plan for and to act against the threat of external attack, and to be able to act as freely as possible to secure its interests in the international arena.[2] It hardly needs to be reiterated that the state's potential for the use of force also underpins the legal process which validates it. Clearly, force applied within a legal framework, prescribed by democratically elected legislators under the guise of popular consent, is in most cases more palatable than indiscriminate state brutality.

Of course, the state also needs to employ both legal and forcible means to protect itself from disaffected and/or destabilising elements from within, whether wholly domestic in origin, or stimulated in some way by a hostile international power or powers.[3] For every example of a nascent or emergent modern state, there can be found examples of attempts to undermine or overthrow it.[4] Given the size of the British Empire at its peak, and the disparity between political and socio-economic development in Britain and its far-flung colonies, it is as no surprise that many such territories provided a breeding ground for widespread subversion and armed insurgency.[5]

It is therefore axiomatic that 'arms' (police and military forces) and 'the state' (democratic or authoritarian government) are synonymous.[6] However, while the history of the conquest and formation of the British state arguably stretches back over the last thousand years, and the development of modern legal, military, police, and political structures can be traced back over the last two or three centuries or so, the formation and development of the colonial state and its attendant paraphernalia is a relatively recent phenomenon, as is decolonisation.

The history of the British colonial state in Kenya is certainly no exception. Military conquest and formal annexation began in 1895. Colonisation of the territory by white and Indian immigrants was encouraged shortly afterwards. Significant numbers of the early European settlers originated from the military and 'officer class', especially after the First World War, reflecting the essentially defensive nature of the colonisation.[7] The British East Africa Police had been established in 1887, as the Imperial British East Africa Company fell into decline. The British East Africa Protectorate was not proclaimed until 1895.[8] This pattern was repeated some twenty years later. The Kenya Police was formed in 1918, two years before Britain declared the Protectorate to be 'Kenya Colony'. As with most of Britain's colonial territories, responsibility for external defence and internal security beyond the capacity of the police was vested largely in local levies, commanded by European officers. The King's African Rifles (KAR) was established from the remnants of earlier units, such as the East African Rifles, in January 1902, as the initial conquest of Kenya drew to an end.[9]

From almost the outset of the occupation, exclusion by European settlers of many Kikuyu from their homeland, a rich agricultural area which came to be known as the 'White Highlands', and their concentration in set-aside reserves, considerably restricted their socio-economic life.[10] This, combined with the imposition of a state-sponsored system of native administration by British-appointed chiefs and headmen, and settler domination of state politics, also severely limited the channels for the expression of any grievance, if they were not effectively closed.[11] Those Kikuyu who did not eke out a living in the reserves were compelled to seek either wage labour in the urban areas or, for the most part, lived as 'squatters' on European farms in the Highlands, working for so many days per year in exchange for the usufruct of as much land as they could cultivate. Meanwhile, mission-educated young Kikuyu proto-politicians vied unsuccessfully for their share of state patronage.

This fragile political and socio-economic situation continued for several years and was alleviated, albeit temporarily, by the contraction of settler agriculture during the 1930s Depression, then by the boom brought about by the Second World War, both of which served as motors for Kikuyu agriculture.[12] By the end of the 1930s and after the war, however, the economic and political resurgence of the settlers, along with conservation-driven agricultural reforms and the abuse of office by many in the 'native' authorities, began to drive an ever-increasing wedge between not only the

Europeans and the Africans, but the Kikuyu 'haves' and 'have nots'.[13] The very nature of the political system in Kenya dictated that the moderate would-be political spokesmen of the Kikuyu would be at best ineffective. As matters became increasingly untenable, with rising urban and rural unemployment, homelessness, and ever-stringent demands on the squatters from the European farmers, an apparent lack of concern, let alone action by the Kenya government led to the gradual onset of the militant action which culminated in the so-called 'Mau Mau revolt'.[14]

By 1945, as the 'second colonial occupation' began, Kenya already had a well-established system of 'native administration' running in parallel with the European settler-dominated central government.[15] Europeans also formed the mainstay of the territorial Kenya Regiment, founded in 1937 to defend against possible Italian aggression, and reconstituted in 1950 for mainly internal security purposes.[16] While 'ill-equipped and poorly trained Tribal Police' operated in the African 'reserves', the regular police Special Branch intelligence structure in Kenya was apparently 'as good a system, if not better, than [in] most colonial territories'.[17] The British imperial state in Kenya seemed to many to be secure, at least until 7 October 1952, when this perception changed dramatically with the assassination of Senior Chief Waruhiu. This was 'an important blow against the colonial regime' and, according to one interpretation, 'provided the pretext for a new offensive' against such expressions of African grievances.[18] Before decolonisation, would come a 'second conquest' or *third* 'colonial occupation' of Kenya.

The 'Mau Mau revolution' of the 1950s had a profound, if by no means immediate, impact upon British plans for the transfer of power in Kenya.[19] The State of Emergency, imposed in October 1952, legalised the repression of the Mau Mau guerrillas and their supporters. Politically, the Emergency facilitated the gradual implementation of socio-economic and constitutional reforms designed to alleviate, again only temporarily, the grievances of those Africans who had not yet chosen to resort to violence, and to stem support for those who had.

However, the major political advances which arguably anticipated 'decolonisation' (the 'Macleod plan' for a majority of seats in the Legislative Council to be elected on an 'open' rather than 'communal' franchise, for example), were not set in train until April 1959, when the British Secretary of State for Colonial Affairs, Alan Lennox-Boyd, announced a future constitutional conference.[20] Lennox-Boyd made his rapid policy reversal in response to pleas from the Governor of Kenya, Sir Evelyn Baring, following the African members' January boycott of the legislature. This breakdown in the political process occurred weeks, if not days, after Lennox-Boyd and the East African governors had 'pencilled in' the date for Kenya's independence as 1975. Significantly, Lennox-Boyd's change of heart came some two years after the apparent defeat of the Mau Mau forest fighters, and in itself raises doubts over the connection between constitutional reform and British counter-insurgency.[21]

In the light of the above, Britain's use of massive force, combined with the introduction of piecemeal political and selective socio-economic reforms during the Emergency can be seen, not as a direct response to Mau Mau, as such, but as a form of continuity. British policy towards Kenya following the Mau Mau Emergency, and in the run up to, and immediately following independence, can only be fully understood in a broader context. Moreover, Britain's efforts to stabilise internal security in Kenya during the 1950s and 1960s clearly represented attempts to rectify the mistakes made before October 1952, and to consolidate economic and strategic interests beyond Kenya's independence in December 1963. It is therefore necessary to consider the British transfer of power in Kenya not simply in the strict chronological sense suggested by the Emergency and its aftermath, but in the broader context of the Cold War and the so-called 'era of decolonisation'. In other words, what did the British government hope to achieve by arming the Kenya state to varying degrees, at certain times over a twenty-year period, in combination with the gradual implementation of constitutional and socio-economic reforms?[22]

Before any attempt can be made to answer this question, it is necessary to consider post-war British defence planning and internal security policy in relation to Kenya. Only then will it be possible to understand the British response to Mau Mau and the various, if intermittent, developments in its aftermath. This chapter therefore examines Britain's defence and security priorities in Kenya during the post-war, pre-Emergency period, as the Cold War apparently threatened to spread throughout the British Empire and beyond.

Cold War: Kenya as Adjunct to British Middle East Strategy, 1945-50

Kenya was annexed by Britain mainly to head off competition from other European powers, and largely for economic and strategic purposes based primarily on the exclusion of those powers. Strategically, it seems that Kenya had very little intrinsic value, except as a land bridge from the Indian Ocean to the source of the Nile, the great lakes in Uganda. It was consistent with Kenya's status as a British colonial possession, if somewhat ironic, that before independence the territory's transient involvement in international affairs came about as a result of the two world wars which, excepting Japanese aggression in the Pacific and Southeast Asian regions, had originated largely from continued and irreconcilable conflict between European states.

In both the Great War and the Second World War, East Africa contributed greatly to the British and Allied campaigns. During the 1914-18 war, the KAR was eventually increased from three battalions (the perceived internal security requirement), to the 22 battalions (over 30,000 troops) which took part in the German East Africa campaign. Between the wars, the KAR in Kenya was frequently engaged in internal security operations in the largely ethnic Somali Northern Frontier District (NFD), and border defence following the Italian invasion of Ethiopia in 1935. The KAR also occasionally broke cover from its discreet position in the background of the colony's life to repress strikes during the mid-late 1930s. During the Second World War, KAR battalions from Kenya fought in Italian East Africa, Madagascar and, by 1944, had been posted as far afield as Southeast Asia.[23]

In Kenya itself, African and European commercial farmers and African peasant cultivators and black market traders benefited from the wartime agricultural boom. Growing land poverty, the corrupt practices of native officials, and consequent disaffection and dispossession only added to population pressures and rising crime, however, as the unemployed and homeless flocked to Nairobi.[24] In January 1945, concern over the prevalence of street gangs and rising crime in Nairobi led to an emergency debate in the Legislative Council. Two members representing African interests, Eliud Mathu (who had only been appointed in 1944, 13 years after African representation was first recommended) and Archdeacon Beecher (who, among others, had pressed for such an appointment), stressed that the crime wave had social and economic causes. However, in what was to become a familiar pattern, the majority of the settlers were more concerned that police manpower and criminal sentences should be increased.[25] While political and socio-economic development in Kenya during the war had been complicated and to some extent held in check by Britain's need to maintain stability and maximise the colony's contribution to the war effort, very little would change following victory.[26]

If anything, the problem posed by the closing stages and end of the Second World War was that the very exigencies of the war (the build up and employment of massive levels of financial, industrial, manpower, and military resources), geared towards victory, actually led to stalemate in Europe. The onset of the Cold War and the consequent potential for renewed global warfare, while not necessarily on the scale seen between 1939 and 1945, was certainly unprecedented in terms of its complexity, duration and inclusiveness. Following any brief overview of the 1939-45 conflict and a passing understanding of the alliances and issues at stake, and given a cursory glance at global political developments in the post-war period, one could be forgiven for questioning the point of it all. Surely, following any global conflict fought ostensibly against 'oppression' and 'tyranny' (thus, *for* 'freedom'), it would not be unreasonable to expect to perceive such an outcome. Yet, the onset of the Cold War, whatever the reasons for it, could hardly be said to have reflected this, despite the ostensible freedoms gained in Asia through independence in the immediate post-war years.

As for Britain's post-war strategic 'grand design', Kenya Colony was never far from British defence planners' thinking, if only ever in a necessarily peripheral sense. Towards the end of the war, the British Resident Minister in the Middle East, Sir Edward Grigg, prepared a memorandum for the soon to be dissolved War Cabinet, in which he outlined 'the nature of British interests and aims in the Middle East'.[27] While the document was primarily a 'political memorandum', Grigg explained that, in line with its title, it also contained 'some tentative ideas upon' the military 'dispositions which seem best suited to maintain security within the political and financial conditions which are likely to govern us'. As is well known, the Middle East was a 'region of life-and-death consequences for Britain and the British Empire in four ways': as 'an indispensable channel of communications'; a 'strategic centre'; 'the Empire's main reservoir of mineral oil'; and 'as a region in which British political method must make good, if the British way of life is to survive'.

Much of Grigg's overview necessarily considered the Middle East states themselves, focusing particularly on Egypt and the problem of integrating Palestine into British strategy given plans for its possible partition. In these early stages of post-war planning, however, little had been done regarding detailed financial and military provisioning, which was being undertaken by various redeployment committees. Kenya and Rhodesia, significantly given their white minority governments, began to be drawn into British strategy in so far as the development of RAF bases in those countries was considered to be 'desirable'. Grigg also perceptively presented this concept in terms not only of imperial defence and overseas strategy generally, but also with regard to colonial internal security: 'Military expenditure is most economically incurred where, so far as possible, it will serve a double purpose and pay two separate dividends. The use of Kenya and Rhodesia as rear bases and of Cyprus as an advanced base would conform to this principle.'[28]

By March 1946, with the war over, and ongoing wrangling over revision of the Anglo-Egyptian Treaty (1936), the case for Kenya becoming the location for major British military installations had progressed little further than Grigg's paper recommendations of the previous year. The British Chiefs of Staff, contrary to the thinking of the Prime Minister, Clement Attlee, had insisted upon the retention of a peacetime garrison in Egypt. The Foreign Office supported the service chiefs' view on the grounds that the Egyptians could not be 'trusted to maintain unaided (or, let us say it frankly, unprompted) the military framework which must exist in peace-time if the area is to be properly defended in war'.[29] However, difficulties in negotiating with the Egyptians prompted Britain to consider in detail the idea of an East

African base.

The decision pivoted as much on whether an 'East African bastion' was a military possibility, as it did on the likelihood of being able to remain in Egypt. According to the Foreign Office, withdrawal from Egypt could not be countenanced '*unless* the over-all defence of the British Empire can be assured by substituting for the Egypt-Palestine-Transjordan-Irak [*sic*] bastion the East African bastion *plus* through communications with West Africa'.[30] Significantly, the option of a base in East Africa apparently held financial as well as political merits, especially when compared with 'the present edifice, whose foundation is the shifting sand of Arab-and Jewish-politics'. The Foreign Secretary, Ernest Bevin, for one, considered it preferable to defend the Middle East from 'British or British-controlled territories and not from foreign territories the governments of which were reluctant to have British forces quartered on their soil. Thus, a large and perhaps the main British base would be at Mombasa and other bases would be in Iraq and Transjordan if, as was probable, the Governments of those territories agreed.'[31]

Before any reports on East Africa's suitability as a location for a major base were forthcoming, the Chiefs of Staff had dismissed the idea. If the defence of the Middle East on a regional basis were to become 'a reality' the 'main headquarters' simply could not be located elsewhere.[32] The only other alternative (at the time) was to base the HQ in Palestine, with store holding facilities in Mombasa and Aden, but with the internal security situation in the former likely to be as precarious as that in Egypt, British policy tended more towards the 'better the devil you know' approach.[33] Yet, Bevin remained unconvinced that the Middle East HQ could not be located in Kenya, or even the Sudan. Immediate commencement of withdrawal from Egypt would not only create goodwill, but also show that Britain's dependence upon the Cairo HQ and the Suez base was far less than the Egyptians had perceived, and could only enhance Britain's negotiating position.[34] Again, the Chiefs of Staff countered, this time because Turkey and the Arab states would not be convinced of Britain's commitment to the defence of the Middle East with troops stationed in East Africa.[35]

With the issue of British policy in the Middle East delicately poised, it seems that Britain's 'left hand' (represented by Bevin) was not so much unaware of what its 'right hand' (the service chiefs) was doing, nor the means or lack of means at its disposal, rather than somewhat schizophrenic regarding the ultimate ends of policy generally. As Kent has demonstrated, British defence policy in the Middle East was complicated to some extent by Bevin's vision of wide-ranging economic, strategic and technical co-operation in Africa between Britain and the other European colonial powers.[36] With this in mind, in the autumn of 1946, Bevin had laid the groundwork for Britain's evacuation from Egypt to be completed by 1 September 1949, with some flexibility to take account of possible future international hostilities. The Foreign Secretary was also encouraged by the 'progress made in examining the potentialities of East Africa as a base'.[37]

Potential was one thing, however, and reality was quite different. The problem from Kenya's perspective, so to speak, was that broad strategic decisions taken in Whitehall often impacted on parochial security issues. Whatever London decided to do with its military forces after the war, Nairobi still had to ensure that in its corner of the British Empire it remained 'business as usual'. As we will see, this turned out to be the greater problem.

Towards the end of the Second World War, in response to the burgeoning crime wave, the Kenya Police had begun to take tentative steps towards improving its coverage of the African reserves, establishing 'regulars' in Kiambu, Nandi and Narok, then Kericho and Kisii, respectively. By 1949, however, large areas of Kenya, including the Rift Valley Province, still lacked a regular police presence.[38] Despite the ongoing increases in manpower, wider dispersal, and measures taken to improve the command structure, the police found it difficult to adapt to its increased responsibilities in both rural and urban areas, as levels of unemployment, housing shortages, and the cost of living spiralled upwards, contributing inevitably to rising levels of crime, particularly minor offences.[39] As crime levels increased, the settler-dominated local governments enacted more and more legislation designed to regulate African activities. 'Poorer Africans, especially Kikuyu, who flocked to the burgeoning shanty-towns around the capital as they were dispossessed by European and African commercial farmers, were common offenders against local ordinances.'[40]

In the early post-war period the colonial state was not preoccupied only with the threat to internal security and economic progress and stability posed by crime. As the Cold War took hold, Kenya's strategic significance was again, if briefly, elevated. By August 1947, given Britain's planned withdrawal from India and Palestine, and continued difficulties in negotiating the future of the vast military complex in Egypt, Kenya Colony now seemed destined to become the principal military stores holding area for the Middle East.[41] Certainly, the military commanders in the Middle East itself had arrived at this, albeit hasty, conclusion. As an enclosure in a despatch from the Chief of Staff, Middle East Headquarters (COS, GHQ, MELF), General Pyman, to the local military commander, General Dimoline, made clear:

> If political decisions take a certain turn it may even be that directing headquarters and even theatre reserves of British fighting units will have to be stationed in peacetime in EAST AFRICA [*sic*]. [...] Therefore military activity is certainly going to increase IN PEACETIME in EAST AFRICA to some and

possibly to a very large degree. That EAST AFRICA will be an important military base in any future WAR is almost without question.[42]

This would add to the 'security problem' in Kenya, because of the need to import skilled labourers for the construction of the MacKinnon Road depot ('Operation Satire II', later renamed 'Leader'): 'careful screening would be necessary'.[43] Kenya's security planners' minds had already been focused by the Mombasa dock strike in January 1947, the Murang'a peasants' revolt later that year, and pro-secessionist agitation by the Somali Youth League in the NFD, as well as the latter's supposed 'link up' with the political voice of African nationalism in the colony, the Kenya African Union (KAU).[44] Moreover, before the end of the war, Officials in Whitehall had begun to express concerns, which on one view were groundless, about the potential threat posed to the internal security of Britain's African colonies by returning demobilised African soldiers.[45] Also, as pressure began to mount for aborting the evacuation from Egypt, because security of tenure in Cyrenaica (yet another possible Middle East HQ) could not be assured, it seemed feasible to station British troops in Kenya for reinforcement of the Persian Gulf.[46] It followed, according to somewhat circular logic after Grigg's earlier recommendations, that the more secure Kenya was as a colony, the more viable it would be as a British base, and the more secure, and so on.

In September 1950, as the result of Britain's eventual decision to stay on in Egypt, the MacKinnon Road project was finally abandoned.[47] Kenya was just too far away from the Middle East to serve as a main base.[48] Despite measures taken to expand and improve the police, the Kenya government's ability to make contingency plans to deal with internal civil disorder had also been weakened by other decisions taken in Whitehall. With the closure of MacKinnon Road, so dwindled any immediate prospect of significant numbers of British troops being stationed in Kenya. While fairly comprehensive plans existed for internal security reinforcement by air, these decisions served effectively to limit the numbers of local military personnel on the ground.[49]

In late 1946, wartime debts and the consequent requirement to economise prompted awareness in Britain that post-war demobilisation would steadily deplete the numbers of locally recruited troops stationed in the colonies when there was a 'grave shortage of white man-power'. This led Attlee to suggest that 'a review be carried out in order to make the maximum possible use of Colonial man-power, both from the military and industrial points of view'.[50] Thus began the review of 'the role of the colonies in war'.[51]

Although presented with reference to efficiency and battle-readiness, with particular attention paid to the colonies' defence schemes, the review amounted to a cost-cutting exercise aimed at reducing, where practicable, the levels of manpower in colonial armed forces. The British Chiefs of Staff were in favour of maintaining 'an internal security force re-organised from the present demobilised East and West African forces, and of maintaining a small armed nucleus capable of expansion in war'.[52] They would not, however, approve the funding of colonial forces in East and West Africa from the service votes, 'which would have to be devoted to raising the British Services to the highest possible standard. Money spent from the votes of the Service Department on African forces could only be at the expense of the British Services.'[53]

Following Attlee's suggestion, the review of colonial forces included an assessment of wartime accomplishments. According to one such evaluation, East African troops had performed creditably in Africa and the Middle East, and achieved their 'main' success in the Far East with an advance down the Kabaw Valley in Burma during the 1944 monsoon. 'In the campaign in Burma, however, reports from Force Commanders show that the East Africans did not reach the standard of other troops engaged, and in fact were somewhat disappointing. When outside the fighting zone, their discipline also caused difficulty at times.'[54] Perhaps there were grounds for Britain's fears of the risk to internal security posed by demobilised African soldiers after all?

One of East Africa's roles in any future war would be to provide a military force to be expanded initially to one division 'for use outside East Africa'. It was decided, however, that until 'further experience indicates whether the defects noted ... can be overcome, it appears wise not to plan for its use outside Africa'.[55] Apart from projected future manpower requirements for pioneer and labour units, mainly for essential industries, this left local troops with responsibility for internal security duties and the 'Army share of defences for Imperial naval and air bases in East Africa'.[56]

With this renewed emphasis placed on the internal security role of local military forces, and given that it was 'common ground' that financial responsibility therefore 'fell on the Colonies concerned', an effective limit on the numbers of troops in Kenya was inevitable.[57] This materialised in the form of a recommendation from the War Office for a reduction in East African forces to a ceiling of 5,000.[58] The 'Expansion for war provision' was to be a 'long term contribution to the war effort which need not [*sic*] affect the peace time planning'.[59] In an effort to minimise the impact of the manpower ceiling, Dimoline proposed that the size of KAR battalions be reduced, rather than their number. Despite objections from Dimoline's successor, General Sir Arthur Dowler, this change was made in early 1949, reducing a four company KAR battalion from 728 African ranks to 656.[60] The inter-war objection to such reductions, that the flexibility required of

African troops in an 'imperial role' would thereby be impaired, had again been superseded by financial constraints.[61]

The East African governors had pressed throughout for the War Office to assume sole responsibility for direct command and control, and financing of local military forces.[62] The War Office, however, found this to be conveniently inconsistent with their status as 'His Majesty's representatives and therefore His Majesty's heads of the Army forces in their territories'.[63] The governors were therefore left to haggle with London over the relative proportions which Britain and the colonial governments should pay towards the cost of maintaining the local forces. This question pivoted on the difference between what the War Office was prepared to pay for the forces' external 'Commonwealth Defence element' and the amount the territories could afford to pay towards their internal security, as well as the extent to which the shortfall could be met by the Colonial Office.[64] Events elsewhere, particularly the June 1948 'Berlin crisis', compounded the problem by complicating and prolonging the colonial defence review.[65] Despite numerous committee meetings in London and East Africa, several conferences, and reams of correspondence, 'the special EA problem could not be settled until decisions had been reached on the larger question' of 'Colonial forces everywhere, and the methods of paying for them. In the meantime, all planning in East Africa had to be on suppositions.'[66]

Among the possible solutions suggested to the actual and, perhaps more important, the potential shortfall in military personnel, were that the Kenya government could either introduce a form of national service, or raise territorial units on the UK model, or both. Since the end of the war, Governor Sir Philip Mitchell had consistently asked Dimoline why (white) 'Kenya youths' were not being conscripted like their British counterparts, who were sent out to serve in Africa.[67] The answer came in August 1947, when the then Secretary of State for Colonial Affairs, Arthur Creech Jones, informed Mitchell that the question of conscription would have to be deferred until completion of the review of colonial forces. He did however agree in principle to the reconstitution of the mainly European Kenya Regiment, which had been disbanded at the end of the war.[68]

Although the Chief of the Imperial General Staff (CIGS), Field-Marshal Lord Montgomery, had enthusiastically praised the potentially vast reserves of African manpower as a means of dealing with 'crises' throughout the Empire, no 'African' solutions to Europe's overseas defence problems were in fact forthcoming.[69] Britain's reversal on Middle East defence policy led, as we have seen, to a proportionate downgrading in Kenya's strategic importance. In the end, the governors themselves rejected the idea of (white) national service in East Africa, not least because of the cost. Besides, such 'reinforcements' would be either too young, and lacking in the quality of leadership needed to serve in East African units or, as with British conscripts generally, their service would be too short-term, 'so that by the time they had become useful in their units they were due to be released'.[70]

As for addressing manpower shortages with part-time reservists, Dimoline was not in favour of re-starting an African territorial unit on the lines of the old 7 KAR. He came to this negative conclusion after the Mombasa dock strike, when Ugandan troops aided the police in restoring order.[71] The problem was addressed again the following year:

> At the meeting of the [East Africa] High Commission held in February, 1948, the High Commission came to the preliminary conclusion that the highly complicated nature of modern military training made it unlikely that Territorial Forces embodying Africans would be practicable. The General Officer Commanding subsequently endorsed this view.[72]

British opinion apparently distinguished between the 'more educated and sophisticated West African, and the greater number of large towns where a territorial unit might be located, and the East African'. Dimoline did not believe that 'the East African' was 'yet ready for Territorial service' and considered that 'any money so spent would be entirely wasted'.[73] That some 225,000 East Africans, including over 20 KAR battalions, had served the British Empire during the war, and largely successfully, did not figure in these calculations.[74] Perhaps demobilised African soldiers did not need refresher courses in marksmanship? The revival of rifle clubs for 'Indians and Europeans', on the other hand, did not seem to pose a security problem.[75]

Unsurprisingly, the same can be said for the reconstitution of the Kenya Regiment, which was finally approved in early 1949 and implemented in 1950. This provided the means by which Europeans would continue to receive military training without the Kenya government resorting to conscription.[76] With limits on the numbers of troops available in the colony, however, and the laboured improvements to the police, some means were still needed to enable the security forces to be brought up to strength in 'emergency conditions'. The Kenya Police Reserve (KPR), which was 'open to all races', was therefore established to take over in 'undisturbed areas' while the regular police dealt with 'disturbed areas'.[77] Another solution to manpower shortages in the event of an emergency, which would have far-reaching implications beyond Kenya's independence, was 'a strong striking force of police available to deal at the earliest possible moment with any outbreak'.[78] In late 1947, in parallel with a similar initiative in the Gold Coast (Ghana), so came about the formation of the Kenya Police 'Emergency

Company', predecessor of the General Service Unit (GSU).[79] It seems that on this occasion the lead was taken in the colonies, with Creech Jones not advocating the widespread adoption of colonial mobile gendarmeries until the end of 1948.[80] In the political and socio-economic spheres, Creech Jones seemed more concerned with developments in 'local' rather than 'self-' government, although he did make the concession, unpopular with most white settlers, whereby Kenya's Legislative Council would receive four appointed (*not* elected) African members. Meanwhile, the socially disastrous agricultural terracing campaign continued.[81]

While Britain's post-war review of colonial defence was undertaken primarily to ensure military effectiveness against external attack, unrest in the Gold Coast highlighted a serious deficiency in colonial internal security capabilities which had implications elsewhere in the Empire. The Accra riots of February 1948, were foreseen by the local military commander, but had utterly surprised the Police Commissioner. This focused the minds of the colonial governments on 'the need for establishing or strengthening intelligence services and special branches', especially given the circular they had received that month demanding 'political intelligence on the threat posed by subversive movements'.[82]

Prompted also by 'crises' in Europe, the Malayan Emergency of June that year, and unrest elsewhere in the Empire, a colonial police adviser, W.C. Johnson, was eventually appointed at the behest of the Minister of Defence, Lord Alexander, in November 1948.[83] The importance of broadcasting and 'propaganda warfare' was also brought home by the 1948 'panic', with the Colonial Office information service taking over the management of the British Council in April. In May 1948, Bevin had asked the Colonial Office to initiate the practice of preparing regular reports on communist activities in the Empire.[84] At around the same time, Bevin recommended that Attlee add a Colonial Office representative to the Joint Intelligence Committee, so as 'to ensure that we have the best possible intelligence about Communist activities in the Colonies, so that we may not be taken unawares'.[85]

Indeed, in early 1948, fear of widespread communist and/or nationalist subversion throughout the Empire, led to a thorough reorganisation at the Colonial Office. Geographical departments were tasked with preparing fortnightly intelligence summaries, collated from the information that they received from the colonies. These summaries were then submitted to the newly established Colonial Office Defence Department, for inclusion in its monthly reports.[86] No sooner had these arrangements been put in place, however, and the colonial governments' contributions been found to be wanting, than the Malayan State of Emergency was proclaimed.[87]

The East African governors had long been aware that African nationalism was likely to arise and would threaten peace and stability in the post-war period. In June 1945, at a conference to assess the problem, they had agreed that 'an efficient political internal security organisation should be established in East Africa and that each territory should take steps to ensure that its own organisation was adequate'. The subsequent enquiry reported that Kenya's political intelligence structure 'cannot be regarded as satisfactory'.[88] By 1947, little had improved, and the authorities were again reminded of the 'lack of an adequate Intelligence organisation for the Civil Police'.[89] As General Dimoline noted:

> I informed HE [Mitchell] that I was apprehensive that the Police Security Int[elligence] in the territory was almost non-existent and that this was amply born [*sic*] out in the Mombasa strike. Moreover, in view of our new visitors [Kenyatta *et al*?], this fact had even greater significance. I further consider that the Special Branch of the Police was not doing its job, although the Chief of the Special Branch, Capt Sandwith, seemed to know his job, but was not allowed to do it.[90]

Reflecting what would become a recurring theme regarding political intelligence gathering in Kenya, if not elsewhere, it seemed that a lack of civil-military-police co-operation, exacerbated by what might be called the 'bailiwick mentality', was at the root of the problem.[91] For example, the then Provincial Commissioner for Central Province, Percy Wyn Harris (later appointed Chief Native Commissioner), while agreeing that there 'might' be a problem in the towns, 'felt that, from the Native Reserves of his Province, he was getting a reasonable amount of information'.[92]

Nevertheless, Mitchell agreed with Dimoline, 'that there was a grave weakness in our Police Int[elligence] and promised to give it immediate attention'.[93] This culminated in a 'Security Conference' attended by the Director-General of the Security Service (MI5), Sir Percy Sillitoe, in late August 1947.[94] The conference made several recommendations. Autonomous Special Branches should be established within each territory's police force. All police recruits from Britain should be trained there prior to departure, with Special Branch recruits taking short MI5 and Special Branch courses in either London or the provinces. Ultimately, 'Central Training Schools' should be established locally. Perhaps most important: 'All information on security matters, from whatever source, should be made immediately available to the Commissioners of Police.' The resulting report would then be passed to the Security Liaison Officer (SLO), representing MI5, who would collate this with 'information reaching him from other sources', and advise the relevant authorities.[95]

These recommendations were all well and good, but their implementation and subsequent effectiveness were another matter. Despite its separate establishment and firmly laid guidelines for the dissemination of political intelligence, Special Branch continued to suffer from manpower shortages, preventing it from developing a 'provincial network for intelligence-gathering'. In June 1948, while communist 'crises' seemingly rampaged throughout the Empire, East Africa Command reported gloomily that 'the "security situation" had "deteriorated considerably in the post war period"'.[96] In 1950, the problem was compounded, ironically, by the formation of the Kenya Police Criminal Investigation Department (CID). Although this released more officers for 'regular' police work, the new department also tended to monopolise the enthusiastic attention of the then Police Commissioner, Michael O'Rorke. While O'Rorke's main concern was the Nairobi 'crime wave', he paid scant attention to the steady flow of Special Branch reports on trade union and 'radical' activity. Thus little effort was made to bring such reports to the attention of the administration or the Attorney General and Member for Law and Order, John Whyatt. The situation was exacerbated by the promotions of several middle-ranking Special Branch officers to other colonies. If that were not enough, in 1950 the Director of Intelligence and Security (DIS) himself, Cecil Penfold, was promoted elsewhere. Penfold's successor lacked his intricate local knowledge, and seemed unable to utilise the information available to him.[97]

Given Britain's post-war financial stringency, the Kenya government was poised dangerously between two stools. On the one hand, a more or less generally perceived lack of any desirability or necessity to concede major political advance to Africans served only to frustrate the efforts of the moderate would-be collaborators in the KAU to gain incorporation into the colonial state. The situation was complicated, of course, by the relatively early independence of India and Burma, juxtaposed by Colonial Office pronouncements on political reform. As a somewhat irritated Mitchell put it to Creech Jones in September 1948:

> At a time when there are frequent declarations of policy to the effect that it is the object of His Majesty's Government to bring Colonial Dependencies to the point of self-government at the earliest possible moment, it is not surprising that ignorant and excitable populations of this kind should suppose that means within [the] next year or two, and accordingly the subversive elements who organise movements of this kind derive a great deal of strength from official statements of policy made at Ministerial level ... these statements of policy have, if I may be frank, been overdone in the recent past.[98]

In this context, the increasingly intolerable socio-economic circumstances of the great majority of Kenyan Africans merely provided the colony's aspirant nationalist politicians with broad-based support. On the other hand, while resources in Kenya Colony were insufficient to make a substantive improvement to many Africans' situation, and what development programmes existed were tarnished by corruption, even the state's emphasis on maintaining internal security was undermined by the very financial hardship which made it necessary in the first place.

'Splendid Isolation?': Strategies to Maintain Stability, 1950-2

Despite financial and manpower constraints, the Kenya government had taken real steps to strengthen its security forces and to repair deficiencies in its intelligence structures, and was clearly 'obsessed with the question of security'.[99] An overview of two aspects of the internal security planning process confirms this. The comprehensive 'Internal Security Scheme (Nairobi/Mombasa)', for instance, detailed the army's 'duties in aid of the civil power' and its precise role in 'emergency conditions'.[100] The scheme was reviewed almost monthly, and updated in accordance with relative manpower levels and the latest intelligence summaries. It recognised 'five possible causes of unrest': racial and inter-racial disputes; economic; religious; subversive influence; and inter-tribal disputes. The 'seven possible types of unrest' included, for example: 'inter-tribal fighting (African)' and 'attacks by Africans on Europeans and/or European property'. Educated Africans, disaffected African ex-soldiers, and African trade unionists were identified, correctly as we now know, as among those persons most likely to cause or lead unrest.[101] (Again, British fears of the threat posed by demobilised African soldiers, it seems, were not necessarily groundless.) As well as covering the major municipalities, the plan catered for the army being called out to 'deal with civil disturbances' in the African reserves. All this planning, however, did not guarantee effective practice. Following a rehearsal in September 1949, and undoubtedly reflecting some of the difficulties outlined above, the army reported that the police 'were not able to participate in the scheme'.[102]

By March 1950, an 'Emergency Scheme for Kenya Colony' had been drawn up to address many such shortcomings. Taking account of probable manpower shortages and in expectation that outbreaks of unrest might well be widespread and occur simultaneously in rural and urban areas, the scheme specified a rigid and clearly defined command structure, with 'emergency committees' at the colony, provincial, and district levels. These would assist in the co-ordination of the exchange of intelligence, so that the security forces could be deployed when and where they were most urgently needed.[103] 'Internal Security' would come 'under the direction of the Commissioner of Police, with the assistance of Headquarters, East Africa Command' which would, if requested, 'supply a Military Liaison Officer to be stationed at Kenya Police Headquarters'. The Police Commissioner would also submit situation reports twice daily.[104]

In May 1950, the Nairobi general strike provided the opportunity for the Emergency Scheme's first real test and, more importantly, proved its success. Armoured cars were seen on Nairobi's streets, and teargas was used to disperse restless crowds in some of the African locations, both for the first time.[105] Significantly, although the Army's rules of engagement made allowances for 'singling out' the 'ringleaders' of angry mobs or riots (a 'shoot to kill' policy), firearms were not used.[106] Order was restored within two weeks, the strike broken.[107] Shortly afterwards, Kenya's Chief Secretary, John Rankine, wrote to General Dowler, thanking him for 'the considerable assistance ... given during the recent strike in Nairobi. [...] The loan of gas grenades and of jeeps was much appreciated.'[108] Ironically, their defeat led Bildad Kaggia and Fred Kubai, the strike organisers, to decide that more militant action was necessary, including infiltration of KAU, and a general oathing campaign directed from Nairobi.[109]

While urban unrest, by definition, was concentrated, thus comparatively straightforward to repress, rural subversion was more fragmented and widespread. Of course, as the colonial authorities in London and Nairobi feared, and were later to experience, simultaneous rural and urban civil disturbances were a different matter altogether. The Kenya government had learned of the existence of Mau Mau in 1948, when Kikuyu labourers on settler farms began to agitate against their conditions.[110] In early 1950, Special Branch first reported the existence of the Mau Mau 'secret society' and its oathing campaign, which was promptly made a criminal offence. In April, the police began to make arrests for 'administering an unlawful oath'. By the end of 1950, there had been 120 convictions.[111]

With emergency schemes and intelligence systems for gathering and collating information in place, the principal task remaining for directors of internal security is threat analysis, or 'targeting'. In August 1950, the decision was taken to establish an Internal Security Working Committee (ISWC) to this end: tasked to 'assess the internal security risk in Kenya in the light of present conditions and trends' and to 'review broadly the scope and nature of existing schemes with a view to assessing generally their adequacy or otherwise to meet the risk'.[112]

The ISWC's first report, submitted in November 1951, covered many of the 'causes' and 'types of unrest' mentioned above. In an appreciation of 'General Factors', which reflected the distinct lack of racial harmony in the colony at the time, the ISWC Report began thus: 'The factors which may affect the internal security situation in Kenya can best be considered separately in relation to the three communities.'[113] (This aspect of the report was omitted from Corfield's summary.) Referring to 'Asian factors', in so far as they might have posed a security problem, the ISWC summarised that these 'lie mainly in the possibility of communal strife arising from events in their own countries, and in the chance that as the tool of Indian politicians, the African might be incited to excesses which he would not otherwise contemplate'. The ISWC also predicted that in the probable event of natural population growth, consequent increases in Asian unemployment might well push some towards communist leanings. On the whole, however, Asians were not considered to be a security risk.[114]

Taking a broad view, the ISWC also reported that 'Europeans may affect internal security in three ways: (a) by acting as an abrasive to other communities; (b) by propagating well meaning but impracticable or misguided advice to Africans; (c) by unlawful actions against the Government or other communities.' Although the decision to form the ISWC had been taken two days before Mau Mau was proscribed, on 12 August 1950, it paid little attention to this apparently unspectacular secret society. In this same first report the ISWC thought the threat to internal security represented by Mau Mau was negligible. It was responsible for little more than encouraging a '"go slow" policy' and 'minor acts of sabotage on farms'.[115]

Significantly, under the various headings relating to the 'African factors' which might lead or contribute to unrest, the ISWC noted: 'an increasing intolerance of interference in the conduct of their affairs by Europeans'; '"corner boys" ... [who] have little to lose by the disruption of the society they exist in, and provide a permanent nucleus of thieves and malcontents in all the larger towns and in the African land units which have contact with them'. Despite its apparent lack of activity, Mau Mau could still be 'a possible instrument for mischief in the hands of agitators, though one of which the potentialities *appear* to be waning'. Most significant of all, it remained 'a fact that the main focus of discontent is at present amongst the Kikuyu'.[116]

As one might expect, the ISWC also assessed the influence of communism as an internal security risk, and considered it unlikely to present a major problem in relation to the numerically inferior Asian and European communities. 'Although Communism [*sic*] has not necessarily any racial limitation, and indeed its known followers in Kenya number only a few Indians and a couple of European fellow travellers, it is suitable, for the purposes of this paper, to consider it as a matter concerning Africans[!]' While the ISWC recognised that there were in fact very few communists in Kenya 'and no known party influence now actually at work', the reasoning behind this distinction was clear:

> Kenya is, however, a country where there exist great disparities of wealth between the African peasants on the one hand, and the European and Asian planters and traders on the other. This class cleavage is accentuated by the coincidence [*sic*] of a colour cleavage, and inevitably gives rise to feelings of

> envy and animosity on the part of the "have nots". No society in which such disparities obtain can be regarded as healthy, and here economic conditions provide a suitable environment for the propagation of Communism.[117]

When read in conjunction with the ISWC's findings on 'Land Hunger', on the one hand the threat of communism is brought into sharp focus. On the other hand, especially given the apparently low risk, or effective non-existence, of Soviet influence in the colony at the time, communism pales into insignificance:

> The land available to certain tribes in Kenya is generally insufficient to support them, as at present utilised, at a reasonable standard of living. The population is increasing very rapidly, and it is doubtful whether improved methods of agriculture, and employment in secondary industries, will be able to offset the natural increase. [...] Africans turn hungry eyes on the [White] Highlands, and many undoubtedly believe that the simple and natural solution of their problem would be to spill over from the Reserves [*sic*] on to the European farms. To the Kikuyu, in particular, this simple solution appears to be the more appropriate, as they have convinced themselves that in adopting it they would merely be repossessing lands taken from them by the white settlers. It is probable that the spectacle of the large areas of the Highlands (much of them admittedly undeveloped), compared with the congested picture of many of the Reserves, constitutes, at the moment, the most potent cause of hostility against Europeans.[118]

The ISWC was also aware that vernacular newspapers in India, West Africa, and in British colonies elsewhere, had been a 'potent source of trouble'. In Kenya, the mainly Kikuyu vernacular press, which was 'deliberately and mischievously disparaging of Government and of Europeans', was a factor, 'if not yet a very considerable one, in fomenting unrest and anti-European feeling'.[119] Matters were not helped, either, by earlier developments elsewhere in the Empire:

> The rapid constitutional advance made in other countries and the flattery of some visitors from England inevitably suggest that quicker progress towards "self-government" should be made in Kenya. The fact that progress has been quicker in the "black countries" focuses still more favourable attention on European settlement in Kenya. It would be difficult, too, for the East African agitator to fail to appreciate that every concession extracted from the British Government, whether in Ireland, Palestine, India, or indeed to an extent on the West Coast, has seemingly been extracted only by violence.[120]

Given the ongoing restrictions on the political means of expression of

African grievances, evidenced by the eventual increase to four Africans appointed to the Legislative Council in 1947,[121] the ISWC's assessment of African political factors as risks to internal security is instructive:

> It is inevitable that the more intelligent and ambitious Africans should seek opportunities to make their mark in politics. [...] Some of the politicians are undoubtedly actuated by a more or less honest desire to promote the interests of their people; others are simply anxious to get rich quick. The disparity of wealth, the shortage of land, and general social grievances furnish the politicians and agitators with potent medicine; the susceptibility of Africans to oratory, and the ignorance of the masses, make them easy game.[122]

As the principal 'official' political voice for Africans, the KAU naturally came under ISWC scrutiny. KAU was considered to be mostly 'moderate and constitutional in method', as evidenced by contacts between some of its members and the African members of the Legislative Council. By contrast, alleged contacts between some members of KAU and the organisers of Mau Mau and various religious sects gave rise to considerable uncertainty within the ISWC. As a factor in internal security risk assessment, however, one thing was certain: 'The Kenya African Union would at present undoubtedly play the major role in any wide scale political agitation, though the personal rivalries of its leading officials make it not improbable that there may be a "hiving off" into other unions or congresses, perhaps based tribally or territorially.'[123] Ironically, this latter prediction would not be fully realised until Kenya moved closer to independence following the lifting of the State of Emergency (1952-60) and subsequent Lancaster House Conference. As will be seen in the next chapter, the Kenya government's approach to those members of the KAU leadership suspected of complicity in Mau Mau, while apparently somewhat belated, would reflect the fears expressed above. Whether these fears were justified is another matter entirely. Certainly, Kenya's Attorney General seemed to have a clear understanding of the gravity of the situation, which is difficult to contradict following even a cursory glance of the ISWC Report.

Reflecting his liberalism, possibly some naïveté, and perhaps the relative lack of information that he received on Kikuyu subversive activities, Whyatt nevertheless drew a prescient conclusion. In his covering letter to the ISWC Report, he emphasised that:

> [The] major problem in Kenya and East Africa generally is social and agrarian and not nationalistic. Moreover, we are at present at a stage when improvement in social conditions and such land reform as is practicable could bring about a marked betterment in the attitude to Government and it is for that reason that we can regard such improvement and reform as major security

measures.[124]

Crucially, alarm bells should have been ringing in the Colonial Office for at least a year before the declaration of Kenya's State of Emergency. However, as Füredi has perceptively argued, it was common throughout the British Empire for warnings such as those contained within the ISWC Report to be ignored until it was too late. 'When disorder broke out, sociological explanations lost ground to those of law and order.'[125]

Certainly, the Cold War paranoia of 1948 had superseded earlier, more moderate approaches to those 'who actively oppose colonial rule'.[126] It seems that Britain could not afford, in terms of financial and other resources, to distinguish between communists and nationalists. While the British were aware that many forms of anti-colonial agitation in the Empire were justified by socio-economic conditions, dissent, rather than quiet acquiescence, was qualification enough for incurring the state's wrath. Britain simply had too much to lose by caving in to nationalist demands everywhere, and Kenya was far too important from both the economic and, albeit transient, strategic perspectives.

Nonetheless, the Kenya government, at least in part, was acutely aware of Kikuyu grievances and the potential threat to security that they posed, if not the full extent of the threat. As for 'existing security arrangements', the ISWC concluded that these were 'generally adequate to meet the scale of risk which can immediately be foreseen, and that the real issues of policy are rather those preceding the violent state; they are those of ensuring that the elements which lead to violence and the means of achieving any serious disorder are denied'. The report also stressed that the emergency schemes 'should, of course, be reviewed from time to time'.[127]

The ISWC also made several recommendations. These included 'the restriction of local agitators who overstep the mark', 'appropriate control over publications whether local or imported', and 'the strengthening of existing legislation relating to arms and explosives'.[128] Documents relating to the Singapore Riots Inquiry would also be circulated among the military and police, so that lessons could be learned.[129] By the time that the ISWC Report had been submitted, 'the strengthening of the legislation relating to arms and explosives' was already 'in train'. Mitchell had even prepared a request for a Royal Commission on land use. Unfortunately, because of changes in personnel, the ISWC did not meet as scheduled, in May 1952, so its second review of internal security risks and contingency plans did not take place.[130] By the time of the next review, due in November 1952, Kenya was already in a State of Emergency.

In the absence of meaningful political and socio-economic development, it follows that pre-emptive action to 'nip' a security problem 'in the bud' should be preferable to a delayed, and often heavy-handed response. The

Kenya government was certainly alive to this proposition, as evidenced by its extensive planning, although its approach to dealing with threats to internal security could hardly be said to have been subtle. The problem was related as much to the dissemination and interpretation of intelligence as to its availability and, as Corfield concedes, Mau Mau was a secret society, bound by an oath.[131] It should also be stressed that the Mau Mau guerrillas were arguably as much a product of state repression as its target. (This will be discussed further in Chapter Two.) That the first detailed intelligence report on Mau Mau, completed in April 1952, took nearly four months to arrive at Government House only made matters worse.[132]

This gives some credence to Lyttelton's tenuous retrospective view that if the Colonial Office had been better informed, and earlier, as might have been possible, 'many security and remedial measures could have been taken earlier', saving many lives and, of course, money and other resources.[133] It is hard to believe that the Colonial Office was unaware of the ISWC Report. Nevertheless, while 'remedial measures' were thin on the ground before October 1952, and fitfully applied thereafter, 'security' measures were certainly 'taken earlier', although the application of such measures could not have been further removed from Whyatt's interpretation.

In early 1952, well before the declaration of the State of Emergency, the Kenya Police began to implement the government's security crackdown, and arrested several key figureheads from the Fort Hall branch of KAU.[134] By May, the police had begun an extensive campaign against Mau Mau in the Rift Valley, in which 150 Kikuyu squatters were detained, and 10 others arrested. The District Commissioners (DCs) of Fort Hall, Kiambu, Laikipia, Meru, Naivasha, Nakuru, Nanyuki, and Nyeri were also given 'the equivalent of Supreme Court powers of punishment for certain offences which are commonly committed by members of the Mau Mau Society'.[135] In July 1952, a 'Special Bureau' was set up to 'combat' Mau Mau. It 'collected and collated all Mau Mau information and organised action against Mau Mau'.[136] In August, the Bureau began to collect evidence against suspected Mau Mau leaders, many of whom were prominent KAU personalities, in readiness for a future arrest sweep.[137] Kenyatta, the nominal head of KAU, was of course on the list.

Following his return to Kenya in 1946, the field administration, the regular police, and Special Branch had closely monitored him. Despite the lack of any real evidence against him, visits to Moscow in 1932 and 1933, respectively, placed Kenyatta, in the eyes of the Colonial Office, and certainly in the settlers' perception, firmly in the Marxist nationalist camp.[138] His equivocal speeches to KAU mass rallies and failure to condemn Mau Mau did not help his case either, although the circumstances surrounding Kenyatta's trial ensured that he would be convicted, regardless of the facts.[139]

Since early 1952, the settlers had pressed for 'firm action' against Mau Mau.[140] In August that year, this culminated in an attempt to intimidate the new Chief Secretary and acting Governor, Henry Potter, when two settler delegations demanded that the government take emergency powers to deal with Mau Mau. Potter rejected these demands, but was sufficiently impressed to warn the Colonial Office of an 'imminent revolution'. Mitchell's tendency to understate matters towards the end of his governorship and the apparent lack of urgency regarding intelligence reports about Mau Mau, led to confusion and disagreement in Whitehall. Some officials dismissed the settlers' views as unnecessarily alarmist. Moreover, Whyatt was not alone in thinking 'fresh and positive measures to remove or alleviate underlying causes of discontent' to be preferable to 'repressive legislation alone'.[141]

Besides, the Kenya government's campaign against Mau Mau was far from lacklustre. By September 1952, 412 persons had been imprisoned for membership of Mau Mau.[142] A further 'mass campaign of arrests' initiated by the police in September landed 547 Kikuyu in 'preventive detention' in the first week.[143] That same month, the Kenya government convened an emergency session of the Legislative Council to 'consider special measures designed to check unrest'. These included legislation which would deny defence counsel the right to cross-examine prosecution witnesses, introduced corporal punishment for forcibly administering an oath, and gave the Kenya government 'complete control of all printing by presses'.[144] The state was certainly armed, and using all the repressive means at its disposal to check unrest and to remove its instigators and perpetrators from circulation. So why, in the end, did the Kenya government (with London's approval) resort to the declaration of a State of Emergency?

Conclusion

Towards the end of the Second World War, as preparations began for the mass demobilisation of African soldiers, British officials in East Africa began to assess the adequacy of intelligence and policing arrangements to cope with an expected upsurge in anti-colonial nationalism. Within a year or two, their woeful findings had been exacerbated by the onset of the Cold War and the related complications of uncertainty in London over the precise nature of future defence policy in the Middle East, and the broad question of colonial defence and security throughout the British Empire.

Overarching these difficulties were the financial and material strains of the war itself, which underlined the necessity to maximise the use of colonial resources in aid of the dollar-starved British economy, while ensuring that what remained of the Empire would have to be run on 'a shoestring'.[145] This impaired the ability of the Kenya government to balance its expenditure on the 'welfare programmes' designed to stimulate the local economy and to alleviate African socio-economic grievances with the costs of projected internal security requirements.

Nevertheless, considerable progress was made in planning for the possibility of a serious breakdown in 'public security' and, despite retrospective protestations to the contrary,[146] the Kenya Police did all in its power to avert a potential security crisis. While there may not have been enough police in Kenya, irrespective of their quality, there were certainly enough pre-emptive arrests, if far too many for Kikuyu sensibilities. Ironically, the almost total failure in London and Nairobi to appreciate that, in the absence of meaningful or sufficient political and socio-economic improvements, repression alone could never win the day, forced Britain to 'fight fire with fire'. While Kenya might not in fact have been in the throes of armed insurrection, the declaration of the State of Emergency and allied repressive measures would soon ensure that a 'terrible beauty' was born.

Notes

1. M.E. Chamberlain, *The Scramble for Africa* (London: Longman. 1980 [1974]), p. 52; Darwin, *Britain and Decolonisation*, p. 126; J.M. MacKenzie, *The Partition of Africa 1880-1900* (London, New York: Methuen, 1983); H.L. Wesseling (Arnold J. Pomerans: trans.), *Divide and Rule: The Partition of Africa, 1880-1914* (Westport, CT, Praeger, 1996), pt. I, chs. 3-6, pts. II-III, passim.; Richard C. Whitting, 'The Suez Canal and the British Economy 1918-1960', in Keith M. Wilson (ed.), *Imperialism and Nationalism in the Middle East: The Anglo-Egyptian Experience* (London: Mansell, 1983), p. 77; Keith M. Wilson, 'Introduction', in idem., *Imperialism and Nationalism*, pp. ix-xi.

2. For an overview of theories regarding the use of force by the state, and the development of colonial policing, see: Morrison, '"Quis Custodiet Ipsos Custodes?"', pp. 13-64.

3. For the relationship between British democracy and legal means of ensuring state, internal, or 'public' security, developments in said legal devices, and the 'repressive' civil means at the state's disposal to enforce law and 'public' order, see, for example: Baxter, *State Security, Privacy and Information*, passim.; Tony Bunyan, *The History and Practice of the Political Police in Britain* (London: Quartet, 1978 [1976]), passim.; Lustgarten and Leigh, *In from the Cold*, passim.; Bernard Porter, *Plots and Paranoia: A History of Political Espionage in Britain 1790-1988* (London: Unwin Hyman, 1989), passim.; Richard Thurlow, *The Secret State: British Internal Security in the Twentieth Century* (Oxford: Blackwell, 1994), passim.; Charles Townshend, *Making the Peace: Public Order and Public Security in Modern Britain* (Oxford: Oxford University Press, 1993), passim.

4. Janet Coleman, *Against the State: Studies in Sedition and Rebellion* (London: Penguin/BBC, 1990), passim.

5. For a broad overview and analyses of imperial insurgencies and efforts to repress them, see: Anderson and Killingray (eds.), *Policing and Decolonisation*, passim.; Blaxland, *The Regiments Depart*, passim.; Michael Carver, *War since 1945* (London: Weidenfeld & Nicolson, 1980), passim.; Mockaitis, *British Counterinsurgency*, passim.; Paget, *Counter-Insurgency Operations*, passim.; Townshend, *Britain's Civil Wars*, passim.

6. This assertion is supported by numerous cases throughout history. With respect to Africa, see: Gutteridge, 'Military and Police Forces in Colonial Africa', pp. 286-319; and Killingray, 'The Maintenance of Law and Order in British Colonial Africa', pp. 411-37. For Kenya, see: David M. Anderson, 'Policing, prosecution and the law in colonial Kenya, c. 1905-39', in David M. Anderson and David Killingray (eds.), *Policing the Empire: Government, Authority and Control, 1830-1940* (Manchester: Manchester University Press, 1991), pp. 183-200. For the parallel rise of modern police forces and the 'dynamic development of the European state system' over a 150 year period, see: Hsi-Huey Liang, *The Rise of Modern Police and the European State System from Metternich to the Second World War* (Cambridge: Cambridge University Press, 1992), passim.

7. John Lonsdale, 'The Conquest State of Kenya 1895-1905', in Bruce Berman and John Lonsdale, *Unhappy Valley: Conflict in Kenya and Africa*, Book One: State and Class (London: James Currey, 1992), pp. 13-44; C.J. Duder, '"Men of the Officer Class": The Participants in the 1919 Soldier Settlement Scheme in Kenya', *African Affairs*, 92/366 (Jan. 1993), pp. 69-87.

8. Foran, *The Kenya Police*, pp. 3-10; Robert B. Edgerton, *Mau Mau: An African Crucible* (London: I.B. Tauris, 1990), pp. 1-32; Anne Thurston, *Guide to Archives and Manuscripts Relating to Kenya and East Africa in the United Kingdom* (London: Hans Zell, 1991), p. xiii.

9. Clayton and Killingray, *Khaki and Blue*, p. 200; Malcolm Page, *KAR: A History of the King's African Rifles* (London: Leo Cooper, 1998), p. 1.

10. Kanogo, *Squatters and the Roots of Mau Mau*, passim.; David W. Throup, *Economic and Social Origins of Mau Mau, 1945-1953* (London: James Currey, 1987), passim., 'The Origins of Mau Mau', *African Affairs*, 84/336 (July 1985), pp. 399-433.

11. Berman and Lonsdale, *Unhappy Valley*, pp. 2, 13-74; Füredi, *Mau Mau War*, pp. 9-12, 22.

12. John Lonsdale, 'The Depression and the Second World War in the Transformation of Kenya', in David Killingray and Richard Rathbone (eds.), *Africa and the Second World War* (New York: St. Martin's Press, 1986, pp. 97-142.

13. For the wartime assimilation of the European settlers by the colonial state, see: George Bennett, *Kenya: A Political History; The Colonial Period* (London: Oxford University Press, 1963), pp. 89-98.

14. *Keesing's Contemporary Archives*, Vol. 9 (1952), p. 12478; *House of Commons Debates* (*HCD*), vol. 505, col. 389, 'Kenya (Mau Mau Activities)', 16 Oct. 1952; Füredi, *Mau Mau War*, passim.; Throup, *Origins of Mau Mau*, passim.

15. D.A. Low and J.M. Lonsdale, 'Introduction: Towards the New Order 1945-1963', in D.A. Low and Alison Smith (eds.), *History of East Africa*, Vol. III (Oxford: Clarendon Press, 1976), pp. 12-6, also reproduced in D.A. Low, *Eclipse of Empire* (Cambridge: Cambridge University Press, 1991), pp. 173-6; Throup, *Origins of Mau Mau*, p. 25.

16. Guy Campbell, *The Charging Buffalo: A History of the Kenya Regiment 1937-1963* (London: Leo Cooper/Secker & Warburg, 1986), pp. 15-7, 29.

17. Throup, 'Crime, politics and the police', p. 129; Cmnd. 1030, *Historical Survey of the Origins and Growth of Mau Mau*, (London: HMSO, 1960), p. 36 (hereafter, Corfield Report).

18. Füredi, *Mau Mau War*, p. 116; Bruce Berman, 'Bureaucracy and Incumbent Violence: Colonial Administration and the Origins of the "Mau Mau" Emergency', in Berman and Lonsdale, *Unhappy Valley*, Book Two: Violence and Ethnicity, p. 252.

19. The Kenya government uncovered the 'Mau Mau movement' on white settler farms in 1948, but the origins of the term 'Mau Mau' remain unclear. The forest fighters had few, if any, connections with the pre-emergency 'Mau Mau' leadership, and did not consider themselves to be 'members', as such. Instead, many called their 'movement' *ithaka na waithi* (land and moral responsibility, or freedom through land), taking on many guises during and after the official State of Emergency (1952-60). Given that at one stage there were up to eight 'Mau Mau armies' from geographically diverse origins, operating in the Aberdares region alone, it seems that the 'Mau Mau' label was a catch-all imposed by the authorities upon all forms of anti-colonial resistance, serving to tar such dissent with the 'atavistic return to savagery' brush, thereby justifying whatever repressive measures were employed. See: Bruce Berman, *Control and Crisis in Colonial Kenya: The Dialectic of Domination* (London, James Currey, 1990), p. 349; Robert Buijtenhuijs, *Essays on Mau Mau: Contributions to Mau Mau Historiography* (Leiden, African Studies Centre, 1982), p. 51; Susan L. Carruthers, *Winning Hearts and Minds: British Governments, the Media and Colonial Counter-Insurgency 1944-1960* (London, Leicester University Press, 1995), p. 134; Frank Füredi, *Colonial Wars and the Politics of Third World Nationalism* (London: I.B. Tauris, 1994), pp. 1, 192; John Lonsdale, 'Mau Maus of the Mind: Making Mau Mau and Remaking Kenya', *Journal of African History*, 31/3 (1990), pp. 393 n. 2, 394, 416 n. 118; Percox, 'British Counter-Insurgency', pp. 47, 66-7; M. Tamarkin, 'Mau Mau in Nakuru', *Kenya Historical Review*, 5/2 (1977), pp. 228-9. For the sake of simplicity, hereafter, the term 'Mau Mau' will be retained.

20. Robert Shepherd, *Iain Macleod: A Biography* (London: Hutchinson, 1994), p. 182; Kyle, *Politics of Independence*, p. 104; Philip Murphy, *Alan Lennox-Boyd: A Biography* (London: I.B. Tauris, 1999), pp. 223-8.

21. Public Record Office, Kew (PRO), CO 822/1819, 'Future Policy in East Africa', memo. by Lennox-Boyd (Secretary of State, Colonial Office), n.d. (c. Jan. 1959). Unless otherwise stated, all documents were consulted at the PRO. See also: Blundell, *So Rough a Wind*, pp. 262-2. The tenuous link

attributed to constitutional reform and counter-insurgency in Kenya is explored further in: Percox, 'British Counter-Insurgency', passim.

22. Consideration of the obvious extension of this question, whether ends justified means, would depend largely upon ideological perspectives and subjective value judgements of British imperialism *per se* and what might be called the 'Cold War scholarly divide'. Given that satisfactory analysis of these and related issues would require endeavours far beyond the current remit, any such interpretations and resulting conclusions must be left to the reader. A Neo-Marxist interpretation of the aims and outcome of British policy in Kenya up to and beyond independence can be found in: Colin Leys, *Underdevelopment in Kenya: The Political Economy of Neo-Colonialism* (London: Heinemann, 1976 [1975]), passim. This is supported to some extent, but with little in the way of primary sources, for obvious reasons, in: Jonathan Bloch and Patrick Fitzgerald, *British Intelligence and Covert Action: Africa, Middle East and Europe since 1945* (Dingle, London: Brandon/Junction, 1983), passim., esp. pp. 43, 47-50, 78, 81-3, 86-9, 105, 132, 143-57, 163, 168, 200, 203. For documentary evidence which indirectly supports some of the contentions in the above works, see the impressive: Wm. Roger Louis and Ronald Robinson, 'The Imperialism of Decolonization', *Journal of Imperial and Commonwealth History*, 22/3 (Sept. 1994), pp. 462-511.

23. Page, *KAR*, pp. 28, 49, 50-1. For details of the establishment of the KAR, its involvement in the 'Mad Mullah' Campaign (1900-20) in the Horn of Africa, the 1914-18 war, and the inter-war years, and the Second World War, see: idem., pp. 1-175; and Clayton and Killingray, *Khaki and Blue*, pp. 200-4, 215, 224-5, 250-4. For the nature and extent of the Second World War role of British colonial African manpower generally, see: David Killingray, 'Labour Mobilisation in British Colonial Africa for the War Effort, 1939-46', in Killingray and Rathbone (eds.), *Africa and the Second World War*, pp. 68-96. See also: James Lunt, *Imperial Sunset: Frontier Soldiering in the 20th Century* (London: Macdonald, 1981), pp. 205-43. Examples of cross-border incidents can be found in: WO 276/521.

24. Throup, *Origins of Mau Mau*, p. 171. See also: Gavin Kitching, *Class and Economic Change in Kenya: The Making of an African Petite-Bourgeoisie 1905-1970* (New Haven and London: Yale University Press, 1980), pp. 188-99.

25. Throup, *Origins of Mau Mau*, pp. 177-8; Bennett, *Kenya: A Political History*, pp. 96-8.

26. Harold Macmillan, *Tides of Fortune, 1945-55* (London: Macmillan, 1969), p. 276.

27. CAB 66/67, CP (45) 55, 'Imperial Security in the Middle East', memo. by Sir Edward Grigg, 2 July 1945, cited in: Kent, (ed.), *Defence of the Middle East*. Part I: 1945-1949, pp. 20-34, doc. 11.

28. Ibid., pp. 29-30.

29. FO 371/53286, no. 942, minute by P. S. Scrivener, 2 March 1946, cited in: ibid., pp. 75-7, doc. 27.

30. Ibid.

31. FO 371/53288, no. 1151, 'FO note of a meeting in Mr Bevin's room on 11 March 1946', cited in: ibid., p. 82, doc. 30. See also: P.S. Gupta, , *Imperialism and the British Labour Movement, 1914-1964* (London: Macmillan, 1975), pp. 286-7.

32. FO 371/53218, no. 3476, minute by R.G. Howe for Bevin, 4 April 1946, cited in: ibid., p. 101, doc. 34. See also: Alan Bullock, *Ernest Bevin: Foreign Secretary, 1945-51* (Oxford: Oxford University Press, 1985 [1983]), pp. 243, 610.

33. FO 371/53292, no. 1723, telegram 81, Commanders-in-Chief, Middle East to Chiefs of Staff, 22 April 1946, cited in: ibid., pp. 111-2, doc. 41.

34. CAB 131/1, DO (46) 17th Meeting, Cabinet Defence Committee, Item 1, 'Strategic Requirements in the Middle East', 27 May 1946. Also cited in: Kent, *Defence of the Middle East*, pp. 125-9, doc. 49.

35. CAB 131/3, DO (46) 80, 'British Strategic Requirements in the Middle East', report by the Chiefs of Staff', 18 June 1946, fo. 9, para. 22. Also cited in: Kent, *Defence of the Middle East*, pp. 146-66, doc. 56.

36. John Kent, 'Bevin's Imperialism and the Idea of Euro-Africa, 1945-49', in Michael Dockrill and John W. Young (eds.), *British Foreign Policy, 1945-56* (London: Macmillan, 1989), pp. 61-2.

37. CAB 131/1, DO (46) 30th Meeting, 24 October 1946, cited in: Kent, *Defence of the Middle East*, pp. 206-8, doc. 84.

38. Throup, 'Crime, politics and the police', p. 129; Clayton and Killingray, *Khaki and Blue*, p. 112.

39. Throup, 'Crime, politics and the police', pp. 129-37.

40. Ibid., p. 131, and idem., *Origins of Mau Mau*, pp. 171-202, 243-4.

41. CAB 131/1, DO (46) 10th Meeting, Item 3, 'Location of Middle East Forces', 5 April 1946, ff. 6-7. See also: WO 216/304, 'Long Term Policy in Egypt', note for the Cabinet Defence Committee by E. Shinwell (War Office), Jan. 1949, paras. 2, 12-3, cited in: Kent, *Defence of the Middle East*, pp. 307-10, doc. 132; Devereux, *British Defence Policy*, p. 18; and Throup, *Origins of Mau Mau*, pp. 47-8.

42. WO 276/10, 'Note on Middle East Strategy', enclosed in Maj.-Gen. H.E. Pyman (COS, GHQ, MELF) to Maj.-Gen. W.A. Dimoline (GOC, EAC), 23 Sept. 1947.

43. WO 276/75, 'Conference in GOC-in-C's Office [Nairobi]', 21 Aug. 1947. See also: WO 276/10, 'Resolutions' from East African governors' 'Security Conference. Nairobi - August, 28th-29th, 1947', f. 3, para. 11, and GC (47) 19, 'SATIRE II and other Defence Matters' paper for 'Conference of East African Governors, October 1947', Office of the Chief Secretary, 10 Sept. 1947, f. 2, para. 9.

44. Throup, *Origins of Mau Mau*, pp. 5, 139-64, 173.

45. For analysis of 'the striking sense of fear [which] permeated imperial discussions of the likely consequences of the demobilisation of colonial troops' and measures taken to address those fears, see: Frank Füredi, 'The demobilised African soldier and the blow to white prestige', in David Killingray and David Omissi (eds.), *Guardians of Empire: The Armed Forces of the*

Colonial Powers c. 1700-1964 (Manchester: Manchester University Press, 1999), pp. 179-97.

46. DEFE 5/11, COS (48) 111, 'Staff Study "Intermezzo"', report by the Commanders-in-Chief, Middle East, to the Chiefs of Staff, 13 May 1948, cited in: Kent, *Defence of the Middle East*, pp. 277-80, doc. 120.

47. Devereux, *British Defence Policy*, p. 42. The projected capacity for the stores holding area had been reduced by almost half in Jan. 1949. See: WO 216/304, 'Long Term Policy in Egypt', note for the Cabinet Defence Committee by E. Shinwell (War Office), Jan. 1949, paras. 2, 12-3, cited in: Kent, *Defence of the Middle East*, pp. 307-10, doc. 132. The MacKinnon Road site did not remain redundant for long, however, and became one of the many holding camps for the 'hardcore' or 'black' (Z1) Mau Mau detainees located outside central Kenya: Clayton, *Counter-Insurgency in Kenya*, p. 16. See also: CAB 131/8, DO (49) 25th Meeting, Item 2, 'Accommodation Problem in the Middle East', 20 Dec. 1949, also cited in: Kent, *Defence of the Middle East*, Part II: 1949-1953, pp. 7-9, doc. 154.

48. WO 216/356, General Sir Brian Robertson (C-in-C, Middle East) to Field Marshal Sir William Slim (GIGS), 6 Oct. 1950, and DEFE 4/36, COS 166 (50) 7 (Annex), 'British Forces in Egypt', report by the Joint Planning Staff (JPS) to the Chiefs of Staff [JP (50) 124, 7 Oct. 1950], 11 Oct. 1950, both cited in: Kent, *Defence of the Middle East*, Part II: 1949-1953, pp. 105-13, 113-6, docs. 180, 181.

49. WO 276/75, notes of conference between GOC and Governor of Tanganyika, Government House, Dar-es-Salaam, 18 Jan. 1947, para. 9; WO 276/104.

50. CAB 131/1, DO (46) 24th, 5, 'The Future of East and West African Military Forces', 7 Aug. 1946, f. 9; David Killingray, 'The Idea of a British Imperial African Army', *Journal of African History*, 20/3 (1979), pp. 433-6; Throup, *Origins of Mau Mau*, pp. 19-20.

51. CAB 134/531, ODC (46) 11, note by J.A.M. Phillips (Secretary to the Overseas Defence Committee), attaching revised draft memo. and papers [ODC (46) 2] on 'The Role of the Colonies in War', 6 Dec. 1946. 'The East African military forces expanded during the war from 11,000 to over 225,000 strong.' (f. 7) See also: CAB 131/4, ODC (47) 10, 'The Role of the Colonies in War', memo by the ODC, 11 April 1947; and CAB 134/532, 533, and 534 for the deliberations of the Oversea Defence Committee between 1946-8.

52. CAB 131/1, DO (46) 24th, 5, 7 Aug. 1946, f. 7.

53. Ibid; Killingray, 'The Idea of a British Imperial African Army', p. 434.

54. CAB 134/531, ODC (46) 11, 'The Role of the Colonies in War', 6 Dec. 1946, f. 7. For a full account of KAR activities in Burma, see: Page, *KAR*, pp. 133-75. On KAR discipline in Burma and generally, see: Clayton and Killingray, *Khaki and Blue*, pp. 237-444, 254.

55. CAB 134/531, ODC (46) 11, 'The Role of the Colonies in War', f. 9.

56. Ibid.

57. CAB 131/1, DO (46) 24th, 5, 7 Aug. 1946, f. 8.

58. WO 276/75, 'Notes on Tour of GOC to Uganda: Discussion between HE The Governor, C-in-C MELF and GOC, 20 February 1948', f. 2, para. 9.

59. Ibid., COS/42, 'Aide Memoire for GOC's Address to East Africa High Commission Defence Session 21st September 1948'.

60. WO 276/76, 'Record of a Meeting with the [New] GOC - 27th January, 1949, Secretariat, Entebbe, Uganda [Civil Version]', HC (49) 6(a) 'Peace-time Requirements', memo. for EAHC Defence Committee, March 1949, 'Third Meeting of the East Africa High Commission held in Nairobi on Tuesday and Wednesday 8th and 9th March, 1949', f. 2.

61. Page, *KAR*, pp. 50-1.

62. WO 276/75, 'Conference Government House Dar-es-Salaam 18 Jan. 1947'; WO 276/76, HC (49) 6(b), 'Financing Defence Requirements', memo. for EAHC 'Defence Session', March 1949, 'Third Meeting of the East Africa High Commission held in Nairobi on Tuesday and Wednesday 8th and 9th March, 1949', f. 2.

63. WO 276/75, 'Notes on Conference with HE The Governor of Kenya, on Friday, 21st February [1947]'.

64. WO 276/76, 141, top secret telegram, Wallace (War Office?) to Dimoline (GOC, EAC), 4 March 1949.

65. WO 276/75, COS/42, 'Aide Memoire', Sept. 1948.

66. WO 276/76, 'Record of a Meeting with the [New] GOC - 27th January, 1949, Secretariat, Entebbe, Uganda [Civil Version]', and 'Third Meeting of the East Africa High Commission held in Nairobi on Tuesday and Wednesday 8th and 9th March, 1949', f. 2.

67. WO 276/75, 'Notes of Conference with HE the Governor on 13th December', by Maj.-Gen. W.A. Dimoline, GOC East Africa, 14 Dec. 1946.

68. WO 276/10, GC (47) 16, 'National Service in East Africa', memo. for East African Governors' Conference, 8-11 Oct. 1947, referring to saving secret telegram 42, Creech Jones (Secretary of State, Colonial Office) to Mitchell (Governor of Kenya), 12 Aug. 1947. For an examination of the question of conscription in the colonies generally in its broader context, see: L.V. Scott, *Conscription and the Attlee Governments: The Politics and Policy of National Service 1945-1951* (Oxford: Clarendon Press, 1993), pp. 247-9.

69. Kent, 'Bevin's Imperialism and the Idea of Euro-Africa', pp. 61-2. Montgomery's report (consulted for the above in FO 800/435; cf. FO 800/451) on his tour of Africa (Nov.-Dec. 1947) can also be found, in whole or in part, in: CO 967/39, PREM 8/923, WO 216/675, and WO 276/251. See also: DO 35/2380, no 1, '[Development of Africa]: memorandum by Field-Marshall Lord Montgomery, "Tour of Africa, Nov-Dec 1947" [Extract]', 19 Dec. 1947, cited in Hyam (ed.), *The Labour Government and the End of Empire 1945-51*. Part II: Economics and International Relations, pp. 188-93, doc. 104; Kent, *British Imperial Strategy*, pp. 148-9; and Morrison, '"Quis Custodiet Ipsos Custodes?"', pp. 67-9.

70. WO 276/75, Notes of meeting between Dimoline and Majs.-Gen. J.E.C. McCandish and J.D. Woodall, n.d. (c. Aug. 1947-Feb. 1948).

71. Ibid., 'Conference, Entebbe', 29 Jan. 1947.

72. Ibid., HC (48) 22, 'Item III Defence (a) Peace-time requirements (ii) Colonial Territorial Forces', 14 Sept. 1948, and HC (48) 23 of the same heading, n.d. (c. 29 Sept. 1948), 'Second Meeting of the East Africa High Commission, held in Nairobi on Tuesday and Wednesday, 21st and 22nd September, 1948'. There was no need for a 'Regular reserve' of Africans 'because they lose their efficiency very rapidly'.

73. Ibid.

74. Clayton and Killingray, *Khaki and Blue*, pp. 200-4.

75. WO 276/75, 'Conference, Entebbe', 29 Jan. 1947.

76. Ibid., 'Notes of Conference with HE the Governor on 13th December' by Dimoline, 14 Dec. 1946, 'Notes on Tour of GOC to Uganda: Discussion between HE The Governor, C-in-C MELF and GOC, 20 February 1948', f. 2, para. 13, 'Second Meeting of the East Africa High Commission, held in Nairobi on Tuesday and Wednesday, 21st and 22nd September, 1948'; WO 276/76, 'Note of Meeting with the Governor of Kenya - 1st Feb. 1949', 'Memorandum of Meeting with HE the Governor of Kenya on 2nd March 1949', 'Third Meeting of the East Africa High Commission held in Nairobi on Tuesday and Wednesday 8th and 9th March, 1949' ('Defence Session', 9 March 1949), f. 6; Campbell, p. 29.

77. WO 276/76, EAHC 'Defence Session', 9 March 1949, f. 10; Clayton and Killingray, *Khaki and Blue*, p. 113. For a breakdown of KPR membership by race in Oct. 1952 and Dec. 1953, see: Throup, 'Crime, politics and the police', p. 141.

78. WO 276/76, 'Record of Meeting with the [New] GOC - 27th January, 1949, Secretariat, Entebbe, Uganda [Civil Version]'.

79. Richard Rathbone, 'Political intelligence and policing in Ghana in the late 1940s and 1950s', in Anderson and Killingray, *Policing and Decolonisation*, p. 84; Clayton and Killingray, *Khaki and Blue*, p. 114. References to the GSUs, along with their alleged implication in atrocities committed by the security forces during the military phase of the Mau Mau revolution can be found in: Clayton, *Counter-Insurgency in Kenya*, p. 37; Edgerton, *Mau Mau*, pp. 156-7; Füredi, *Mau Mau War*, pp. 167, 181; Maloba, *Mau Mau and Kenya*, pp. 93, 110-1; B.A. Ogot, 'The Decisive Years 1956-63', in B.A. Ogot and W.R. Ochieng' (eds.), *Decolonization and Independence in Kenya 1940-93* (London: James Currey, 1995), p. 74; Throup, 'Crime, politics and the police', pp. 143-4, 151, 154.

80. Füredi, *Colonial Wars*, p. 92; Morrison, '"Quis Custodiet Ipsos Custodes?"', pp. 79-82.

81. Kyle, *Politics of Independence*, pp. 41, 43, Throup, *Origins of Mau Mau*, pp. 4-5, 6-7, 66, 79-81, 139-64, 151, 203, 205-6, 209, 215-7.

82. Füredi, *Colonial Wars*, p. 91.

83. Ibid., pp. 88-90; Morrison, '"Quis Custodiet Ipsos Custodes?"', p. 82; Rathbone, 'Political intelligence and policing', pp. 84-5.

84. Füredi, *Colonial Wars*, pp. 90, 92-3.

85. Cited in: CAB 158/20, 'Colonial Security. Part I: The Form Which Intelligence Reports from the Colonies Should Take and the Material They Should Contain', Annex to JIC (55) 28, 'Colonial Intelligence and Security',

report by the Joint Intelligence Committee (JIC), 23 March 1955, fo. 9, para. 20. Also cited in: CAB 129/76, CP (55) 89, 'Security in the Colonies', note by the Lord Chancellor, Viscount Kilmuir, 22 July 1955, with attached 'Report on Colonial Security, by General Sir Gerald Templer, GCMG, KCB, KBE, DSO', 23 April 1955, p. 19, para. 81.

86. Füredi, *Colonial Wars*, p. 91.

87. Ibid., p. 92.

88. Kenya National Archives (KNA), GO 3/2/72, Corfield Report (secret - unpublished version), ch. III, 'The Organisation of Intelligence', para. 5, cited in Heather, 'Counterinsurgency and Intelligence', p. 14. See also: idem., 'Intelligence and Counter-Insurgency in Kenya', p. 61.

89. WO 276/75, 'Conference Nanyuki 27 Jan. 47'.

90. Ibid., 'Notes on Conference with HE the Governor of Kenya, on Friday, 21st February [1947]'.

91. Ibid., 'Conference in GOC-in-C's Office - 21 August 1947'; Throup, *Origins of Mau Mau*, pp. 224-36.

92. WO 276/75, 'Conference Nanyuki 27 Jan. 47'.

93. Ibid., 'Notes on Conference with HE the Governor of Kenya', 21 Feb. 1947.

94. Ibid., 'Conference in GOC-in-C's Office - 21 August 1947'. Sillitoe's involvement in efforts to improve political intelligence-gathering capabilities in East and Central Africa in 1947 is less well known than his two visits to Kenya in November 1952 and April 1953, respectively. See, for example: Blundell, *So Rough a Wind*, p. 187; Clayton, *Counter-Insurgency in Kenya*, p. 33.

95. WO 276/10, 'Security Conference. Nairobi - August, 18th-29th, 1947. Resolutions'. The Nairobi SLO, W.F. Bell, formerly with MI6, was recruited by Sillitoe in 1949: Nigel West, *A Matter of Trust: MI5 1945-72* (London: Weidenfeld & Nicolson, 1982), pp. 54, 66-7.

96. Füredi, *Colonial Wars*, p. 89.

97. Throup, 'Crime, politics and the police', pp. 135, 137-9.

98. Rhodes House Library, Oxford (RHL), Creech Jones papers, box 55, file 4, 'Governor P. Mitchell to A. Creech Jones', 16 Sept. 1948, cited in: Füredi, *Colonial Wars*, pp. 93-4, 289 n. 20.

99. Frank Füredi, 'Kenya: Decolonization through counter-insurgency', in A. Gorst, L. Johnman, and W. Scott Lucas (eds.), *Contemporary British History, 1931-1961: Politics and the Limits of Policy* (London: Pinter, 1991), p. 144.

100. The existence of a similar internal security scheme for Uganda, among others, suggests that Britain's approach to preventing insurgency in the empire was very deliberate, and reflects fears of the likelihood of widespread civil unrest. See: WO276/103, 'Uganda - Internal Security', June 1947-July1950.

101. J. 'Bayo Adekson, 'Ethnicity and army recruitment in colonial plural societies', *Ethnic and Racial Studies*, 2/2 (1979), p. 158.

102. Percox, 'British Counter-Insurgency', pp. 53-4.

103. Ibid., pp. 54-5. Dimoline had 'disagreed' with provisions in the earlier internal security schemes for Kenya and Uganda, which entailed deploying

troops, rather than the police, to guard 'vulnerable points' (VPs), WO 276/76, 'Note of Meeting with the Governor of Kenya - 1st Feb. 1949', 'GOC/HE Governor, Uganda Conference Draft Notes', n.d. (c. 27 Jan. 1949).

104. WO 276/106, 'Emergency Scheme for Kenya Colony', March 1950.

105. Throup, *Origins of Mau Mau*, pp. 10, 194-6.

106. Clayton and Killingray, *Khaki and Blue*, p. 115.

107. Throup, loc. cit.

108. WO 276/102, Rankine (Chief Secretary, Nairobi) to Dowler (GOC, EAC), 7 June 1950.

109. Throup, *Origins of Mau Mau*, pp. 10, 194-6.

110. Lonsdale, 'Mau Maus of the Mind', p. 394; Tamarkin, 'Mau Mau in Nakuru', pp. 228-9.

111. Berman, 'Bureaucracy and Incumbent Violence', p. 250.

112. Percox, 'British Counter-Insurgency', pp. 55-8.

113. WO 276/519, 'Report of the Internal Security Working Committee', 12 Nov. 1951 (hereafter, ISWC Report).

114. WO 276/519, ISWC Report.

115. Ibid.

116. Ibid. (Emphasis added.)

117. Ibid.

118. Ibid.

119. Ironically, in June 1948, Whitehall had intervened in Kenya to prevent Mitchell from attempting to deport a newspaper editor to India. 'This was the latest in a series of clashes between the governor and the Colonial Office over proposals for state repression.' See: Füredi, *Colonial Wars*, p. 95.

120. WO 276/519, ISWC Report.

121. Kyle, *Politics of Independence*, p. 43.

122. WO 276/519, ISWC Report.

123. Ibid.

124. Ibid.

125. Füredi, *Colonial Wars*, p. 94.

126. Ibid., p. 95.

127. WO 276/519, ISWC Report.

128. Ibid.; Corfield Report, p. 117.

129. WO 276/519, ISWC Report, 12 Nov. 1951.

130. Corfield Report, p. 36.

131. Ibid., p. 117.

132. Ibid., pp. 132-3; Richard A. Frost 'Sir Philip Mitchell, Governor of Kenya', *African Affairs*, 78/313 (Oct. 1979), p. 551; Heather, 'Counterinsurgency and Intelligence', pp. 20-1.

133. Oliver Lyttelton, *The Memoirs of Lord Chandos* (London: Bodley Head, 1962) p. 393.

134. Berman, 'Bureaucracy and Incumbent Violence', p. 251.

135. Füredi, *Mau Mau War*, p. 116.

136. RHL, MSS Afr s 746, Blundell papers, 'Minutes of the Meeting of Legislative Council Committee for the Preservation of Law and Order at the Attorney General's Chambers on July 24th, 1952' (hereafter, LCCPLO); Throup, 'Crime, politics and the police', pp. 139-40.

137. Heather, 'Counterinsurgency and Intelligence', p. 30.

138. Maloba, *Mau Mau and Kenya*, pp. 76, 98, 111; Murray-Brown, *Kenyatta*, pp. 163-71, 255-76.

139. Maloba, *Mau Mau and Kenya*, pp. 98-100; Throup, *Origins of Mau Mau*, pp. 6, 52-3, 152, 228-9.

140. Füredi, *Mau Mau War*, p. 116.

141. Percox, 'British Counter-Insurgency', pp. 59-60; Throup, *Origins of Mau Mau*, pp. 11, 230-2.

142. Kanogo, *Squatters and the Roots of Mau Mau*, p. 137.

143. Füredi, *Mau Mau War*, p. 116.

144. CO 822/437, Sir Thomas Lloyd (Permanent Under-Secretary, Colonial Office) to Lyttelton (Secretary of State, Colonial Office), 10 Sept. 1952.

145. Popplewell, '"Lacking Intelligence"', p. 337.

146. DEFE 7/415, '[Colonial armed forces]: brief by Sir H Parker for Mr Macmillan', 27 Nov. 1954, cited in: Goldsworthy (ed.), *The Conservative Government and the End of Empire* Part I: International Relations, doc. 16, pp. 51-2.

CHAPTER TWO

British Counter-Insurgency in Kenya, 1952-56

Introduction

It is a commonly held fallacy that in response to numerous challenges to colonial rule throughout the Empire, Britain conceded varying measures of constitutional advance, the precursor to decolonisation, as part of a broad strategy of counter-insurgency. Indeed, the fact that Britain made such concessions so readily has been attributed to vast experience in combating insurgency, and has also been interpreted as contributing greatly to Britain's arguable success in the field.[1] It would clearly be unreasonable, and misinformed, to suggest that political reform did not in any way help to avoid or bring about the end of many insurgencies in the British Empire, as most clearly, if tragically demonstrated by Britain's withdrawal from India.[2] However, given the relative lack of detailed scholarship focusing on internal security in a pre- or post-emergency context, it is fair to say that too much emphasis has been placed on political reform, with insufficient attention paid to the timing of such reform in relation to broader issues. This has been detrimental to our understanding of the precise function of political reform on a territory-by-territory basis, and has ignored the strong element of continuity in post-war British colonial policy, especially regarding matters of overseas defence.

It is unnecessary to provide an encyclopaedic or exhaustive account of the military aspects of the so-called 'Mau Mau revolt'.[3] By considering the military and policing aspects of the Emergency in relation to the nature and timing of political and socio-economic reforms, this chapter will demonstrate that British counter-insurgency in Kenya amounted to a comprehensive strategy for regaining control, rather than an attempt to devise a satisfactory formula for the transfer of power.

'Phoney War': Kenya's 'Imminent Revolution', October 1952-May 1953

With the arrival of the new governor, Sir Evelyn Baring, on 30 September 1952, so began the next, and apparently decisive phase in Britain's efforts to regain control of Kenya Colony. Draft legislation to strengthen the government's 'hands in maintaining law and order' had been completed, and the Royal Commission on land use would soon be established. Despite criticism over the delay in the new governor's departure, Lyttelton had told Churchill that it would have been a mistake to send him to Kenya beforehand.[4] Clearly, the Colonial Office wanted to ensure that he had all the legal and political tools perceived necessary at the time to restore order to the colony. Baring had not arrived in Kenya with the intention of declaring a State of Emergency, however, and immediately began a tour of the African reserves, leaving instructions for Kenyatta to be invited to meet him for talks.[5] This all changed following the assassination of Senior Chief Waruhiu on 7 October.

Baring contacted Lyttelton on 9 October, and explained that it was in fact necessary to declare a State of Emergency. Kenya was 'facing a planned revolutionary movement' which, if left unchecked, would give rise to 'an administrative breakdown, followed by bloodshed amounting to civil war'.[6] The Colonial Office advised that although the Secretary of State 'was absent at the time of despatch, would wish to consult his colleagues and there might be a delay before his decision would be communicated, ... planning should proceed'.[7] Baring wasted little time, and immediately began to make military arrangements. He also extended the police curfew to the entire Kikuyu Reserve.[8]

By 14 October, Lyttelton had been persuaded that a State of Emergency was 'drastic but necessary to prevent deterioration' of the situation.[9] The Secretary of State also agreed that because those arrested for 'connection with subversive activities' would include 'certain respected public figures', the operation ('Jock Scott') might give rise to widespread Kikuyu violence. He therefore abandoned the earlier Colonial Office reluctance to despatch a British battalion from the Middle East as a pre-emptive measure.[10] Baring and the local military commander, General Sir Alexander Cameron, considered a British battalion to be necessary on two grounds. At best, the psychological effect of the arrival of British troops might prevent 'riots and bloodshed'. At worst, there would be a 'general uprising' of the whole Kikuyu tribe 'half a million strong'. They also thought it to be 'only a question of time before unauthorised European retaliation' began, as a result of the 'wanton' Mau Mau attacks.[11] A second battalion was already 'being ear marked and prepared' in case further reinforcements should be required.[12]

When viewed from the 'government side' (administration, loyalists, security forces, settlers), the first five months of the Emergency (the 'phoney war' phase), was somewhat short of results.[13] Between 20 and 21 October, the Kenya Police, supported by the army, arrested 89 of the 139 targeted suspects.[14] This was about as late in the day as a pre-emptive strike could get. Given the delay in Lyttelton's response to Baring, the earlier reluctance in the Colonial Office, as well as in the Kenya government to declare a State of

Emergency, and Baring's initial opinion that 'the emergency was unlikely to last more than a few weeks',[15] Füredi's assertion that emergencies 'were as much pre-planned attempts at the political management of anti-colonial forces as belated responses to an unexpected challenge to the imperial order' is, in this case, questionable.[16] So too is his suggestion that declarations of states of emergency allowed Britain to maintain 'the pretence of normal civil rule'.[17] This is especially so if Füredi's earlier remark, that the response to Mau Mau was 'poorly thought-out and panicky' is taken into account.[18]

Clearly, Füredi has a point, given that states of emergency, as a concept, did indeed allow for the introduction of political and socio-economic reforms, *viz* the 'political management of anti-colonial forces'. However, it is equally, if not more clear that in practice, during a state of emergency, such arguably 'progressive' reforms could only ever be introduced as a subordinate aspect of the resource-intensive and 'repressive' military and policing measures, or *first* 'prong' in any counter-insurgency campaign. If for no other reason, logic dictates that given a situation of ongoing and widespread anarchy, often incorporating violence, the introduction of reforms might well be impracticable. Besides, by the time that such 'Emergency' reform becomes necessary, it would surely amount to too little, too late, and 'terrorism' cannot be seen to have gained concessions from the body politic. As will be seen below, this view seems in accordance with practice during the Kenya Emergency.

Within a week of Baring's request, London had agreed to the declaration of an Emergency, and plans were put into effect to airlift one battalion of British troops into Kenya to support the police during the 'Jock Scott' arrests, due to coincide with the Emergency declaration at midnight, 20 October.[19] It cannot be overstated that recourse to legal means of repression, and the monopoly of such, is a significant weapon in any state's armoury. By resorting to the device of a State of Emergency, however, the British and Kenya governments were not simply exercising this monopoly in order to brand the nationalist politicians as lawbreakers, as Füredi has suggested.[20]

The legal mechanisms defining and underpinning a 'technical' state of emergency, the Emergency Powers Order in Council (1939) were derived essentially from the Emergency Powers (Defence) Act (1939), which had been introduced as a precaution against invasion before the outbreak of the Second World.[21] Although in Britain there were protests concerning certain provisions of the Act, notably detention without trial of potential subversives, and despite Füredi's contention that emergencies were declared throughout the British Empire as pre-emptive catch-alls to help in combating anti-colonial resistance, there is evidence to suggest that the device was not used indiscriminately.

Certainly, when it came to the Special Branch arrest lists of the alleged 'Mau Mau managers', Baring had removed the names of those against whom there was *no* evidence of association with Mau Mau. Rather, the British authorities had to keep one eye on international opinion and the growing body of international law, and could only take militarily supported action against suspected subversion if a state of emergency were deemed to exist. By taking action under Emergency Regulations in this context, Britain could avoid contravening the European Convention on Human Rights.[22] It should be stressed that Baring had hoped initially that the Emergency would last until the end of the year, at worst; a position supported by Lyttelton, who hoped that it would end quickly enough to save him embarrassment at Westminster. Surely, if Britain had intended to curtail all nationalist tendencies in Kenya under the guise of an Emergency, this would have been planned from the outset, and concerns to end it as quickly as possible would be absent from the documentary record; this is not the case. Besides, it could be argued that indiscriminate tactics had already been employed by the Kenya Police up to two years before the State of Emergency.

Moreover, the 'Jock Scott' arrests did not bring about the expected widespread disturbances which had apparently necessitated the arrival of British military forces in the first place.[23] However, Mau Mau activities were not curtailed by the arrests of their alleged leadership, with seven 'loyalist' Kikuyu and a European being murdered within a week of the declaration of the Emergency; 'oath-taking ceremonies were being held and an unknown number of young Kikuyu had taken to the hills and forests'.[24]

On the day of the declaration of the Emergency, Lyttelton explained to the Commons that the situation in Kenya had 'become progressively worse', that troops had been deployed 'as a reserve', and that 'all action now being taken is by the Police'. He added, 'I am leaving for Kenya next week, not to discuss the present measures - which ... have my full support, but to see for myself what is happening and to consider, with the Governor, plans for the future development of the Colony'.[25]

Following Lyttelton's arrival in Kenya on 28 October, Baring outlined his government's plans to combat Mau Mau.[26] The Kenya government's priorities were to obtain evidence for the prosecution of the 'Class A' prisoners and to re-establish its authority in Kikuyuland.[27] The Kenya Police would be further expanded in the African reserves, and a Kikuyu Home Guard would be established.[28] What better test of 'loyalism' was there than to allow the Kikuyu to combat Mau Mau themselves? Baring thought that if '20 or so leaders could be put out of the way for a long time, Mau Mau would die, but it was vain to hope for quick success'. Far from having the 'breathing space' of an Emergency in Kenya to enable the 'political management of anti-colonial forces', Lyttelton was more concerned that it should be over quickly, in order that he could avoid the embarrassment of Opposition questions in Westminster.[29]

On 11 November, Baring increased the powers of local officials in 11 Kikuyu areas to punish Mau Mau supporters, or anyone who failed to 'make a "reasonable effort" to help the Security Forces'.[30] Resident Magistrates were given further enhanced powers, while many sentences for crimes associated with Mau Mau were increased. New regulations were introduced, enabling the authorities to confiscate cattle and other possessions, to introduce communal fines, and to forcibly remove resident labourers from settled areas and send them back to the reserves.[31]

The police and the military had already begun 'extensive sweeps' of the Kikuyu Reserve. By 12 November, around 2,000 suspects had been arrested, while 3,775 cattle, and 6,095 sheep and goats had been seized in a 'punitive action' for non-co-operation with investigations into the murder of yet another Kikuyu, Senior Chief Nderi.[32] On 14 November, Baring announced that Kikuyu Independent Schools Association (KISA) and the Kikuyu Karinga Education Association (KKEA) 'had been dissolved on the ground that they were "societies dangerous to the good government of the Colony"'.[33] Towards the end of November, in response to the murder of another European, Meiklejohn, a further 2,200 Kikuyu men, women, and children, along with their livestock and household possessions, were removed from their homes in the Thomson's Falls area, and placed in detention behind barbed wire.[34] In December, a special 'punitive' tax (also designed to help pay for the Emergency), and compulsory registration were imposed upon the Kikuyu.[35] Again, such measures could hardly be called pre-emptive, their very *reactionary* nature serving to demonstrate just how little control the colonial authorities in fact, or at least perceived, they had.

Despite several protests about the repressive nature of government measures, including Lyttelton's doubts about the likely effectiveness of communal punishment, Baring's proposals remained largely intact. This reflected not only the large degree of authority vested in Britain's colonial governors, but also the over-riding desire in Whitehall to see a rapid conclusion of the Emergency.[36] The 'lessons of Malaya' concerning the counter-productive nature of blanket repression clearly did not apply in Kenya. This suggests that the panic brought about by the earlier failure to avert an insurgency held sway over any pre-planned attempt at political control of the situation.

Between 20 October and 15 November, Mau Mau had allegedly murdered seven Africans and a European settler.[37] In response, the security forces had arrested 8,500 suspected Mau Mau supporters (most of whom remained in detention), and had 'screened' a further 31,450.[38] In addition, Kikuyu squatters were expelled *en masse* from settlers' farms, and endured '[b]eatings, forced confessions and summary executions' at the hands of some settlers.[39]

Far from intervening on behalf of the Kikuyu, the Kenya government was more concerned that such incidents should be 'hushed up'.[40]

In the government's eagerness to suppress Mau Mau, dare one say pre-empt an insurgency, by arresting oath-takers and administrators, and punishing thousands of Kikuyu for the crimes of a few, it actually accelerated the onset of the armed conflict which it sought to avoid.[41] Many Kikuyu who had not originally supported Mau Mau felt angrily compelled to join, in response, it should be stressed, to the security forces' and the settlers' repressive measures: 'If one were treated as Mau Mau by police, it looks as if it seemed prudent to become one'.[42] Many others joined the guerrillas in the forests because they believed, ironically, that if Kenyatta was indeed the leader, as the Kenya government argued, then Mau Mau was probably not such a bad thing after all.[43]

Neither the Kenya government, nor the security forces were aware of the extent of the inadvertent mobilisation of Mau Mau forces. On 5 November 1952, Cameron reported that 'most of the young [Kikuyu] men have disappeared from their villages. There have been stories of them assembling in force in the forest areas of the Aberdares and Mount Kenya, but there is little evidence to substantiate this and it seems more probable that they are lying up in the woods and valleys within the reserve.' The GOC had hoped that the guerrillas would assemble 'in force ... in only one place' so that the security forces 'could have hit them'.[44] Cameron realised that Mau Mau was 'far more deep-seated' than was previously known, and according to 'the Government experts', the movement would take 'at least nine months to eradicate'. General Robertson, overall commander in the Middle East, went as far as to suggest that he 'should not be surprised if it took longer'.[45] With Mau Mau successfully evading the security forces in the forests, the government's priorities were to obtain the convictions of the detained Mau Mau leadership, and to discourage further action in support of, or by Mau Mau.[46]

By the end of November 1952, apparently to 'save numbers of innocent persons being caught up in the net', 'large-scale sweeps by troops and police' were abandoned 'save in exceptional circumstances', and would be confined to the areas where 'disturbances' had occurred, as in Thomson's Falls, following the Meiklejohn murder.[47] The contradiction of targeting those Kikuyu who failed to take 'reasonable steps to *prevent* crime committed in their locality', when this could only be, and *was* measured *after* the event, is obvious.[48] Even localised sweeps, which also involved the innocent, were to prove counter-productive. At the time, however, avoiding the alienation of the innocent took second place to putting down 'as ruthlessly as is necessary, and no more ruthlessly than is necessary, crimes against law and order'.[49] On 15 December, it became official policy to evict Kikuyu from areas where alleged Mau Mau crimes had occurred.[50]

The policy of punitive sweeps and mass evictions of Kikuyu from Mau Mau crime areas continued unabated into 1953. By the end of February 1953, 58,864 'Africans' had been screened. Although 39,000 were subsequently released, 2,249 were held on remand while 17,613 were sent for trial.[51] From November 1952 to April 1953, between 70,000 and 100,000 Kikuyu were either forcibly evicted, or departed voluntarily from the Rift Valley and Central Provinces, mostly ending up in the already overcrowded Kikuyu Reserve.[52] The evictions only added to the desperation of many young Kikuyu males who, with few prospects in the reserve, began to drift to the relative security of the forests in early 1953.[53] If African political and socio-economic grievances and the consequent crime and unrest, combined with state repression, had not in fact brought about Kenya's State of Emergency, the measures taken from 20 October onwards certainly did.[54]

Nevertheless, as early as 28 October, despite official insistence that Mau Mau had no economic causes, Baring had announced development plans for Kenya, which he later called his 'second prong' in the campaign.[55] Indeed, the State of Emergency, while enabling Britain to adopt wide-ranging coercive powers, also facilitated the implementation of reforms which, if undertaken earlier, might well have averted the crisis preceding the Emergency.[56] As for 'progressive measures', although the Emergency had prompted Baring's announcement of some £7 million for development and reconstruction, this would include only £328 thousand (less than five per cent of the whole) to 'continue general agricultural betterment'.[57]

The greater part of the development funds would be allocated to road-building and water projects, for the building of community centres, hospitals, schools, urban housing, village halls, and a new airport for Nairobi. In addition it was possible that an oil refinery would be constructed at Mombasa, while 'the Government was ... carrying on negotiations about the granting of oil exploration licences "over a considerable area of the Colony"'.[58] Despite Baring's retrospective remark that 'we thought ... if you have a policy in which you are repressing a terrorist movement, you must try and do something that will try and make life tolerable when the thing's over',[59] the intention at the time was that the Emergency should end before development plans could be undertaken. Baring made it clear that the development plans 'could not be carried out "in an atmosphere of unrest and anxiety"; and said that it was hoped to carry out the ... development schemes in the next 12 months'.[60] Of course, Baring hoped at the time that the Emergency would be well over by then.

By proposing the introduction of agricultural reforms it was hoped not only to win the 'hearts and minds' of the Kikuyu, but to provide an incentive to prevent other African ethnic groups from participating in Mau Mau. However, the Kenya government did not start to negotiate the funding for the programme until August 1953.[61] By then, there were already three British battalions stationed in Kenya, in addition to the 5,000-strong local military contingent, about 12,000 police, and several thousand Kikuyu Guards.[62] While Britain eventually granted £5 million for agricultural reform, which Baring restricted to Kikuyuland despite it being designated for the whole of Kenya, this apparently progressive measure was a one-off payment, and amounted to less than ten per cent of Emergency expenditure.[63] The plan itself was not published until February 1954.[64] Moreover, the Colonial Office firmly rejected Finance Minister Vasey's additional request for a grant to expand African education.[65] Educated Africans had already proved to be far too much of a problem. Surely, if such reforms represented a facet of the 'managed' gradual relinquishment of political power, as Füredi and others would contend, the money would have been better spent sooner, as Whyatt had suggested in 1951.[66] Given the emphasis on restoring order, and the cost of the military and policing aspects of the Emergency, as opposed to ameliorative measures, it is clear that defeating Mau Mau was not just a priority, but also an end in itself. Repression first was certainly the order of the day.

From the outset of the Emergency, Whyatt was put in charge of co-ordinating security forces' measures against Mau Mau, reflecting the emphasis on the restoration of law and order. Information was collated, and decisions made by a 'Sitrep' (Situation Report) Committee, chaired by the Governor, and attended by Whyatt and other leading officials 'closely concerned with the campaign'.[67] However, the Sitrep Committee had 'no official status', as such, was not 'part of any overall chain of command and it lacked a staff to ensure that its decisions were carried out in the field'. Thus, it was 'not of sufficient authority or efficiency to fight a campaign'.[68] Ironically, until many Kikuyu were pushed into active participation in Mau Mau by the very nature of government repression, which in turn had added to the unfavourable intelligence situation, there was no campaign to fight. Moreover, this was compounded by the relative lack of an early offensive role for the army, which acted mainly in support of the under-manned police, or was widely scattered on defensive duties.[69]

Although Whyatt had supplanted the Police Commissioner as nominal head of internal security measures, 'the responsibility for making policy rested with' the governor.[70] Upon his arrival, Baring had requested an expert adviser on intelligence gathering, to review the situation. In late November 1952, Sir Percy Sillitoe was again despatched to Kenya, and soon recommended a thorough restructuring of the intelligence organisation.[71] It would be quite some time before the recommendations could be implemented, let alone show results.[72] Meanwhile, Baring hoped to make other improvements.

On 24 November 1952, he requested the appointment of a Director of Operations, in the rank of at least Major-General, similar to that which existed in Malaya.[73] The British service chiefs, endorsed by Lyttelton, refused, claiming that the problem in Kenya was not 'parallel' to that in Malaya. Baring would have to be contented with the appointment of Colonel G.A. Rimbault as 'Personal Staff Officer to the Governor'.[74] Rimbault lacked authority, seniority and staff, and therefore found it difficult to co-ordinate operations.[75] The 'bailiwick mentality' continued to prevail, as evidenced by the relative autonomy of the District Administration and the police.[76] Ironically, on the one hand government repression was leading to the insurgency that it was intended to prevent. On the other hand, the effective conduct of counter-insurgency was hindered by London's insistence that Mau Mau was a police problem rather than a military one.

By the end of 1952, the Kenya Police had found the bodies of 121 'loyal' Africans, including some who had given evidence against suspected Mau Mau members.[77] Mau Mau had also murdered three European settlers and one Asian woman.[78] Following a frustrated Baring's appeal direct to Churchill, and the intervention of General Robertson, Lyttelton finally approved the appointment of Major-General W.R.N. Hinde as 'Chief Staff Officer to His Excellency the Governor' on 16 January 1953. By then, two more settlers had been killed. Baring announced Hinde's appointment on 26 January, the same day as 1,500 settlers marched on Government House to protest over the inadequacy of government counter-measures, following the murders of a further three Europeans two days earlier.[79]

The Kenya government had not been complacent, however. By the time Hinde took up his appointment on 1 February 1953, Whyatt had been made to relinquish his responsibility for the conduct of the campaign to Potter.[80] Magistrates were given greater powers, and the first Provincial and District Security Committees were established.[81] In January, the security forces even began offensive sweeps of the forest fringes adjacent to the Kikuyu Reserve.[82]

Despite his rank, Hinde had little more authority than his predecessor, however, and was not in a position to take overall command of the campaign. The emphasis of the campaign was to remain on policing, with the military in support, and the policies of food denial and the 'protection' of the Kikuyu settled areas were to be rigorously adhered to. In line with the other 'doves', he also recommended 'social measures for the betterment of the inhabitants' to go 'hand in hand with military and police measures for the restoration of law and order', and a scheme of rewards to encourage active participation against Mau Mau and the provision of information. If re-absorption of the displaced Kikuyu should prove impracticable, 'uncontrolled movement' would be 'reduced to manageable proportions' by increasing the number of 'reception areas and camps'.

Hinde was also aware that the security forces were 'not yet built up to their full strength', and that the army should be released from static defensive duties as soon as was practicable. If offensive action by air should be required 'the soundest plan will be to ask for an RAF squadron'. Significantly, he was also aware that the financial 'shoe' was 'beginning to pinch'.[83] More troops would cost more money, but both propositions did not accord with some views in Whitehall.[84] Nevertheless, as the insurgency dragged on some further measures would be required to bring it to a rapid and successful conclusion.

Following a visit to Kenya in February 1953, General Sir John Harding (CIGS) recommended the despatch of two additional battalions and a further brigade headquarters to cater for the wider dispersal of troops.[85] Hinde would also be given executive authority over the 'small emergency committee' that Baring had recommended should be established to direct the campaign.[86] Harding was concerned that unless measures were taken quickly the 'disease' would spread. He did not want to see 'a growing and costly commitment, as happened in Malaya'.[87] Two British battalions were therefore despatched to Kenya in April 1953, arriving shortly after four Harvard aircraft from Rhodesia, which were to be used for strafing and bombing Mau Mau hideouts in the forests.[88]

As if to confirm fears in both London and Nairobi, and to pre-empt the arrival of 39 Brigade, Mau Mau carried out its first major offensive on the night of 26 March 1953. More than 300 men, divided into smaller groups, hacked and burnt to death 97 men, women, and children, and wounded 29, in the Lari area of Kiambu District. Simultaneously, a Mau Mau gang of about 80 attacked a police station in Naivasha, killing two African policemen and a KPR officer, released 173 prisoners, and raided the armoury.[89] The Mau Mau forest fighters had, in what was to prove a rare large-scale offensive action, at long last demonstrated their credentials as a guerrilla force to be reckoned with.

The panic instilled by the Lari massacre and the raid at Naivasha led to a reappraisal of the operational command structure. On 11 April, in a bid to step up the campaign against Mau Mau, Hinde's appointment was at last upgraded to Director of Operations.[90] Hinde was still subject to Baring's authority, and despite his nominal promotion exercised command over military forces only. Although military incursions into the forests began in May, they achieved little success until early June.[91] The settlers nevertheless continued to express their dissatisfaction with 'the way in which matters are progressing out here' and with Hinde. Two consequent reports from the GOC, General Cameron, and the overall commander in the Middle East, General Nicholson, respectively, brought about an apparently dramatic change. At the end of May, the War Office announced that East Africa Command would be established in its own right, and General Sir George Erskine, an experienced counter-insurgency campaigner, was appointed with full operational control of 'all Colonial, Auxiliary, Police and Security

Forces'.[92] Ironically, Erskine was among the first in Kenya to suggest the importance of political solutions to the 'KIKUYU [*sic*] problem'.[93]

Unfortunately for Kenyatta, although the Colonial Office had by then almost determined that neither he nor Mau Mau had any association with communism, reaching this conclusion in July 1953, the imperatives of government propaganda, as the campaign against Mau Mau was once again reinvigorated, ensured that no mitigation would be forthcoming, at least in public.[94] The Lari massacre had ensured equally that the colonial authorities would give no quarter to even a nominal nationalist figurehead. While one of the settlers, Ewart 'Grogs' Grogan, had suggested in 1953 that only Kenyatta had sufficient authority to bring an end to Kikuyu violence, and canvassed opinion with a view to his early release, the rest considered this to be a 'crazy idea'.[95] Indeed, it was Kenyatta's very significance to the Kikuyu, if not Kenyan African nationalism as a whole, that ensured he would remain under some form of detention for the next eight years. There would be only one victor in the forthcoming military conflict, irrespective of how hollow that victory may have appeared to some. As the following overview of the British military campaign will demonstrate, neither African nationalism nor African grievances would gain meaningful redress until the 'shooting war' was over.

'Limited War': the Colonial State 'Hits Them', June 1953-November 1956

In terms of 'arming the state' and thus bringing the military campaign against Mau Mau to an early and apparently successful conclusion, it was not simply Erskine's appointment, but clarification of the powers of the office of the military commander in itself, which proved to be decisive. It is unnecessary to provide an encyclopaedic overview of the details of the military phase of the Mau Mau revolution from the British perspective. It should be stressed, however, that Erskine was in a much stronger position than his predecessors had been, as evidenced by his immediate redeployment of the army on offensive, rather than 'guard' duties, and his later insistence on the formation of the four-man War Council at the apex of the command structure. Erskine was still hindered by the relatively slow expansion of the police, and did not hesitate to call for more military reinforcements for large-scale 'sweeps' in the reserves and operations against Mau Mau in the forests. RAF heavy bombers were also deployed at Erskine's request. Erskine can also be credited with the apparent 'turning point' in the campaign, 'Operation Anvil' (24 April-9 May 1954), a cordon and search of Nairobi involving four battalions of troops, during which some 19,000 adult males were detained.[96] Nevertheless, Erskine's request that a permanent garrison of British troops should be established in Kenya, which received considerable support from

British politicians following Britain's July 1954 agreement to withdraw gradually from Egypt, fell on deaf ears.[97] Besides, such considerations were academic given the numbers of British military personnel already stationed in Kenya at the time.

The very success of Erskine's offensive against Mau Mau had brought its own problems. As Erskine reported: 'The trouble with NAIROBI [*sic*] is that a great many "displaced" KIKUYU who were turned out of the RIFT VALLEY or who have deserted from the forest have found their way into NAIROBI. There is no livelihood for them in the Reserve and so the problem is social and economic as well as police.'[98] The problem was even more serious from the military perspective:

> There is evidence that for some time the central direction of Mau Mau came from the City [*sic*], and though this is probably no longer the case, Nairobi remains an important source of funds, firearms, supplies and recruits for the gangs. As a result, although petty crime is (because of greater police activity) less than for many years, there has been a serious increase of armed robberies and political assassinations, the suppression of which present a problem quite different to that facing the security forces elsewhere. The situation is aggravated by the influx of many thousands of Kikuyu whose removal is essential and re-settlement is being studied.[99]

Operations in Nairobi between October 1953 and January 1954, had only temporarily disrupted Mau Mau. Within weeks of the arrests of various leading members of the organisation, others had moved in to replace them. Daylight attacks by Mau Mau in Nairobi became increasingly frequent.[100] The plans for 'Anvil' had also suffered a setback because of abortive mass surrender negotiations which had been initiated earlier in the year. Ironically, Erskine could not spare troops for 'Anvil' until they had completed the process of receiving the surrender of a possible 2,000 insurgents.[101] Following the collapse of the negotiations in the second week of April, Erskine immediately launched 'Operation Overdraft' which, capitalising upon the intelligence gained during the surrender negotiations, resulted in the capture of about 1,000 Mau Mau supporters in the reserves. With the security of the reserves sufficiently ensured, Erskine could release troops for the Nairobi operation.[102]

With Mau Mau at last isolated in the forests, the District Administration proceeded with renewed vigour to step up the hitherto fitfully applied policy of 'villagisation'. Large-scale military operations continued. Erskine had hoped that these operations would place the 'government side' in a strong enough position to enable him to make yet another surrender offer towards the end of March 1955.[103] Although there had been encouraging reports in December 1954 of a willingness on the part of the guerrilla leadership to discuss peace, this was not Erskine's principal motive.[104] Throughout 1954, allegations of brutality and the practice of 'summary justice' against the Kikuyu Guard had increased. It was feared that some members might even defect to Mau Mau, rather than face judicial proceedings by their own side.[105] The situation had been exacerbated by charges of perjury against some law enforcement officers, and interference by the District Administration with criminal investigations into brutality. This led to a 'breach' between the police and some officials, and was the main reason for Police Commissioner Sir Arthur Young's early relinquishment of his post.[106]

In September 1954, the War Council decided to reorganise the Kikuyu Guard, then numbering some 25,000, into a reduced but paid professional force, to be effective from 1 January 1955. This would also enable the government to issue a 'strong and unequivocal warning ... to the loyalist tribesmen making it clear that the Government would not tolerate unlawful practices'.[107] In order to prevent Kikuyu Guard defections based upon this instruction, an amnesty was declared for all offences committed before that date. This left the way clear for the death sentence to be lifted for Mau Mau offences committed before the date of the new surrender offer, thereby removing the main obstruction to mass surrenders.[108] The amnesty and the surrender terms were therefore announced simultaneously on 18 January.[109]

The planning and execution of 'Operation Anvil' were not only significant in terms of the immediate effect on Mau Mau recruitment and organisational capacity, and the longer-term impact of the formation of the War Council. Many of Erskine's proposals for 'Anvil' and the outcome of the operation were to prove important to the arguably non-military aspects of the counter-insurgency campaign. They are particularly significant when considering measures taken to 'improve the lot of the African' and the broader debate over decolonisation.[110] The expression 'winning hearts and minds' was in many ways a euphemism. What mattered most was ***winning, not*** 'hearts and minds'.

In August 1953, when the Colonial Office granted £5 million for agricultural reform, and at the same time rejected the Kenya government's request for money for the expansion of African education, Lyttelton clarified exactly what the intention of reform was. It was important to 'win the people over' by securing their protection and introducing development schemes, in order to avoid a protracted struggle like that in Malaya.[111] Unlike the public pronouncements of October 1952, there was no mention of development for its own sake, nor of improving conditions for the African *per se*. This ambiguity again reflected the anxiety in Whitehall that the Emergency should be brought to a rapid conclusion. While reform nevertheless pressed ahead, if fitfully at first, the characteristic carrot and stick approach was explained by Erskine: 'Because other tribes are closely watching to see if the Kikuyu will derive any benefits from Mau Mau ... schemes so far put forward by the Committee on African Advancement have been confined to tribes other than the Kikuyu. [...] Stress in propaganda is laid on the progress achieved by Africans in the untroubled areas of Kenya.'[112]

While Mau Mau remained undefeated it was important, at least so far as the Army was concerned, that the 'hearts and minds' aspects of the counter-insurgency campaign remained subordinate to military tactics. For Erskine, the significance of the 'Development Plan' for the 'non-Kikuyu' was that it was only intended to be 'short-term'.[113] Moreover, the GOC made it clear that 'Administrative measures' were important to provide 'Incentives to Other Tribes'.[114] The 'stick' for the Kikuyu would include measures such as the confiscation of the land of Mau Mau supporters, the forcible imposition of villagisation, the prohibition of 'all movement out of villages except that of communal labour parties', replacement of 'all Kikuyu in employment outside [the] reserves', and suspension of Kikuyu political activity. The other tribes, in exchange for their non-participation in Mau Mau, would enjoy the 'carrot' in the form of 'entry into Kikuyu held jobs', a small increase in wages, 'better living standards for chiefs and headmen', the promise of development funds from Britain, and the 'cheap sale of confiscated Kikuyu cattle'.[115] It is notable that the immediate benefits to the 'other tribes' would be provided at the expense of the Kikuyu. More significant, however, is that Erskine's 'recommendations of a political nature' were 'designed to obtain short term results favourable to the military operations'.[116]

In assessing the relative importance of military victory compared to reform in the perceptions of the Kenya government and Whitehall, it is significant that the draft estimates of the cost of 'Operation Anvil' (non-recurrent and recurrent for one year), not including the costs of transportation of the detainees, nor the actual military costs of the operation, amounted to £1,580,250.[117] Of course, 'Anvil' actually ended up costing more, while 'Emergency expenditure' for 1954-5 ran at a rate of 'something over' £14 million per annum, more than twice the estimated level.[118] Conversely, a project to develop African housing in urban areas received a *loan* of £2 million.[119] To put this in perspective, by July 1954 'Emergency expenditure' was running at about £1 million a month. Approximately a third of this was 'for military forces and operations', the rest covered the 'cost of closer administration, the increase in the police forces, the cost of detention and rehabilitation camps, and emergency public works'. Moreover, the figure was expected to be 25 per cent higher for the remainder of 1954.[120]

While Erskine's proposals did not herald the introduction of political reform (the arguable precursor to decolonisation), they certainly helped, if they did not directly bring about the granting of the first government ministry to an African in Kenya. In late 1953, Baring suggested to Lyttelton that a means of increasing trust and improving relations between the peoples of Kenya would be to allow them to share 'in the responsibility of government'. As Baring somewhat naïvely put it: 'If men of different races take executive positions in government they will be compelled to work together'. Baring's proposals did not, however, conceive of African political representation in the immediate future. Three Europeans, two Asians, and an Arab were to fill the proposed six new positions in the government.[121] Discussions with European political representatives began in January 1954, and the Asian community was approached some time between January and February.[122]

Plainly, the Lyttelton Constitution of March 1954 was intended to demonstrate the government's willingness to accept African desires for political representation on a par with the other (numerically-inferior) Kenyan communities. It certainly reinstated earlier Colonial Office proposals intended to institute a multi-racial polity in Kenya. This was a far cry from decolonisation, though. Surely, a principal aim at the time was to deflect the non-Kikuyu tribes from supporting the political aims of Mau Mau. The Lyttelton Constitution was intended to last until 'the next [Kenyan] general election, which was to take place six months after the Governor had proclaimed that the State of Emergency had come to an end, or on June 30th, 1955, whichever was the later'.[123] Obviously, that meant when the security forces had won, and the Kenya government's negotiating position on political matters would be correspondingly strong. It is noteworthy that by the time the registration of African voters for elections to the Legislative Council began in late 1956, the military campaign against Mau Mau was apparently all but won.[124]

This interpretation is confirmed by the ban, until 1960, of African political organisations above the district level, designed more to foster political representation among the non-Kikuyu African ethnic groups (who largely had not resorted to the *radical* politics of violence), despite increases in 1956 and 1958, in African representation in the Council of Ministers. Moreover, even as late as 1959, the date for eventual Kenyan independence was 'pencilled in' as 1975, while Lyttelton's successor, Alan Lennox-Boyd, told the House of Commons that 'I cannot now foresee a date when it will be possible for any British Government to surrender their ultimate responsibilities for the destiny and well-being of Kenya.'[125]

Another arguable feature of the so-called 'hearts and minds' aspect of the anti-Mau Mau campaign, villagisation, also pivoted on 'Operation Anvil'. While the District Administration had earlier felt unable to consolidate its position in the reserves sufficiently to impose villagisation, following the success of "Anvil" the policy began to be officially implemented on a large scale.[126] Hitherto, some Kikuyu apparently loyal to the government had begun voluntarily to co-operate with villagisation, in order to gain protection from the Guard Post around which each village was built.[127] Indeed, such co-operation was taken as a 'fair test of loyalty'.[128]

The purpose of villagisation was clearly not just to provide protection for loyal Kikuyu. As early as December 1952, O'Rorke had suggested that 'both from the short-term police point of view, and the long-term social point of view, he would like to see all Africans in the Reserves living in villages instead of scattered about as they were at present'.[129] While villagisation did enable the introduction of various social improvements, such as the training of Kikuyu women in 'practical hygiene', the establishment of schools and churches, facilitated agricultural reform, and did indeed increase residents' security, it also served a more practical purpose from the security forces' perspective.[130] As Erskine had envisaged, villagisation made 'the maintenance of law and order as simple as possible'.[131] Not only could curfews be imposed upon those villagers found, for whatever reason, to be still supplying Mau Mau guerrillas with food, but a whole range of communal punishments and control measures could be imposed more easily.[132] The 'carrot and stick' approach was applied from the outset, by rewarding 'loyal' Kikuyu with economic and social provisions in 'model villages', while those considered to be disloyal were concentrated into 'punitive villages', which remained unclean and under-developed.[133] Anyone who remained 'tardy in moving' into a village had their hut burned down, leaving them little choice but to co-operate.[134] Most important, the effect on Mau Mau of concentrating the Kikuyu into villages, as opposed to leaving them scattered about the reserve, was to force the guerrillas once and for all to remain in the forests, where their isolation would be almost total.[135] From then onwards it would be just a matter of closing the military net.

Post 'Anvil' military operations proved to be so successful that by 1955 the monthly 'killing rate' was raised to 66, compared with 39 in 1953 and 49 in 1954.[136] Although there was still work to be done, Erskine was convinced that the Emergency had entered its last phase, and suggested that 'it is not optimistic to expect a reduction in the RAF and the Army later in the year'.[137] Nevertheless, the failure of surrender negotiations led Erskine's successor, General Sir Gerald Lathbury, to resume military operations against the 5,000 guerrillas estimated to have remained in the forests. Lathbury also increased the number of 'pseudo-gang' (mainly surrendered Mau Mau) patrols, resulting in the numbers of guerrillas being reduced by half by December 1955.[138] This apparently vindicated Lathbury's decision, announced that September, to withdraw 3,500 British and African troops and a brigade headquarters by the end of the year.

In January 1956, with yet still no sign of surrender, Lathbury decided to focus the pseudo-gang operations on capturing the guerrilla leadership.[139] By the end of July, a further 1,430 guerrillas had been accounted for, and two more British battalions had been withdrawn. With the capture of guerrilla leader Dedan Kimathi on 21 October 1956, and remaining Mau Mau strength estimated at approximately 450, Lathbury could announce that 'we now return therefore to the normal state of affairs in any British territory, where the Police are responsible for law and order'.[140] Superiority of arms, numbers, and tactics had apparently won the day. However, as British efforts to consolidate victory and 'vital' interests over the next three years (while maintaining a 'technical' State of Emergency) demonstrate, the 'state of affairs' was far from 'normal' (see Chapter Five).

Britain's task, or rather that of the Kenya government, was not made any easier by the ever-increasing cost to the British Treasury of maintaining internal security throughout the Empire, a burden which threatened to impair, rather than assist, broad defence strategy. As the Chair of the Cabinet Committee on Defence Policy, Lord Salisbury, explained in July 1954: 'We were instructed to review, in the light of recent developments in atomic weapons, the strategic assumptions underlying current defence policy and the scale and pattern of defence programmes, military and civil. In doing so, we have sought to secure all practicable economies in defence expenditure in 1955 and subsequent years.'[141] These economies would include a reduction in the size of the British Army by April 1956 from 435,000 to 400,000, but far more important was the necessity to bridge the gap of £130 millions in projected defence expenditure and available finances.[142]

The colonies were among the first targets where projected reductions in military expenditure could be expected, especially given the view in the MoD that the Colonial Office had failed to keep abreast of subversion in the territories for which it was responsible. As the Permanent Secretary, Sir Harold Parker, complained to the then Defence Minister, Harold Macmillan:

> We have drifted into trouble in many Colonial territories-Malaya, Kenya, British Guiana. The S of S for War and the Chiefs of Staff feel that had our local intelligence and our local security forces been better organised, we might never have got into the mess, or, alternatively, if help had to be given by the Army it might have been given earlier in the day. [...] To put it in other words, the Army argues that the Colonial Office gets into a mess and then asks the Army to help it out. [...] The Colonial Secretary will probably not accept this view. He has his difficulties. Personally, I have always felt that the share of the budgets of the various Colonies devoted to law and order may well be inadequate.[143]

Defence reviewers in London therefore saw room for considerable improvement in colonial police and intelligence structures, as well as the necessity to 'build up local Colonial forces in order to reduce the demands on our own Army'.[144]

Further deliberations on these questions led to the formation in January 1955 of a Ministerial Committee to examine colonial security, under Lord

Swinton's chairmanship (later replaced by Lord Kilmuir).[145] This committee then invited General Sir Gerald Templer to make enquiries about the causes of the emergencies in British Guiana, Cyprus, Kenya, Malaya, and elsewhere, and the state of colonial intelligence and security generally.[146]

While detailed consideration of the Templer Report, at 79 pages, must remain beyond the current remit, several crucial points can be made. First, upon reading the report, it is difficult to accept Goldsworthy's view, based on his reading of 13 of a possible 464 paragraphs, that it 'is generally regarded as having little impact on policy'.[147] For a start, the Cabinet accepted all of Templer's recommendations regarding colonial intelligence, policing, and security establishments, with one exception. Lennox-Boyd had objected to Templer's suggestion that a 'reverse colour bar' should be imposed on the recruitment and promotion of locals within colonial police forces (in preparation for future independence), because of the probable negative effects on serving European officers' morale.[148] However, Templer's argument that major changes were necessary to Britain's approach to colonial security were approved and, it seems, implemented widely. This was not least within the Colonial Office itself, where separate police, and intelligence and security, desks were established. A permanent Colonial Office appointment was also made to the Joint Intelligence Staff in order to augment the department's work with the JIC. The JIC, in turn, would have its Charter withdrawn and 'reissued jointly' by the Foreign Secretary, Minister of Defence and, for the first time, by the Secretary of State for Colonial Affairs.[149]

As for colonial armed forces, the major impact of Templer's report, unsurprisingly, involved the reversion of financial 'responsibility' to the colonies themselves. As Templer explained:

> The last time that a comprehensive review of the Colonial forces took place was in 1949. That review was written against the background of the second world war [*sic*] and at a time when fears of a third war were prominent in the minds of both Ministers and of the Chiefs of Staff. [...] Now that the chance of a third war has receded and with the practical certainty that we have ahead of us many years of cold war, during which the Colonies and dependent territories will form one of the main battle fields, it has become apparent that the whole matter should be reviewed afresh, in the light of our new strategy.[150]

Of course, the ever-increasing cost of imperial military commitments generally, as well as the inter-departmental tensions brought about by the fact that for the most part the colonial governments were expected to pay bills determined in advance by the War Office, had a considerable bearing upon all of this.[151]

Certainly, the Chiefs of Staff had already concluded that with global war unlikely in the foreseeable future, and even in such an event, the principal role of colonial armed forces would be to 'provide for' internal security and 'as far as possible, for their own local defence'.[152] Crucially, 'it would be more in accordance with the normal principles of British Colonial administration [preparation for 'self-government'] if the administrative control and policy direction of the Colonial forces were devolved on to Colonial Governments'.[153] This would also conveniently provide annual savings of some £980,000 on the War Office vote, thus to the Treasury, of maintaining local armed forces in East Africa (not including Emergency expenditure).[154] The local governments would also have to settle for reduced army contingents (from seven to c. five battalions).[155] Given the situation in Kenya at the time, these military recommendations could not be implemented immediately, although it did not take long for the principle to be established.[156]

In September 1955, Lennox-Boyd outlined Templer's recommendations to the governors, and informed them of the change which was likely to take place in the summer of 1957, recalcitrant Mau Mau allowing.[157] As will be seen in Chapter Five, the colonial state would therefore have to employ an ever more sophisticated armoury, in both political and socio-economic terms, and especially regarding matters of defence and internal security, if it was going to retain a foothold, let alone any influence, in 'fortress' Kenya. Yet, as will be shown in the next chapter, unbeknownst to all concerned in late 1955, the strategic assumptions regarding East Africa, which were set to entail considerable local financial difficulties, would change rapidly within a year. Rather less rapidly, the local colonial administrators would eventually see the fulfilment of even their most wildly optimistic defence and internal security *desiderata*, if not for long (see Chapters Six and Seven).

Conclusion

Between 1945 and 1950, increasing African socio-economic hardship and political marginalisation led to a steady rise in crime, civil disobedience, and anti-colonial militant action, including the murders of Europeans and loyalist Kikuyu alike. As government repression led to the onset of the Emergency it was designed to forestall, so the level and sophistication of that repression had to be increased. Irrespective of the piecemeal political reforms and selectively targeted socio-economic developments introduced during the 1952-6 period, British counter-insurgency was clearly not designed to pave the way for the transfer of power to anti-colonial nationalists. What mattered to Britain, first and foremost, was that it reassert its authority and control. By the end of 1956, this had largely been achieved, well at least apparently. As will be seen in the next two chapters, this was all well and good for Britain given that its broad regional strategic priorities would change, albeit coincidentally, within days of the Mau Mau guerrillas' defeat.

Notes

1. Popplewell, '"Lacking Intelligence"', pp. 336-52.

2. Judith M. Brown, *Modern India: The Origins of an Asian Democracy* (Oxford: Oxford University Press, 1994), pp. 251-359; Townshend, *Britain's Civil Wars*, pp. 127-55.

3. In addition to the works already cited, see: Charles Allen, *The Savage Wars of Peace: Soldiers' Voices 1945-1989* (London: Michael Joseph, 1990, pp. 125-38; Carver, *War Since 1945*, pp. 28-43; Michael Dewar, *Brush Fire Wars: Minor Campaigns of the British Army Since 1945* (London: Robert Hale, 1984); pp. 50-62; Lawrence James, *Imperial Rearguard: Wars of Empire, 1919-1985* (London: Brassey's, 1988); pp. 172-95; Philip Anthony Towle, *Pilots and Rebels: The Use of Aircraft in Unconventional Warfare, 1918-1988* (London: Brassey's, 1989), pp. 95-106.

4. PREM 11/472, Lyttelton to Churchill, 12 Sept. 1952.

5. Clayton, *Counter-Insurgency*, p. 5, n. 9.

6. CO 822/443, Baring to Lyttelton, 9 Oct. 1952, also cited in Corfield Report, p. 159; KNA, GO 3/2/73, 'Corfield Report (Confidential - Not for Publication)', ch. 17, fo. 1, mimeo., seen by courtesy of John Lonsdale (hereafter, 'Corfield - Confidential'). See also: RHL, MSS Afr s 1675, Corfield papers.

7. KNA, GO 3/2/73, 'Corfield - Confidential', ch. 17, fo. 3.

8. KNA, GO 3/2/73, 'Corfield - Confidential', ch. 17, fos. 1-4; PRO, WO 216/810, GHQ, MELF to War Office, 10 Oct. 1952; *Keesing's Contemporary Archives* p. 12570.

9. PREM11/472, 'Cabinet Committee, CC(52) 85th Conclusions, Minute 1', 14 Oct. 1952.

10. WO 216/810, War Office to GHQ, MELF, 10 Oct. 1952; PREM 11/472, C (52) 332, 'Top Secret Memorandum by the Secretary of State for the Colonies', 13 Oct. 1952; WO 216/810, 'Personal, for VCIGS, from Major-General in charge of Administration [MGA]', 15 Oct. 1952.

11. WO 216/810, loc. cit.; Lonsdale, 'Mau Maus of the Mind', p. 408.

12. WO 216/810, GHQ, MELF to War Office, 11 Oct. 1952.

13. Berman, *Control and Crisis*, p. 348.

14. CO 822/444, 'Top Secret and Personal Telegram 627', 'Immediate, Top Secret and Personal Telegram 630', Baring to Lyttelton, 17 Oct. 1952; CO822/438, Post Office telegram, 21 Oct. 1952; Heather,

'Counterinsurgency and Intelligence', pp. 30-4. It has also been suggested that initially 83 out of 154 suspects were arrested, KNA, GO 3/2/73, 'Corfield - Confidential', ch. 17, fos. 5, 6.

15. Douglas-Home, *Evelyn Baring*, p. 230.

16. Frank Füredi, 'Creating a Breathing Space: The Political Management of Colonial Emergencies', *Journal of Imperial and Commonwealth History*, 21/3 (Sept. 1993), p. 90.

17. Füredi, *Colonial Wars*, p. 1.

18. Füredi, 'Kenya: Decolonization through counter-insurgency', p. 147.

19. Percox, 'British Counter-Insurgency', pp. 60-2.

20. Füredi, *Colonial Wars*, pp. 1, 192.

21. CAB 134/1202, CA (56) 21, 'Powers of Colonial Governors to Preserve Order', memo. by Lennox-Boyd, 31 May 1956; Clive Emsley, *The English Police: A Political and Social History* (Hemel Hempstead: Harvester Wheatsheaf, 1991), p. 158; Füredi, *Colonial Wars*, pp. 1-3; Keith Jeffery and Peter Hennessy, *States of Emergency: British Governments and Strikebreaking since 1919* (London: Routledge & Kegan Paul, 1983), pp. 143-4; Thurlow, *The Secret State*, pp. 217, 220-1; Townshend, *Britain's Civil Wars*, p. 23, *Making the Peace*, ch. 6, esp. pp. 112-5, 131.

22. The declaration of a State of Emergency was also desired by administrative field officers in the Central and Rift Valley Provinces, who had long believed that action should be taken against the African politicians who were, they thought, actively fomenting armed rebellion. Apparently, these field officers considered it unwise to act alone against this supposed 'conspiracy' for fear that they might be charged with exceeding their authority. See: Berman, 'Bureaucracy and Incumbent Violence', p. 251.

23. Percox, 'British Counter-Insurgency', pp. 62-3.

24. 'Government House Meeting to Discuss Jock Scott Operation, 6:30 pm, 29/10/52', notes of minutes, seen by courtesy of David Throup (hereafter, 'Meeting, 29/10/52'). Those present included: Lyttelton, Potter, Whyatt, Davies (CNC), Cameron (GOC, East Africa Command), O'Rorke, and Hall (Principal, East Africa Section, Colonial Office).

25. *HCD*, 505, col. 865,'Kenya (Mau Mau Activities)', 21 Oct. 1952.

26. *Keesing's*, p. 12571; 'Meeting, 29/10/52'.

27. 'Meeting, 29/10/52'. 'Class A' were those considered to be the 'central planners' of Mau Mau, including Jomo Kenyatta, Heather, 'Counterinsurgency and Intelligence', p. 33. KISA, the Kikuyu Independent Schools Association, was thought to be a recruiting ground for Mau Mau 'terrorists'.

28. By the end of Nov. 1952, this voluntary unit had reached a strength of about 1,400, RHL, MSS Afr s 746, LCCPLO, 1 Dec. 1952.

29. 'Meeting, 29/10/52'.

30. Heather, 'Counterinsurgency and Intelligence', p. 38; *Keesing's*, pp. 12571, 13065. It should be stressed that these powers were granted *before* the murder of Meiklejohn, on 22 Nov., *not* 'shortly after', as Heather claims.

31. Heather, 'Counterinsurgency and Intelligence', p. 38, n. 19.

32. *Keesing's*, p. 13065. Again, the dates and figures differ from those for which Heather provides the same references, idem., 'Counterinsurgency and Intelligence', pp. 38-9.

33. *Keesing's*, loc. cit.

34. *Keesing's*, p. 13068; Füredi, *Mau Mau War*, p. 119. This appears to have been an action subsequent to the wider sweeps that took place between 20 Oct. and 7 Nov.

35. Heather, 'Counterinsurgency and Intelligence', pp. 39-40.

36. Ibid.; John W. Cell, 'On the Eve of Decolonisation: The Colonial Office's Plans for the Transfer of Power in Africa, 1947', *Journal of Imperial and Commonwealth History*, 8/3 (May 1980), pp. 235-57; David Goldsworthy, *Colonial Issues in British Politics, 1945-1961* (Oxford: Clarendon Press, 1971), p. 28. For example, in 1947, the intervention of governors in East Africa caused the Colonial Office to abandon plans to introduce a substantive measure of African self-government to the region, instead settling for minor reforms to local governments. These included, for example, a change in the nomenclature of 'Local Native Councils' to 'African District Councils'. See the extensive documentation on 'Native administration policy', reproduced in: Hyam (ed.), *The Labour Government and the End of Empire 1945-1951*. Part I: High Policy and Administration, pp. 103-306, esp. docs. 40-52, 58-62.

37. *Keesing's*, p. 12569. Not everyone was convinced that Mau Mau was responsible for all of the crimes committed during the period. O'Rorke, for example, 'said that he did distinguish between ordinary criminals and Mau Mau, but one was cashing in on the other', RHL, MSS Afr s 746, LCCPLO, 17 Nov. 1952. An example of such an incident may well have occurred in late Nov. 1952, when ten Kikuyu attacked two Asian shopkeepers, shouting "We are the Mau Mau", *HCD*, 508, col. 256, 25 Nov. 1952. As the perpetrators were never knowingly caught, unfortunately, this can never be ascertained.

38. *Keesing's*, p. 12574.

39. Berman, *Control and Crisis*, p. 349; Füredi, *Mau Mau War*, pp. 118-9, (1991), pp. 147-8; John Newsinger, 'Revolt and Repression in Kenya: The Mau Mau Rebellion, 1952-1960', *Science and Society*, 45/2 (Summer 1981), p. 169.

40. CO822/468, Robertson (C-in-C, MELF) to Harding (CIGS), 12 Jan. 1953, cited in Heather, 'Counterinsurgency and Intelligence', p. 41, n. 29.

41. Susan L. Carruthers, *Winning Hearts and Minds: British Governments, the Mass Media and Colonial Counter-Insurgency, 1944-60* (London, New York: Leicester University Press, 1995) p. 134.

42. Lonsdale, 'Mau Maus of the Mind', p. 396.

43. Ibid., pp. 396, 409.

44. WO216/811/3, CIC 87696, Cameron to Redman (War Office, VCIGS), 5 Nov. 1952.

45. WO216/811/4, Robertson, (GHQ, MELF) to Redman, 5 Nov. 1952.

46. WO216/811/3, Cameron to Redman, 5 Nov. 1952.

47. CO822/439, 'Statement by the Secretary of State', drafted by P. Rogers (Colonial Office), 25 Nov. 1952, cited in Heather, 'Counterinsurgency and Intelligence', p. 40, n. 25; *HCD*, 508, cols. 255-58, 25 Nov. 1952.

48. Heather, loc. cit. (emphasis added).

49. Ibid.

50. Füredi, *Mau Mau War*, pp. 119-20.

51. Heather, 'Counterinsurgency and Intelligence', p. 46, n. 44.

52. Ibid., pp. 40-1.

53. Füredi, *Mau Mau War*, p. 120.

54. Rosberg and Nottingham, *The Myth of "Mau Mau"*, p. 276.

55. RHL, MSS Afr s 1574, 'Lord Howick, Interview', loc. cit.; Keesing's, loc. cit.

56. John W. Harbeson, 'Land Reforms and Politics in Kenya, 1954-70', *Journal of Modern African Studies*, 9/2 (1971), p. 234; RHL, MSS Afr s 1574, 'Lord Howick (Evelyn Baring), Interview with Dame Margery Perham, 19 Nov. 1969', fos. 24-5; *Keesing's*, p. 12573; Anne Thurston, *Smallholder Agriculture in Kenya: The Official Mind and the Swynnerton Plan* (Cambridge: Cambridge University Press, 1987), p. 72.

57. Harbeson, 'Land Reforms and Politics in Kenya', loc. cit.; Anne Thurston, *Smallholder Agriculture*, loc. cit.

58. *Keesing's*, loc. cit.

59. RHL, MSS Afr s 1574, 'Lord Howick, Interview', loc. cit.

60. *Keesing's*, loc. cit.

61. Thurston, loc. cit.

62. *Keesing's*, p. 13066.

63. RHL, MSS Afr s 1574, 'Lord Howick, Interview', loc. cit.

64. Charles Chenevix Trench, *Men Who Ruled Kenya: The Kenya Administration 1892-1963* (London, New York: Radcliffe Press, 1993), p. 68.

65. Douglas-Home, *Evelyn Baring*, p. 263.

66. Füredi, 'Kenya: Decolonization through counter-insurgency', passim., 'Creating a Breathing Space', passim., and *Colonial Wars*, passim.; R.F. Holland, 'The Imperial Factor in British Strategies from Attlee to Macmillan,

1945-63', in R.F. Holland and G. Rizvi (eds.), *Perspectives on Imperialism and Decolonisation: Essays in Honour of A.F. Madden* (London: Frank Cass, 1984), p. 175; WO 276/519, 'ISWC Report', 12 Nov. 1951.

67. Heather, 'Counterinsurgency and Intelligence', p. 48.

68. RHL, MSS Afr s 1580, Hinde papers, 'Brief for C-in-C', 6 June 1953.

69. Paget, *Counter-Insurgency Operations*, p. 91.

70. RHL, MSS Afr s 1580, 'Brief for C-in-C', loc. cit.

71. Heather, 'Counterinsurgency and Intelligence', pp. 50-1; Keith Jeffery, 'Intelligence and Counter-Insurgency Operations: Some Reflections on the British Experience', *Intelligence and National Security*, 2/1 (Jan. 1987), p. 125.

72. See: Heather, 'Counterinsurgency and Intelligence', passim., for details of the evolution of the intelligence organisation.

73. Carver, *War since 1945*, p. 34; Heather, 'Counterinsurgency and Intelligence', pp. 48-9.

74. Heather, 'Counterinsurgency and Intelligence', p. 49.

75. Ibid., p. 50.

76. Ibid., pp. 57-8.

77. Throup, 'Crime, politics and the police', p. 140.

78. *Keesing's*, pp. 12569, 13065.

79. Carver, *War since 1945*, p. 34.; Douglas-Home, *Evelyn Baring*, p. 236; Heather, 'Counterinsurgency and Intelligence', pp. 56-9; Paget, *Counter-Insurgency Operations*, pp. 92-3.

80. RHL, MSS Afr s 1580, 'Brief for C-in-C', loc. cit.

81. Heather, 'Counterinsurgency and Intelligence', pp. 50, 56-7, 59. It is noteworthy that the March 1950 'Colony Emergency Scheme' had provided for local emergency organisations if circumstances dictated. This had become the case after less than three months.

82. Heather, 'Counterinsurgency and Intelligence', p. 57.

83. RHL, MSS Afr s 1580, 'Appreciation of the Situation by Major-General W.R.N. Hinde', 5 March 1953; Heather, 'Counterinsurgency and Intelligence', p. 62.

84. T 225/771, Treasury minute, Bancroft/Johnston, 2/3 March 1953. 'The Treasury do not consider that the United Kingdom Defence Budget should bear the cost, as it does for the Malayan operations, because the operations in Kenya are quite different from the campaign in Malaya (which is in essence one facet of the world-wide anti-communist struggle). [...] Moreover, the Mau Mau troubles are an internal security problem and quite unlike the Communist rebellion in Malaya.'

85. PREM 11/472, COS (53) 134, Chiefs of Staff Committee, 'Appendix Report by the Chief of the Imperial General Staff on his Visit to Kenya, 19th-24th February, 1953'.

86. Ibid.

87. Ibid., Alexander (MoD), to Churchill, 5 March 1953.

88. Blaxland, *The Regiments Depart*, pp. 272-3; Philip Towle, *Pilots and Rebels: The Use of Aircraft in Unconventional Warfare 1918-1988* (London: Brassey's, 1989) p. 101.

89. Blaxland, *The Regiments Depart*, p. 273; Füredi, *Mau Mau War*, p. 122; Heather, 'Counterinsurgency and Intelligence', pp. 69-73. It is now the consensus that the Lari massacre was not a Mau Mau attack at all, but the result of a 'long-simmering land dispute' between specific parties. See: David M. Anderson, 'The Lari Massacre', Seminar Paper, University of Cambridge, Centre for African Studies, 31 Oct. 1995; Berman, *Control and Crisis*, p. 349. However, given that many Kikuyu grievances were in one way or another based upon the land issue, it could be suggested that the distinction is largely irrelevant.

90. RHL, MSS Afr s 1580, 'Brief for C-in-C', 6 June 1953; Paget, *Counter-Insurgency Operations*, p. 93.

91. W.J.P. Aggett, *The Bloody Eleventh: History of the Devonshire Regiment. Vol. 3: 1915-1969* (Exeter: Devonshire & Dorset Regiment, 1995), p. 555; Blaxland, *The Regiments Depart*, pp. 274-6; and idem. *The Farewell Years: The Final Historical Records of the Buffs, Royal East Kent Regiment, 1948-1967* (Canterbury: Queen's Own Buffs Office, 1967), p. 70; Heather, 'Counterinsurgency and Intelligence', pp. 81-8, 95.

92. WO 216/851, Blundell to Harding, 18 April 1953, Cameron to Redman (VCIGS), 30 April 1953; WO 216/852, 'Report on the Commander-in-Chief, Middle East Land Forces, Visit to Kenya, 11-16 May 1953'; PREM 11/472, Lyttelton to Churchill, 27 May 1953; Imperial War Museum, London (IWM), 75/134/1, Erskine papers, 'Top Secret Directive to C-in-C East Africa', 3 June 1953; Clayton, *Counter-Insurgency*, p. 6; Füredi, 'Kenya: Decolonization through counter-insurgency', p. 150. Heather, 'Counterinsurgency and Intelligence', p. 91.

93. WO 216/863, (file heading: 'Appreciation of the Situation in Kenya and Proposals by General Erskine'), Erskine to Harding, paras. 2, 3, 27 Jan. 1954 (hereafter, 'Anvil proposals').

94. Maloba, *Mau Mau and Kenya*, pp. 11, 98-100, 111-2.

95. Edgerton, *Mau Mau*, p. 210.

96. Percox, 'British Counter-Insurgency', pp. 75-82.

97. For the detailed deliberations on Erskine's proposals, see: CO 968/462. See also: PREM 11/581, C.J.M. Alport to Churchill, 29 July 1954, cited in: Goldsworthy (ed.), *The Conservative Government and the End of Empire* Part I: International Relations, doc. 70, pp. 202-3.

98. WO 216/860, 'Situation Report as at the end of September 1953', by Erskine, 29 Sept. 1953.

99. WO 216/861, 'The Situation in Kenya', report by Erskine, 3 Oct. 1953.

100. Heather, 'Counterinsurgency and Intelligence', pp. 129-32.

101. WO 236/18, 'The Kenya Emergency, June 1953 - May 1955: Report by General Erskine', para. 48; G.W. Croker, 'Mau Mau', *Journal of the Royal United Services Institute*, 100 (Feb.-Nov. 1955), p. 53.

102. WO 236/18, 'The Kenya Emergency, June 1953 - May 1955', paras. 54, 60.

103. Ibid., para. 104.

104. Ibid., para. 105.

105. Ibid.; RHL, MSS Afr s 1694, Whyatt papers, Hill (District Officer, Mathira Division) to District Commissioner, Nyeri, 4 Dec. 1954, D. MacPherson (Assistant Commissioner of Police, CID) to Colonel A.E. Young (Commissioner of Police), 23 Dec. 1954.

106. Ibid., Acting Director of Public Prosecutions to Whyatt, 16 Dec. 1954; WO 216/879, Erskine to Harding, 20 Dec. 1954, Erskine to Redman, 29 Dec. 1954; RHL, MSS Brit Emp s 486, Sir A.E. Young papers, MacPherson to Young, 10 Dec. 1954, Young to Baring, 14 Dec. 1954. Young, had experience of Palestine and Malaya, and was seconded from the City of London Police at Baring's request, CO 822/692, Baring to Lyttelton, 29 Oct. 1953. Despite Baring's expressed hope for a police force 'strong in quality as well as in quantity', Young became increasingly frustrated by an apparent lack of government measures to increase efficiency, and the tendency to release recent police recruits 'into the field' before they had completed their training, CO 822/692, Baring to Lyttelton, 17 July 1953.

107. WO 236/18, 'The Kenya Emergency, June 1953 - May 1955', paras. 106, 107.

108. Ibid., para. 107.

109. Ibid., para. 108; WO 216/876, Erskine to Redman, 20 Jan. 1955.

110. John Darwin, 'British Decolonisation since 1945: A Pattern or a Puzzle?', in R. F. Holland and G. Rizvi (eds.), *Perspectives on Imperialism and Decolonisation: Essays in Honour of A. F. Madden* (London: Frank Cass, 1984), pp. 187-209, and idem., *Britain and Decolonisation*, passim., summarises and rightly dismisses accounts that British decolonisation 'exactly followed a master plan laid down in Whitehall'.

111. CO 822/692, Lyttelton to Baring, n.d. (c. 12 Aug. 1953).

112. WO 216/861, 'The Situation in Kenya', 3 Oct. 1953.

113. RHL, MSS Afr s 1580, Hinde to Erskine, 7 Jan. 1954.

114. WO 216/863, 'Anvil proposals', para. 13, (d) (x), 27 Jan. 1954.

115. Ibid., para. 13, (d) (iii).

116. Ibid., para. 3.

117. CO 822/796, 'Colony and Protectorate of Kenya Enclosure: Operation Anvil, Outline Plan (Copy No. 3: File No. ADM 45/65/6)', JPC/1/17, 'Operation Anvil: Outline Plan by Joint Commanders', Appx. E, 'Draft Estimates for Operation Anvil', fo. 236, n.d. (c. Feb.-March 1954).

118. T 220/386, Gorell Barnes (Assistant Under-Secretary of State, Colonial Office) to Lyttelton, 19 June 1954.

119. PRO file T 220/417 provides details of the levels of finance provided for 'African development'.

120. *HCD*, 530, col. 476, 14 July 1954.

121. Douglas-Home, *Evelyn Baring*, pp. 271-2.

122. Heather, 'Counterinsurgency and Intelligence', p. 154.

123. Bennett, *Kenya: A Political History*, p. 137. See also: Cell, 'On the Eve of Decolonisation', passim.; Lyttelton, *Memoirs*, p. 407. Kenya's pre-Emergency political system certainly did not lend itself to African aspirations. It should be stressed that the numerical formula for the Council of Ministers, adopted under the Lyttelton Constitution was still weighted in favour of Europeans, even though victory over Mau Mau was by no means a certainty: Low and Lonsdale, 'Introduction: Towards the New Order', pp. 56-7. By June 1958, when Mau Mau had been defeated, 'Baring was still determined to hold the "politicals"': Füredi, 'Kenya: Decolonization through counter-insurgency', p. 144.

124. Conversely, Malaya gained independence in 1957, while still in the throes of a state of emergency which was not lifted until 1960: Lapping, *End of Empire*, pp. 176-7, 187.

125. Bennett, *Kenya: A Political History*, pp. 140-1; Bethwell A Ogot and Tiyambe Zeleza, 'Kenya: The Road to Independence and After', in Prosser Gifford and Wm. Roger Louis (eds.), *Decolonization and African Independence: The Transfers of Power, 1960-1980* (New Haven and London: Yale University Press, 1988) pp. 401-26; Darwin, 'British Decolonisation since 1945', pp. 191, 198-200; Douglas-Home, *Evelyn Baring*, p. 283.

126. Trench, *Men Who Ruled Kenya*, p. 265.

127. CO 822/692, Baring to Lyttelton, 30 Dec. 1953.

128. RHL, MSS Afr s 1580, Hinde to Erskine, 7 Jan. 1954.

129. RHL, MSS Afr s 746, LCCPLO, 1 Dec. 1952.

130. Trench, loc. cit.

131. WO 216/863, 'Anvil proposals', para. 29.

132. RHL, MSS Afr s 1784 (20), memoirs of Maurice K. Akker (Assistant Commissioner of Police, Nairobi), fo. 14; Trench, loc. cit.

133. Heather, 'Counterinsurgency and Intelligence', pp. 179-81.

134. Trench, *Men Who Ruled Kenya*, p. 267.

135. Füredi, 'Kenya: Decolonization through counter-insurgency', p. 157.

136. WO 236/18, 'The Kenya Emergency, June 1953 - May 1955', paras. 100, 103, 119, 121.

137. WO 216/884, Erskine to Harding, 12 April 1955.

138. WO 216/892, Lathbury to Field Marshall Sir Gerald Templer (CIGS), 5 Dec. 1955. See also: Frank Kitson, *Gangs and Counter-Gangs* (London: Barrie & Rockliff, 1960).

139. WO 216/892, 'Appreciation by the Commander-in-Chief East Africa, January 1956', 23 Jan. 1956.

140. Ibid.; Lathbury to Templer, 30 July 1956; WO 276/4, 'Appreciation by the Commander in Chief East Africa July 1956', 28 June 1956; WO 276/517, 'The Kenya Emergency, 3 May 1955 - 17 November 1956', report by Lathbury, 14 Dec. 1956, paras. 74-80, 88, 'Order of the Day by Lieutenant-General Sir Gerald Lathbury, KCB, DSO, MBE, Commander-in-Chief East Africa, 13 November 1956'.

141. CAB 129/69, C (54) 250, 'Report by the Committee on Defence Policy', memo. by Salisbury, 24 July 1954, cited in: Goldsworthy (ed.), *The Conservative Government and the End of Empire* Part I: International Relations, doc. 14, p. 45.

142. Ibid., pp. 46 para. 6, 49 para. 16.

143. DEFE 7/415, '[Colonial armed forces]: brief by Sir H Parker for Mr Macmillan', 27 Nov. 1954, cited in: ibid., doc. 16, pp. 51-2.

144. CAB 129/71, C (54) 329 (Annex), 'Defence Policy', report by Lord Swinton (CRO), 3 Nov. 1954, cited in: ibid., doc. 15, p. 51, para. 20.

145. CAB 131/14, D (54) 43, 'United Kingdom Defence Policy', memo. by COS, 23 Dec. 1954, cited in: ibid., doc. 17, pp. 52-7; CAB 129/72, C (54) 402, 'Internal Security in the Colonies', memo. by Macmillan, 29 Dec. 1954, cited in: ibid., doc. 18, p. 58; Macmillan, *Tides of Fortune, 1945-55*, pp. 572-3.

146. CAB 129/72, C (54) 402, 'Internal Security in the Colonies', memo. by Macmillan, 29 Dec. 1954, cited in: ibid., doc. 18, p. 58, n. 3. For the JIC contribution to Templer's enquiries, see: CAB 159/18, JIC (55) 18th Meeting, Item 4, 'Colonial Security', 24 Feb. 1955, JIC (55) 24th Meeting, Item 7, 'Colonial Intelligence and Security', 17 March 1955; CAB 158/20, JIC (55) 28, 'Colonial Intelligence and Security', report by the JIC, 23 March 1955.

147. CAB 129/76, CP (55) 89, 'Security in the Colonies', note by the Lord Chancellor, Viscount Kilmuir, 22 July 1955, with attached 'Report on Colonial Security, by General Sir Gerald Templer, GCMG, KCB, KBE, DSO', 23 April 1955; John Cloake, *Templer: Tiger of Malaya* (London: Harrap, 1985), p. 332; Goldsworthy (ed.), *The Conservative Government and the End of Empire*, p. 58, n. 3.

148. CAB 128/29, CM (55) 26th Meeting, Item 6, 'Security in the Colonies', 26 July 1955.

149. CAB 129/76, CP (55) 89, 'Report on Colonial Security', pp. 3, 12, 14-5, 18-20, 22- 3, 32, paras. 20, 22, 42-5, 74-88, 101-10, 178-9.

150. Ibid., p. 32, paras. 178-9.

151. Ibid., para. 181.

152. Ibid., p. 33, para. 188 (a) (i) (ii).

153. Ibid., pp. 38-9, para. 221.

154. Ibid., pp. 36, 60, paras. 208-9, 368.

155. Ibid., pp. 34, 44, paras. 194, 263.

156. Ibid., pp. 44, 45, 48, paras. 264, 270, 302-3. See also: CO 968/468.

157. CO 968/468, telegram circular despatch 1489, Lennox-Boyd to Baring, Uganda (930), Tanganyika (1356), Mauritius (468), Zanzibar (336), 30 Sept. 1955.

CHAPTER THREE
East Africa, East of Suez, 1956-7

Introduction

Lathbury's announcement in November 1956 of the withdrawal of all but one battalion of the British Army from Kenya following the apparently successful completion of counter-insurgency operations coincided, ironically, with Britain's humiliating retreat from Suez.[1] The 'Suez affair' led not only to a reassessment of Britain's options in the Middle East under the auspices of the ongoing review of long term defence policy, but to an almost overnight upgrading of Kenya's strategic importance.[2] As a result, British soldiers would be back on Kenyan soil much sooner, and in far greater numbers than the military run-down and the process of electoral reform, which began there in June 1955, might have suggested. This chapter examines post-Suez British decision-making concerning the deployment in Kenya of an element of the United Kingdom Strategic Reserve. In doing so, it illuminates a hitherto largely neglected, but significant, sub-text to the diminution of the British Empire in East Africa. The implementation of Kenya's constitutional reforms in 1958 did not occur in isolation from Britain's overseas defence planning. 'Fortress Kenya' would remain largely unassailable, at least until March 1959.

'The Long Retreat'? The Decision to Establish the UK Strategic Reserve in Kenya

The reversal of British defence policy on Kenya followed soon after the Suez operation. In early February 1957, the British Chiefs of Staff submitted a memorandum to the then Defence Minister, Duncan Sandys. They 'proposed that an infantry brigade should be positioned in Kenya, with the equipment for some supporting arms, to act as a reserve to reinforce any threatened area east of Suez'.[3] The reasons for the change in policy were listed succinctly as:

(a) the present air barrier which divides the Middle East is likely to remain, at least as a potential threat, for the foreseeable future.
(b) similarly, there can be no guarantee that the Suez Canal will not be closed to movement of our forces by adverse political decision from time to time.

> (c) the potential commitments south of the air/sea barrier are likely to increase, and because of the existence of the barrier, speedy intervention from the Eastern Mediterranean becomes doubtful.
> (d) there is some uncertainty on the long term reliability of even the West African air route under all circumstances.[4]

These 'problems' would be 'to a great extent overcome by the stationing of a force in Kenya'. Moreover, the Chiefs of Staff now apparently accepted, in line with Baring's earlier arguments, that 'the presence of some land forces in the area would help to ensure the tranquil development of British territories in East and Central Africa'.[5]

Of course, with the 'role in war' of Africa south of the Sahara already downgraded, Kenya would still constitute simply an adjunct to British defence strategy in peacetime. Britain's main concern, especially in the wake of the abandonment of the Suez operation, was the defence of its supplies of Middle East oil. For this reason the Chiefs of Staff were unequivocal in explaining the role of the proposed new Kenya garrison: 'The primary purpose of the force is the maintenance of the internal security and territorial integrity of dependent territories in the Arabian Peninsular [*sic*], Central and East Africa, and the Indian Ocean'.[6] The existence of 'a permanent UK garrison', it was thought, would not only provide readily available assistance in the event of serious internal troubles 'beyond the capabilities of the local forces' in Kenya and elsewhere in East and Central Africa: the existence of the base 'would itself tend to inhibit further troubles'.[7] Clearly, given the apparent recent victory over the Mau Mau guerrillas, on the one hand Kenya was considered to be safe ground for British strategic thinkers. On the other hand, the presence of a permanent garrison of British troops, it seems, would help to keep it that way.

The estimate by the Chiefs of Staff of the likely future commitments east of Suez, and the extent of such commitments, was crucial in gaining approval for their recommendations. Nasser's 'victory' had contributed to 'a general worsening' of Britain's position in the Arabian Peninsula. This, combined with the 'vital importance' of the area made it essential for Britain to be able to 'reinforce rapidly'. The proposed new reserve force for Kenya would not necessarily be confined to operations in East and Central Africa, and the Arabian Peninsula. The clearest possible indication of the albeit extrinsic strategic significance that the Chiefs of Staff now ascribed to Kenya was provided by the extent and varied nature of the other possible future commitments which any British troops based there might be called upon to undertake: 'In addition to the two battalions planned to be stationed in Aden, there is a requirement for reinforcements by up to four battalions'; up to one brigade was earmarked for British Somaliland; one battalion was committed to reinforce Central Africa while the 'Central African battalion' was deployed in Malaya ('We would be unwise to assume that this represents the full extent of our commitment in the long term'.); 'The current commitment to reinforce Zanzibar, Mauritius and Rodriques [*sic*], with up to one battalion, is likely to be a continuing one'.[8]

Furthermore, the possibilities for deployment of British soldiers to be stationed in Kenya extended far beyond the environs of their immediately projected 'out of area' role:

> There is a current commitment to reinforce Singapore in the event of Internal Security troubles with up to two brigades. There are also commitments to ANZAM[*] in the event of limited war. Immediate reinforcement of the Far East could be mounted more quickly from Kenya than from [the] UK. [...] With the present political alignment in the Middle East, we might reinforce the Baghdad Pact Area with more certainty from Kenya than from Cyprus, in spite of the greater distance. However, a more realistic contribution to the Baghdad Pact might be the maintenance of tranquility [*sic*] in the Persian Gulf during an emergency, and for this the force from Kenya would be invaluable.[9]

Given the extent of the above operational commitments, the Chiefs of Staff concluded that 'ideally' a full infantry brigade group should be sent to Kenya. In reality, financial and manpower shortages limited the size of the force available for deployment in Kenya to 'the equivalent of three major units' only. Artillery was not required for normal internal security purposes, so a brigade headquarters, two infantry battalions, and a field squadron of engineers 'should be included'.

As for future command arrangements, the fact that the proposed Kenya garrison and the Aden base were over 1,000 miles apart made it impracticable for them to be 'linked' under the same commander. Accordingly, the Chiefs of Staff recommended that the British brigade to be stationed in Kenya should be placed under the administrative command of the GOC, East Africa, and under the operational control of the C-in-C, MELF:

> Under the present trial command of the Arabian Peninsular [*sic*] there are two brigadiers with operational powers, in the Persian Gulf and Aden respectively. Units despatched from Kenya to one of these areas would need to be placed under the local commander. It is only if the Kenya brigade moves as a formation to a new area of operations in the Peninsular, [*sic*] that the command system would need to be modified.[10]

Implementation of the new scheme was further complicated by 'current plans' for East Africa. Templer's report on colonial intelligence and security of 23 April 1955 had led to a reassessment of the administrative, command, and financial arrangements for locally-recruited armed forces in Kenya.[11]

The consequent redoubling of the emphasis on the internal security role of local forces led to yet another reversal in policy and related command arrangements. Intensification of the Mau Mau Emergency had provided the impetus for the somewhat belated establishment of East Africa Command in its own right in May 1953.[12] The GOC was henceforth responsible directly to the War Office, and in operational command of all military, police, and auxiliary forces.

By November 1956, the effective withdrawal of British soldiers from military operations in Kenya, and the consequent resumption of responsibility for internal security by the police, left the way clear for the implementation of 'Longshot III'. From 1 July 1957, East African forces would be under the operational control of the governor of the territory in which they were stationed; GOC, East Africa would be the military commander; and the East Africa High Commission (EAHC) would be responsible for overall administration. Crucially, while 'Imperial units' would be paid for by the British government, the colonial governments 'will be entirely responsible through the High Commission for financial control of the East African Forces'.[13] This in itself would create problems, both financially and politically, for the respective East African administrations.

The 'Longshot' plan also envisaged that the Kenya government would meet the extra cost of stationing the British infantry battalion and 250 administrative personnel due to remain there until the middle of 1958 under separate arrangements made with Baring.[14] While the Chiefs of Staff were aware that consultation with the administrative and military authorities in East Africa 'would be essential before the administrative plan for the UK force in Kenya' could be drawn up, they also anticipated the likely response of the colonial East African governments to the news of its implementation: 'There can be no question of reversing LONGSHOT III [*sic*] and the UK force will therefore need its own chain of supply'. There would be a sop or two to the Kenya government, though:

> However some integration of administrative arrangements with the local forces might be possible. Since the whole force would be retained in Kenya primarily for strategic reasons, it will probably no longer be possible to ask the Government of Kenya to meet the costs of any Imperial units in Kenya, other than the costs of internal security operations there.[15]

Significantly, the estimates for completion time and the cost of accommodation for the new force served as a good indicator of how long the British military intended, or believed it would be able, to stay in Kenya:

> Building resources in Kenya are limited and even semi-permanent accommodation is at present estimated to take about 6 years [*sic*] at a cost of ...

> [£5.5 million - roughly £55-60 million at current values] ... (excluding a war reserves depot). This cost should however be measured against the big reduction in the long term building costs in the Mediterranean due to the reduction in the projected garrisons in that area. The annual cost of maintaining a force of this size in Kenya rather than in the UK would be about £600,000 [£6 million]. Against this should be set the reduction in movement costs for emergency moves to meet likely commitments in the area.[16]

Proposals and plans were one thing. Implementation turned out to be something completely different. Lathbury, for one, complained to the War Office that the new proposals rendered obsolete certain aspects of the 'Longshot III' plans. In particular, the plan for a centralised administrative body for all East African local forces would have to be scrapped. Not only would the existence of such a body 'working parallel' to a similar body for British forces prove to be 'inefficient and uneconomical', but it was doubtful that the governments of the East African territories would accept it.[17] As will be seen below, this hinged largely on the East African governors' reluctance to find additional funds to cover the administration of soldiers for internal security purposes in East Africa when, clearly, given Kenya's enhanced strategic significance, it was now in Britain's interests to do the utmost to ensure the continuing stability of the region. The Uganda government had its own specific concerns: administering the East African forces centrally, on a quasi-federal basis, would have clear 'imperial' overtones, and would be unacceptable to Africans at a time when Ghana in West Africa had just been granted independence.[18] There seemed to be a clear distinction between *Ugandan* and *Kenyan* Africans.

Before any plans could be finalised, let alone implemented, a War Office planning team had to 'study the administrative problems of stationing an infantry battalion in KENYA [*sic*] within 18 months in semi permanent accommodation'.[19] The planning team had the following tasks:

> The team will recommend a site for a permanent barracks for the infantry battalion. The following factors will be taken into consideration:-
>
> (a) Availability of Crown Land.
> (b) Existing accommodation and site facilities.
> (c) Availability of hirings for married quarters.
> (d) Amenities for the troops.
> (e) Communications.
> (f) Adequate water supply.
> (g) Availability of public utilities.
> (h) Training facilities.

> As a general guide the site selected should be in the general vicinity of NAIROBI. It should be capable of expansion later to accommodate the whole force ... [2,200 personnel].

British soldiers would therefore be stationed within easy reach of Eastleigh Airport, should the need arise for quick despatch to other 'trouble spots' in the Empire; equally, if not more important, within close proximity to HQ, East Africa Command; the offices of the EAHC; and the seat of British colonial administration in the principal territory of the region, which had until so recently been the main urban area for Mau Mau activities and organisation. Nairobi was also entering into a new phase of heightened political activity with the recent African elections to the Kenya Legislative Council.

Given the post-Suez reassessment of strategy in the Middle East, enunciated in Paragraph 26 of the April 1957 Defence White Paper, Britain's other military deployments had been placed under close scrutiny. Following a tour by the Vice-Quartermaster-General of Britain's military bases in the area, in early April, Templer (Field Marshal and CIGS since September 1955) reported that Lieutenant-General Sir Geoffrey Bourne, the new C-in-C, MELF, 'and local political leaders and commanders' had concluded that 'not more than half the present infantry battalion in the Persian Gulf is now needed there ... [and] ... no further British infantry is at present required in Aden. These are in fact very convenient conclusions because of our difficulties in providing hot-weather accommodation in the Arabian Peninsula.'[20] Templer accordingly recommended the withdrawal of roughly half of the First Battalion, Scottish Rifles (1 Cameronians),[21] or 370 'all ranks' from Bahrain and Sharjah to Kenya 'where they can be held in readiness to return to the Arabian Peninsula if required'.[22]

This was all 'very convenient' for the military, the main concern being the administrative problems which might arise from stationing British soldiers in Kenya at a time when East African forces were to become the responsibility of the colonial governments. Lathbury was asked to confirm that temporary accommodation could be made available for the 370 personnel by 1 May 1957, 'without detriment to plans for Longshot III'. The planning team would also investigate the extent to which the administration of the British force could be integrated with that of the local forces.

With politics in Kenya entering into a new phase as the newly-elected African Members of Legislative Council (MLCs) prepared to take their seats, the Colonial Office had to take account of broader considerations. As Lennox-Boyd put it to Baring: 'You will no doubt be able to settle the practical difficulties direct with Lathbury but if you, or the other Governors to whom I am repeating this, foresee adverse political or other repercussions arising out of this proposed move I should be grateful for your very early views.'[23]

The replies to Lennox-Boyd's enquiry from two of the governors concerned are instructive. They reflect different priorities as a function both of political developments within the territories themselves, and estimates of their future course, and because of the more immediate restrictions likely to result from limits on financial and manpower resources. As Baring explained:

> The news of the establishment of a British base in Kenya is very welcome indeed. It will give the country a sense of security and of permanency. It will, therefore, assist in the attraction of capital. The administrative arrangements will not be easy. I hope that no final decisions will be taken until the various alternatives have been carefully considered on the spot. There is a tendency in the War Office to forget that the number of capable officers available in East Africa is very limited and in fact that any East African administration and pay machine can only cope with a limited force.[24]

The response from the recently appointed Governor of Uganda, (Baring's former deputy) Sir Frederick Crawford, while positive, expressed a significant reservation:

> Neither I nor my advisers foresee any adverse political or other repercussions to the stationing of British troops in East Africa so long as it is made quite clear that these troops will not be stationed in Uganda and that control over internal security forces in East Africa remains as proposed in Longshot III with individual Governors in their capacity of Commander-in-Chief.[25]

However, such albeit guarded reassurance about the local impact of news of the force had to be weighed against both British domestic and international opinion. Referring to the War Office planning team, Lennox-Boyd, in reply to Crawford, explained that:

> Their presence is in any case likely to excite comment and speculation. In reply to any enquiries they will state that their task is to examine the implications of [the] last two sentences of paragraph 26 of [the] Defence White Paper (Cmd. 124) [*sic*] which read: "In the Arabian Peninsula Britain must at all times be ready to defend Aden Colony and Protectorates and the territories on the Persian Gulf for whose defence she is responsible. For this task, land, air and sea forces have to be maintained in that area and in East Africa". They have been instructed not to go beyond this in any public statements. You will no doubt wish to adopt [a] similar line in answering Press or other enquiries. In discussions which might become public they would not wish to disclose [the] contemplated strength of [the] force involved.[26]

Meanwhile, the size of the eventual British force to be deployed in Kenya, in itself was brought into question. Post-war pressures on the British economy, coupled with a potentially overwhelming defence burden in Europe and overseas, had led the 1951-5 Churchill administration to produce *Global Strategy Paper 1952* (GSP 1952). In advocating that in future much greater reliance 'should be' placed upon nuclear deterrence than upon conventional forces, GSP 1952 sought to equate defence means and ends, and was a significant precursor to the 1957 Defence White Paper, heralding the reduction in British armed forces personnel so irksome to the British service chiefs and several government ministers.[27] Ironically, Sandys' first statement to the Commons as Defence Minister on 13 February 1957, when he announced the shift in defence policy to deterrence, and the intention to end National Service as soon as possible, coincided roughly with the appraisal by the Chiefs of Staff of the need to deploy British soldiers in Kenya.[28]

This apparent contradiction led to difficulties at the most basic planning level. At a meeting held in the War Office on 5 April 1957 (the day that the Defence White Paper was published), 'to resolve outstanding points necessary for the briefing of the War Office team', Brigadier D.C. Mullen, the Adjutant to the Director of Military Operations (A/DMO), explained that 'the long term War Office task is to establish in KENYA a brigade'. Clearly aware of the renewed emphasis on financial stringency in the Defence White Paper, the lack of any strategic certainty in the immediate aftermath of the Suez operation, and the likely effect of political developments elsewhere in Africa, Mullen continued:

> As security of tenure and the operational commitment is subject to change it was proposed, in the interest of economy, that the brigade would be established by stages. The War Office therefore propose to concentrate first on building adequate accommodation for one battalion within 18 months; this would avoid the dangers inherent in embarking on large scale projects for which the plans may have to be changed.[29]

As will be seen below, Britain did its utmost to ensure that political developments in Kenya would accord with strategic plans for the area. This, of course, was the responsibility of the Colonial Office and the Kenya government.

Meanwhile, the War Office concerned itself largely with the administrative and financial mundanity involved in planning to establish a British garrison in Kenya, which seemed to depend upon broader policy issues. Given that the 1957 Defence White Paper 'promised reductions in our overseas commitments', the minutes of the April War Office meeting show that at least one Treasury official, T.J. Bligh, kept his eye firmly on the bigger picture. Bligh stressed that although his department would not object to the planning team being sent to Kenya, he 'would wish to reserve their position on the stationing of the brigade' there. As tends to be the case with new policy initiatives, of whatever nature, plans are all well and good, while paying for them is a different matter.

Clearly, Bligh had needed to be more emphatic in the face of Colonial Office and War Office determination. As he put it to Mullen in a subsequent letter:

> It was my understanding at the meeting that the Working Party would not in any way at all be making any commitment on future policy about either a battalion or a brigade. [...] I said that although the Treasury did not want to object to the Working Party going we would certainly have to reconsider our attitude if the very fact of their going implied a firm commitment. [...] I think that the drafting of ... the minutes has been rather economical, and I would find it more suitable if the sentence ran "Mr. Bligh said that there would be no Treasury objection to a team going to Kenya provided that no commitments of any sort were entered into ..."[30]

In the light of the above, and given that the full-scale military building programme in Kenya was scheduled to take six years, Phillip Darby's retrospective remarks deserve consideration:

> That Kenya attained full internal self-government less than six years after the decision was made to proceed with the cantonment, and that the last British troops left Kenya little more than five years after work first began on the major construction project, is now common knowledge. What is not so clear is how the defence establishment came to undertake building the base in the light of the territory's uncertain future as a colony. The answer seems to lie in changed political objectives and lack of co-ordination within the government machine.[31]

Undoubtedly, Britain's political objectives in East Africa did change, and this, along with the implications for defence planning, and British efforts to secure a strategic foothold in Kenya will be considered in Chapters Six and Seven. As will be shown below, it would be inaccurate, however, to suggest a lack of co-ordination between government departments so far as defence and political, and related matters were concerned. This is not to say that there were not disagreements over ends and means, particularly given the at times seemingly mutually-exclusive 'global strategy' concerns of defence ministers and planners, and the arguably more parochial local political focus of the Colonial Office juxtaposed, of course, by the financial restraint imposed by the Treasury.

It should be stressed that, at least until January or March 1959 and, as Darby concedes, in 1957 'when the Ministry of Defence decided to go ahead with the scheme to station troops in Kenya, independence for the East

African territories seemed several generations away'.[32] Indeed, as will be argued below and in subsequent chapters (Six and Seven), Britain did the utmost to ensure this, with a combination of piecemeal political concessions and attempted delaying tactics, along with strictly targeted, and limited, financial and military aid packages. Moreover, British efforts to foster divisions between the African nationalists were intended to promote the 'moderate' African politicians who, it was thought, would be more amenable to the 'responsible government' constitutional model that gave Britain the best hope of safeguarding 'vital' economic and strategic interests.

The emergence of the Middle East air/sea barrier brought about renewed speculation concerning the requirement for a British military base in East Africa. *The Times* 'concluded that there was undoubtedly a need for some sort of half-way house in the area, although it was doubtful whether a full-scale garrison in Kenya was the answer'.[33] This, and further newspaper speculation quickly came to the notice of the new African MLCs. As Reuter's News Agency reported in April 1957: 'There has been opposition from some African politicians in Kenya who suggest [that] the establishment of a British military base here will needlessly involve Kenya in any future war and will enable the British Government [to] counter their political demands with the argument that an essential military base cannot be compromised.'[34]

This report, based upon a statement attributed to the African nationalist, Tom Mboya, again prompted Crawford to request that he be allowed to make a statement to the effect that it was not the intention to station British soldiers in Uganda.[35] Meanwhile, the War Office gave clear instructions to Lathbury and Bourne: 'The following statement may be made to the Press if the Press raise the matter and only if they raise it. ["]A detachment of 1 CAMERONIANS is being moved in the first half of May from the PERSIAN GULF to KENYA as a routine matter["]'.[36]

It seems that the British desire for minimal publicity regarding the subject of the possible British force for Kenya had little to do with concerns for African sensibilities. As *The Times* had speculated, there was no guarantee that a suitable site would be found for the size of force envisaged, especially given the increasing requirement in the British Army for 'accompanied postings' overseas.[37] The move of the Cameronians from the Arabian Peninsula to Kenya might well have ended up as simply 'routine'. Also, the physical separation of local commands south of the air barrier from Middle East Command in Cyprus had imposed a review of the overall command structure in the area. Kenya was being considered as a possible location for the proposed new headquarters: 'In view of this it is most important to prevent [the governments of the] East African Territories hearing rumours perhaps through [the] Colonial Office that [a] new Command in these parts is under consideration. [The] ... [e]ffect of [the] possible return of [the] War Office might be most disruptive to LONGSHOT'.[38]

Given the refusal of the Kenyan African MLCs to participate in government following the March 1957 elections, and that they would not, in any case, have any direct involvement in defence and security related decisions until independence in December 1963, it is clear that what mattered in this regard was the intention of the British defence establishment that the administration, where possible, and the financing, in particular, of the East African Land Forces (EALF) should not continue as a direct British responsibility. There was also the matter of the practicality of competition between 'Imperial' forces and the EALF for land and facilities upon which any base might be built. Certainly, when demonstrating the British government's apparent lack of concern or understanding for local African objections, Lennox-Boyd, perhaps somewhat disingenuously, stated to the Commons on 1 May that 'he disagreed with a suggestion that there was widespread anxiety in Kenya about its use as ... a base'.[39]

On 23 April 1957, the War Office planning team recommended Kahawa, ten miles from Nairobi, as the 'most suitable' site as a base for 'Imperial troops'. This was followed at the end of April by a statement by John Hare, the Secretary of State for War: 'In addition, as indicated in the policy statement on defence, plans are being prepared to enable certain British forces to be stationed in East Africa to help to safeguard our general interests in the Middle East and the Persian Gulf'.[40] Further statements in Kenya's Legislative Council, and ever-increasing newspaper speculation led Sandys to decide to tour Aden, Kenya and Libya in mid-June, in order to assess the situation for himself.[41]

While in Kenya, Sandys was briefed by Baring and Lathbury. Baring, tending more towards imperialist 'hawk' than decolonising 'dove', went to great lengths to convince Sandys of the efficacy of the plan for the British garrison:

> The United Kingdom has, I believe, a chance to maintain in Kenya both a stable state and an important point of British influence in eastern Africa. Admittedly such points of influence are threatened in these days by emotional and unthinking nationalism. In other parts of the world this threat has proved irresistible. All the same the circumstances of Kenya differ from those of most of the territories which we have abandoned. Thus - [...] The element of stability in Kenya, which is lacking both in West African colonies and in Arabic speaking territories, is a permanently settled European population. [...] This element of stability, this existence as an important section of the Kenya population, of people determined to maintain the British connexion, [*sic*] is by far the most important and re-assuring feature which distinguishes Kenya from many other territories.[42]

Baring went on to explain that the relative lack of contact between East Africans and Europeans compared with West Africa, and the consequent lack of sufficiently educated Africans in the area had given rise to a situation whereby Kenyan Africans were ill-prepared to run the country. On the other hand, as this situation improved, an external threat 'from the Arabic speaking world would give the impetus to make a mixed government in Kenya not only a working success - *as it has already been* - but also something with a popular appeal to many men and women in all communities'.[43]

Fully aware of the developing pressures for independence, not only in East Africa, but from within Britain, Baring elaborated:

> Provided Britain does not herself lose her nerve, the future of Kenya need not be the bleak prospect of an incompetent African government attaining independence and then trying to cope with problems far beyond its capacity. Admittedly there are many in Britain who wish to see independence at any cost and who, if in power, might be prepared to exercise the constitutional right of the United Kingdom Government so to alter the constitutional arrangements of Kenya that an independent African government would come into being quite soon. Whatever the constitutional position may be, there is however reason to believe that a move in this direction would present the United Kingdom Government of the day with a series of troubles and a series of decisions which it is most unlikely that it would be prepared to face when the time came.

Among these difficulties, Baring cited the fact that a 'large section of the government activities of the country is run by Europeans not in Government service'. Many government servants owned land in Kenya and had children educated there,

> and intended to retire in Kenya and *to become Kenyans*. An attempt, therefore, to "impose" a very drastic constitutional change from the United Kingdom ... would lead first to the paralysis of Government since the attempt would cause a flow of resignations. Then this would almost certainly be followed by an outbreak of violence ... [from within the] ... considerable Afrikaner element in this country ... [who] ... cannot pack up and remove themselves quietly to Cheltenham! Their natural instinct would be to resist by force any attempt to bring the new changes into practice and they would follow that natural instinct. [...] I doubt whether the sort of United Kingdom Government likely to wish to impose changes leading to "Ghana in our day" would also be the sort of government likely to face and to quell a violent movement. [...] If it is worth making an effort to succeed in the far from hopeless task of preserving Kenya in stability and in close connexion with Great Britain, then an important factor contributing to success will be the presence of British troops.[44]

Moving on to explain that the various telegrams from the Colonial Office, public statements by British and Kenya government ministers, and intense newspaper speculation about the new British base were tantamount to a *fait accompli*, Baring played his trump card:

> All this is not by itself a decisive point. But the general public here, both European and African, have read in the newspapers of announcements by Ministers both in the United Kingdom and in Kenya that British troops will be stationed here. They have read of an attack on this decision by the African Members of the Legislative Council. If there is now an announcement that no British troops will be stationed here, whatever is said they will draw the conclusion - especially if they are Africans - that Mr. Mboya has forced the United Kingdom Government to change its mind.[45]

Summing up, Baring then reiterated that the presence of British soldiers would 'give a sense of the permanence of the British connexion'. Curiously, given his earlier remarks about the 'Afrikaner element', he also explained that: 'All African political movements, if faced with resistance, are liable to become violent and the British troops would have a strong preventive and deterrent effect'. Certainly, the former would be less fearful for their future. Finally, referring to the 'Longshot III' arrangements in as much as they implied a loosening of the connection 'in defence matters' between East Africa and Britain, and with one eye clearly on the broader picture, Baring concluded, shrewdly, that such a 'danger' would be averted by the presence of the garrison, 'either as a support for troops in the Arabian peninsula or as a place to which, if things go wrong, they could retreat from Arabia'.[46]

With half the Cameronians from the Persian Gulf already in temporary accommodation in Gilgil, some 80 miles from Nairobi, Lathbury's major concern was to determine the exact size of the force to be stationed in Kenya. As he reported to the War Office, 'although the accommodation is reasonable as a temporary measure for half a battalion and a few families, it could in no way be considered as satisfactory from the long term point of view, nor could it take all the battalion families. It will therefore be necessary to build barracks and Kahawa seems to be the most suitable site.'[47] Apparently unconcerned by such minutiae, Sandys remained non-committal, making it 'quite clear' that no final decision had been taken on 'what troops would be stationed where in the East African and South Arabian area'. As if Baring's note were not enough, the Defence Minister also 'closely questioned' him on 'the future of Kenya'.[48]

Upon Sandys' return, continuing newspaper speculation suggested that the base project for Kenya would be pushed forward.[49] Labour MP Fenner Brockway, apparently prompted by Kenyan African nationalists, asked in the

Commons for a statement from Sandys about the matter. He was told that Sandys 'hoped to be able to announce some of the decisions regarding the strength and disposition of forces in Aden, Kenya and Libya in the near future'.[50] While the subsequent implementation of construction work in Kenya would serve to demonstrate that, at least in the short term, Sandys had been persuaded by Baring's arguments, no announcement was made until five months later. This was partly because the proportion of forces to be allotted between Aden, the Persian Gulf, and Kenya depended upon Sandys striking a balance between the size of the forces that could be stationed south of the air barrier as a function of both the economies in conventional forces set out in the 1957 Defence White Paper, and a combination of broader strategic considerations and the immediate security requirements of the governors of Aden and Kenya.[51] While Sandys had ruled out stationing a whole brigade group in Kenya, Baring had hoped for at least four companies (c. 320 personnel), equating roughly to those soldiers already stationed in Gilgil.[52] This would also help the Kenya government to make economies by disbanding the 2nd/3rd King's African Rifles (23 KAR) reserve battalion which had been raised during the military phase of the Kenya Emergency.[53] It seems that the matter of a definitive announcement on the future of forces to be stationed south of the air barrier, rather than the actual decision, was in itself the cause of the delay.[54]

Shortly after Sandys returned from Kenya, his Chief of Staff, Marshal of the Royal Air Force, Sir William Dickson (the nominal Chief of the Defence Staff), had submitted a report outlining the 'more likely possibilities' for troop deployments. These were summarised as follows:

> (a) to accommodate one battalion in Kenya, one battalion in Aden and one in the Persian Gulf less two companies in Kenya and married quarters for the whole of this battalion in Kenya;
> (b) ... one battalion in Aden and ... half the Persian Gulf battalion in Kenya with married quarters for the whole of this battalion;
> (c) to accommodate in Kenya half the Aden and half the Persian Gulf Battalions [*sic*] with married quarters for the whole of both battalions.[55]

The Colonial Office naturally favoured solution '(a)' because of Baring's long-standing desire that a full battalion be stationed in Kenya on a permanent basis, and because the Governor of Aden, Sir William Luce, had amended his requirements from two companies to a full battalion.[56] This latter decision had arisen because of a general increase in widespread anti-British unrest in the Middle East, which in turn was heightened by British military intervention on 23 July 1957, in support of the Sultan of Muscat and Oman against a Saudi-backed revolt.[57] More importantly, the fact of the

Oman operation in itself, and the lessons learned, added fuel to the fire of those government ministers, including the Foreign Secretary, Selwyn Lloyd, and Lennox-Boyd, who opposed Sandys' shift to a defence policy reliant on nuclear deterrence, and the consequent projected reductions in conventional forces.[58]

Lloyd's statement to the Commons on 29 July, explaining Britain's motives for intervention in Oman, and that there was 'no need to emphasise the importance of the Persian Gulf' was crucial in this regard. Equally so was the Foreign Secretary's exposition of the British government's 'interpretation of its commitments in the Persian Gulf':

> the difference between a formal obligation and the obligations of a long-standing relationship of friendship is not readily apparent to the local rulers and people. If we were to fail in one area it would begin to be assumed elsewhere that perhaps the anti-British propaganda of our enemies had some basis to it, and that the Government were no longer willing or able to help their friends.[59]

The implication of this statement, that the likelihood of Britain's military intervention to preserve the *status quo* in the area would increase, and its corollary, that sufficient forces would have to be maintained in order to undertake such commitments, has been well noted by Darby. Added to the key military lesson of the Oman operation, that air power was no substitute for soldiers on the ground, the tide began to turn back in favour of those defence chiefs and ministers who opposed large-scale reductions in conventional forces.[60]

Sandys waited until 7 November 1957 to state publicly that 'an element of the strategic reserve would be stationed in Kenya'. Hare added, in response to questions from the Labour Party, that this might entail one or two battalions. At the same time, Sandys announced the creation of a separate integrated command in Aden for British forces in the Arabian Peninsula and British Somaliland. On 10 July he had announced the review of the command structure in the Middle East.[61] This latter decision had been made effectively by the end of that month.[62] It is difficult to ascertain what, exactly, caused the delay in any announcement being made. Apart from the summer recess, for example, and the wish of the Foreign Office to avoid further inflaming Arab opinion with mention of the Persian Gulf, a few points regarding Kenya can be brought together tentatively.[63]

Firstly, in response to agitation from Mboya in particular against the proposal to establish any form of British military base in Kenya, Baring had argued that should Sandys decide *not* to go ahead with the project, this would not only prove to be embarrassing for the Kenya government, but would also show the British government to have retreated in the face of such pressure. This in turn would provide further encouragement to the African nationalists to press for more rapid constitutional advance than Britain was prepared to concede, along with the concomitant dangers that Baring had outlined, and could well have serious repercussions elsewhere. Certainly, Lennox-Boyd, in support of Baring's viewpoint, had pressed Sandys in July 'not to make an announcement to the effect that no base would be set up there at the present time'.[64]

Secondly, it surely must have been no mere coincidence that Sandys' and Hare's statements to the Commons on 7 November were made the day after Lennox-Boyd sent a telegram to Macmillan informing him of the decision to replace the Lyttelton Constitution with 'minimum delay'.[65] Of course, this is not to suggest that the final decision on the British force for Kenya was made, then announced, within 24 hours, although this would not be far wide of the mark. It *is certain* that on 4 November 1957, following discussions with Baring and the new GOC, General Tapp, Lennox-Boyd requested that an announcement on the stationing of British soldiers in Kenya should be made on 11 November: 'We [Lennox-Boyd and Baring] also both feel that it would be politically unwise for me to make the announcement myself at my final press conference here'.[66] Hare's reply, transmitted on the same day, is instructive:

> I am anxious that we should make a statement ... but owing to recent developments in Oman we are not yet able to give a final decision on the future of the Persian Gulf battalion. We shall get this resolved as quickly as we can and shall then be able to agree something suitable. As matters now stand I am sure you will appreciate that we cannot agree to putting anything out for the present. Meanwhile I am discussing [this] with the Minister of Defence.[67]

A month earlier, having examined the administrative and accommodation difficulties with Tapp, Bourne had already recommended that the bulk of two British battalions should be stationed in Kenya; all that remained was to decide the size of the element, if any, of the Cameronians to be left in the Persian Gulf.[68] Nevertheless, it is surely significant, if 'in retrospect laughable', that at the same time as Lennox-Boyd announced his amendments to the Kenya Constitution, he also 'promised' that the proportions of communal representation in Kenya's Legislative Council would not be changed again for ten years. In the Commons a week later he stated that 'I do not foresee a date ... when it will be possible for the Colonial Office to relinquish control'.[69] Equally important, despite Mboya's subsequent protests that the British government still had not made any firm commitments regarding Kenya's ultimate 'destiny', in Britain the 'Lennox-Boyd plan received a broad initial welcome across the political spectrum'.[70]

It should be stressed, also, that well before Lennox-Boyd's October visit to Kenya in order to attempt to remedy the political 'deadlock' there, Baring already knew Sandys' decision on the British base. Indeed, on 2 August 1957, the Assistant Under-Secretary at the Colonial Office, Gorell Barnes, sent a telegram to Kenya explaining that '[the] Secretary of State has been informed by [the] Minister of Defence that whilst "no final conclusion has yet been reached, it seems probable that we shall decide normally to station in Kenya one battalion of the central reserve for which permanent accommodation would be required"'.[71] It was also vitally important that the decision received no publicity, ironically, to give as 'little handle for agitation as possible to Mboya. We should need to agree text, timing and place of issue between us and I shall need to consult ministers.'[72]

In the end, the announcement of the British battalion for Kenya was made before the decision on British forces in the Gulf. There can be little doubt that implementation of the Lennox-Boyd Constitution helped to secure this. It seems that while British strategy in Aden and the Gulf, and imperial policy in Kenya were becoming synonymous, in being so they were also precariously inter-dependent. While the veil of renewed constitutional stability in Kenya apparently provided conditions suitable for Britain's strategic requirements south of the air barrier, by somewhat circular logic, that stability in itself depended to a certain extent upon the presence of British soldiers. More will be said about this in relation to politics and internal security in Chapters Five and Six.

Meanwhile, a good indication of Lennox-Boyd's early awareness of the uneasy connection between political development and security in Kenya, and the perceived vital role, at least initially, of the new British base in this regard, is provided by some correspondence following Sandys' and Hare's respective Commons statements of 7 November 1957. This, and the other political aspects of the implementation of the decision are examined in the next chapter.

Conclusion

If for no other reason, Britain's decision to 'permanently' station elements of the Strategic Reserve in Kenya, above all, confirms that the political and socio-economic reforms introduced during the military campaign of the previous four years were designed to ensure British control of the colony. Prospects for the planned transfer of power to an African majority government could not have been further from British defence planners' minds. Indeed, while military planners concerned themselves largely with the administrative and logistical niceties of moving troops to Kenya, the Colonial Office went to great lengths to smooth the way politically, at least in theory. While with hindsight it would be easy to suggest that Britain's strategic flirtation with Kenya was doomed from the start, it certainly did not look that way to those involved at the time.

Notes

1. WO 276/517, 'Order of the Day by Lieutenant-General Sir Gerald Lathbury, KCB, DSO, MBE, Commander-in-Chief, East Africa, 13 November 1956'; Keith Kyle, Suez (New York: St. Martin's, 1991), passim., 'Britain and the Crisis, 1955-1956', in Wm. Roger Louis and Roger Owen (eds.), Suez 1956: The Crisis and its Consequences (Oxford, Clarendon Press, 1991 [1989]), pp. 103-30; Richard Lamb, The Failure of the Eden Government (London: Sidgwick & Jackson, 1987), pp. 198-305.

2. DEFE 4/94, JP (57) 8 (Final), 'Long Term Defence Policy', memo. by the Joint Planning Staff, 24 Jan. 1957, fos. 194-205, cited in Ovendale (ed.), British Defence Policy since 1945, pp. 111-3.

3. DEFE 5/73, COS (57) 34, 'Long Term Defence Policy', memo. by the Chiefs of Staff, 5 Feb. 1957; CO 968/693, annex to MO1/LM/5683/507, 19 Feb. 1957, 'Draft ECAC [Executive Committee of the Army Council] Paper: Stationing of an Army Reserve in Kenya', note by the VCIGS, 18 Feb. 1957, fo. 1.

4. CO 968/693, loc. cit.

5. Ibid.

6. Ibid., fos. 2, 8.

7. Ibid., fo. 3.

8. Ibid.

9. Ibid., fos. 3, 8. * Michael Carver, Tightrope Walking: British Defence Policy since 1945 (London: Hutchinson, 1992), p. 50: 'Australia, New Zealand and Malaya - a vaguely defined defence agreement between Britain and those countries to cooperate [sic] in the defence of Malaya and the surrounding area'.

10. CO 968/693, 'Stationing of an Army Reserve in Kenya', fo. 6.

11. CAB 129/76, CP (55) 89, 'Security in the Colonies', note by Viscount Kilmuir, 22 July 1955, with attached 'Report on Colonial Security, by General Sir Gerald Templer, GCMG, KCB, KBE, DSO', 23 April 1955; Cloake, Templer: Tiger of Malaya, p. 332.

12. Füredi, 'Kenya: Decolonization through counter-insurgency', p. 150.

13. CO 968/693, 'Stationing of an Army Reserve in Kenya', fo. 7.

14. Also in Kenya as a 'carry over' from the British counter-insurgency campaign were one field survey squadron of Royal Engineers (due to remain until mid-1959), and a permanently established signals squadron (Commonwealth Communications Army Network - COMCAN).

15. CO 968/693, 'Stationing of an Army Reserve in Kenya', fos. 7-9.

16. Ibid., fo. 8.

17. Ibid., extract from Signal 30686, C-in-C, East Africa to War Office (WO), 31 March 1957.

18. Ibid., loose minute to BM1 to 0165/3895 (MO3), Lt.-Col. J.N. Thomas, p.p. A/DMO, East Africa Command, 1 April 1957; Crawford (Deputy Governor, Kenya) to Lennox-Boyd, 27 March 1957. Brian Lapping, End of Empire (London: Guild, 1985), p. 389.

19. CO 968/693, 'Terms of Reference for Kenya Planning Team' (draft), n.d. (c. April 1957).

20. DEFE 5/74, COS (57) 80, 'Army Deployment in the Arabian Peninsula' note by the Chief of the Imperial General Staff (MO1/P (57) 254), 1 April 1957; Blaxland, The Regiments Depart, p. 495.

21. Blaxland, The Regiments Depart, p. 485; Ian S. Hallows, Regiments and Corps of the British Army (London: Cassell, 1994 [1991]), p. 282.

22. DEFE 5/74, loc. cit.

23. CO 968/693, telegram 25, Lennox-Boyd to Baring, 5 April 1957.

24. CO 822/1252, GH 1953/5/39/II, letter, Baring to Lennox-Boyd, 10 April 1957. See also: CO 968/693, telegram 301, Baring to Lennox-Boyd, 6 April 1957.

25. CO 968/693, telegram 16, Crawford to Lennox-Boyd, 6 April 1957. See also: ibid., Crawford to Maj.-Gen. N.P.H. Tapp (GOC, EAC), 10 Sept. 1957.

26. Ibid., telegram 16, Lennox-Boyd to Crawford, 6 April 1957. Cmnd. 124, Defence. Outline of Future Policy (London: HMSO, April 1957), cited in Ovendale, British Defence Policy since 1945, p. 115.

27. Colin Gordon, 'Duncan Sandys and the Independent Nuclear Deterrent', in Ian Beckett and John Gooch (eds.), Politicians and Defence: Studies in the Formulation of British Defence Policy 1845-1970 (Manchester: Manchester University Press, 1981), pp. 138-9.

28. Ibid., p. 144.

29. CO 968/693, 'Stationing Part of the Strategic Reserve in Kenya', summary of a meeting held in the War Office, 5 April 1957.

30. Ibid., Bligh (Treasury) to Mullen (War Office), 11 April 1957.

31. Darby, British Defence Policy East of Suez, p. 205.

32. Ibid.

33. Ibid., p. 124.

34. CO 968/693, teleprint, Reuter (Nairobi), n.d. (c. 10 April 1957).

35. Ibid., telegram 17, Crawford to Lennox-Boyd, n.d. (c. 11-24 April 1957); 'Stationing of Part of the United Kingdom Strategic Reserve in Kenya', brief (draft) for the Secretary of State, n.d. (c. April/May 1957).

36. Ibid., 14177 (MO4), TROOPERS (WO) to MIDEAST MAIN FORCE NAIROBI HQ BFAP [British Forces Arabian Peninsula], 25 April 1957.

37. Darby, British Defence Policy East of Suez, p. 205. CO 968/693, 'Stationing of Part of the United Kingdom Strategic Reserve in Kenya', brief (draft), n.d. (c. April/May 1957).

38. CO 968/693, telegram 31092/SD, Lathbury to VCIGS, 25 April 1957.

39. Ibid., teleprint, Reuter (Nairobi), 3 May 1957.

40. Ibid., brief for Sandys by Baring, 20 June 1957, fo. 3.

41. Ibid., Reuter, 23 April 1957; Darby, British Defence Policy East of Suez, pp. 124-5; The Daily Telegraph, 'New Kenya Base Not Rush Project', 30 April 1957; The Times, 'Strategic Base in Kenya', 2 May 1957, and 'British Base in Kenya. Mr Sandys to See Possible Site', 15 June 1957.

42. CO 968/693, brief by Baring, 20 June 1957, fo. 1.

43. Ibid., fo. 2 (emphasis added).

44. Ibid., fos. 2, 3 (emphasis added).

45. Ibid., fos. 3-4.

46. Ibid., fo. 4.

47. Ibid., 'Note by C-in-C East Africa Command - Stationing British Troops in Kenya', 20 June 1957.

48. Ibid., Baring to Lennox-Boyd, 21 June 1957.

49. Darby, British Defence Policy East of Suez, pp. 124-5.

50. CO 968/693, 'Establishment of United Kingdom Base in Kenya - Stationing British Troops in Kenya', brief for John Profumo (Parliamentary Under-Secretary of State, Colonial Office), 31 July 1957, fo. 1.

51. Ibid. The 1957 Defence White Paper had proposed reducing the British armed forces from 690,000 personnel to 375,000 by 1962, Murphy, Alan Lennox-Boyd, p. 128.

52. CO 968/693, Lennox-Boyd to Sandys, 9 July 1957.

53. Ibid., telegram 639, Baring to Lennox-Boyd, 1 Aug. 1957.

54. Ibid., telegram 109, Hare (Secretary of State, War Office) to Lennox-Boyd, 4 Nov. 1957. 'War Office however confirm that although wishing to avoid publicity at this juncture, reply does not affect plan to locate one infantry battalion in Kenya. No announcement to this effect is however contemplated at present'.

55. Ibid., 'Establishment of United Kingdom Base in Kenya - Stationing British Troops in Kenya', brief, fo. 2.

56. Ibid.; Lennox-Boyd to Sandys (Minister of Defence, MoD), 9 July 1957.

57. Darby, British Defence Policy East of Suez, pp. 129-30; Glen Balfour-Paul, The end of empire in the Middle East: Britain's relinquishment of power in her last three Arab dependencies (Cambridge: Cambridge University Press, 1994 [1991]), p. 118.

58. Darby, loc. cit.

59. HCD, 574, col. 872, 29 July 1957, cited in ibid., pp. 130-1.

60. Ibid., pp. 131-3.

61. HCD, 577, cols. 334, 446, 7 Nov. 1957; HCD 573, cols. 49-50, 10 July 1957, cited in ibid., p. 125, nn. 88, 89, and 91.

62. CO 968/693, 'Establishment of United Kingdom Base in Kenya - Stationing British Troops in Kenya', brief, fo. 3.

63. Ibid., Hare to Lennox-Boyd, 22 Nov. 1957.

64. Ibid., 'Establishment of United Kingdom Base in Kenya', brief, fo. 3.

65. Kyle, Politics of Independence, pp. 81-2; Murphy, Alan Lennox-Boyd, pp. 223-4. Under the Lennox-Boyd Constitution the African Elected Members (AEMs) were provided with six additional seats in Legislative Council, giving them parity with the European members (MLCs).

66. CO 968/693, telegram 873, Lennox-Boyd (from Kenya) to Hare, repeated to the Earl of Perth (Minister of State for Colonial Affairs), 4 Nov. 1957.

67. Ibid., telegram 110, Hare to Lennox-Boyd, 4 Nov. 1957.

68. Ibid., Maj.-Gen. J.R.C. Hamilton (War Office) to A. Campbell (Principal, Colonial Office Defence Department), 10 Oct. 1957.

69. HCD, 577, cols. 1112-4, 14 Nov. 1957, cited in Kyle, Politics of Independence, p. 82; Murphy, Alan Lennox-Boyd, p. 223.

70. Kyle, loc. cit.

71. CO 968/693, telegram 60, Gorell Barnes to Baring, 2 Aug. 1957.

72. Ibid., telegram 64, Gorell Barnes to Baring, 19 Aug. 1957.

CHAPTER FOUR

East Africa, East of Suez II, 1957-9

Introduction

This chapter will confirm that Britain's strategic plans for Kenya Colony were far from being an irrelevant side-show to political developments. Rather, assurances from the men on the ground, combined with political concessions which can only be understood in terms of constituting a holding operation, served to increase confidence among British defence planners, as evidenced by the steady increase in the levels of military personnel stationed in the territory. Colonial administrators in East Africa were more concerned about the administrative and financial burdens imposed by establishing the UK Strategic Reserve in Kenya, and the implications for their internal security provisioning, than they were about its political effects. Only when the outward appearance of political progress and stability was unceremoniously undermined by the Africans' refusal to validate the process any longer in January 1959, did Britain even begin to reassess the all too convenient strategic assumptions which had underpinned the decision to station British troops 'permanently' in Kenya in the first place.

The Politics of Implementation

Two weeks after the announcement that an element of the UK Strategic Reserve would be stationed in Kenya, Hare informed Lennox-Boyd that 'we have this very day been able to confirm our intentions for the future of the Persian Gulf battalion and I can now agree to be rather more precise though we have to take account of Foreign Office views in our references to the Persian Gulf'.[1] It had been decided that, from April 1958, 1 Cameronians would replace the First Battalion, King's Shropshire Light Infantry (1 KSLI), which had been held over in Kenya at Baring's request. In addition to the replacement of one battalion by another, and the transfer of its status from residual internal security duties to element of the strategic reserve, this force would be bolstered by 'a detachment' of the First Battalion, Royal Fusiliers (1 RF). Sandys made it clear that he did not want references to the extra battalion included in any public statements.[2]

While this again seems simply to be a matter of determining the precise size of any forces required for the Persian Gulf and gauging the sensitivity to Britain's actions and intentions in the area, Lennox-Boyd was quick to show the importance that he attached to a more substantial contingent of British soldiers being stationed in Kenya. Although the Secretary of State was aware that the British soldiers in Kenya were not 'primarily there in that Colony's interest', he explained to Sandys:

> I know from my recent talks with the Governor in Nairobi, that he puts much store by the issue of an early and positive announcement to bolster local confidence at a difficult constitutional stage. The Governor set out the position very forcibly to you in his minute of 20th June when you yourself were in Kenya. This confidence can best be engendered by a statement that British troops and their families, in excess of the battalion already in the Colony, will be stationed there: [...] I hope therefore you will reconsider your view that no reference should be made to the second battalion, its name and time of arrival in Kenya.[3]

Significantly, Lennox-Boyd had not visited East Africa in October 1957 with the sole purpose of ending the political stalemate in Kenya. Initially, he flew to Uganda for a conference with the East African governors 'on future policy'.[4] This coincided with the visit of General Bourne to Nairobi in order to consider the administrative implications of stationing British soldiers in Kenya, Aden and the Persian Gulf in the wake of Sandys' visit and the Oman operation.[5]

The Entebbe conference covered the whole spectrum of policy, from 'political and constitutional' and 'economic development', to 'defence, police and internal security'. The papers for circulation at the conference were prepared by the Colonial Office, in consultation with the local governments and Whitehall departments, and were provided as additional briefs for Lennox-Boyd prior to his departure for the region. An important paper in this regard, EAC (57) 6, 'Defence, Police and Internal Security', was amended by the Colonial Office in order to reflect the reassessment by the Chiefs of Staff 'of the employment in the Middle East of Commonwealth and Colonial forces in the post-nuclear phase [of global war]'.

While in the late 1940s and early 1950s it had been British military policy that, apart from their local internal security role, soldiers recruited in East Africa would contribute to the defence of Egypt, the loss of the Suez base and subsequent developments brought about a change. Thereafter British defence planners 'did not envisage any primary global war requirement for East African forces outside their area'.[6] However, the internal security role would not necessarily be confined to assisting in the maintenance of the economic and political stability of the region and its individual territories in peacetime. In the event of global war, East African soldiers, apparently,

> would be profoundly disturbed by events in Europe, and likely developments

> in the Middle East, and ... the political and economic situations of the territories will be severely shaken. For these reasons it is thought that the situation is unlikely to be stable enough to warrant Governors risking the release of troops for excursions outside their own territorial borders.[7]

If anything, this underpinned the rationale behind stationing British soldiers in Kenya. While 'global war' was not expected in the 'foreseeable future', recent political developments in Africa and increasingly vocal African nationalists, juxtaposed by their anti-British counterparts in the Middle East, made it politically, if not militarily, inexpedient to rely upon East African forces for even the most minor of 'fire brigade' duties elsewhere in the Empire. If it was politically unacceptable to use East African soldiers in an internal security role beyond their own area, why was it any more acceptable, or even feasible, to put faith in 'guided' political development, leading to independence 'within a generation', thus relatively long-term security of tenure for the British base?

The conference paper on East African political and constitutional matters reiterated the strategic importance of the region and Britain's economic interests. Apart from Kenya's climatic and geographical suitability for British soldiers, there were three 'major airfields' in the region - Dar-es-Salaam, Entebbe, and Nairobi - and two smaller ones at Kisumu and Mombasa, also in Kenya; two commercial sea ports at Dar-es-Salaam and Mombasa, the latter having 'certain rudimentary naval facilities which could be improved with some expenditure of time and money'; with the possibility that an oil refinery would be built at Mombasa. 'At the present time the airfields of the region are essential links in the air reinforcing route from South Africa to the Middle East and from Europe and West Africa to the Arabian Peninsula and the Far East'. Significantly, the sources of the Nile in Uganda constituted, 'while under British control, at least a psychological threat to Egyptian ambition'.[8]

So far as economic interests were concerned, Britain had a surplus of visible trade with East Africa. For example, diamonds (a significant source of dollar earnings) were imported from Tanganyika (over £3 million in 1955), and East Africa was 'almost the sole supplier of sisal [99.8%] to the United Kingdom and the principal supplier of coffee [58.8%]'.

> The relative importance of East Africa in the United Kingdom market for ... [such] ... commodities ... is a post-war phenomenon, resulting from the dollar shortage, but as far as can be seen there will always be a substantial advantage in having these sterling sources of supply at competitive prices. [...] If the possibility of denial of supplies is envisaged, the principal difficulty would arise with sisal, for which there is no obvious alternatives [*sic*] available in the sterling area.[9]

There was therefore every reason why Britain should wish to exercise control of the defence and security arrangements, and to retain trading links with the whole of the East Africa region.[10] It is axiomatic that this would be made all the more simple by retaining control of political developments.

This of course had a considerable bearing upon the discussions at the Entebbe conference. The more commonly known of East African governors' conference at Chequers in January 1959 can arguably be seen as a watershed in terms of British policy towards East Africa, albeit in the ironic sense, because dates for independence were 'pencilled in', then revised within a matter of months, if not weeks. However, the October 1957 conference had not been convened with a view to providing a timetable for the transfer of political power. Lennox-Boyd's November statements concerning political development in Kenya had been pre-empted in discussion at Entebbe:

> In summing up on the problem of a statement of ultimate intention ... the *Secretary of State* said that it was agreed that a portentous statement aimed to cover the whole of East Africa was certainly undesirable, and probably impossible at the present stage. If any such statement were required it must be related to individual territories. The conference accepted, as being a good basis for responding to questions in Kenya and Tanganyika, something on the following lines: -
>
> "It is our intention to promote gradual evolution towards democratic forms of government in a controlled and orderly way but not to abandon our ultimate responsibilities until there is a reasonable prospect that, when we have done so, all who have made their homes here will be able to continue to live here and pursue their occupations in security".[11]

The conference paper EAC (57) 6, covering defence, police and internal security had been prefaced with African nationalists' demands for more rapid constitutional advance and statements of British intentions in mind: 'A prerequisite of orderly political progress in East Africa is the ability of the East African Governments, backed by Her Majesty's Government, to maintain law and order and to counter outside interference'.[12] On the latter point, the paper explained, in somewhat contradictory terms that, in wartime

> no direct military threat to East Africa is expected, at least initially. If such a threat should eventually materialise it would be mainly from the north-east [Somaliland], and since it would most probably arise in a confused post-nuclear phase the United Kingdom could not be counted on to give fresh assistance to back up East African forces. The proper defence in global war of East Africa, indeed of the African Continent, lies in the Middle East, and existing strategic plans concentrate on the provision of forces, particularly of air forces with nuclear capability, in that theatre. In such circumstances East Africa's role

> must be primarily one of a staging area and in this context the special function of the local forces must be the maintenance of internal security, as much for their own as for the Imperial interest.[13]

Lennox-Boyd summarised the above as 'the latest views of the Chiefs of Staff on the role, or absence of one, of East African Forces in global war'.[14] While all this would have provided little comfort to Mboya except, that is, as further grounds to campaign against the establishment of the Kahawa cantonment, an 'external threat to the East African territories short of global war may be discounted; in so far as any lesser external threat exists it is likely to be confined to one arising out of a breakdown in effective administration in neighbouring territories'.[15] Gorell Barnes and Baring both stressed that this latter point did not take into account current political uncertainty in Italian Somaliland which, in peacetime, could well lead to 'every possibility of a military, as distinct from a police situation developing as a result in northern Kenya'.[16] Lennox-Boyd therefore undertook to inform the Defence Committee in London that it was the 'unanimous view' of the conference that the military appreciation in the paper had to be qualified accordingly.

As a significant precursor to defence and security considerations in the context of political negotiations on the eve of Kenya's independence in December 1963, a date hardly envisioned in October 1957, the conference also considered 'the problem of co-ordinating East African defence'. Despite the 'Longshot' re-organisation for primarily internal security purposes, the Chiefs of Staff considered that there was

> every advantage from the Imperial as well as the East African point of view in treating local defence on a regional basis and the East African forces as a unified instrument. The problem for the future is how to maintain the existing defence co-ordination if the three East African territories increasingly diverge in their political development. Should one attain independence before the others this would automatically make it difficult, and, if the territory in question joined the neutralist camp, impracticable, to maintain inter-territorial defence co-ordination. The only effective way of countering this may be to foster the concept of East African instead of territorial land forces, to encourage local interest in defence planning, particularly among local unofficials undergoing the education of Ministerial office, and to propagate the necessity of regarding East African defence as a regional and not a territorial problem. The maintenance of HQ East Africa Command will help to foster this concept.[17]

This seems to have been perfectly acceptable at Entebbe, with only Crawford remarking that 'so long as defence remained in the hands of the Governors' (thus Britain) co-ordination on a regional basis should not pose a problem. Significantly, supporting the above premise that co-ordination could be maintained even if one territory became independent, in all likelihood involving treaty arrangements, Crawford added that 'he hoped it would be possible, even then, to *persuade* East African Governments to deal with defence on a joint basis'.[18] While Chapters Six and Seven will show the extent of British *persuasion* in this regard, as the pace of constitutional advance in the East African territories accelerated significantly from 1959, the main issues of the Entebbe conference, as outlined above, are noteworthy in several respects.

Although the possibility of independence for any of Britain's East African territories was not discounted entirely, it was certainly not considered as a short-term prospect: timetables were conspicuous by their absence. This clearly accorded with the contemporary views of the Colonial Office and defence planners in London. Given the foregoing examination of British strategic provisions, for both internal security in East Africa and the Middle East, and the broader defence assessment, especially as it related to Kenya, one point is particularly notable. The 'men on the ground' expressed very little, if any, disquiet concerning East Africa's viability in the British imperial, thus strategic, connection. Baring, again, reiterated his welcome for British soldiers: 'because they provided a sense of security and permanency. It was precisely for these reasons that African politicians' opposed the move. Besides, 'experience in India, the Sudan and elsewhere had shown that the presence of such troops was no barrier to independence'.[19]

Most important is the backdrop that all this provided for Lennox-Boyd's subsequent negotiations with Kenya's African politicians and the constitutional 'award' of six extra seats in Legislative Council, giving parity with the European Elected Members. Clearly, defence and security did not amount to a side issue when it came to constitutional matters. It could be suggested reasonably that when Lennox-Boyd introduced his ten-year 'standstill' on any further alterations to the proportions of communal representation, he did so with one eye firmly, and necessarily, on Britain's broader strategic interests. It should be noted, also, that this all took place while a legal State of Emergency was still technically in being. Although, with the benefit of hindsight, it could be argued that the British colonial project in Kenya, as elsewhere, was doomed from 1945 onwards, it is not stressed enough that policy-makers had to act, as they saw it, on what could be predicted as reasonably likely. The unforeseen often undercut such assumptions.

Thus, having made and announced the strategic and constitutional decisions concerning Kenya by the end of 1957, with new elections due in March 1958, it remained for Britain to begin to implement the plans for the garrison for the strategic reserve.[20] For logistical and security purposes, the precise timing of the transfer of status of the British soldiers already in Kenya had not been set when the initial decisions were taken. The gradual movement of elements of 1 Cameronians from the Gulf to Kenya related as much to the readiness of locally recruited forces, such as the Oman Scouts, to take over from the British, as to the availability of accommodation. Equally, 'conditions in the Arabian Peninsula' had dictated that the size of the detachment of 1 RF bound for Kenya would remain uncertain.[21]

In addition, Baring's residual internal security requirements had to be taken into account. 1 KSLI were due to be relieved between April and May 1958, and it was 'generally understood within the War Office' that Baring would not require a British battalion in a 'purely' internal security role after May 1958, making the relief the ideal time for the role of the battalion to change.[22] The 'actual relief' was scheduled to extend over a number of weeks, while the War Office hoped to bring the change into effect in order to coincide with the reorganisation of the command structure in the Middle East, particularly the date when Headquarters British Forces Arabian Peninsula (HQ, BFAP) in Aden would become autonomous, on 1 April 1958.

Before this could go ahead, however, approval had to be obtained from East Africa Command, regarding matters of accommodation, for example, and from the Kenya government via the Colonial Office. This amounted simply to a matter of administrative routine. As Lennox-Boyd explained:

> In our view, the earlier the transfer takes place the better, particularly as this should save you £100,000 on [the] month of April alone on [the] Emergency Fund in respect of [your] contribution towards [the] upkeep of [the] KSLI. Grateful if you will telegraph [your] concurrence to [the] agreement which we have already provisionally given.[23]

While acceptance of the proposal was correspondingly routine, some points should be highlighted.[24]

Firstly, although on the face of it Baring would be losing a British battalion for internal security purposes, the transfer of status amounted effectively to no loss at all, especially given the increased establishment. Obviously, the presence of British soldiers in Kenya at little or no cost to that territory was a considerable boon, from both the financial and the security perspectives. On the latter point (as has been suggested above and will be developed further in Chapter Five) it should be reiterated that, in both Whitehall and Government House, political and security conditions in Kenya were not considered to be stable enough to end the State of Emergency.

If anything, the major problems to beset Britain's plans to station troops in Kenya, at least initially, were matters of administrative, financial, and logistical integration with local forces, and extraneous circumstances which brought about frequent reassessments of troop deployments south of the air barrier. When it became clear, in October 1957, that 'there may be fairly substantial Imperial Forces stationed in Kenya as a strategic reserve', C.H. Hartwell, Chief Secretary to the Uganda government, took up the former matter with East Africa Command, explaining that

> this is likely to necessitate engineering workshops and other facilities which would not otherwise be required at all. It may also be necessary for the GOC and his staff, and the civil organisation coming under his control, to perform services for and in respect of the Imperial Forces stationed in East Africa. It follows, therefore, that it will be necessary when more detailed information is available ... to work out in detail the financial arrangements which will be necessary between the War Department on the one hand and the East African Governments on the other.[25]

In April 1957, when the War Office planning team began to consider where in Kenya the strategic reserve would be located, the East Africa Defence Committee (EADC) convened a working committee (EADWC) to examine the administrative and financial questions. The preliminary view of the EADWC was:

> "(a) that the War Department should pay the whole cost of any organisation or facility which is necessitated wholly by and works only for the Imperial Forces; and
> (b) that the War Department should pay an appropriate share, to be agreed between it and the Governments, of the cost of the Command and civil organisations, on account of the service performed by them for the Imperial Forces." ... it is still the view of the Uganda Government on the subject, and I shall be grateful if you will take note of this.[26]

By November, of course, such views had to be taken into account, especially given the wish of the War Office that, in the interests of economy, while in East Africa the British force should 'be as far as possible integrated with the East African Land Forces for [the] purposes of training and administration'.[27] For similar reasons, it was also considered desirable that the GOC, East Africa Command, should command and administer the British soldiers through 'his EALF Command Headquarters'. Cost saving would also, where possible, extend throughout the range of '"Q" Services' (equipment).

For example, although there would be separate 'WD' and EALF storage depots, 'the maximum possible use' was to be made of EALF resources. For this reason, the War Office requested that Tapp ascertain whether the EALF could deal with the 'receipt, storage, maintenance and issue of clothing and General stores; returned stores (inc. technical); storage of reserve vehicles (if cheaper than if WD depot [were] responsible); storage of reserve ammo?' Also, so far as possible, stores would be purchased locally through EALFO.

Cost saving would also extend to the numbers of staff to be added to the EALFO establishment for the additional administrative requirements for the 'Imperial troops'.

While all this might have caused problems for East Africa Command, the very *ad hoc* nature of the planning for integration in itself gave the greatest cause for concern, especially regarding '"Q" Services'. This was highlighted in January 1958 at a War Office meeting to discuss command and administrative arrangements. D. Rees, Command Secretary, East Africa,

> explained the problems facing HQ East Africa Command under the War Office proposals which entailed two separate financial responsibilities and sources of revenue. The crux of the problem is: - where do the stores come from, who pays for them and what officer controls them? He then gave various examples pointing out the difficulties attaching to the War Office proposal that responsibilities should be split making the best possible use of EALF resources, and suggested that the solution was to hand over the complete responsibility to EALFO.[28]

On the one hand, this was considered to be an acceptable proposal because tasking one organisation with administrative responsibilities for all military forces in East Africa would avoid duplication of staff, thus unnecessary expense. On the other hand, a crucial aspect of the principal reason for British soldiers being sent to Kenya in the first place had to be taken into account. As Buttenshaw, the War Office '"Q" (Ops)' representative put it,

> the criterion must be the capability of the Imperial Forces to operate as a strategic reserve at short notice. We must be certain that the day to day administration meets this, as second best will not do. Because the GOC is finally responsible he should decide whether the EALFO solution would meet this requirement. Seconded British officers should be made available if he requires them. The War Office should, therefore, accept the EALFO solution if the GOC East Africa is satisfied that it can be made to work, bearing in mind that the battalion must be properly equipped.[29]

Allowing the decision to rest with Tapp was significant because proposals for various 'methods' of administration that he had submitted in October 1957 had been either rejected by the Colonial Office and War Office, respectively, because of relative cost to the East African or British governments, or were subject to the difficulties considered in the January War Office meeting. The War Office now agreed that, whatever the outcome, the GOC should be asked to 'propose a solution which would satisfy the requirement to maintain the Imperial Forces at the correct standard and state of readiness and without being influenced by previous War Office views'.[30] This would give Tapp greater flexibility in tailoring his proposals to suit the capabilities of

East Africa Command and the EALFO, and, equally important, would enable him to cater for the objections and requirements of the East African governments.

Before any new solutions could be proposed, let alone adopted, planning fell down at the preliminary stage. A prerequisite for planning to begin was that the governments of the East African territories should agree to Tapp being requested to command and administer the British units, in addition to his local responsibilities.[31] What had seemed to be simply a matter of routine, especially in discussion in the War Office, quickly brought to light a set of problems which had hardly been anticipated when the strategic reappraisals of the previous two years or so had been undertaken. It should be stressed, in line with the earlier analysis, that *political* problems, as such, did not figure in any of this.

In early February 1958, a somewhat impatient War Office official enquired whether the Colonial Office had yet made a formal approach to the East African governments requesting their agreement to Tapp taking command of the British soldiers, as its representative had undertaken to do during the January meeting.[32] A month later, the head of the Colonial Office Defence Department, A. Campbell, explained that the delay was the result of

> some disagreement in East Africa on the role of the [EALF], and consequently on the form and functions of the [EALFO]. There appear also to be financial difficulties in connection with the administration of the [EALF], and consequently some mis-apprehensions as to what looking after the United Kingdom garrison in Kenya might entail. We therefore felt it necessary to dispose of these matters before approaching [the] Governors ... in order to avoid a possible danger that your requirements might become entangled with and overlaid by the problems of the [EALF], and a favourable decision thereby delayed.[33]

On the matter of 'financial difficulties' the Colonial Office hoped that the War Office would extend the concession of 'Estimates Customer status' (ECS) to the East African territories 'in respect of stores items in common use' by the British and local forces.[34] The 'great financial help' that this represented would 'undoubtedly be a big factor in securing wholehearted ... co-operation'. With this agreed by the War Office representative, apparently as a matter of routine, Lennox-Boyd wrote to the East African territories, formally announcing the decision on the Strategic Reserve, and making the requisite enquiries regarding Tapp's assumption of administrative command of the British units from 1 April.[35] While also summing up the key points from the earlier deliberations over the Strategic Reserve, the Secretary of State dangled the ECS carrot. Significantly, Lennox-Boyd added that, whatever administrative and financial arrangements were eventually finalised, they would have to be 'capable of providing for any expansion of the force which [HMG] with the agreement of the Governor of Kenya may consider necessary in the future'.

The *coup d'état* in Iraq in July 1958 would ensure that *future* British strategic necessities would alter much more quickly than planners in London had anticipated. This would again lead to an upgrading of Kenya's strategic status. Meanwhile, the EADC agreed to the War Office proposals concerning the administrative and command arrangements for all military units 'now in Kenya'; the EALFO 'could accept complementary responsibilities'. The EADC also agreed that there should be a fully-integrated headquarters, with administrative arrangements to be agreed between the GOC and the governments of the East African territories.

Yet, the EADC continued to protest against any possibility that the new arrangements would prove to be financially disadvantageous to the East African governments. Moreover, 'modifications which would result in fundamental alterations to our present policy for the administration of the EALF and the composition and organisation of their supporting installations etc. [*sic*] would be unacceptable'.[36] This was not simply a case of the East African governments wanting to have their cake and eat it:

> It is now clear that the figures and assumptions on which the Longshot stores handover was based - and on which the territorial Governments had, perforce, to make their financial arrangements - contain an unreasonable margin of error. This is a serious embarrassment to us and, in consequence, we would find it necessary to request an adjustment of the provisions of the Longshot Agreement (Comd 281) [*sic*] relating to stores and scalings as part of any negotiations concerning the arrangements for the UK Central Reserve.[37]

The EADC would simply not 'accept any financial burden on [the] East Africa governments for [the] administration of British Troops Kenya [BTK]; we were convinced that we could not undertake responsibility for UK units unless the EALFO was granted estimates customer status ...'

If anything, the very mundanity and the routine nature of all this demonstrates the 'matter of fact' and workman-like approach to these military arrangements taken by both the British and East African governments. It also underlines the apparent, if transient, importance given in London to the views of the administrators 'on the ground'. Certainly, in May 1958 the Colonial Office stressed the desirability of a 'very early agreement on temporary financial arrangements so as to avoid creating unnecessary financial confusion in East Africa. Such confusion could only lead to a sharpening of the East African Governments' bargaining attitude'.[38] The EALFO, for its part, argued that the ECS proposal should be implemented 'forthwith', because even if the War Office were to end up resuming administrative (and financial) responsibility for EALF this would end up being the case.[39] Implementation of the former would certainly help to facilitate that of the latter.

With well over a year having passed since the Chiefs of Staff had made their initial recommendations, and six months since Sandys' announcement to the Commons, the requirement that command and administrative arrangements for all military forces in East Africa should take account of Britain's and East Africa's respective strategic, local defence and internal security commitments, while remaining cost effective, created a kind of bureaucratic stalemate. By June 1958, the command and administrative arrangements for British and 'local' forces stationed in East Africa had by no means been finalised. While proposals were being put forward for yet another War Office planning team to visit East Africa in order to resolve this, in effect attempting to 'marry' the British demand for high standards for the UK Strategic Reserve detachment with East African financial, material and practical necessities and limitations, no final decision on financial matters could be taken. As a result, there would be 'no further consideration of proposals for interim financial and provision arrangements'.[40] In practical terms, therefore, the War Office could not, or rather *would* not grant the EALFO 'Estimates Customer status', thereby effectively negating the earlier negotiations and proposals upon which the East African governments' agreement had been based.

The difficulties that this presented did not amount simply to a matter of principle. Clearly, achieving administrative and financial efficiency in the command and control of all of the military forces in East Africa was in the interests of all parties concerned. Yet, as Tapp explained to the War Office, uncertainty regarding what on the face of it might appear to be simply a matter of who should pay, and how much should be paid, for EALF stores procurements would have 'serious repercussions'. The EALFO was already experiencing considerable monetary difficulties for the financial year beginning 1 July 1958:

> In spite of drastic economies planned and discussions lasting 6 [*sic*] months [the] territories have not yet agreed [the] budget for funds considered [to be the] absolute [minimum] for [the] effective [operation] of EALF. [...] Gap is nearly 4% [*sic*] of total estimate or £100,000 [£1 million]. Delay in decision of [administrative] arrangements will cause [the] gap to widen because [the] estimates as framed are based on [*sic*] [the] assumption [that] EALFO would enjoy ... [ECS] ... with lower average prices, quicker [supply] and lower freight rates. Prolongation [of the] system of [supply] through Crown Agents [is] therefore [a] serious matter. [...] Provided [the] final decision is [for an] integrated system under either WD or EALF and EALFO [ordnance supply] will presumably be through normal WD channels. [...] Strongly recommend

> therefore [that] EALFO [be] granted ...[ECS] ... immediately in anticipation of what seems [the] *inevitable outcome* as far as [ordnance stores are] concerned.[41]

Remarkably, given the earlier agreement in the War Office that Tapp should be allowed to make the final decision over the command arrangements in East Africa, this latter plea was rejected. With the report of the War Office working party having only just been submitted prior to the planning team's visit to East Africa, it was by 'no means inevitable' that future administrative and command arrangements for the UK strategic reserve in Kenya would be integrated with EALFO. There was, therefore, no justification for granting ECS to EALFO 'at this stage if at all and regret your request cannot be agreed. There are strong reasons for restriction of [ECS]'.[42] Despite already conceding that ECS should be granted to the EALFO, the War Office was 'in the process of winding up this procedure, and by 1960 the only force which will still enjoy such status is the Canadian Brigade in Germany, which is so integrated with the British forces that it can be treated as part of them'.

As Lennox-Boyd (undoubtedly briefed by the War Office) explained, there was an important distinction:

> This is not the case with the KAR. To grant "full" estimates customer status would compel the War Office to order, hold and supply stores and equipment which would not at any time be needed by the British Army, and this would both tie up capital funds for a considerable time before recovery, and also involve use of extra manpower in depots, offices, etc.[43]

This last point seemed to be contradicted by the probability that the British Army would establish its own ordnance depot in Kenya. Nonetheless, the War Office did at least agree to provide 'common use items' which the East African forces could draw 'as required'. This, Lennox-Boyd suggested, would enable the East African governments to make savings in their estimates for forward provisioning, 'given no need to build up stocks of such items'. Although Lennox-Boyd apparently accepted the War Office line, joining in presenting the governors of the East African territories with a *fait accompli*, the matter did not rest there.

In the meantime, Tapp had continued to press for the effective reversal of the 'Longshot' arrangements, arguing that although integration of the administration and command of all military forces in East Africa under the EALF and EALFO 'could be made to work, it would be to everyone's advantage if the War Office resumed control of all forces in East Africa Command'.[44] This would be facilitated because he already commanded all military forces in British East Africa.

A principal reason for the GOC to press for the policy reversal was that, in his view, the EALFO establishment was understaffed. Moreover, the organisation was top-heavy with civilian administrators, thought suitable only for 'the standards that are needed in a force maintained for purposes of internal security and a measure of local and regional defence'. He added: 'My Headquarters [*sic*] and the administrative machine available would have been inadequate to accept responsibility for operational War Department units'.[45] In addition, the very nature of the interim administrative and financial measures gave rise to a situation in which there were two sources of funds (EALFO and the War Office), two sets of 'estimates, allotments and financial regulations, and two systems of financial advice, control and audit. This arrangement has even meant [*sic*] that civilians, not only in different units working side by side, but actually within my Headquarters, have served on different rates of pay and conditions of service.' Tapp stressed that this situation 'was acceptable only as a purely temporary measure. Its operation has been a great strain on all concerned.'[46]

With British forces in Kenya likely to number around 3,500 'for at least a year and in all probability for considerably longer' Tapp thought it 'necessary to weigh carefully the disadvantages of the integration of their command and administration under the [EALF] and [EALFO]'.[47] From the GOC's perspective, these disadvantages can be summed up as follows. Firstly, there was a 'pressing need' for just one source of funds and a single, rational administrative system, without which 'effective integration' would be 'impracticable'. Because the annual cost of stationing British forces in Kenya (£6 [60] million) amounted to more than twice that for EALF (£2.8 [28] million), in Tapp's view it seemed 'logical for the contributor of the larger amount to control the whole'.

Secondly, the East African governments' refused to meet the shortfall between their financial provisioning and Tapp's minimum requirements. While this could be addressed with pressure being applied on the territories from various quarters, Tapp felt that 'the system would be at best ponderous and at worst ineffective'. Thirdly, the territories had already insisted that all financial systems

> generally should depart to some extent from the procedures used in the British Army, and I have little doubt that pressure towards conformity with Colonial Government practice will continue. There are serious disadvantages to subjecting British officers, posted to East Africa Command for purely Imperial purposes to unfamiliar financial systems and to financial dependence on officials who are not answerable to the War office in any way.[48]

Finally, and perhaps most damning, was Tapp's observation that the governments of the East African territories 'are unused to the administration of a military force'. Although this might have been overcome with time, the greater 'complication' of the British force's equipment and higher costs 'would greatly increase these difficulties'.[49]

While Baring, for one, might have disagreed with some of the bases for Tapp's arguments, he certainly would not have rejected their substance nor, for that matter, the GOC's conclusion. Tapp continued:

> We have always assumed that reversion to War Office control was entirely unacceptable to both the War Office and the Colonial Office for political reasons. It appears, however, that this is not necessarily so. Kenya, who opposed the transfer of control in 1957, would of course be delighted to change back and I do not believe that Uganda and Tanganyika would seriously object to a return to the pre-July 1957 arrangements, provided that their annual expenditure on defence thereby fell or at any rate did not increase other than in ordinary inflationary ways, that they were told in some detail how their contributions were applied, and that they could still exercise some measure of control over the strengths and standards of the King's African Rifles. [...] In conclusion I would again stress the urgency of integration one way or the other, and I request that the possibility of an early return to a system of War Office control of all the forces in East Africa Command should be examined.[50]

Tapp's intervention could well have been decisive and, as will be seen below, were it not for the determination of policy-makers in London to adhere to recent 'political' decisions regarding the administrative and financial control of colonial forces by their local governments, the GOC's views might have won the day.

In the same month as Tapp put forward the case for the War Office to resume control of all military forces in East Africa, the working party 'on the future method of command and administration of imperial forces in East Africa' submitted its report. This outlined the three methods of administration that had been proposed by the GOC, but dismissed his main recommendation:

> <u>METHOD 'A'. For the War Office to reassume [*sic*] control of all forces in East Africa</u>. From a military point of view, this is most desirable and it is recommended by GOC East Africa. However, it is against HMG policy of making Colonial Governments responsible for their own local forces, and therefore, it is not acceptable politically. There would also be serious financial objections. This method is, therefore, not examined any further.[51]

Method 'B' entailed placing all 'Imperial troops' in East Africa under EALFO administration, requiring adequate financial provision to be made by the War Office, while method 'C' involved providing 'Imperial administrative backing' for the strategic reserve, thereby establishing the 'Imperial force in East Africa independent of EALFO'.[52]

The working party had obtained the views of the various interested War

Office branches on methods 'B' and 'C', regarding, among other matters, accommodation, financial responsibilities, secondment of British officers and other ranks (OR) 'into key positions', and manpower requirements. It then assessed the relative impact on the 'standard of service' and ability of BTK to operate anywhere south of the air/sea barrier at short notice, comparing the respective advantages and disadvantages of both methods.[53] The working party concluded that the 'only real disadvantage' of method 'C' (the 'Imperial establishment' solution) was that it would involve dividing the existing Command HQ into three separate headquarters (East Africa Command, Imperial Forces East Africa, and EALF District).[54] While an increase in manpower to enable the effective working of ECS for the EALFO had been cited as a principal reason for the initial War Office proposal to be rejected, it seems that the increased establishments required to staff three separate, if in many ways functioning in parallel, military administrative organisations was a different matter.

Conversely, because method 'B' (the 'EALFO system') had not been tried out,

> it is difficult to say with any certainty whether or not it will definitely maintain 24 Infantry Brigade Group at the correct standard. War Office branches are suspicious of the system and there is a strong doubt if it will work in practice. This cannot be considered as acceptable for a formation of the UK Strategic Reserve. The EALFO system will also entail complicated financial arrangements and it is likely to prove no more economical than Imperial administration. For these reasons, Method "C", i.e. Imperial administrative backing for 24 Infantry Brigade Group, should be adopted.[55]

Thus, the working party recommended that the War Office planning team should use method 'C' as its basis for discussions with Tapp on how exactly the administrative structure would take shape. It also recommended that manpower allocation should be re-examined accordingly, and that accommodation requirements should be submitted by the War Office branches on that basis. That was not the last of the matter.

The working party had also examined the feasibility of setting up a system whereby the 'Imperial Organisation' in Kenya would supply 'common user services and items' to EALFO on an 'agency basis', and had recommended that method 'C' be modified to provide this service.[56] However, as might be expected, the War Office was less concerned with placating the East African colonial governments than it was with maximising the effectiveness and the efficiency of the 'Imperial units'.

Having examined the working party's report and Tapp's letter, Brigadier I.C. Harris, Assistant Under-Secretary of State in the War Office, was alarmed that, despite the GOC's recommendations, method 'A' for administering all soldiers in East Africa (under War Office control) had been so readily dismissed. Given Tapp's views, Harris considered that 'the political and financial aspects of Method "A" should be re-examined, with a view to determining whether or not a detailed examination of this method should be made'.[57] For reasons which remain unclear little, if anything, seems to have been done in this regard. Whether the result of administrative procedure or simply time available, or because of concerns for the situation in the Middle East following the *coup d'état* in Iraq in July 1958, there were no further substantive military discussions on Kenya in the War Office until August.

Notably, the agenda for that War Office meeting betrayed a surprising amount of indecision on policy generally. It seems 'official War Office policy, which has never been countermanded', was that 'Imperial troops' should be administered by EALFO.[58] Earlier objections regarding the 'standards' for BTK, and the working party's recommendation that separate 'Imperial administration for the brigade' was therefore essential 'to its proper functioning as part of the Strategic Reserve', nevertheless left the issue of policy open to question. This had to be decided before the minutiae of the command structure in East Africa could be determined.

The only constant to work with was the British government's seemingly contradictory policy (in this particular instance), based upon the Templer Report, that colonial governments should administer and finance their 'local' military forces. Nevertheless, it seems all the more surprising given Britain's experience with colonial military exploits, garrisons overseas, and command and control of local levies, for example, that the principles for administering and financing British and local forces established essentially in parallel had not hitherto been cast in bronze. Much of this, of course, reflected the traditional British practice of dealing with each situation on its own merits, what might be called an *ad hoc* approach, and the relative novelty of the situation pertaining to Kenya.

In many respects these latter points were demonstrated by the third item on the agenda for the August War Office meeting. Provided that items one ('Imperial administration' of BTK) and two ('common user' stores for EALFO) were agreed as matters of policy, the proposed 'solution' was that there should be in East Africa one HQ, with parallel staffs for EALF and BTK, respectively.[59] By then, however, Tapp had become aware that reversion to War Office control seemed increasingly unlikely, and had modified his earlier objections to the current system, despite the difficulties of dual financial responsibilities.[60] Apparently, the War Office had to clarify whether or not this objection still applied, as well as deciding if staff of similar rank serving in the same HQ should receive the same rates of pay and, indeed, whether or not the proposed planning team should even go to Kenya. Only then could the draft paper on policy be approved or amended, let alone implemented.[61]

It seems that, in terms of both broader and immediate policy considerations, examining each case based upon its merits imposed far more restrictions on action than the flexibility that might have been expected, and which might have been achieved, by more firmly established policy guidelines. Again, it should be reiterated that the financial and political objections referred to above were matters of inter-governmental policy and had little, if any, relation to African sensibilities. This was confirmed in early June 1958, when ministerial approval was given to the recommendation of the Chiefs of Staff that 'until 1963 at least an infantry brigade group should be established in Kenya', and by the latter's view that Britain's operational requirements south of 'the Barrier' could be met only by doing this 'on a permanent basis'.[62]

By the time of the August 1958 War Office meeting, Lennox-Boyd had become even more convinced that EALFO should be allowed to continue its functions in respect of EALF, and that control of the East African forces should *not* therefore revert to the War Office. British government policy aside, the Secretary of State felt that it was 'only natural' that any new organisation was bound to have 'teething troubles', and that any difficulties could be 'adjusted locally'.[63] In Lennox-Boyd's view, a year was simply not long enough to have concluded (as the governments of Kenya and Tanganyika had) that the organisation should be 'wound up' entirely. Besides, in Uganda, Governor Crawford's views had 'hardened against any reversion [to War Office control] because:- (i) It is politically difficult for him to convince his Government of the necessity. (ii) He is not satisfied that it would be cheaper'.[64] Thus, with no unanimity between the governors of the three territories, the case for adhering to current British policy was strengthened and, moreover, with no perceived requirement to station any British troops in Uganda, it was clearly unnecessary to risk unsettling African opinion there. With the 'technical' State of Emergency still in place, and Lennox-Boyd's ten-year 'standstill' on further political concessions, Britain was therefore apparently firmly 'in control', and this latter consideration did not seem to apply in Kenya.

There seemed to be only one justification remaining for the War Office to resume administrative and financial control of all military forces in East Africa: the current assessment of the potential threats to East African security. As Tapp put it:

> In July 1957 when the East African Governments became responsible for their own forces there was no serious external threat and, therefore, the EALF was organised for a purely internal security role. At that time it was not proposed to station an Imperial force permanently in East Africa. [...] In the next three to four years it is possible that Imperial forces will have to operate alongside

EALF in meeting an external threat from the SUDAN, ETHIOPIA or SOMALILAND.[65]

Although Tapp cited the above as his reasons, 'from a military point of view', for recommending reversion to full War Office control, he now recognised that this was impracticable, and realised that, in any case, British soldiers would be made available to help combat any such external threats to East Africa.[66]

Moreover, the Colonial Office had determined with the governments of Kenya and Tanganyika that external threats could be sub-divided into three types: '(i) Unorganised tribal raiding. (ii) Tribal raiding encouraged by an independent SOMALILAND. (iii) Frontier warfare of the type now being experienced on the YEMEN/ADEN frontier'.[67] While (iii) was considered to be unlikely in 'the reasonably foreseeable future', the other two threats could be dealt with by the KAR.[68] Tapp and Baring agreed with most of the above, but they 'could not agree with the Colonial Office view that the KAR are correctly organised to meet tribal raiding encouraged by an independent SOMALILAND'.[69] Plans for the War Office and the Colonial Office to convene jointly a 'high level committee' to examine the situation 'on the ground' in East Africa had been postponed until the three governors had 're-examined and reorganised the structure of EALFO on the lines suggested by [the] Secretary of State for the Colonies'.[70]

In summary, Lieutenant-General Sir Harold Pyman, the Deputy Chief of the Imperial General Staff (DCIGS), reiterated that the present organisation in East Africa was based upon a Cabinet decision, and that any reorganisation would require Cabinet approval. The issue was therefore held in abeyance, and the meeting moved on to discuss 'the present problem' of determining the overall command structure for East Africa.[71] Much of what has already been outlined above in this regard was then painstakingly considered, the principal conclusions being that 'Imperial administration must be provided as soon as possible for the strategic reserve brigade', and that a 'local examination' should take place, but the approval of the three governors should be obtained beforehand.[72]

With this latter condition satisfied as a matter of routine, it remained to inform the East African governments officially that the proposals for the War Office to resume control of all forces there, or for EALFO to administer the strategic reserve, had both been rejected.[73] After some subsequent confusion, it was also made clear that any Colonial Office representative attached to the planning team due to visit East Africa in October, would be acting in the interests of that Office, and *not* on behalf of the East African governments, which would not be allowed to second their own representatives as 'members' of the team. ('Team will of course work in close consultation with EALFO.')[74] Despite several protests from the three governments in East Africa, the War Office planning team would be tasked to deal 'purely with military organisation and not with Governmental matters' which, given the preceding account, appear almost certainly to be related more to fiscal and financial concerns than 'political' issues, as such.[75]

As an indication of the British government's single-mindedness, if not a quiet confidence, the secrecy surrounding the precise nature of previous War Office visits to Kenya regarding the strategic reserve, and the earlier reticence regarding longer-term plans, were then abandoned. In an apparent signal of Britain's determination to protect its interests in the Middle East, and certainly to remain in Kenya for several years, the War Office announced in August that 'new barracks now being built in Kenya were "part of our policy of long-term planning" and was "a natural development". It also said the new accommodation would not be ready for two or three years'.[76] In late September, the Kenya government followed this up, and announced the imminent arrival of the War Office team, 'to consider command changes necessary when additional troops are stationed in Kenya'.[77]

The War Office team duly arrived in Kenya on 5 October 1958.[78] In anticipation of this, Tapp had consulted the three governments, and had prepared detailed proposals to be put to the team regarding the changes required to the command and administrative structures.[79] Essentially, both parties were agreed and, the minutiae aside, settled on a system whereby both the 'Imperial' and EALF establishments would exist as separate units, except for the matter of dividing the EALF into two categories. 'Category "A"' would include the GOC, Chief of Staff, Aide-de-Camp (ADC), General Staff, signals staff, and chaplains from East Africa Command, who would be responsible for both 'Imperial and EALF matters'. The War Office would make a financial contribution to EALFO for the use of these staff, along with making financial provision for other costs incurred by EALFO as a direct result of any arrangements made to cater for 'Imperial requirements'. 'Category "B"' would, of course, 'include staff and services required solely for EALF purposes'.[80] It was expected that the Executive Committee of the Army Council (ECAC) would agree to the planning team's recommendations as a matter of course; unsurprising given the earlier lengthy deliberations. In the War Office it was hoped that the proposals could be 'put into effect ... with the minimum of delay' (1 April 1959), so all that apparently remained was to formally obtain the approval of the East African governments.[81]

Meanwhile, concerns in East Africa over interim arrangements for the placing of orders for 'common user' military equipment with Crown Agents, which would result 'overall in considerable extra costs' compared with items purchased under ECS, were allayed by the Colonial Office instruction to hold back such orders in preparation to submit them to the 'WD Depot'.[82] By the end of November 1958, Brigadier Harris had informed East Africa Command that, 'in anticipation of the Army Council agreeing the War Office Team's report there is no objection to the Imperial Ordnance Depot in Kenya [Kahawa] supplying EALF with common user items on repayment, provided there is no detriment to British needs'. In response, Lisle felt it necessary to reiterate that the East African governments did not expect EALF requirements 'automatically to have a second priority'.[83]

> Indeed, I have no doubt that one of the fundamental factors which influenced their representatives in favour of proposals which would entail the large scale surrender of their "rights" in Kahawa was that they believed that the plan would provide the EALF with supply arrangements better than an adequately stocked EALF Depot. Sub-paragraph 10 (b) of Appendix "A" to the latest draft of the War Office Team's report emphasises this as part of the quid pro quo [*sic*].[84]

Conversely, while the ECAC agreed the War Office planning team's proposals, as had been expected, it rejected Tapp's recommendation that staff on both the 'Imperial' and the EALF establishments should be on 'Imperial' terms of service (i.e. lower pay), rather than secondment terms of service, as currently enjoyed by EALF staff, in order to avoid friction among ranks serving together.[85] As the ECAC saw it, it was unfair to reduce the pay for EALF staff because other staff seconded on other colonial duties enjoyed secondment pay: 'The East African Governments offer such terms as they see fit to attract the right quality and sufficient quantity of British ranks to serve with the EALF.'[86]

By January 1959, all of the major problems concerning the command and administrative control, and the financing of military forces in British East Africa appear to have been resolved. The East African governments had given their agreement 'in principle' to the War Office and Colonial Office proposals, subject to the successful completion of all related 'detailed negotiations'.[87] The reorganisation of the military command structure in British East Africa as a whole and, more importantly, on the ground in Kenya, therefore seemed set to take place on 1 April 1959. In the meantime, various officials in the War Office, the Colonial Office, East Africa Command, and EALFO, continued to disagree over relatively minor issues like whether the command paymaster should serve on the HQ EALF (shared) establishment (thereby attracting a financial contribution from the War Office), and whether some of the motor spares required by EALF might not 'strictly speaking, be "in common use between the two forces"'.[88]

While these various government departments continued to 'split hairs', political considerations in East Africa had already begun to militate against Britain's longer-term strategic and political plans. British policy-makers and defence-planners had spent three years deciding whether to station British soldiers in Kenya 'on a permanent basis', finding the most suitable location and determining how large such a force should be, as well as going to great lengths to iron out the complexities of administration, command and control, and finance. Britain now had to begin the process of aligning its strategic requirements in East Africa more closely with political developments, instead of *vice versa*. This response was far from immediate, however, and would take the best part of five years to conclude to Britain's, and independent Kenya's satisfaction. British attempts, from January 1959 onwards, to secure 'vital interests' in Kenya, while making further political concessions to African nationalists, will be examined in the subsequent chapters.

Conclusion

With Mau Mau apparently defeated, and following the imposition of the Lennox-Boyd Constitution, political development in Kenya appeared to have been aligned with Britain's strategic requirements in East Africa. This left British defence planners, interested government departments, and officials on the ground free to haggle over the related administrative, financial, and military implications of implementing the new strategy. While the nationalists adhered to the substance, if not the spirit, of the Colonial Office standstill on further constitutional advance, little regard had to be paid to African political sensibilities. Yet, at the very moment that all of the numerous problems associated with stationing British troops in Kenya seemed to have been settled, ironically, political considerations returned to the fore. Only then would Britain begin to seriously contemplate its strategic options in Kenya with regard to the Africans' refusal to legitimise the process further with their participation. As Britain's political legitimacy in Kenya was brought increasingly into question, the grounds for retaining its military bases there became all the more difficult to justify. Yet, as will be seen in the subsequent chapters, Britain's efforts to solve its Kenyan defence and internal security conundrum were far from hasty. Three years of painstaking military planning and implementation would not be thrown to the wind.

Notes

1. CO 968/693, Hare to Lennox-Boyd, 22 Nov. 1957.
2. Ibid., Campbell, minute for Carstairs and Mathieson (Colonial Office), 26 Nov. 1957.
3. Ibid., Lennox-Boyd to Sandys, 29 Nov. 1957.

4. CO 822/1818, 'Colonial Office, African No. 1191, Not for Publication: Proceedings of the Conference with East African Governors on Future Policy', 7-8 Oct. 1957. See also: CO 822/1807.

5. CO 968/693, 'Brief for the Secretary of State', (probably by A. Campbell), 30 Sept. 1957; telegram CIC/10188, Bourne (War Office) to Tapp, 23 Sept. 1957; telegram 18336 (MO4), Director of Military Operations (DMO), War Office, to Force Nairobi, 19 Sept. 1957; letter MO4/733, Maj. D.M. Pontifex (War Office) to T. O'Neill (Colonial Office, Defence Department), 25 Sept. 1957. 'Foreign Office wish to avoid reference to OMAN or reinforcement of the PERSIAN GULF in any press release concerning the visit. Explanation to press should be limited to saying that the visit is to a neighbouring Commander for purposes of routine liaison', telegram 18574 (MO4) to MIDEAST (INFORMATION: FORCE NAIROBI), 1 Oct. 1957. See also: CO 822/1813.

6. CO 968/693, minute by Campbell to Mathieson, 30 Sept. 1957.

7. Ibid.

8. CO 822/1806, extract from East African Governors' Conference paper EAC (57) 1, 'East Africa: Political and Constitutional', n.d. (c. Sept. 1957), fos. 11-12.

9. Ibid., fos. 12-14.

10. It is significant that when Kilmuir presented Macmillan with his colonial 'profit and loss' account in June 1957, economic considerations were 'evenly matched'. In other words, it would make no difference, from the economic point of view, whether Britain retained or disposed of its colonies: Ritchie Ovendale, 'Macmillan and the Wind of Change in Africa, 1957-1960', *Historical Journal*, 38/2 (1995), pp. 459-60; John Ramsden, *The Winds of Change: Macmillan to Heath, 1957-1975* (Harlow: Longman, 1996), p. 22.

11. CO 822/1818, 'Proceedings of the Conference with East African Governors on Future Policy', 7-8 Oct. 1957, p. 48, para. 209.

12. CO 822/1813, EAC (57) 6 (Final), 'Defence, Police and Internal Security', n.d. (c. Sept./Oct. 1957), fo. 1.

13. Ibid.

14. CO 822/1818, 'Proceedings', 7-8 Oct. 1957, p. 48, para. 210.

15. CO 822/1813, EAC (57) 6 (Final), fo. 1.

16. CO 822/1818, 'Proceedings', 7-8 Oct. 1957, p. 48, para. 211. Baring referred to the possibility that Italian Somalia might fall under Soviet influence, as had happened in the case of Syria. This view was derived from intelligence appreciations concerning Italy's desire to relinquish its Trusteeship. Independence for Italian Somaliland, leading to pressures for a 'Greater Somalia', would not only affect British Somaliland, but would also add to calls for secession by the Somali peoples in Kenya's Northern Frontier District. Such pressures, including violent action to varying degrees,

were also expected from within the British Somaliland Protectorate if Britain's position in the Arabian Peninsula were to deteriorate, CAB 158/31, JIC (58) 15 (Final) (Revise), 'Likely Developments in the Arabian Peninsula over the Next Five Years', report by the Joint Intelligence Committee, 11 Feb. 1958.

17. CO 822/1813, EAC (57) 6 (Final), fo. 2.

18. CO 822/1818, 'Proceedings', 7-8 Oct. 1957, p. 48, para. 212 (emphasis added).

19. Ibid., para. 227.

20. In the end, Sandys acceded to Lennox-Boyd's request that an announcement be made about a 'detachment' of 1 RF being sent to Kenya in addition to the Cameronians in April 1958, CO 968/694, telegram 147, Lennox-Boyd to Baring, repeated to Tanganyika (743), Uganda (P 80), and Sir Bruce Hutt (Administrator, East Africa High Commission) (309), 10 Dec. 1957; telegram 20397 (MO4), War Office to Force Nairobi, 11 Dec. 1957. The announcement was made jointly in London and Nairobi on 23 Dec. 1957, ibid., 34660 SD, Force Nairobi to War Office, 21 Dec. 1957; Press Office Handout No. 1181, 'British Troops in Kenya', 23 Dec. 1957.

21. CO 968/694, telegram 147, Lennox-Boyd to Baring, repeated to Tanganyika (743), Uganda (P 80), and Administrator, EAHC (309), 10 Dec. 1957. It remains uncertain as to why, precisely, this was the case. Speculating, it would seem to be simply a matter of not wishing to publicise troop movements in the area in order to deny any freely-available intelligence to agitators and those disposed towards violent unrest.

22. Ibid., letter MO4/309, Colonel J.A. Hunter (War Office) to Campbell, 3 Jan. 1958.

23. Ibid., telegram 21, Lennox-Boyd to the Officer Administering the Government (OAG) of Kenya, 10 Jan. 1958.

24. Ibid., telegram 34908, Force Nairobi to War Office, 13 Jan. 1958, telegram 89, Governor's Deputy to Secretary of State, 31 Jan. 1958, A.J. Fairclough (Colonial Office, Defence Department) to Hunter, 5 Feb. 1958.

25. CO 968/695, letter S 8398, Hartwell (Chief Secretary, Entebbe) to Brig. J.C.D'A. Dalton (Chief of Staff, HQ, EAC), 5 Oct. 1957.

26. Ibid., memo. by Hartwell, under cover of letter S 7032, 18 April 1957.

27. Ibid., 'Command and Administration of a Strategic Reserve Battalion in Kenya. Record of decisions taken at a Meeting held in the War Office (Main Building), Room 237 on Monday, 4 Nov. 1957'; memo. 0165/3888 (SD2b), by Brig. I.C. Harris (War Office, p.p. Maj.-Gen. [DSD - Permanent Under-Secretary of State]) to Tapp, 11 Dec. 1957.

28. Ibid., 'Minutes of a Meeting held in Room 220 Main Building on Friday, 24 Jan. 1958 to discuss the Command and Administration of a Strategic Reserve Battalion in Kenya', para. 3.

29. Ibid., para. 3, c).

30. Ibid., para. 20; Harris to Tapp, 11 Dec. 1957.

31. Ibid., 'Command and Administration of a Strategic Reserve Battalion in Kenya. Record of decisions taken at a Meeting held in the War Office (Main Building), Room 237 on Monday, 4 Nov. 1957'; memo. 0165/3888 (SD2b), by Harris, to Tapp, 11 Dec. 1957.

32. Ibid., 16/Abroad/4978 (F1), T.A.G. Charlton (War Office) to A. Campbell, 10 Feb., 1958.

33. Ibid., Campbell to Charlton, 13 March 1958.

34. 'ECS' amounted essentially to credit terms at cost price for stores plus a percentage to cover 'UK departmental expenses and freightage to Mombasa', hand-written notes in margin, unattributed, in ibid., 856/58, Baring to Lennox-Boyd, 12 April 1958. The procedure was introduced during the Second World War 'when colonial and other overseas forces were using identical equipment supplied along the same supply lines', ibid., secret savingram 33, Lennox-Boyd to Sir Bruce Hutt (Administrator, EAHC, and Permanent Secretary, EALFO), repeated to Kenya (1240), Tanganyika (886), and Uganda (803), 16 July 1958.

35. Ibid., Charlton to Campbell, 20 March 1958, Lennox-Boyd to OAG, Kenya (482), Crawford, Uganda (326), Twining, Tanganyika (337), Hutt, Administrator EAHC, Private Secretary, EALFO, 21 March 1958.

36. Ibid., 856/58, Baring to Lennox-Boyd, 12 April 1958. See also: ibid., 57405 SD, Tapp to J. Amery (Parliamentary Under-Secretary of State, War Office), 13 March 1958.

37. Ibid., Baring to Lennox-Boyd, 12 April 1958.

38. Ibid., N.B.J. Huijsman (Colonial Office, Defence Department) to H.W. Browne (War Office, F1), 7 May 1958.

39. Ibid., un-numbered secret telegram, EALFO (Hutt or Lisle?) to Lennox-Boyd, 28 June 1958.

40. Ibid., 36951/SD, Tapp to WO (MAGIC LAMP) [*sic*], 17 June 1958.

41. Ibid. (emphasis added). By July, the shortfall between the financial provisions made by the East African governments and Tapp's 'minimum requirements' had apparently more than doubled to £221,000, as the colonial authorities continued to press for the granting of estimates customer status. 'This will inevitably mean reappraisal of the whole scheme for [EALF] in spite of our views, shared by Uganda, that Tapp's requirements are minimum necessary for effective operation of [EALF]. I bring this matter to your attention at once as I have no doubt you would wish to consult Turnbull [Governor, Tanganyika] with the object of making pressing representations to the War Office that EALFO be granted [ECS] as envisaged by the S of S in paragraph 8 of his despatch No. 482. I understand Tanganyika Government would agree that such representations should be made', ibid.,

telegram 504, W.F. Coutts (Chief Secretary, Nairobi) to Baring (visiting S of S, London), 8 July 1958.

42. Ibid., 25820/Q (Ops)1, Troopers (WO) to Tapp, 1 July 1958.

43. Ibid., secret savingram 33, Lennox-Boyd to Hutt, repeated to Kenya (1240), Tanganyika (886), and Uganda (803), 16 July 1958.

44. Ibid., 57405 SD (copy), Tapp to Amery, 10 June 1958.

45. Ibid.

46. Ibid.

47. Ibid.

48. Ibid.

49. Ibid.

50. Ibid.

51. Ibid., 0165/3920 (SD2b), 'Report by War Office Working Party on the Future Method of Command and Administration of Imperial Forces in East Africa', by Maj. L.W.A. Gingell, Maj. P.R. Richards, Maj. S.P.H. Simonds, and D.J. Harwood, June 1958, fo. 2. (Underlining in original.)

52. Ibid., fo. 3.

53. Ibid., fos. 3-6.

54. Ibid., fos. 4-5, 7.

55. Ibid., fo. 7.

56. Ibid., Appendix 'A' to 0165/3920 (SD2b), 'Provision of an "Agency Service" for EALFO by the Imperial Organisation proposed for Kenya', n.d. (c. June 1958), fos. 1-3.

57. Ibid., secret loose minute to 0165/3920 (SD2b), 'Future Method of Command and Administration in East Africa', by Brig. I.C. Harris (War Office, DSD, 2), 19 June 1958.

58. Ibid., 'Agenda for DSD's Meeting on Future Organisation in KENYA, to be held in Room 218 Main Building on 11 August at 1430 hrs', n.d. (c. June/July 1958), fo. 1, para. 1.

59. Ibid., paras. 1-3, 'Proposed War Office Policy on the Future Organisation in Kenya', (draft), n.d. (c. June/July 1958), fos. 3-4, para. 16.

60. Ibid., 'Agenda', fo. 1, para. 3, 'Proposed War Office Policy', loc. cit.

61. Ibid., 'Agenda', fos. 1-2, paras. 3-6.

62. Ibid., 'Proposed War Office Policy', fo. 2, para. 9; DEFE 5/84, COS (58) 150, 'UK Policy in the Arabian Peninsula', memo. by the Chiefs of Staff, 9 June 1958.

63. CO 968/695, DEF 78/6/010 (copy), Lennox-Boyd to Baring, 31 July 1958.

64. Ibid., 'Minutes of a War office Meeting on Future Organisation in East Africa held in Room 218 Main Building on 12 August 1958', taken by Maj. L.W.A. Gingell (Secretary, War office, SD, 2), 12 Aug. 1958, fo.2, para. 5 (d). 'The Secretary of State for the Colonies has therefore informed the

three Governors that they should re-examine the structure of EALFO with a view to making it work more efficiently, and that until it had been proved that EALFO could not be made to work he would not attempt to reverse HMG policy.'

65. Ibid., fo. 1, para. 3.

66. Ibid.

67. Ibid., fo. 2, para. 5.

68. Ibid.

69. Ibid., para. 6.

70. Ibid., paras. 7-8.

71. Ibid., fos. 2-3, para. 9.

72. Ibid., fo. 4, paras. 19-20.

73. Ibid., telegram 98, Macpherson (Colonial Office), to Baring, repeated to Turnbull, Tanganyika (394), and Hartwell, Uganda (38), 14 Aug. 1958; telegram 567, Baring, (478) Turnbull, (27) Uganda, to Lennox-Boyd, n.d. (c. Aug. 1958); Harris, p.p. Maj.-Gen. DSD, to Tapp, 22 Aug. 1958; DEF 127/74/05, telegram 1561, Lennox-Boyd to Baring, repeated to Tanganyika (1128),.Uganda (1022), Permanent Secretary, EALFO (47), Administrator, EAHC (600), 5 Sept. 1958.

74. Ibid., telegram 33, Hartwell (Uganda) to C.Y. Carstairs (Colonial Office), 6 Sept. 1958; telegram 45, Carstairs to Hartwell, 9 Sept. 1958; telegram 530, Turnbull (Tanganyika) to Carstairs, 9 Sept. 1958; telegram 607, Cusack (Deputy Governor, Kenya) to Carstairs, 12 Sept. 1958; Maj.-Gen. DSD to Tapp, 10 Sept. 1958; restricted, un-numbered telegram, Troopers (War Office) to Tapp, 11 Sept. 1958; Carstairs to Hartwell, 22 Sept. 1958; savingram 872 (S 8390), Acting Governor, Uganda [Hartwell], to Lennox-Boyd, 23 Sept. 1958; telegram 556, Deputy Governor, Tanganyika [A.J. Grattan-Bellew?], to Lennox-Boyd, 25 Sept. 1958; letter S.8398, Hartwell to Carstairs, 26 Sept. 1958; telegram 633, OAG Kenya to Lennox-Boyd, 26 Sept. 1958.

75. Ibid., telegram 633, OAG Kenya to Lennox-Boyd, 26 Sept. 1958; DEF 127/74/05, telegram 1561, Lennox-Boyd to Baring, repeated to Tanganyika (1128),.Uganda (1022), Permanent Secretary, EALFO (47), Administrator, EAHC (600), 5 Sept. 1958.

76. Ibid., teleprint, Reuter (Nairobi), 27 Sept. 1958.

77. Ibid.

78. *The Times*, 6 Oct. 1958.

79. CO 968/695, 57405 SD, 'Report by a Working Party convened by the Chief of Staff to consider organisational changes in East Africa Command', 19 Sept. 1958, Tapp to the Under-Secretary of State (SD 2), War Office (J. Amery), 23 Sept. 1958.

80. Ibid., 0165/3920 (SD2b), 'Paper by DCIGS for consideration by ECAC: Future Organisation in East Africa' second draft, attached to loose minute by Brig. I.C. Harris, DDSD 'A', 22 Oct. 1958, para. 32 c) (i)-(iii), d), PS/S/30 V., savingram 27/58, J.T. Lisle (Permanent Secretary, EALFO) to J.A. Sankey (Principal, Colonial Office, Defence Department), 23 Oct. 1958, Lisle to Sankey, 24 Oct. 1958.

81. CO 968/696, 0165/3983 (SD2b), Maj.-Gen. G.S. Thomas, (Under-Secretary of State [DSD], War Office), to Amery, 11 Dec. 1958, savingram, Lennox-Boyd to OAGs, Kenya (2078), Tanganyika (1566), Uganda (1478), Lisle (Permanent Secretary, EALFO) (61), 16 Dec. 1958.

82. CO 968/695, Lisle to Sankey, 31 Oct. 1958, PS/S/30 V, DEF 127/74/05, Sankey to Lisle, 5 Nov. 1958.

83. CO 968/696, PS/S/30 VI/26, Lisle to Sankey, 29 Nov. 1958.

84. Ibid.

85. Ibid., minute by Maj.-Gen. G.S. Thomas, 4 Nov. 1958, ECAC/P (58) [0165/3920 (SD2b)], 'The Executive Committee of the Army Council: Future Organisation in East Africa', paper by DCIGS, Dec. 1958, 0165/3983 (SD2b), Brig. I.C. Harris, p.p. DSD (Thomas), to Amery, 23 Dec. 1958.

86. Ibid., 0165/3983 (SD2b), draft letter, War Office to GOC, East Africa, n.d. (c. Jan. 1959), J.R. McGregor (War Office) to Tapp, 20 Feb. 1959.

87. Ibid., savingram 119/59 [DEF 54/2AA-IV], Acting Governor, Kenya, on behalf of OAG, Uganda, and OAG, Tanganyika, 19 Jan. 1959.

88. Ibid., 39905/SD, Brig. P.W.P. Green, p.p. Tapp, to H. Fraser, (Under-Secretary of State [SD3], War Office), 13 Jan. 1959, Gingell to Sankey, 21 Jan. 1959, PS/S/30 VII/13, Lisle to Browne, 26 Feb. 1959, PS/S/30 VII/14, Lisle to Sankey, 26 Feb. 1959.

CHAPTER FIVE

Internal Security and Decolonisation, 1956-9

Introduction

It is virtually a commonplace that the financial and material strains of the Second World War, more than any other factor, made it inevitable that the British Empire's days were numbered.[1] The steady, if gradual, transition of several countries to independence after 1945 supports this interpretation.[2] With Ghana's independence in 1957 it was only a matter of time before the rest of Africa followed suit, subject to the requisite constitutional and administrative, and 'collaborative' arrangements being put in place.[3] Successor governments were 'encouraged' to remain within the western or 'free world' orbit, non-aligned at worst, and to retain trading links with their former suzerains, serving the same purpose.[4] It has been suggested that 'constitutional and administrative' development were 'the two major areas of policy' in this regard.[5] Of course, this can hardly be disputed given that administrative and constitutional development represent the legal and practical instruments which underpin and succeed any ceremonial transfer of power. The substantive aspects of political decolonisation in Kenya, particularly the constitutional and administrative, have therefore received considerable scholarly attention.[6]

But decolonisation did not amount simply to an administrative exercise. Important as administrative and constitutional arrangements were, transferring power to local nationalist politicians was not just a matter of finding the 'right man' (or men) for the job; the conditions had to be right too. More recently, the arguably subordinate area of policy, internal security, particularly the 'ubiquitous presence' of the colonial police, has received more attention than had hitherto been the case.[7] For example, David Throup examines the 'role and functions' of the various police departments in Kenya in the context of the problems of wartime expansion to combat rising crime, post-war 'political policing' and, of course, decolonisation.[8] As with other works on colonial policing, Throup's essay is also concerned with the problems of adaptation to these new circumstances, particularly the pressures of nationalism and accelerated decolonisation.

While all such studies are invaluable in increasing our knowledge and understanding of the intricacies of colonial rule and disengagement from Kenya they tend, understandably, to concentrate on the 'events' of crime, rural and urban unrest, and nationalist protest, especially in the late colonial period, in the context of negotiated constitutional development. Yet, this focus on the relative success of the Kenya Police in maintaining internal security between the apparent military defeat of Mau Mau and independence obscures the real significance to Britain of internal security issues in Kenya during the transfer of power.

This is not to say that internal security policy is ignored by these studies; the opposite is, of course, the case. As Anderson and Killingray make clear, the rapid progress towards independence in Africa in the late 1950s and early 1960s put many strains upon the colonial police in general.[9] However, the maintenance of internal security in Kenya was not solely the concern of the police, and the situation in Kenya was not always as peaceful as the authorities portrayed it to be.

It is well known that the British Army became actively involved in counter-insurgency operations and in support of the police and the KAR during the Mau Mau Emergency.[10] Indeed, all studies of British counter-insurgency necessarily examine the British Army's experience in Kenya, stressing the 'duties in aid of the civil power' aspects of this, and the determination to hand back responsibility for law and order to the police and civil administration. However, particular emphasis is still laid on the role of political reform, especially decolonisation, in British counter-insurgency.[11] Although this approach is persuasive, it tends to over-simplify and, in some respects, to over-estimate the *process* of decolonisation.

This over-emphasis on Colonial Office planning and the readiness to grant political concessions in order to combat insurgency, has been mirrored by certain works which suggest that the declaration of the State of Emergency in Kenya in itself, as in other colonies, represented plans for a 'managed' withdrawal.[12] This approach ignores the reluctance of the Colonial Office to agree to Baring's initial request to declare an emergency, let alone to commit British troops. Equally, the three year gap between the military defeat of Mau Mau and Britain's acceptance that African majority government would have to be conceded sooner, rather than later, sheds doubt upon such interpretations.[13]

In a recent study, Murphy has argued that: 'The most orthodox and self-serving of myths surrounding the decolonisation of the British Empire was that this was the natural culmination of a political mission to prepare colonial peoples for democratic self-government'.[14] More recently, he has suggested 'that if one wants to discover why the pace of constitutional reform in Africa accelerated so dramatically after 1959, one needs to look to Africa and not to Whitehall'.[15] Of course, it was not simply events in Africa which dictated

Colonial Office policy there.[16]

Yet, the idea that after the Second World War Kenya's independence was a foregone conclusion, especially given the implementation of political reforms after the apparent defeat of Mau Mau, has been so persuasive that studies of post-war British overseas defence policy have paid scant regard to Kenya's significance.[17] The albeit essentially correct view that Kenya was largely an adjunct to the Middle East and Far East theatres in British 'global strategy' has gone hand-in-hand with those illustrated above.[18]

Effectively, this can be summarised as follows: counter-insurgency and political (and socio-economic) reform in Kenya were synonymous; therefore Britain could only ever expect, and indeed did expect, limited security of tenure; and the withdrawal of British Land Forces Kenya (BLFK) to Aden following Kenya's independence was the logical culmination of a seemingly holistic process. As this and the next chapter will show, by the time of Macmillan's 'wind of change' speech and the January Lancaster House conference, and even as late as the 'Independence Conference' of September-October 1963, British withdrawal from Kenya was by no means a formality.[19]

It is not intended here to examine the details of the political bargaining, constitutional reform, and the devolution of political power, which have been covered by the studies referred to earlier, among others.[20] If anything, detailed examination of internal security policy and planning sheds new light on the background to the transfer of power in Kenya, the significance of security issues to this *process* and, given this significance, the very real sense in which it could be said that independence on 12 December 1963 was far from inevitable, that is, until literally months beforehand. It should also be stressed, as Kyle has shown, that the British government's October 1963 decision to back the Kenya African National Union (KANU) administration as the means by which a civil war in Kenya would be most likely avoided did not allay British fears of that eventuality.[21]

This last point is demonstrated clearly by the British government's willingness to intervene militarily in Kenya to evacuate the European settlers at the last minute if a political settlement were not reached and if the security situation had in fact deteriorated. The survey of the internal security aspects of the seven years between the defeat of Mau Mau and independence, in this chapter and the next, demonstrates the precariousness of Britain's position, as the colonial power sought to balance the 'shaping' of Kenyan politics with offsetting pressure from African nationalists for a 'quick withdrawal', while attempting to secure 'vital' economic and strategic interests.[22]

As the next section will show, British concerns for internal security in Kenya in the context of limited resources following the apparent military defeat of Mau Mau cast doubt over the commonly held interpretation of events during the latter half of the State of Emergency. Far from having the luxury of simply introducing incremental constitutional reform, the British authorities faced the prospect of renewed challenges to their rule on a par with Mau Mau, while they struggled to construct a political settlement in Kenya, and made desperate attempts to portray a situation of 'normality'.

'The Consolidation of Reaction', 1956-9

The three years between the defeat of Mau Mau and ending the State of Emergency were very much a period of political and socio-economic tutelage. The British authorities certainly hoped that this would be seen to be the case. For the British, a crucial aspect of the consolidation of victory was the legitimisation, thus stabilisation, afforded by the normalisation of politics in the territory. Yet, defence and security matters had a considerable bearing on British policy, and go far in explaining the retention of the 'technical' State of Emergency until 1960.

In this respect the political reforms of 1957-1958 can be seen not so much as means of 'guiding' the nature and pace of developments in the name of some higher and noble cause, such as 'nation-building', but rather as a significant weapon in Britain's policy armoury. Only by keeping a firm grip on the political process, and by maintaining internal security, could Britain hope to sustain 'vital' economic and strategic interests in Kenya, while at the same time being seen to make concessions to the increasingly radical 'African' political consciousness which had gained impetus from Ghana's independence in 1957.

Prior to the resumption of responsibility for the maintenance of law and order by the police in November 1956, the security situation, future prospects, and future policy had to be decided. At a meeting of the War Council in December 1955, Lathbury concluded that 'as the number of terrorists at large was now so few, routine patrols and large-scale operations became less rewarding. If all security forces were maintained at their present strength it might be that the Emergency would be finished a little earlier but a balance had to be drawn between the effort and the result.'[23] Lathbury also had to bear in mind the ongoing reduction in the numbers of British Army personnel.[24] 'Pseudo-gang' operations would therefore be the best way to eliminate the remaining 'terrorists', clearing the way for a further reduction by two battalions of the British Army by May of the following year. This would leave just one British battalion, 1 KSLI, alongside the KAR in support of the police.

Besides these and other manpower and tactical considerations, there were other matters of security policy discussed which, while not of immediate concern, were significant in respect of the future post-military phase and ultimate end of the State of Emergency. A matter of considerable importance was the fate and release rate of Mau Mau detainees.[25] On this point Baring 'drew attention to the statement that the release of detainees was unlikely to present a serious security problem if the release was governed by the ability to provide land or work'. To this he added that the 'release rate was inevitably governed by the ability to absorb those released'. Although detention and rehabilitation policy is not the concern of this study, given that detainees, by definition, cease to be a direct security threat, Baring's implicit awareness of the potential for problems later on is in itself significant.

This is especially so in the light of the necessarily limited success of land consolidation, and its impact on post-Emergency Kikuyu militancy and politics.[26] Again, the concern here is not with reforms, as such, but with Britain's approach to planning for a breakdown in internal (or public) security, the ultimate expression of a perceived failure of reform. Also, by assessing the severity and extent of Emergency planning in its latter stages, it is possible to gauge the seriousness with which ministers and officials in London and Nairobi took threats to security vis-à-vis their perceptions of the success of reform. In short, how close, and how frequently, did the British and Kenya governments believe they had come during the seven or eight years since control was militarily re-imposed in Kenya, to again losing that control, and what were they prepared to do about it? This, more than anything, it could be argued, is the true measure of the success of socio-economic and political reform in the run up to Kenya's independence.

The security situation in December 1955 gave Kenya's then Commissioner of Police, Richard Catling, sufficient reason to hope to reduce the African KPR 'element by about a sixth and also to disband some of the GSU Platoons during the second half of 1956' in line with the withdrawal of the British Army. However, the seemingly improving situation did not give the War Council reason to throw caution to the wind. While Farm Guards were still considered essential for food denial, requiring them to be kept at full Emergency strength, along with the Regular Tribal Police and Tribal Police Reserve (TP[R]), it was considered inadvisable to keep large numbers of Kikuyu 'under arms' if the army was to be run down.

Although Kenya's then Minister for Internal Security and Defence, J.W. Cusack, had suggested that the plan for a reduction of tribal police elements should 'be amended to draw attention to the need to relate reductions in the [TP(R)] to the run-down of the Army', the consequent requirement to maintain the strength of the 'civil arm' in readiness for the likely future releases of detainees, prompted another solution. The Tribal Police would be disarmed, as they had been before the Emergency. Replacing the rifle with the baton at the end of 1956, therefore, did not just represent an improvement in the security situation: it was a means of ensuring that security risks were minimised.[27] So, by reducing the potential threat of armed Kikuyu, the War Council was also able to make provision for the 'policing' of released detainees.[28] Baring had already decided that one British battalion would have to stay in Kenya 'at least until the end of the Emergency situation'. As a further precaution, the War Council decided that 'as a means of maintaining a nucleus of the police force trained in forest operations, both the Army and Police [GSUs] should continue to operate in the Prohibited Areas until the end of the Emergency'.[29]

Lennox-Boyd was far from confident about all of this. He expressed his fears to Crawford, then Baring's deputy: 'I feel some misgivings about the effect so steep an overall reduction of forces might have on control of the reserves in the future especially after December'. The Secretary of State was also greatly concerned that the strength of the TP(R) would be too *great* without sufficient 'military control'. With the prospect of 'some 40,000' detainees remaining at the end of 1956, Lennox-Boyd's most pressing concern was whether there would be 'sufficient forces left to deal with any situation which may arise in the reserves from [the] release of detainees during 1957?'[30]

Lennox-Boyd's fears had been prompted by his realisation that the improving situation would bring 'pressure from various quarters for the speed up [*sic*] of the release rate, without regard to the degree of rehabilitation and the capacity of the reserves to absorb released detainees'. Crawford's reply was unequivocal:

> I note with some misgivings your reference to pressures from various quarters to speed up release and should like to reaffirm that the Council of Ministers and the War Council are firmly of the opinion that the rate of release can only be determined by security conditions, including rehabilitation and absorptive capacity of the country and that pressure on any other grounds must be firmly resisted from the outset.[31]

Crawford also dismissed fears that manpower levels would be insufficient, explaining that following a proposed review of the situation in June 1956, if it were found to be necessary, African military personnel could be increased. 'In addition, in emergency call can be made on four KAR in Uganda and six KAR in Tanganyika, a total of about 1,000 troops. Strength of [the] police in [the] emergency area in January 1957 ... will be the same as now [c. 8-9,000] except that the KPR may be reduced to 2,500'. Also significant in terms of potential manpower for the security forces was that at least one British Army battalion earmarked for Aden would stay in Kenya until 'about January 1957, go to Aden for the cool season, and probably return to Kenya in the spring of 1957'.

With the effective end of military operations in November 1956, and the expansion of the Kenya Police to over 12,000 personnel, it seems that despite the temporary absence of the KSLI in Arabia, standing manpower and provisions for emergency expansion would have given cause for optimism.[32] After all, economic and social reforms were well under way, as evidenced by the ongoing implementation of land consolidation under the Swynnerton Plan; and March 1957 would see the first elections of Africans to Kenya's Legislative Council. Life in Kenya was 'essentially back to normal', with the main interest of the press being politics. The Emergency received little attention and, if at all, then only on the back pages.[33] Indeed, as Throup shows, the police had to adapt to 'renewed African political activity', especially the growing number of mass meetings.[34] Yet, *normality* did not herald the immediate termination of the State of Emergency.

Ironically, the apparently successful conclusion of Britain's military campaign in Kenya had coincided with the forced withdrawal from Suez at the hands of US diplomatic and economic pressures. The subsequent imposition of the Middle East 'air barrier', leading to Britain's decision to locate a permanent British Army garrison in Kenya only added to the irony. More importantly, however, this latter decision (and its implementation) confirms that the political concessions made before Lennox-Boyd's April 1959 Commons statement served in many ways as a holding operation, aimed at legitimising politics according to a British model, and in doing so attempted to demonstrate that nationalists could achieve more by eschewing any recourse to violence. Crucially, the *delay* rather than acceleration in the transfer of power implicit in Britain's policy of 'gradualness' might well have bought more time were it not for the divisive aspects of socio-economic reforms and the upsurge of African political consciousness during the Emergency. With Ghana independent in 1957, it must have seemed peculiar, to say the least, for Kenyan Africans to still be living under a State of Emergency, especially as this had been no barrier to Malaya's independence that same year.

Prior to his October 1957 visit to East Africa, Lennox-Boyd had been aware that there was likely to be pressure to end the Emergency, 'or at least a reduction in Emergency measures'. Although it was 'the acknowledged policy to dispense with those as soon as possible' there were several security-related problems. 'The official and legal termination of the Emergency would mean the automatic withdrawal of all Emergency Regulations and the powers assumed under them. This would create both immediate and more distant difficulties'. The immediate difficulties included the mass release of 20,000 detainees and the cessation of 'psychological discipline' for some 50,000 who were already at liberty. Added to this was the problem of the 'irreconcilables' who were perceived, probably correctly, to be a considerable security risk and could not be released *en masse*.

The main problem was that if the Emergency were to be revoked the Kenya government intended to enact legislation enabling it to retain powers to detain 'trouble-makers without trial', to continue to hold the 'hard core', compelling them to work 'where necessary', and to 'forestall would-be subversive movements, including political movements, which they at present wield by Emergency Regulation'. The difficulty with this, according to the Colonial Office, was the British government's adherence to several international Conventions, particularly the European Convention on Human Rights and the International Labour Organisation (ILO) Forced Labour Convention (1930), with a second, 'more rigid' ILO Convention in the process of ratification. Accordingly, the introduction of such non-Emergency legislation as the Kenya government required would mean an open breach of 'these international obligations'.

It is clear that, given the problems associated with the reabsorption of detainees, the only course of action was to retain the legal Emergency. So, what of political restrictions? As a Colonial Office brief explained:

> Secondly, the disappearance of all Emergency checks on African political life could quickly lead to a deterioration in security, so that a further emergency would be created requiring special measures. [...] In the last resort we must be prepared to sustain existing practises [*sic*] deemed essential for the maintenance of peace in Kenya even if we stand frankly in default of international obligations. [...] The conclusion must be that for as long as possible the Emergency must be kept alive and that attempts for its revocation should be resisted.[35]

There are essentially two ways that all this could be interpreted. First, the detainees other than the 'irreconcilables', if released, did not represent a significant or direct threat to internal security and what mattered, as evidenced by the restriction on colony-wide political activity, was the likelihood of the former Mau Mau adherents' affiliation to radical, anti-colonial political movements. There is undoubtedly some truth in this, but a second possibility is more convincing. As Baring and Crawford noted in late 1955 and early 1956, detainees simply could not be released to an uncertain future which might only serve to breed further disaffection and militancy; certainly not 20,000 in one go, and certainly not the unrehabilitated or 'irreconcilable'. Releasing the detainees and simultaneously lifting restrictions on political activity, given the potential for a return to violence, along with the capacity to organise on a colony-wide basis, it seems, was just too much of a risk to take.

Of course, *control* was what mattered, but not simply control of the political process. While there can be no doubt that Baring and Lennox-Boyd were disturbed by the prospect of political 'deadlock' in the Legislative Council, and efforts by Mboya and Odinga to co-ordinate political action with Ugandan and Tanganyikan nationalists, it is clear that the granting of parity to the African Elected Members (AEMs) was not intended to lead to the 'destruction of the multi-racial idea, the road along which Africans would advance to an ultimate overall majority on communal polls'.[36]

It seems that the Lennox-Boyd Constitution represented as much an attempt at offsetting pressures for an end to the Emergency, as it did a concession to the Africans' refusal to participate in the legislature.[37] This almost classic example of a 'half-measure' in itself, then, was motivated by broader security considerations than simply 'meeting the demand for constitutional advance fast enough to keep the peace and retain a guiding influence over developments'.[38] For all the apparent improvements in the security situation, it should not be forgotten that in late 1957 Kenya was still very much in the 'shadow' of Mau Mau.

If the retention of Emergency Regulations was simply a device for maintaining control of the political process, it would not be unreasonable to expect a fairly optimistic view of the security situation, especially in the run up to and immediately before the revocation of the State of Emergency. However, de-militarisation, if it can be called that, and political concessions in themselves brought new security risks. Although throughout 1957 Mboya had made statements to the effect that 'if African wishes for increased representation were not met, the results would be far worse than anything Mau Mau produced', this was not taken too seriously. In itself, the threat of civil disobedience might not have caused too much concern but, combined with political consciousness at the grass roots level based largely on ethnic origin, a resurgence in urban crime, and the persistence of Kikuyu subversion in one form or another, highlighted many of the security problems faced by the Kenya government.

As Baring explained to Lennox-Boyd in early 1957:

> What is more significant is that Kodhek and some of his supporters are beginning to talk openly about starting a form of passive resistance. They mention plans for organised bands of Africans deliberately to break some of the less important or more unpopular laws. They foolishly go on, though not in public, to speak of organised attempts to intimidate watchmen and arrange crimes from which Europeans and Asians will suffer. [...] While this news has come in from Nairobi, in the overcrowded area of the southern locations of North Nyanza there are signs of the possibility of the same sort of trouble.[39]

This, along with the 'recrudescence' in Nairobi 'of the type crime of which there was far too much before the Emergency', related to African unemployment and housing shortages, was a matter for the police. Yet, while 'these straws in the wind in Nairobi and in Nyanza' were not considered to be a 'very big affair', they served as 'an indication of the sort of trouble which we can expect in the future if things go wrong'.

It is noteworthy that by February 1958, a month before the elections under the Lennox-Boyd Constitution, Kenya's ISWC had prepared a draft of a revised Colony Internal Security Scheme. Based upon 'the experience gained in the last [five-and-a-half] years, and in the light of the Kenya Intelligence Committee's (KIC) most recent appreciation', the scheme recognised that: 'In any future Emergency, trouble is likely to take the form of strikes, civil disobedience, sabotage, and the dislocation of transport and supplies rather than armed insurrection.'[40]

The Kenya government had already set up an Economic Priorities Committee, headed by the leading white settler politician, Sir Michael Blundell, then European Minister without Portfolio, 'to study supply problems in such an eventuality' in April 1957, a month after the first African elections to the Legislative Council.[41] This would continue in being under the auspices of the revised internal security scheme. The principal aim of the scheme, as one might expect, was: 'In the event of unrest to prevent the breakdown of law and order, to maintain services essential to the community, and where necessary, to safeguard life and property.'[42]

This was quite natural, of course, but betrays a sense that despite the 'normal situation', officials in Kenya feared that everyday law enforcement might not be sufficient. Of greatest concern to the ISWC was that while sufficient 'resources', or 'Colony reserves' (i.e. personnel) were available to deal with perceived threats to internal security as they stood: 'If a serious threat were to materialise in the Northern Province, necessitating the use of two battalions of troops ... the combined military and police forces available might not be adequate to meet simultaneously internal security situations without the addition of further [GSU] platoons.'[43]

There was also the problem of civilian manpower to maintain essential services. It is again noteworthy that while the Tribal Police were placed at the disposal of the Provincial and District Security Committees, and were not, therefore, available for colony-wide provisions, as such, additional reserves were comparatively meagre. Apart from only 2,600 convicts from a colony total of over 16,000 (not including Mau Mau detainees), the rest being available to the Provinces, the ISWC could only rely on 'a register of some 13,000 male Europeans liable to call-up under the Compulsory National Service Ordinance'.

Yet, ironically, the very effort to make contingencies for a breakdown in the security situation, albeit at the economic level, had its attendant risks. Expansion of the numbers of GSU platoons as a colony reserve, and of the police that might be required for the Nairobi area could not be undertaken without 'equivalent economies'. While it was decided that Asians and Africans should be registered as volunteers, the latter, it was thought, 'would be particularly susceptible to intimidation'. The greatest difficulty with the registration of *any* volunteers, it seems, was that the preparation of nominal rolls of European volunteers in particular 'would cause alarm and despondency, exacerbate African feeling and serve little purpose since the lists would soon be out of date'.[44] However, despite the potential pitfalls, the War Council agreed, within weeks of the forthcoming African elections, that 'it was particularly important to be prepared during the next few months'. Publicity was to be kept to a minimum.

This contradictory approach, minimising publicity so as not to 'scaremonger', yet wishing to be seen to be making adequate preparations for all eventualities, was a constant feature of internal security planning, as were re-appraisals to take account of possible renewed threats to security. By December 1958, it appeared 'from recent utterances of certain African politicians' that a 'plan of "positive action"' focused on Nairobi, Mombasa, and Nakuru was imminent:

> The Director of Intelligence and Security [DIS] in his brief to the Security Council in September anticipated that this campaign might develop in early 1959. He was of the opinion that the campaign would take the form of boycotts, spasmodic industrial strikes, and general civil disobedience. [...] In these circumstances it can be anticipated that racial relations will deteriorate with a consequential increase in anti-European and anti-Asian incidents. It may even be that in an atmosphere of racial disharmony, the economic affect [*sic*] on strikers may well lead to an increase in attacks on non-African property. At worst a planned campaign against unprotected and easy targets such as old folk and isolated women might develop.[45]

The short-term solution to this potential problem was to reconstitute the *Asian* and *European* Home Guard system that had operated during the anti-Mau Mau campaign. Significantly, these Home Guards would not be issued with firearms, and every effort would be made to ensure that the 'jittery' Asians and Europeans were led to believe that the government was 'quietly taking action to meet the eventuality of "positive action" being accompanied by sporadic violence'. To help perpetuate this semi-fiction, which was intended to restore confidence, even government officials were instructed that the measure was precautionary 'but in no way foreshadows serious trouble'.

Both of these aspects of internal security contingency planning were, of course, consistent with the aim of maintaining Kenya's economic viability, by dealing with both direct threats and the related issues of domestic and international confidence. However, even the requirement that the 'Regular Police' contact the ex-leaders of the Asian and European Home Guards to get plans underway met with difficulties. In discussion, Catling explained that 'the hands of the Police were already full, and they should not be expected to undertake the responsibilities which it was suggested in the memorandum should be required of them; they were very short of European Police Officers'.[46]

Manpower shortages were a perennial problem for the Europeans concerned with Kenya's internal security management.[47] This was reflected particularly in the arrangements for the protection of Colony Vulnerable Points that included, for example, water supplies, airports, oil installations, hospitals, and 'certain factories'.[48] In some cases steps were taken 'to enlist employees in essential services as Special Constables; in the event of an emergency they would assist in the protection of their own installations while performing their normal, essential duties'. It was fortunate, perhaps, that: 'Members of the staffs of many essential installations were already in the KPR.'

Yet, even then manpower was still thin on the ground: 'It would be impossible to provide guards for all the Vulnerable Points, and Provincial Security Committees would have to decide, if and when the need arose, how they could best dispose the forces available to them.'[49] The view of at least one Colonial Office official on this matter is telling:

> I hope it will be possible to "leak" the manpower preparations to the general public. The next few months will be crucial and weakness never has paid off; public knowledge that the Gov[ernmen]t are rigid in their determination to act quickly and vigorously against any threat would allay disquiet felt by Europeans both here and in Kenya and make even the most extremist of the African "black nationalists" think twice before agreeing to a full-scale campaign of disobedience and non-co-operation. [...] Mr Rolfe would no doubt like to see these papers in case Tanganyika are preparing a similar scheme, or in case they are not (!)[50]

Security considerations after the apparent military defeat of Mau Mau were not just confined to politics and the economic survival of the colony. For example, an outbreak of Mau Mau oathing in Meru in late 1957, although relatively small and quickly dealt with, raised concerns because it had taken three or four months before the government had become aware of it.[51] This apparent failure to anticipate trouble was all too familiar, and no less disturbing. By contrast, potential unrest in Nyanza Province in early 1957 had been detected early on as a result of 'increased and extended' coverage by Special Branch, no doubt because of the prominence of Luo politicians in the run up and subsequent to the election.[52] However, because the successful candidates had apparently been elected because of tribal affiliation 'rather than their political opinions', the assessment of future security prospects was not overly sanguine. In reviewing the security situation in Nyanza, the War Council reported:

> There is no doubt that these newly Elected Members are well aware of this fact and they will be compelled to give considerable attention to local tribal

> interests, *despite their desire to promote African unity in order to further their nationalist policies.* [...] Their activities may further unsettle those sections of the population, particularly in Central and North Nyanza, which are already disturbed by their increasing economic difficulties.[53]

A particular economic difficulty was presented by the greater availability of Kikuyu labour, whether former detainees or those displaced by mechanisation or a failure to obtain or retain land under the land consolidation schemes.[54] This corresponded with the need in Kiambu District, for example, to 'de-villagise' in order that land consolidation could proceed uninterrupted. It seemed inevitable that the African politicians would exploit many Africans' 'justifiable fears' for their economic security, and that the African intelligentsia, especially those who looked to 'the ultimate establishment of an African state in Kenya', would become increasingly concerned with politics: 'In view of these inevitable political trends the establishment of a Central Convention of District Political Associations should be delayed, at least until the present predominance of Nyanza tribesmen amongst the African Elected Members has been countered by the return of the Kikuyu into political life'.[55] What at first appears to a be concern to avoid ethnic tensions rather than to manipulate them, seems more likely to represent the cynical, if pragmatic, approach of the old policy of 'divide and rule'! Certainly, the prevalence of African 'tribalism' in Kenyan politics only highlighted the failure of the Emergency policy of restricting African political participation to the local level, a policy which inevitably proved to be counter-productive given British hopes for implementing a 'multi-racial' state. Moreover, the prominent Luo politicians, particularly Mboya, were proving to be far too successful in furthering the *African* nationalist cause.

Indeed, even piecemeal political concessions, in an atmosphere of aggravated socio-economic hardship, created more problems, at least potentially, than they solved. At the grass roots level the best that the administration could hope for was to remove or alleviate the causes of African grievances: 'It is clearly important on security grounds, that there should be increased agricultural production and that the fertility of the soil should be maintained and improved.' In Central Province 'Welfare Centres' were considered to be a useful option, if for more cynical purposes: 'In my view, it is important to provide some form of recreation and mental stimulus for the African employee during his leisure hours, lest his activities turn to less desirable channels.'[56]

While thought unlikely, a major concern remained that the various reforms and mechanisms of supervision and control could still fail. Aware of the potential for widespread African disaffection as the Kenya government was, frequent reminders of Mau Mau proved to be more than a little unnerving.

Again, this was not so much because the administration felt unable to deal with security risks, but because the extent and potential of such risks, as ever, had often been under-estimated. The emergence of *Kiama Kia Muingi* (Council/Society of the People), or KKM, was a case-in-point.

At one level, it was the popular perception of KKM that gave cause for concern.[57] In explaining that the movement was spreading, and that there had been an increase in violent crime, including the murder of a European farmer, Baring wrote to Lennox-Boyd in April 1958, and explained that: 'The security position gives cause for some anxiety, but not for the fears expressed by some people in this country.'[58] The expansion of KKM 'particularly on farms of Europeans who are not good employers' did, however, give enough cause for anxiety that a week earlier Baring had concluded that

> this is yet another proof that as long as detainees and convicts are being released into the country, and as long as they are being absorbed into employment, we cannot afford to abandon Emergency powers. A still more important conclusion is the strength of the habit of playing with secret societies in the Kikuyu mind. I hope you will agree that this is a very strong argument in favour of having on our permanent Statute Book certain important powers to replace those which we will abandon when the Emergency comes to an end.[59]

Lennox-Boyd's reply to Baring is instructive:

> In many ways your task must present itself as a race to get these people safely back into permanent work before they are got at by KKM, and so either turned into missionaries in their eventual homes or inhibited from being resettled at all. [...] I have never felt that we could revert entirely to the legal position as it was before the Emergency and shall feel very sympathetic to any proposals you put forward to strengthen your anti-subversive powers, although as you know some of the suggestions which are now being examined present peculiar difficulties [see pp. 152-6].[60]

Yet, the apparent emergence of KKM from the so-called Mau Mau 'passive wing' in Embu and Nairobi and the adjoining reserve had been discovered in March 1955, and as a measure of how seriously it was at first taken, the movement was not proscribed until January 1958.[61] The Kenya government's reaction to KKM was not, therefore, as swift as has been suggested.[62] This seemingly belated response was again a function of changing intelligence appreciations and, more importantly, an apparent desire not to be too 'heavy handed'. This, in itself, was a security expedient, aimed at avoiding unnecessary antagonisation of Africans and the consequent potential for political disaffection and its attendant difficulties. Consideration of Britain's response to KKM, and the timing of that response, is crucial to understanding how the authorities perceived the balance between political progress and the likelihood of a repeat of Mau Mau.

By being seen to be helping to secure the surrender of the remaining guerrillas, KKM hoped that all Emergency restrictions on the Kikuyu would thereby be lifted. However, as the Secretary to the War Council (and later author of the now infamous report into the origins and growth of Mau Mau), Frank Corfield, explained to the Colonial Office, 'the real but undeclared aims of the body were to unify the Kikuyu-speaking peoples as a first step and then to strive for the acquisition of more land, the eviction of Europeans and, ultimately, self-government as a second'. Despite this early realisation that KKM's aims were synonymous with those of Mau Mau, its apparently 'passive' nature, lack of central direction, and limited geographical extent precluded proscription. Regardless of Colonial Office protestations, it seems that the Kenya government considered that, so long as KKM did not resort to subversive activities, it could be regarded as a quasi-legitimate expression of those Kikuyu aims which had been shown to be unobtainable by violence.[63] Besides, proscription would have merely given the organisation 'undesirable publicity'.[64]

Although by January 1958 KKM had apparently committed no violent acts, its similarity to Mau Mau in terms of being a secret society, bound by an oath, and the discovery that the movement was in fact better organised than had previously been thought, were sufficient legal grounds for its sudden proscription.[65] Indeed, there was a firm belief that KKM too closely followed 'the same pattern as did Mau Mau in the period leading up to [the] outbreak of violence which brought on [the] Emergency'. With the forthcoming elections under the Lennox-Boyd Constitution, and the imminent arrival of BLFK, the erstwhile secret compilation by KKM of lists of Kikuyu 'loyalists' and their families may not simply have raised concern for their safety.[66] The Kenya government was not only concerned that KKM sought to 'undermine the authority of African administration in [the] Reserves'. As Kenya's then Chief Secretary, Richard Turnbull, explained to Lennox-Boyd:

> Activities of this Society must be particularly dangerous at the present time when [the] most difficult type of rehabilitated detainee is being returned to [the] Reserves in increasing numbers and it is essential [that] conditions should be stable. Existence of [an] organisation deliberately seeking to undermine established authority would present [a] serious threat to [the] rehabilitation and re-absorption programmes.[67]

With the March 1958 elections on the way, the Colonial Office was anxious that KKM should not be seen as another Mau Mau. Political solutions to

Kenya's difficulties should be seen to be working, especially by observers in Britain: 'Suggest that, if further public references cannot be avoided, it would restore perspective to refer to [the] ease with which embryo [*sic*] secret societies of this nature are now uncovered because of African co-operation and [the] desire to prevent their growth.'[68] Equally, if not more important, so long as African nationalists adhered to the Colonial Office formula for constitutional advance, Britain could, or hoped at least, to proceed with strategic plans for the area. Britain had hoped, therefore, that the veneer provided by the Lennox-Boyd Constitution would not only demonstrate a willingness to make reasonable concessions to nationalist demands, but in doing so would provide an incentive for the African politicians to adhere to the spirit, and the delay implied by the Colonial Office policy of 'gradualness'.

This may well have prompted Baring to be a little economical with the truth in his April 1958 assessment. What is certain, is that for the remainder of 1958, as arrests of KKM oath administrators and 'manager types' proceeded apace, more information gathered about the organisation gave increasing cause for concern. Not only did the KKM oath 'include a pledge to kill loyal Africans and Europeans', with 'plans to resort to violence at some future date if it did not achieve its aims by non-violent means'. There was also evidence of KKM taking on 'military ranks' and, more ominous, the movement was much more widespread than previously thought, with 'probably 20,000' members in Kandara Division of Fort Hall District alone.[69]

Also integral to KKM plans was the year 1960 when, it was believed, Kenyatta would be released, and European supremacy in Kenya would naturally come to, or rather be fairly rapidly brought to, an end. In Kihara Division, KKM had another name: '*Kiama Kia* 1960'.[70] The Kenya government was already aware that proscription of KKM in itself would not prevent its re-emergence under other names, and 'will deepen and perpetuate the rift between the loyalists and the rest of the [Kikuyu] tribe. The society will continue to exist more secretly than before.'[71] As the ringleaders and oath administrators were being arrested, the tried-and-tested techniques of 'Closer Administration' were applied: curfews (sometimes 23 hours), restrictions on movement, the closure of markets, and good old confessional barazas.

KKM apparently received 'stimulus' from 'the intemperate utterances of African politicians'. While 'Mboya and his associates in the production of the [newspaper] "Uhuru"' received warnings, the fear was that pressure on KKM might not be maintained indefinitely 'owing to the present difficulty in obtaining suitable Special Branch staff'.[72] The British Army kept a close eye on the situation: 'From the evidence available it would appear that Mau Mau has never been eliminated. There is no requirement for troops at the present stage but should the growth of the society out-run the efforts of the Security Forces, military assistance might be required in about three months time.'[73]

Fortunately for the Kenya government, a re-run of the early phase of the anti-Mau Mau campaign was avoided. (Although it could be suggested that levels of political and socio-economic development were by this time sufficient to offset the 'negative' aspects of the police counter-subversion campaign.) By September 1958, it appeared that curfews and barazas had brought an end to the KKM 'crisis', with 217 committees 'known to have been destroyed since April 1958', compared with only two attempts 'known to have been made to reform [*sic*] a committee'.[74] Any expansion had at least, apparently, been put in check.[75] The head of Special Branch, Ian Henderson's assessment was that while

> KKM or a similar movement under another name, would inevitably continue to smoulder [...] with our present organisation we should catch such a movement before it became very strong or resorted to large-scale violence. On the other hand, like all people who know the Kikuyu well, and who have had active experience of the troubles of the last six years, he ended with the warning that we must be prepared for a series of surprises.[76]

Henderson's warning very quickly turned out to have been prescient. By December 1958, KKM had re-emerged in Fort Hall and Embu.[77] This in itself gave little cause for concern, but the discovery of contacts between the Limuru branch of Mboya's Nairobi Peoples' Convention Party (NPCP) and 'prominent KKM personalities' was another matter. While the apparent involvement of KKM in the open arena of political discourse might well have represented the successful combination of action against KKM subversion and political development, there were a number of reasons to be cautious: 'The new approach is not the same as the approach of the first half of 1958. Thus, there is hardly any mention of poisoning - the emphasis is on the Kenyatta Cult and on future action at an unspecified but comparatively distant date.'

This led, in particular, to the decision to slow down the release rate of KKM detainees. The last thing the administration wanted was for proven or potential militants to be given access to the coverage afforded by political organisations, nor did it want a blurring of the distinction between politics and violence. The KKM detainees who could be released, however, were that small number who had not only confessed, but in doing so had also implicated others. This limit on numbers, it was thought, would enable the police to 'scrutinise' the whole of Kiambu, Fort Hall, and Embu for KKM throughout 1959 without risking a resurgence of subversive activity. The release of KKM detainees would also depend upon the extent of subversion in their home areas.[78]

Security planning for 1959 was all well and good, but the failure of Britain's political strategy in Kenya brought future policy-making into sharp relief. Britain's plans for Kenya were not helped, either, by events elsewhere in East Africa and the Hola controversy. No sooner had Britain got its strategic plans for Kenya well underway, and the colony's future set within the acceptable limits of 'gradualness', than British ministers were forced to reassess their approach to maintaining a 'guiding influence' in the territory's political affairs. The next chapter will examine the increasingly sophisticated, if sometimes desperate, measures taken to ensure that Kenya, and Britain's 'vital interests', would remain stable and secure until, and beyond, independence.

Conclusion

Having achieved an end to the Mau Mau insurgency, Britain did its utmost to be seen to make concessions to legitimate African nationalist aspirations. In doing so, it was hoped that Kenya would remain stable enough for Britain to 'guide' future political developments at its leisure, thereby securing existing economic interests and facilitating the post-Suez regional strategy. However, the imperatives of economic efficiency, and limited financial resources, ensured that a great many Africans would not benefit from selective socio-economic reforms, such as land consolidation, and there were simply not enough jobs to go around. With resultant crime and militancy on a par with levels seen before the Emergency, and the seemingly perennial dearth of resources to cater for all perceivable internal security contingencies, the myth of 'normality' in Kenyan society could only ever be perpetuated while the African nationalists continued to legitimise Britain's interpretation of the nature and pace of political developments in Kenya through their participation. Once this was withdrawn, Britain would have to meet the nationalists halfway in an effort to avoid a repeat of Mau Mau and the dangerous prospect of an irreversible loss of control.

Notes

1. For example, see: Betts, *Decolonization*, pp. 19-36; John Darwin, *The End of the British Empire: The Historical Debate* (Oxford: Blackwell, 1991), pp. 40-55, idem. *Britain and Decolonisation*, pp. 69-125, and 'British Decolonization since 1945', pp. 187-209; J.D. Hargreaves, *Decolonization in Africa* (Harlow: Longman, 1990 [1988]), passim.; Holland, *European Decolonization*, pp. 37-8, and idem., 'The Imperial Factor in British Strategies', pp. 165-86; A.N. Porter and A.J. Stockwell (eds.), *British Imperial Policy and Decolonization, 1938-64*. Vol. 1: 1938-51 (London: Macmillan, 1987), pp. 46-51.

2. For a summary of scholarly explanations of Britain's withdrawal from Africa and the Empire generally, see: Darwin, *The End of the British Empire*, pp. 1-9; and Ovendale, 'Macmillan and the Wind of Change', pp. 455-7.

3. D.R. Thorpe, *Alec Douglas-Home* (London: Sinclair-Stevenson, 1996), p. 195. Note that during 'the decade after 1947 recruitment into the colonial service increased by 50 per cent': David Reynolds, *Britannia Overruled: British Policy and World Power in the Twentieth Century* (Harlow: Longman, 1991), p. 221. See also: Anthony Kirk-Greene, *On Crown Service: A History of HM Colonial and Overseas Civil Services, 1837-1997* (London: I.B. Tauris, 1999), pp. 39-61.

4. Louis and Robinson, 'The Imperialism of Decolonization', passim; Murphy, 'Lennox-Boyd at the Colonial Office', pp. 2-3.

5. Cranford Pratt, 'Colonial Governments and the Transfer of Power in East Africa', in Prosser Gifford and Wm. Roger Louis (eds.), *The Transfer of Power in Africa: Decolonization 1940-1960* (New Haven and London: Yale University Press, 1982), p. 249.

6. See, for example: George Bennett and Carl Rosberg, *The Kenyatta Election: Kenya 1960-1961* (London, New York and Nairobi: Oxford University Press, 1961); Bennett, *Kenya: A Political History*, pp. 135-61; Berman, *Control and Crisis*, pp. 377-423; Füredi, *Mau Mau War*, pp. 149-224, and *Colonial Wars*, passim.; Kanogo, *Squatters and the Roots of Mau Mau*, pp. 162-78; Ogot and Zeleza, 'Kenya: The Road to Independence and After', pp. 401-26.

7. Anderson and Killingray, *Policing and Decolonisation*, pp. 1-2; Mockaitis, *British Counterinsurgency*; Paget, *Counter-Insurgency Operations*, pp. 83-113; and Townshend, *Britain's Civil Wars*.

8. Throup, 'Crime, politics and the police', pp. 127-57. Other notable works on policing and law and order in Kenya include, for example: David M. Anderson, 'Policing, prosecution and the law in colonial Kenya', in D.M. Anderson and D. Killingray (eds.), *Policing the Empire: Government, Authority and Control, c.1830-1940* (Manchester: Manchester University Press, 1991), pp. 183-200; the general study by Clayton and Killingray, *Khaki and Blue*, which is an amalgamated reproduction of earlier surveys by the authors of documents collected under the auspices of the Oxford Development Records Project (ODRP), many of which were used in Throup's essay, supplemented by volumes of the *Kenya Police Annual Review* (KPAR), which are available in the PRO under reference CO 544; W. Robert Foran, *The Kenya Police 1887-1960* (London, 1962); and two other more recent general surveys, William F. Gutteridge, 'Military and Police Forces in Colonial Africa', and David Killingray, 'The Maintenance of Law and Order in British Colonial Africa', *African Affairs*, 85 (1986), pp. 411-37.

9. Anderson and Killingray, *Policing and Decolonisation*, p. 18.

10. For the background and course of the Mau Mau Emergency and decolonisation in Kenya from the political and socio-economic perspectives, with some reference to the British counter-insurgency campaign, see: Bennett and Rosberg, *The Kenyatta Election*; Bennett, *Kenya: A Political History*; Berman, *Control and Crisis*; Berman and Lonsdale, *Unhappy Valley*; Edgerton, *Mau Mau*; Füredi, *Mau Mau War*, *Colonial Wars*; Heather, 'Intelligence and Counter-insurgency'; Kanogo, *Squatters and the Roots of Mau Mau*; Kyle, *Politics of Independence*; Maloba, *Mau Mau and Kenya*; Ogot and Zeleza, 'Kenya: The Road to Independence and After'; B.A. Ogot and W.R. Ochieng' (eds.), *Decolonization and Independence in Kenya 1940-93* (London: James Currey, 1995); Throup, *Origins of Mau Mau*; Robert L. Tignor, *Capitalism and Nationalism at the End of Empire: State and Business in Decolonizing Egypt, Nigeria, and Kenya, 1945-1963* (Princeton, NJ: Princeton University Press, 1998).

11. Füredi, 'Kenya: Decolonization through counter-insurgency', 'Creating a Breathing Space', and *Colonial Wars*; Mockaitis, *British Counterinsurgency*, pp. 64-5: 'The need to use force in a highly selective manner compelled the British to develop a comprehensive counter-insurgency strategy, one that combined limited military action with broad-based social, economic and political reform. Reform attacked the causes of unrest on which the insurgency fed, while military operations provided a shield behind which reform could be implemented. [...] This progress was not uniform, nor was every campaign an unqualified success. The British were much quicker to grasp the importance of civil-military co-operation than they were to engage in reform. [...] Only when the Second World War made the dissolution of the empire clearly inevitable were the British willing to grant what was for many the ultimate political concession, independence'; Paget, *Counter-Insurgency Operations*, pp. 83-113; Popplewell, '"Lacking Intelligence"', p. 337: 'Britain's achievements in suppressing insurgency were the result not only of counter-insurgency operations, but also of the major political concessions which the British were prepared to make. Most of Britain's successes occurred in the context of the end of Empire [*sic*] when the British were no longer concerned with maintaining their physical presence but with securing a smooth transition to independence and maintaining close relations with the newly independent states and the former metropolis'; and Townshend, *Britain's Civil Wars*.

12. Frank Füredi, 'Britain's Colonial Wars: Playing the Ethnic Card', *Journal of Commonwealth and Comparative Politics*, 28 (1990), pp. 70-89, 'Kenya: Decolonization through counter-insurgency', 'Creating a Breathing Space', and *Colonial Wars*.

13. Percox, 'British Counter-Insurgency', passim.

14. Philip Murphy, *Party Politics and Decolonization: The Conservative Party and British Colonial Policy in Tropical Africa, 1951-1964* (Oxford: Clarendon Press,

1995), p. 2. Murphy successfully builds on the ideas of Darwin and Holland. See, for example: Darwin, *The End of the British Empire*, *Britain and Decolonisation*, and 'British Decolonization since 1945'; Holland, *European Decolonization*, and 'The Imperial Factor in British Strategies'.

15. Murphy, '"Holding Back the Tides"? Alan Lennox-Boyd at the Colonial Office, 1954-59', University of London, Institute of Commonwealth Studies Postgraduate Seminar Paper, 28 March 1996, mimeo. courtesy of the ICS, p. 2.

16. Anderson and Killingray, *Policing and Decolonisation*, p. 14; Murphy, 'Lennox-Boyd at the Colonial Office', p. 3.

17. See, for example: Ovendale, *British Defence Policy since 1945*, p. 7, which, while mentioning British Army deployments in Kenya between 1952 and 1956, provides no references to the strategic reserve in Kenya (1958-64), nor the 'base strategy'. See also: David Sanders, *Losing an Empire, Finding a Role: British Foreign Policy since 1945* (Basingstoke and London: Macmillan, 1990), pp. 87, 88, 99, 227, 274, 289.

18. David R. Devereux, 'The Middle East and Africa in British Global Strategy, 1952-56', in Richard J. Aldrich and Michael F. Hopkins (eds.), *Intelligence, Defence and Diplomacy: British Policy in the Post-War World* (Ilford: Frank Cass, 1994), p. 173. 'However, Africa was more important to British strategic thinking in the mid-1950s than has traditionally been portrayed. It is now known that British and American uranium came from the Belgian Congo as part of a 1944 agreement, and both countries viewed the strategic minerals of Southern Africa with considerable envy, leading to active attempts to woo South Africa despite its racial policies.'

19. Keith Kyle, 'The End of Empire in Kenya', University of London, Institute of Commonwealth Studies Postgraduate Seminar Paper, 14 March 1996, [courtesy of the ICS]; Murphy, *Party Politics*, 'Lennox-Boyd at the Colonial Office'; Kenneth Young, *Sir Alec Douglas-Home* (London: Dent, 1970), p. 114.

20. For an excellent recent study of the transfer of power in Kenya, see: Kyle, *Politics of Independence*.

21. Kyle, 'End of Empire', p. 26.

22. DEFE 7/1014, Gorell Barnes to A.D. Peck (Treasury), 11 May 1959.

23. CO 822/772, War Council Minute 1594, 'Appreciation of the Situation by the Commander-in-Chief East Africa', n.d. (c. Dec. 1955).

24. WO 216/856, Head to Lyttelton, 17 Aug. 1953.

25. CO 822/772, WAR/C 817, 'Emergency Policy. Note by the Secretary of the War Council', 12 Dec. 1955.

26. Füredi, *Mau Mau War*, pp. 149-224; Monone Omosule, 'Kiama kia Muingi: Kikuyu Reaction to Land Consolidation in Kenya, 1955-1959', *Transafrican Journal of History*, 4/1-2 (1974), pp. 115-34.

27. CO 822/772, 'Note on the Kenya War Council's Views on the Future Role of the Security Forces', n.d., (c. Jan. 1956). See also: Throup, 'Crime, politics and the police', p. 149.

28. CO 822/772, Baring to Lennox-Boyd, 28 Jan. 1956.

29. Ibid., 'Note on the Kenya War Council's Views on the Future Role of the Security Forces', n.d. (c. Jan. 1956).

30. Ibid., telegram 222, Lennox-Boyd to Crawford (Deputy Governor, Kenya), 3 March 1956.

31. Ibid., telegram 266, Crawford to Lennox-Boyd, 7 March 1956.

32. Blaxland, *The Regiments Depart*, p. 412; Throup, 'Crime, politics and the police', p. 149.

33. CO 822/1229, 'Brief for the Secretary of State's Visit to Kenya, 1957', n.d. (c. Oct. 1957).

34. Throup, 'Crime, politics and the police', pp. 150-1.

35. CO 822/1229, 'Brief for the Secretary of State's Visit to Kenya'.

36. CO 822/1252, GH 35/5/39/Vol.II, Baring to Lennox-Boyd, 27 Feb. 1957, GH 1953/5/39/Vol.II, Baring to Lennox-Boyd, 10 April 1957, Lennox-Boyd to Baring, 20 May 1957; Bennett, *Kenya: A Political History*, pp. 141-2.

37. Bennett, loc. cit.; Ogot and Zeleza, 'Kenya: The Road to Independence and After', p. 410.

38. CAB 129/76, CP (55) 97,'Singapore Constitutional Crisis: Memorandum by the Minister of State for Colonial Affairs' (Henry Hopkinson), 10 Aug. 1955, cited in Murphy, 'Lennox-Boyd at the Colonial Office', p. 3; Dennis Austin, 'The Transfer of Power: Why and How', in W.H. Morris-Jones and Georges Fischer (eds.), *Decolonisation and After: The British and French Experience* (London: Frank Cass, 1980), p. 29.

39. CO 822/1252, GH 35/5/39/Vol.II, Baring to Lennox-Boyd, 27 Feb. 1957.

40. CO 822/1306, WAR/C 1105, 'The Colony Internal Security Scheme: Memorandum by the Internal Security Working Committee', 21 Feb. 1958. For discussion of the pre-Emergency internal security scheme see: Chapter One; and Percox, 'British Counter-Insurgency'.

41. CO 822/1306, WAR/C 1105, 'The Colony Internal Security Scheme'; Bennett, *Kenya: A Political History*, p. 141.

42. CO 822/1306, 'Annex "A" to WAR/C 1105: Kenya Colony Internal Security Scheme'.

43. Ibid., WAR/C 1105, 'The Colony Internal Security Scheme', para. 10. 'Resources available' included: 207 Royal East African Navy (REAN) personnel; two Kenya KAR battalions 'so far as not committed to operations on the Northern Frontier or elsewhere; the [East Africa] Command Reserve KAR battalion 'available if not committed elsewhere in the Command'; one

British infantry battalion of the UK Strategic Reserve, 'which is normally stationed in Nairobi - available with War Office approval, but may at any time be serving outside East Africa'; part of a British infantry battalion of British Forces, Arabian Peninsula (BFAP), normally stationed at Gilgil 'available with War Office approval, but its presence in Kenya cannot be guaranteed'; the Kenya Regiment (Territorial Force), comprising about 700 men, 'available except for members whose civilian employment is in essential services'; the UK Colonial Internal Security Brigade, 'available on application to and approval by Her Majesty's Government'; 12 GSU platoons, comprising 432 men; and five Prison Department Special Platoons, c. 180 men. The latter 'would be required to guard convicts if any considerable number of convicts was enlarged to work on essential services such as the operation of Mombasa Port'.

44. Ibid., War Council Minute 2284, n.d. (c. 13 March 1958).

45. Ibid., SC 44, 'Security Council Advisory to the Governor: Memorandum by the European Minister without Portfolio [N.F. Harris] - Security in Urban Areas', 9 Dec. 1958.

46. Ibid., S/C/MIN 156, 'Security in Urban Areas', n.d. (c. 22 Dec. 1958).

47. CO 822/1255, CM (57) 140, 'War Council Business, 1st March, 1957 to the 30th April, 1957', note by the Secretary to the War Council (Corfield), 2 May 1957. One of the problems, for example, was that 'only about 30 percent [*sic*] of members of the Kenya Regiment were at present fulfilling their statutory duties ...'

48. CO 822/1306, SC 58, 'Protection of Vulnerable Points', memo. by A.C.C. Swann (Minister for Defence, Nairobi), 21 March 1959.

49. Ibid., S/C/MIN 220, n.d. (c. March 1959).

50. Ibid., Colonial Office, hand-written minute, signature illegible (W.J. Dunn?), 27 March 1958.

51. CO 822/1254, 'Mau Mau Oathing in Meru District', memo. by the Office of the Director of Intelligence and Security, 24 Jan. 1958.

52. CO 822/1278, EMER 45/77/1A/253, E.W.M. Magor (Ministry of Defence, Nairobi) to J.L.F. Buist (Colonial Office), 24 April 1957, Annex to WAR/C 1047, 'A Review of the Security Situation in Nyanza Province', by the Kenya Intelligence Committee (KIC), n.d. (c. April 1957).

53. Ibid., Annex to WAR/C 1047, 'A Review of the Security Situation in Nyanza Province' (emphasis added).

54. By April 1958, there were less than 15,000 detainees, the release rate being about 1,000 per month. See: CO 822/1252, Baring to Lennox-Boyd, 8 April 1958.

55. CO 822/1255, CM (58) 83, 'War Council Business, 4th Dec., 1957 to the 4th March, 1958', note by F.D. Corfield (Secretary to the War Council, Nairobi), 13 March 1958.

56. CO 822/1280, WAR/C 1082, 'Markets and Welfare Centres in Settled Areas', memo. by W. F. Coutts, (Special Commissioner [for African Elections]), 3 Dec. 1957.

57. Oginga Odinga, *Not Yet Uhuru: the autobiography of Oginga Odinga* (London, Ibadan, Nairobi: Heinemann, 1969 [1967]), pp. 161-2.

58. CO 822/1252, Baring to Lennox-Boyd, 8 April 1958.

59. CO 822/1347, Baring to Lennox-Boyd, 2 April 1958.

60. Ibid., Lennox-Boyd to Baring, 6 May 1958. Colonial Office and Kenya government deliberations over post-Emergency or 'twilight' legislation included proposals for pre-emptive measures to deal with potential subversion, and legislation to enable the restriction of 'specified detainees', thereby circumventing the limitations of the ILO and Human Rights Conventions. See, for example: CO 822/1334, CO 822/1337, CO 822/1420, CO 822/2090, and CO 822/2091.

61. CO 822/789, telegram 1041, Crawford to Lennox-Boyd, 16 Sept. 1955, Annex to WAR/C 731, 'Kiama Kia Muingi: An Appreciation by the Kenya Intelligence Committee', n.d. (c. 6 June 1955); CO 822/1346, telegram 32, R.G. Turnbull (Chief Secretary, Nairobi) to Lennox-Boyd, 13 Jan. 1958. Omosule, 'Kiama kia Muingi', gives details of the seemingly complex aims of KKM, which appear to have been very much an extension of those of the so-called Mau Mau, albeit exacerbated by the dispossessions and disaffection resulting from land consolidation. See also: Füredi, *Mau Mau War*, pp. 149-224.

62. Omosule, 'Kiama kia Muingi', p. 127.

63. 822/789, CAB 18/7, Corfield (Kenya War Council) to Mathieson (Colonial Office), 17 Sept. 1955, EAF 15/61/01, Mathieson to Corfield, 29 Sept. 1955, INT 38/10A.43, E.W.M. Magor (MoD, Nairobi) to M. Scott (Colonial Office), 16 Dec. 1955, EAF 16/61/01, Mathieson to Crawford, 16 Jan. 1956, CAB 25/14, Crawford to Mathieson, 31 Jan. 1956, 'Extract from Minutes of War Council Meeting held on 16 April 1956: Kiama Kia Muingi'.

64. Ibid., 'Kiama Kia Muingi: Appreciation by the Kenya Intelligence Committee', 4 April 1956.

65. CO 822/1346, telegram 32, Turnbull to Lennox-Boyd, 13 Jan. 1958.

66. Ibid.; Omosule, 'Kiama kia Muingi', p. 125.

67. CO 822/1346, Turnbull to Lennox-Boyd, 13 Jan. 1958.

68. Ibid., Roberts (Colonial Office) to Griffith-Jones (Member for Legal Affairs, Nairobi), 17 Jan. 1958.

69. Ibid., telegram 386, Baring to Lennox-Boyd, 19 May 1958, Annex to SC 5, Security Council Advisory to the Governor, 'Kiama Kia Muingi: Report by the Director of Intelligence and Security', 20 May 1958, KIC (FINAL) 4/58, 'Kenya Intelligence Committee: Kiama Kia Muingi', 25 June 1958, Secret Saving 1692/58, Coutts to Baring, 5 July 1958.

70. Ibid., 'Kiama Kia Muingi: Report by the Director of Intelligence and Security', 20 May 1958.

71. Ibid., KIC (FINAL) 2/58, 'Kenya Intelligence Committee: Kiama Kia Muingi', 10 Jan. 1958.

72. Ibid., Secret Saving 1692/58, Coutts to Baring, 5 July 1958.

73. WO 276/375, Major, GSO 2 (INT) to Maj.-Gen. Sir N. Tapp, (GOC, EAC), 2 May 1958.

74. CO 822/1346, 'Extract from K.I.C. Appreciation No. 9/5 for period 1-31.8.58'. In August 1958, the Secretary to the Cabinet was able to report to the Council of Ministers that given the measures taken against KKM 'so it was possible gradually to relax some of the restraints on the movement of KEM with effect from the 1st June; these include the employment of former detainees in forest villages, an extension of the process of allowing approved tenant farmers to move out to live on their holdings; and in allowing cattle to be moved out of the villages to manyattas', CO 822/1255, 'Review of the Business of the Security Council Advisory to the Governor up to the end of July 1958', note by the Secretary to the Cabinet, 7 Aug. 1958.

75. CO 822/1346, Baring to Lennox-Boyd, 4 Sept. 1958, 'Extract from KIC Appreciation No. 10/58 for period 1-30.9.58'.

76. Ibid., Baring to Lennox-Boyd, 4 Sept. 1958.

77. Ibid., Security Council Minute 150, Dec. 1958, GH 1953/5/17 VI/, Baring to C.M. Johnston (Minister for African Affairs), 23 Dec. 1958.

78. Ibid., 'Extract from KIC Appreciation No.1/59', 'Extract from KIC Appreciation No.5/59', 'Extract from KIC Appreciation No. 7/59'.

CHAPTER SIX

Internal Security and Decolonisation II, 1959-65

Introduction

As the pace of constitutional advance in Kenya began perforce to accelerate in 1959, and the nationalists made maximum capital of ongoing and widespread African socio-economic grievances, Britain had to be seen to make sufficient concessions to maintain political credibility. Military victory over Mau Mau in 1956 had not been decisive, and selective reforms, by definition, still left too many disaffected Africans for threats of subversion to simply go away. The first section of this chapter (1959-63) will show how, as pressure increased for a quick withdrawal, Britain had to combine political tactics designed to foster 'moderate' government with ever-sophisticated means of ensuring that internal security did not collapse. There was just too much to lose.

The next section (1963-5) will show that once Britain was presented with the kind of African nationalist leadership in Kenya with which it could do business, considerable risks were taken to ensure that this government would be seen, so far as possible, to possess impeccable nationalist credentials. The supposed 'extremists' would be given no quarter. This was the only credible alternative to a return to widespread violence and even civil war. It was also imperative that, given Kenyatta's newfound acceptability, the utmost be done to ensure that he, or his 'moderate' colleagues, would remain in power after independence. Britain therefore redoubled its efforts to build up Kenya's security services, this time in Kenyatta's favour. Only then could Britain safeguard its 'vital interests' without risking a blood bath and the ignominy of having to retain formal administrative control.

Securing 'Vital Interests': Britain's Efforts to Maintain Control, 1959-63

In July 1959, Kenya's then European Minister without Portfolio, N.F. Harris, cited the discovery of yet another secret society, *Kiama Kia Thayu* (Council/Society of Peace), to justify the continuation of the State of Emergency. Yet, events had already dictated that this would not continue for long.[1] As is well known, the murder of 11 detainees by African wardens at the Hola Detention Camp in March had caused considerable political embarrassment for the British government, both at home and abroad.[2] This added urgency to Lennox-Boyd's April announcement of future constitutional talks, in response to pleas from Baring following the Africans' January boycott of Legislative Council.[3] The announcement was, of course, as much a domestic and international political bridge-building exercise in the wake of Hola as a palliative for the African MLCs.[4] What matters here, though, is that for constitutional talks to take place (with African participation), let alone work, the State of Emergency would have to be lifted. Baring 'felt that if it should be possible to do this some time in advance of the opening of the Constitutional Conference, that might do much to ensure a reasonable political atmosphere for negotiation'.[5]

The prospect of ending the Emergency presented both the Colonial Office and the Kenya government with a dilemma. Much depended on the readiness of security legislation to replace the Emergency Regulations. As Webber in the Colonial Office put it to Kenya's then Minister for Legal Affairs, E.N. Griffith-Jones:

> We are tentatively exploring [the] idea of ending [the] Emergency on say 31st December and announcing [the] intention of so doing before Baring goes. We wish to advise Ministers urgently whether, leaving aside all other considerations, it is realistic to assume that such replacement legislation as must (repeat must) be enacted before [the] Emergency is lifted could in fact be enacted before 31st December. [...] [I]t would be helpful to know now your assessment of [the] political effects of ending [the] Emergency and seeking, as a prelude, to enact [a] body of pretty controversial legislation. Would it strengthen or embarrass moderates of all races? What has been your latest thinking on [the] likely date of ending [the] Emergency?[6]

The Kenya government agreed with the Colonial Office's timetable 'which accords with our own thinking', provided that 'we would be authorised to enact the Preservation of Public Security [PPS] Bill ... before the ending of the emergency'. Griffith-Jones continued:

> Political effect would be generally good. The operation would be conducive to success of conference in the new year and would remove certain targets of political agitation and generally clear the air. [...] Moderates would, we think, be strengthened and encouraged rather than embarrassed. Replacement legislation would be welcomed by moderates but would be strongly opposed by African extremists. Divisions among Africans might become more acute. Generally speaking responsible opinion recognises both sides of Fairn's penny, which we have accepted, i.e. end the emergency as early as possible but replacement legislation essential.[7]

Crucially, the PPS Bill was intended to provide for Regulations to enable the continued detention and restriction of 'the residue'. Other legislation to pre-empt subversion would be enacted to replace the Emergency Regulations dealing with public meetings, seditious publications, control of printing presses, and control of movement. Effectively, the Kenya government would retain Emergency powers in all but name. Moreover, the arguably most controversial measure was the replacement of Ordinance L.N.37 (1956) 'for control of African Colony wide political Associations to such an extent as can be justified ... either by amendment ... or perhaps more acceptably, as [a] temporary measure by Regulations under the [PPS] Bill'.[8]

There are two ways that this can be interpreted. The most cynical, and perhaps obvious intention was, by using the threat of subversion, to ensure that African political progress would thereby be kept in check, enabling the perpetuation of the colonial state. There is certainly some truth in this, and the measure undoubtedly met with settler approval. However, as others have shown, the Colonial Office and the East African governors had, in early 1959, already conceded that Kenya would become independent, albeit some time between 1970 and 1975. Yet, events in Tanganyika, and 'deadlock' in Kenya's Legislative Council brought an early reassessment of the timetable; Hola certainly added to these pressures.[9] Indeed, Murphy shows clearly that, in March 1959, the Secretary of State was more than a little perturbed by the lack of any reference to an eventual African majority in the Kenya government in the draft statement on policy provided by Baring. It seems that only Blundell's formation of the 'multi-racial' New Kenya Group persuaded Lennox-Boyd to remove the 'punch line' from his April speech to the Commons.[10] There was at least a 'good chance' that the 'moderate' option would still work.

So, was the 'twilight' legislation intended to put a brake on African nationalism *per se*, and only veiled under the issue of security? In his 10 November speech announcing the legislation, Baring's successor, Sir Patrick Renison, outlined the provisions in the PPS Bill for stricter controls over public meetings and over the registration of colony-wide political associations:

> The Bill is therefore both an insurance against future troubles and a means of giving notice to any would-be trouble-makers of the Government's determination to maintain law and order and to take any measures essential to that end In pursuance of that determination and because I am satisfied that it is not possible, or compatible with the interests of security, to abandon completely the present controls under the Emergency legislation of political organisations and public meetings, it is my intention to make regulations under the [PPS] Bill, on its coming into force, to provide for the continuance of these

> two controls for the time being in such form as I may then consider to be still called for. I shall be guided not by race or racial politics but solely by my judgement of the needs of law and order. [...] Please understand that I am not trying to restrain politics but to ensure peace for our development.[11]

Should Renison be taken at his word? It is clear that, like his predecessor, the new governor did not wish to restrain politics so long as it was of the moderate variety. It is fair to argue, therefore, that the legislation, and even its announcement, was intended to serve as a warning to Africans to play by the Colonial Office and Kenya government's political rules. Moderate government was, after all, the best safeguard of Britain's interests in Kenya. The same motives could be said to have applied, if indirectly, to the maintenance of powers of restriction and detention on the so-called 'politicals'. This was both a warning against subversive activity, and a precaution.

In justifying the need to continue to exercise controls over the alleged Mau Mau managers Koinange, Mouria, and Murumbi should they return to Kenya, one Colonial Office official wrote: 'Although these people have sat out the Emergency in this country [Britain], they are dangerous men, who hold high places in the mythology of Mau Mau and if allowed freely at large in Kenya at the present time would be a focus for disaffection and a constant threat to peace and security'.[12] Again, it was perception that mattered. The African had to be shown that the only way of achieving political progress was to abide by Colonial Office interpretations of the appropriate means to that end. The risk to the Colonial Office of Africans pursuing a militant alternative was just too great.

The concept of 'twilight legislation' to reinforce powers to maintain law and order in a pre- or post-emergency situation had been under consideration since Lord Salisbury's visit to Africa in early 1956. Salisbury noted a 'defect' in 'our machinery for preserving law and order in our Colonial territories ... At present, it seems to be geared only to deal with two completely different sets of circumstances, what may be called normal times and what may be called emergencies.'[13] That summer, Lennox-Boyd argued that existing powers were sufficient. Nevertheless, the CPC invited the Secretary of State to consider whether the powers of colonial governors 'needed to be reinforced'.[14]

It is difficult to ascertain when, exactly, Lennox-Boyd's review of the governors' powers began. It is certain, and significant, that the examination was completed by the end of 1957, when the Lennox-Boyd Constitution and the decision to station a 'permanent' garrison of British troops in Kenya were public knowledge. The existence of 'adequate powers to deal with subversion' it seemed 'could be useful in itself as a stabilizing influence in the background of a Colony's political life'. As suggested in previous chapters, stable political conditions would also be useful to British defence strategists.

Because there might well have been multiple factors which could contribute to unrest in any given colony (many of which would be territory-specific) it was considered too difficult to formulate 'a general policy'. Given the perception in Government House and Whitehall that proposals for reinforcing security powers in Kenya should be examined prior to the withdrawal of Emergency Regulations, the colony was therefore singled out to become the 'guinea pig'.[15] All the more important given Britain's strategic aims in the area.

However, the lead was taken in Northern Rhodesia, where an ordinance was enacted enabling the governor to make regulations 'to correct a situation which, if allowed to occur or continue, would be likely to lead' to the declaration of a State of Emergency. This provided for a situation whereby, under Article 15 of the European Convention on Human Rights, Article 5, which prohibited detention without trial, could be derogated: 'such derogation must be limited "to the extent strictly required by the exigencies of the situation". Whether or not an emergency exists is a question of fact.'[16] Another advantage of dispensing with the need for a formal proclamation of an emergency was that it would be less damaging to 'morale and to the economic and political situation in a territory'.

By June 1959, however, as pressure increased to bring the Kenya Emergency to an end in the wake of the Hola affair, concomitant political tensions created a paradox. In considering the prospects for ending the emergencies in Kenya and Nyasaland, Lennox-Boyd was concerned that 'in present political circumstances' the introduction of legislation effectively giving colonial governors emergency powers when a State of Emergency did not formally exist 'would provoke serious controversy'.[17] Much pivoted on the fact that the need for 'twilight legislation' depended on 'how important it was to end the technical state of emergency'.

In Lennox-Boyd's view it was not essential to do so at the time because the continuation of the 'technical' Emergency 'did not really make the possibility of native African co-operation with the administration more unlikely, nor did it in reality reduce the chances of capital investment in the territories'. Equally important, given the forthcoming British general election, was that an early announcement of permanent security legislation might lead the Labour Party to make a commitment to reverse the policy. If the legislation were withdrawn subsequently 'it would mean that the Governors would be entirely deprived of the powers they needed'.[18] It was hoped that the Fairn Committee (Hola) and the Devlin Committee (Nyasaland Emergency) might recommend the continuation of detention without trial of those incarcerated during 'emergency conditions', thereby enabling the legislation to be limited, thus less controversial. The British government would not therefore authorise the introduction of the legislation before the summer recess: Lennox-Boyd would state in the Commons that no decision on the matter had been taken; and both governors would be authorised to continue to annul any Emergency Regulations that were no longer necessary.[19]

By 5 November 1959, when security powers in Kenya were again discussed in the CPC, the Conservative Party had retained office and Iain Macleod had succeeded Lennox-Boyd at the Colonial Office. In Macleod's view the situation in Kenya had been transformed since his predecessor's policy announcement in April and the emergence of moderate political groups. He had hoped initially to 'refer to Kenya "in some detail"' in Colonial Debate in the Commons on 2 November, but there was insufficient time for Renison to examine the final proposals for the post-Emergency, or 'twilight' legislation and to convince his Council of Ministers of their adequacy.[20] Accordingly, the new Secretary of State proposed that Renison should be authorised to announce the end of the 'formal' Emergency simultaneously with the introduction of the new legislation when opening the Legislative Council on 10 November.[21]

To overcome the difficulty of any possible infringement of human rights, Macleod proposed a 'two-tier system of emergency powers':

> The first tier would enable the Governor, after making an appropriate announcement, to assume certain strictly defined powers, such as those concerning public meetings, societies, publications and movement, but not the all-important power of detention without trial; these powers would be used either in a situation where there appeared to be a gradual development of unrest, intimidation and lawlessness, or in circumstances such as those existing in Kenya at present, where certain powers were needed but a full State of Emergency was no longer necessary. The second tier would enable the Governor, after issuing the necessary proclamation, to assume more drastic powers, including the right of detention without trial, in circumstances where the safety of the nation was being endangered.[22]

The declaration of the ending of the Emergency would also coincide with the announcement of an 'act of grace' whereby 300 detainees 'and others convicted of certain offences in connection with the emergency' would be released. This would also allow the release of six 'African loyalists convicted of offences against Mau Mau sympathisers' and 'two junior European officers'.[23] Kenyatta, however, would remain under restriction, at least for the time being.[24]

The ending of the State of Emergency and the concession of further constitutional advance in Kenya had broader implications for British policy, particularly overseas defence strategy. This applied at two levels. First, there was the matter of the UK Strategic Reserve, a Brigade Group stationed at

Kahawa since June 1958, for internal security operations in Arabia and the Persian Gulf and, if necessary, to reinforce the KAR in East and Central Africa (see Chapters Three, Four and Seven). Then there was the KAR itself. While the British troops in the UK Strategic Reserve had always remained under War Office control, and what mattered for Britain with regard to future constitutional development in the territory was the security of tenure of their base, the KAR, as East Africa's 'local' military force, was far more intricately connected with Kenyan politics.

In July 1957, following the end of active military operations against Mau Mau, the Templer Report was implemented, and control of the KAR reverted back to the governments of the East African territories, eventually under the administrative auspices of the East African Land Forces Organisation (EALFO). Almost from its inception, the EALFO suffered from financial problems, despite its military administration by the GOC, East Africa Command (see Chapters Three and Four). This difficulty arose primarily from the practice of each of the three territories being responsible for its share of the EALFO estimates, which led to there being three separate, if not too dissimilar, yet competing sources of revenue. Invariably there were difficulties because one or another, if not all, of the territories could not find its full share.

As we have seen, throughout 1957-60, this led to protracted negotiations concerning the relative administrative, financial, and military merits of a reversion back to War Office control, or variations on that theme.[25] It is unnecessary to cover old ground by a more detailed examination of these aspects of the subject here, but one policy decision in particular warrants greater attention: the British decision, after three years of resisting the change, that the War Office should resume financial and administrative control of the EALF after all.

Murphy tells us that Iain Macleod's 'first major battle in the Cabinet in 1960 was not over the speed of constitutional advance in the colonies but rather over his proposal that the British government should resume financial responsibility for the East African Land Forces'.[26] As his predecessor had done, Macleod suggested that this could be presented as a means by which local revenues could be freed up for 'more constructive purposes, such as the development of agriculture and education'.[27] This, Macleod thought, 'might have a decisive effect' on the forthcoming Lancaster House conference. Although there were protests, particularly from the Chancellor of the Exchequer, D. Heathcoat Amory, who argued that the proposal represented a reversal of normal British policy towards its colonies, ultimately Macleod's argument concerning the 'military and administrative advantages' of the change won the day.[28] Accordingly, in a contrived spirit of magnanimity, the Cabinet agreed to announce the change along with a British pledge of a £5 million loan for land development.[29] So, what were these 'military and administrative' advantages?

Since the 'Chequers decisions' of January 1959, and the adoption of the policy of 'gradualness' (a euphemism for 'delay') towards decolonisation, the issue of the EALF had been under considerable scrutiny. At the administrative, financial, and military levels it made perfect sense, from the points of view of both the Army and the East African governments, if the control of all military forces in East Africa were resumed by the War Office.[30]

Politically, the motives for Britain's policy reversal were far less mundane. As Gorell Barnes put it to Baring the day before questions in the Commons on the Hola affair:

> In the first place we have to "sell" the policy of gradualness to those who would have us out of East Africa within the next few years. To do this we must make it clear that we are going to assist the local governments so far as we possibly can to finance programmes of development aimed at increasing prosperity and bringing the local people on in sufficient numbers to be able, more or less, to run things for themselves when the time comes. [...] In the second place, we do not want what will in fact be a fairly rapid move forward to internal self-government (even on the middle road policy) to prejudice our own interests. [...] If HM Government are to retain ultimate responsibility whether for defence or for ensuring that African or predominantly African Governments do not turn out the Asians or Europeans, or both, they will need the ultimate sanction of force. Furthermore, in so far as HMG's interests remain "strategic" they will have an interest in the internal security of the area. [...] At this moment the situation is secure because we are doing the governing. But our middle road policy envisages the beginning of responsible government for Tanganyika and Uganda and conceivably Zanzibar (possibly also Kenya) by 1965. From that time onwards we can expect increasing friction with Elected Ministers and Legislatures over the forces if the money has to be voted locally. Any attempt to take over the cost of the forces then would be met with violent opposition. But if we do it now (i.e. 1960), if we are prepared to talk fairly freely about when responsible government can be achieved and if we demonstrate that we are prepared to assist Governments to spend money on the really important things, we stand a fair chance of not being accused of planning to depend on force not so much to maintain our position in East Africa but to hold back the Africans from catching up with the more advanced communities.[31]

This admittedly long quotation (which barely does justice to the letter from which it is extracted) is necessary because it provides a good indication of the general thrust of Colonial Office policy towards East Africa at the time. However, even this seems sanitised when compared with Gorell Barnes' justification to the Treasury within a week of publication of the Hola Inquiry report:

> The probability that political advance towards self-government will have to be faster than we desire or think right leads us to the conclusion that we should, as a brake on that advance, do all we can now, before it is too late, to insulate all the internal security forces of the territories from local political control, and secure them in the hands of the Governors and so Her Majesty's Government. [...] The fact that it will not be possible to divorce administration of the police altogether from local politics does not, fortunately, affect the general value of such a change, as the Governor's unfettered control of the military forces will give him the necessary backing in the event of serious trouble, and restore to us one political counter which we need.[32]

Clearly, the first Lancaster House conference on Kenya's constitutional future was no radical political watershed, despite appearances.[33] Moreover, Britain would have to employ increasingly elaborate tactics as the devolution of power in Kenya moved into the endgame.

Meanwhile, as if to validate British concerns, it did not take long for Mboya, as ever, to remind the administration of the dangers presented by apparently radical African politicians. No sooner had the Emergency been lifted, and the first Lancaster House conference concluded, than the young Luo, concerned by his political rivals' efforts to undermine his support base by branding him a colonial collaborator, began to threaten a campaign of civil disobedience if African demands for majority government were not met.[34]

Throughout 1960-3, constitutional negotiations and the electoral process were punctuated by civil disturbances and the threat of, if not actual inter-ethnic and racial violence, as Kikuyu subversive organisations continued to proliferate.[35] The very real fears of 'another outbreak of Mau Mau' which, were it to occur, would have to be 'crushed at great cost and effort' and 'leave us in no better position', compelled Britain to persist with efforts to secure a constitutional solution to 'the grave dangers of the Kenya situation'. For example, this thinking had necessitated the decision to remove the restriction on Kenyatta becoming a member of the legislature, conceded in principle in November 1961.[36] It should be stressed that this, and similar concessions, demonstrated Britain's capacity for shrewd political manoeuvring in the face of such fears. Britain was not, however, going to leave anything to chance, as will be shown below.

In the wake of the Emergency, the ISWC, necessarily, had to review security provisions for the colony. In May 1960, its conclusions differed little from those of 1958: the main threat to internal security was still 'positive action' rather than armed insurrection. The ISWC's thinking on the likely extent of such action is particularly significant: '[T]o be effective, a Colony-wide campaign of positive action must depend on the prior existence of:- (i) united and definite African leadership at the centre; (ii) a Colony-wide organisation, all embracing and disciplined, to give effect to decisions taken at the centre; (iii) a sufficiently popular cause to provide a clear objective'.[37]

The logic of the legitimisation of the political process itself had compelled Britain to grant a constitutional conference to the African nationalists, necessitating an end to the State of Emergency. However, the aftermath of the conference soon dispelled any hopes that 'gradualness' and multi-racialism, with all the implications for British interests, would win the day. The inevitable outcome of earlier gestures towards political reform was demonstrated by the post-conference formation of colony-wide political parties which were divided largely along ethnic lines. Leaks to the Nairobi press about Macleod's constitutional proposals were interpreted as meaning imminent independence, and led to some African rioting.[38]

Although the ban on colony-wide political parties had been lifted, the united African front of Lancaster House had soon reduced down to the ethnic divisions incorporated by KANU and the Kenya African Democratic Union (KADU).[39] While this may have suited Britain to some extent because in Tanganyika the existence of a popular, colony-wide African nationalist party, the Tanganyika African National Union (TANU), had accelerated the pace of decolonisation, in Kenya continued ethnic and racial tensions served only to exacerbate an already fragile situation.[40]

In 1960, violence was erupting all over Africa: first in newly independent West Cameroon; inter-tribal warfare in the Belgian Congo grew progressively worse; then came the 'Sharpeville massacre' in South Africa. Worst of all, the situation in the Congo came to a head that summer. Following independence, on 1 July 1960, the Congolese Army mutinied against its Belgian officers, European civilians came under attack, and the country descended into civil war. This did not bode well for Britain's future plans in Kenya. More immediately, the arrival of several thousand Belgian refugees in Kenya prompted angry reactions from African crowds who shouted, ominously, "the same will happen to Europeans here".[41]

While this prompted Kenya's white settlers to call for the creation of a European Defence Force, as well as stockpiling supplies and weapons at 'strongpoints', on 25 July Mboya told President Kennedy in New York, 'I can definitely say that Kenya is ready for independence.' Perhaps coincidentally, the following day Britain took steps to ensure against the worst-case scenario, and despatched a battalion of troops by air to reinforce Kenya. Shortly after this, the aircraft carrier HMS *Bulwark* arrived in Mombasa, along with an additional complement of 600 Royal Marines (RM).[42] Plans were soon tabled, too, for an exercise ('Kerry Blue') to practise and assess capability for the airlift of a brigade of British troops to Kenya.[43]

All this brought the potentially volatile situation in Kenya into sharp focus. The ISWC recognised that the absence of colony-wide organisations did not rule out the possibility of a campaign of civil disobedience 'as circumstances could quickly change', and that if the 'Kenyatta issue' were the '*raison d'être* for the campaign ... the whole of Central Province would be involved from the start'. This would provide just the scenario whereby, under the 'twilight' powers, the governor would be empowered to make regulations 'in the security field, provided His Excellency "is satisfied that it is necessary for the preservation of public security so to do". The ISWC assume that this subjective test would be discharged by a campaign of civil disobedience.'[44] Effectively, the same sanctions that had been applied against Mau Mau and KKM would be available to prevent the governments' hands from being forced on any issue.[45]

In the immediate aftermath of the Emergency, the importance to Britain of maintaining stability in Kenya after independence was illustrated by the emergence of the Kenya Land Freedom Army (KLFA, or LFA) from the ashes of KKM and Mau Mau, followed by over a dozen more pretenders to the ethnic sub-nationalist crown.[46] Reflecting the KLFA's apparent lack of activity, and Britain's desire for politics to be seen to be working, in essence if not in fact, the organisation was not proscribed until September 1962.

Beside the considerable body of work on constitutional negotiations and so on, there have also been two creditable studies of the increasing disaffection and militancy of Kikuyu squatters and wage-labourers in the post-Mau Mau era, as a function of the non-inclusive policies adopted under the Swynnerton Plan.[47] It emerges from these works that the major vehicle of such discontent was the KLFA which, seeking an equitable distribution of land as its name suggests, represented a fundamental and diametric opposition to the Kenya government's policy of creating a class of African yeomen, or 'moderates'. 'A closer inspection of events shows that agitation for land was restricted to illegal squatting and civil disobedience ...'[48]

As Füredi rightly suggests, this 'absence of violence' does indeed show that the police action against the KLFA was pre-emptive. By 1962, the authorities were not going to take any chances. There had already been too much volatility in the open political arena, especially during the registration of voters for the February 1961 elections based upon the 1960 Lancaster House ('Macleod') Constitution. Many of the KANU leaders had campaigned on a 'free Kenyatta now' ticket, and refused to take office unless this demand was met.[49] Britain's initial response to all this was to assign KAR battalions and British troops from 24 Brigade 'spheres of influence' under the auspices of 'Operation Prophesy'.[50] The Chiefs of Staff had already begun to re-evaluate plans for the air-reinforcement exercise which had been tabled during the previous summer.[51]

Potential subversion remained a constant threat in the form of the KLFA. If anything, the gravity of the problem with the KLFA, as with KKM and Mau Mau, was that they amounted essentially to the same thing. A 'possible resurgence of Mau Mau' could not be ruled out.[52] Notably, the origins of the KLFA, or 'Kenya Parliament', were traced back to Nairobi between 1953 and 1955, when it had apparently been one of the unsuccessful cells vying for control of Mau Mau. Although at first the KIC did not consider the KLFA to be a colony-wide threat, its apparent aim of achieving 'Kikuyu domination after independence, a domination to be exercised by and for KLFA members' certainly placed it in a serious category.[53]

By 21 July 1961, the KLFA was known to have been in existence for about 15 months, and the KIC was well aware of its lack of activity to date, but one factor in particular gave serious cause for concern:

> Most KLFA members will undoubtedly be members of ... KANU - every individual so far arrested in connection with KLFA activity has been in possession of a KANU membership card - and certain aims of KANU, for example, the release of Jomo KENYATTA [*sic*] and a redistribution of land, form part of the fundamental faith of the Land Freedom Army.[54]

As with KKM, it was considered important to secure the co-operation of the African political leaders, particularly the Kikuyu, 'in the campaign against' the KLFA. As Kenya's Minister for Defence, A.C.C. Swann, reported on 28 July 1961:

> This cooperation [*sic*] is very necessary for two reasons - first we must convince them of the dangers of the threat, how it will grow, and how much more difficult it will be to tackle if it is not tackled now; secondly, we must strive to make them see that KLFA restrictees are not political martyrs, and that restriction is vital to the security of the State if we are to proceed peacefully to independence.[55]

The timing of all this was crucial. Earlier in the month, Renison had pressed Macleod to release Kenyatta, following this up with a phone call on 25 July. Renison's own change of heart occurred not only because he hoped to prevent the KADU-NKP (and therefore multi-racial) coalition government from resigning, but because of a seemingly reluctant *volte face* by Special Branch, which 'now felt that Kenyatta had better come out while the British were still firmly in command'.[56] Perhaps more important, KANU had won the February 1961 election by 16 seats in Legislative Council to KADU's nine.[57] While earlier refusals to release Kenyatta may well have served British purposes by temporarily keeping KANU out of office, the KADU leadership, if not that of the NKP, surely realised that they could not command widespread support, even in a coalition, while not at the same time talking up Kenyatta's cause. It is only possible to speculate here whether the British authorities hoped, by releasing Kenyatta, to kill several birds with one stone. While his release removed the pretext for the KADU AEMs to resign, it also allowed the security forces to gauge the impact on popular disaffection. The Kenya government certainly hoped to enlist Kenyatta's co-operation in denouncing the KLFA.[58]

Indeed, the very issue of KLFA subversion vis-à-vis KANU constitutionalism provided further proof of Kenyatta's 'moderate' credentials.[59] In October 1962, Kenya's DIS, Mervyn Manby, reported on Kenyatta's recent denunciations of the KLFA:

> The reciprocal attitude of the KLFA towards KENYATTA [*sic*] is unfavourable. It regards Oginga ODINGA as the only true nationalist in the top KANU leadership, although he is not Kikuyu [...] KENYATTA it regards as an old man, a spent force, *far too moderate*, and probably "sold to the imperialists". The KLFA also, of course, disapproves of his limited co-operation not only with Europeans and Asians, but also with members of other Kenya African tribes: he is indeed a tribalist, but not enough of one for the KLFA.[60]

By September 1962, despite denunciations from Kenyatta and other African politicians, the movement had spread, with an estimated 3-4,000 members in Rift Valley Province alone: 'military drills' were becoming more common; oaths tended increasingly towards violence; and, since January, over 200 precision and home-made guns had been seized from KLFA adherents and members of other Kikuyu subversive organisations.[61] This was especially significant, given the KADU-KANU feud over regionalism, control of the police, and access to the White Highlands that had simmered since the February 1962 constitutional conference, and which by September threatened to explode in violence at any moment.[62]

In March 1963, further disagreements between KADU and KANU, this time prompted by the findings of the Regional Boundaries Commission, seemed ever more likely to push Kenya towards another civil war.[63] All had 'gone well up to now in difficult and tedious talks with Kenya Ministers', who accepted the then Secretary of State, Duncan Sandys', decisions on outstanding points of disagreement:

> However at the last moment KADU (D for DONKEY) [*sic*] Ministers are threatening to resign and to provoke riots and bloodshed unless KITALI district is transferred from the Rift region [*sic*] to the Western Region. It seems quite likely that ... [the commission] ... made a mistake ... But since both parties agreed in advance to accept the commission's findings and since some of its ...

> decisions went against KANU (N for NOBODY) it is extremely difficult for me to make a change without precipitating immediate resignation of KANU (N for NOBODY) Ministers, who are being as unhelpful as possible on this question.[64]

In the NFD, soon to be renamed the North Eastern Region, the ethnic Somali *shifta* rebels were being equally unhelpful.[65] Civil unrest during the fortnight or so before the announcement on the future of the area prompted the Kenya government to request that 70 Brigade, with British units in support, be placed on 12 hours' notice (Operation 'Instalment').[66] The ongoing fear that civil disturbances throughout Kenya might coincide with the commitment of most, if not all, of these units to the NFD, while the rest of the British troops in Kenya were earmarked for operations elsewhere, brought about the contextually novel situation whereby plans to reinforce the territory from Britain might have to be reactivated.[67] Once again, the shoestring was starting to pinch.

While the KADU-KANU feud threatened to explode in violence between the parties' 'Youth Wings' at any moment, any increase in Kikuyu subversion had to be taken very seriously.[68] Swann's recommendation to the Council of Ministers that the KLFA should be proscribed therefore served several purposes. Firstly, the determination of the colonial state to resist any illegal challenges would again be re-iterated, this time with the legitimacy apparently gained from the blessing of the elected African politicians. They, in turn, would be seen to be taking action against a subversive movement with which some of them may well have had links, certainly serving to distance them. Perhaps more important, given Britain's evolving political strategy, the proscription of KLFA provided Renison with the opportunity to press upon the African ministers the importance of dealing with security issues on a national and non-party-political (thus non-racial) basis, leading to a 'political truce'.[69] If matters were to get seriously out of hand subsequently, the British will to maintain security in Kenya until independence would not just rely on the 'longstop' of 24 Brigade, the reserve stationed at Kahawa. By March 1963, the British had prepared plans to 'reinforce Kenya for internal security purpose with a Brigade Group of up to three Infantry Battalions'.[70]

By June 1963, the formation of Kenyatta's 'well balanced' cabinet might well have allayed many British security fears, at least on the surface.[71] However, bitter rivalry between KADU and KANU continued, prompting Kenya government officials to act swiftly to remove the internal security portfolio from the Home Ministry to which communist-funded Odinga had been appointed. This reduced the ability of one of Kenyatta's main rivals to use his position to further his personal political ambitions, while reducing the KADU leaders' disquiet at the prospect of future communist interference with the nascent polity.[72]

In this context, Sandys' decision to press for 12 December 1963 as the date for Kenya's independence is significant. In putting his proposal to the Cabinet, Sandys explained

> that in the light of developments in recent weeks there was now a reasonable prospect that a Federation of Kenya, Uganda and Tanganyika would be established. Such a development would be welcome since, apart from the economic advantages, a Federation would tend to reduce the risk of tribal dissension in Kenya and to reinforce the position of other minority groups.[73]

Much earlier, Britain had hoped to be able to 'foster the concept of East African rather than territorial' defence.[74] Of course, a Federation would have facilitated such ends, as well as 'achieving stability' in the region.[75] Because of the apparent desire of the three governments to create the Federation by the end of the year, in order to retain their goodwill, and for procedural reasons, the British government could no longer put brakes on the transfer of power in Kenya. All that was now required was a conference in September to finalise the Constitution. However, the early realisation that the Federation would not materialise soon put an end to any hopes for that solution to Kenya's security problems, and Britain's defence requirements.

Despite ongoing efforts to repress the KLFA, including further denunciations from Kenyatta and attempts to stem the movement's infiltration of KANU with the arrests of 11 officials from the Naivasha and Gilgil branches of the party, it had continued to expand.[76] The landless and unemployed Kikuyu were just too viable a constituency, as evidenced by continued invasions of European farms, stock thefts and destruction of farm property.[77] In October 1963, at the end of the 'deadlocked' constitutional conference, the security situation seemed potentially more unstable than ever.[78] Sandys therefore decided to hedge his bets by supporting KANU's proposed centralist amendments to the Constitution, in the hope of minimising the 'danger of civil war and damage to British interests'.[79] Kenyatta had shown that he was moderate enough and, more importantly, would not countenance violent attempts to undermine the state.[80] In a sense, the erstwhile 'leader to darkness and death' had become Britain's 'man in Kenya'.

It follows that Kenyatta's position would be bolstered by the very fact of holding the reins of power of a strongly centralised government. All parties to the September/October 'Independence Conference', bar KADU, accepted KANU's proposals for strengthening the centralisation of control of the police. The newly-formed National Security Council would have powers to determine the maximum and minimum police establishments in the regions, while the Inspector-General of the Police (appointed by the centrally-controlled Police Service Commission) would enjoy 'sole responsibility' for all police postings. The Inspector-General would also be empowered to transfer 'sufficient Police officers' to any region that had not filed its minimum establishment, and without reference to that region's Law and Order Committee.[81]

In contrast to February 1962 (see p. 204), the British had also done their utmost to avoid 'forcing a split between the moderates and the extremists in the Government which might have strengthened Odinga's hand'.[82] While the British had not yet entirely abandoned the white settlers, they had wrested the mantle of 'gamekeeper' from KADU, gambling all on erstwhile 'poachers' KANU. Having sided with the Kenyatta faction before independence, Britain was not about to squander its political investment.

This was indeed a gamble. Only days before Sandys' decision to back KANU, preparations were made for a meeting of the British Cabinet to discuss contingency plans for a likely KADU backlash, including threats of civil war and secession. Concluding a brief on the subject, the Cabinet Secretary, Burke Trend, asked 'is there any risk that British troops will be required to support Kenyatta in repressing the KADU tribes who, on the whole, were our friends in the days of the Mau Mau troubles? There could be no more ironical conclusion to the history of our administration of Kenya.'[83]

Nevertheless, the likelihood of a violent response from KADU supporters to the KANU success, and British fears of civil disturbances beyond the capacity of the police and the KAR, prompted the Cabinet to instruct the C-in-C, Middle East Land Forces (MELF), General Sir Charles Harington, to make 24 Brigade available for internal security operations in Kenya.[84] He was also asked to consult with Renison's successor, Malcolm MacDonald, on the local plan for the evacuation of Europeans. 'It was, however, most important that no news of these consultations should reach Kenya Ministers, and the strictest security precautions should be taken to prevent this.'[85]

On 15 October 1963, following discussion of the problem, the Cabinet invited the Minister of Defence, Peter Thorneycroft, in consultation with Sandys, 'to examine, as a matter of urgency, the steps which should be taken if tribal warfare broke out in Kenya, with particular regard to the need to afford the maximum degree of protection to the Europeans in the Colony'.[86] On this point, the acting Governor, Griffith-Jones, reassured the Colonial Office that while 24 Brigade remained in Kenya 'there are adequate means of controlling any foreseeable security threat and protecting [the] European population in the same way as others, either locally or by concentration in safe areas, whence evacuation outside Kenya could be improvised, in the unlikely event of the need'.[87] It should be stressed that Griffith-Jones also explained that in preparation for what the Colonial Office termed 'Stage 3' (the likely withdrawal of 24 Brigade from Kenya at the end of 1964) plans should be drawn up for the subsequent introduction of British troops for the protection or evacuation of the European settlers.[88]

The policies of repression and targeted socio-economic engineering, along with strict control of the political process and the encouragement of moderate African politicians following the collapse of multi-racialism appeared to have worked. In the end, British troops were not required to restore order, well not yet anyway, and the temporary truce between KADU and KANU enabled an apparently smooth transition to independence. Yet, the early political history of Kenya shows that the socio-economic and ethnic divisions which were arguably both created and contained by the British colonial regime, were certainly not alleviated by decolonisation.

The British had been well aware of this problem in advance of independence. Although they had been seen to successfully devolve power to a moderate and stable African government, this was a close run thing indeed. The British were also aware of their luck in this matter. On the eve of independence MacDonald reported that there were 'a number of shafts of sunlight to illuminate the scene despite one or two thunder clouds ahead'.[89]

> On the other hand among the have-nots, especially among the Kikuyu in the Central Region and Nairobi there is increased activity, and organisation; although at present those with grievances lack leadership, it is to be feared this leadership may be forthcoming from among those political prisoners to be released under the independence amnesty, resulting in a growth of [a] more organised subversives movement. [...] In the North Eastern region unfortunately the horizon is uniformly black.[90]

Against this background, the victory of the 'moderates' in the KADU parliamentary group, the isolation of KADU 'extremists', the defection of four KADU MPs to KANU, and the 'very marked *détente* in KADU - KANU rivalry', seem all the more fortunate for the British government.[91] While Britain would no longer administer Kenya, as such, it did its utmost to ensure that Kenyatta would remain in power well beyond 1964, with a little inadvertent help, that is, from disaffected elements in the Kenya Rifles, Somali secessionists in the North Eastern region, and a certain Mr Odinga.

Preventing War: Insuring Kenya's 'Independence' and British 'Influence', 1963-5

On 19 December 1963, concern over ongoing *shifta* violence in Kenya's North Eastern Region prompted a far from optimistic assessment from

Thorneycroft. The Defence Minister informed Prime Minister Sir Alec Douglas-Home: 'I think you should know that, although Kenya is now independent, there remains a risk of our military involvement there.'[92] These were prescient words indeed. Although, in the first instance British troops were not called upon to repress the *shiftas*, nor the disgruntled KADU supporters, who had been mollified to some extent by the defection of four of their MPs to KANU; nor even the Kikuyu have-nots, as might have been expected. The threat from the militant dispossessed and ethnic Somali secessionists would be curtailed later by an arguably more subtle approach, so far as Britain was concerned, anyway.

In terms of the threat posed to the stability of the newly sovereign Kenyatta regime, the January 1964 'copycat' mutiny by the Kenya Rifles had very little real significance.[93] Far more importantly, the intervention of 24 Brigade to assist in quelling the revolt demonstrated in no uncertain terms that Kenya still relied upon British military *largesse*. This was especially important for Britain given the forthcoming defence and financial negotiations over the levels of military aid to be given in exchange for certain military 'facilities' (see next chapter). Equally important, given the far reaching implications for independent Kenya's future internal security, the *bonhomie* created by Kenyatta's independence amnesty for KLFA members still at large in the forests had begun to break down when it became clear to the ex-guerrillas and their supporters that free land was not part of the deal. The amnesty was brought to an end on 15 January, when the 'oxen ran out'. Moreover, the guerrillas had by no means surrendered in their entirety.[94]

On 23 January 1964, Kenyatta requested that British forces be authorised to intervene to help restore law and order, 'without prior reference to HMG' and apparently 'he wanted to make this fact public'. Britain wasted little time, with Sandys announcing the request openly the following day. On 25 January, 41 RM Commando was despatched as reinforcements, to arrive in Nairobi at 17:35 hrs.[95] British troops already in Kenya were assigned to assist the police in protecting 'key points', including the Kenya Broadcasting Station and Nairobi Airport. By 20:00 hrs, on 26 January, British troops had 'maintained their positions dominating Kenya Army units in the Nairobi area', and the Lanet Barracks of 11 Kenya Rifles, in Nakuru, was 'firmly under British control'.[96]

At the same time, in a seemingly desperate attempt to defuse the situation, Kenya Radio announced that Kenyatta's government would set up a commission to examine army grievances, and had decided to recruit an extra one thousand soldiers. This would be good news for the British Army Training Team (BATT), but there was a sting in the tail. All British officers in 'executive command appointments' would be replaced by Africans by the end of the year. To add to Britain's chagrin, following the successful conclusion of the operation to put down the mutiny, Kenyatta refused to make the required public pronouncement of gratitude. The 'old man' was fully aware of the political risks inherent in such a gesture, and even went so far as to question the 'scope of the consent he had given as to the limits of British troop movements in East Africa', which were in Kenya 'at present merely on sufferance until the new defence agreement was worked out'.[97] Britain's earlier contingency planning would have to come into its own. In the meantime, Kenyatta took steps to ensure stability within the Kenya Army by infiltrating all units with intelligence personnel. They would alert the government at the first hint of dissent within the ranks.[98]

Towards the end of January, in the wake of the East African mutinies, British officials began to consider whether more action should be taken to stabilise the local governments, and saw a renewed defensive and political opportunity. Perhaps the governments of the three countries might now be persuaded to co-operate in a 'joint defence force'? Of course, British officers would be made available for training and advice in setting up the force. 'Co-operation of this kind in the defence field might give new impetus to the proposals for a political federation (which should, if possible, include Zanzibar) which had been halted by the reluctance of the Uganda Government to take full part.'[99]

With a view to 'arresting the spread of Communism in this part of the world', given Britain's 'substantial financial and economic interests in East Africa', and 'for strategic reasons', there was 'clearly a strong case for' Britain 'responding to requests for either military or economic help from the Governments concerned'.[100] As the Defence and Oversea Policy (Official) Committee explained to ministers:

> In parallel with the training mission, special effort would have to be devoted, less obtrusively, to increased British assistance to local police forces and Special Branches. If an additional training mission for this purpose were accepted, it could work to some extent in parallel with the defence forces on the intelligence side and might assist in preventing a reoccurence [*sic*] of the recent type of trouble.[101]

Kenyatta was far from an innocent pawn in all of this, however, especially given the forthcoming detailed defence negotiations between British and Kenyan ministers and officials (see next chapter). Defence agreements tend, by their very nature, to be reciprocal affairs. The detailed defence negotiations had hardly concluded when Kenya's Prime Minister decided to test Britain's resolve to fulfil its side of the bargain. Much like the rest of Kenya, the North Eastern Region had not suddenly become peaceful at independence; far from it.[102] Following the murder of the brother of a Kenyan MP by *shifta* rebels on 1 April, Kenyatta decided to abandon his earlier 'restraint and compassion', and declared a State of Emergency in the trouble spot. He also instigated planning for an all out military assault to end the problem once and for all. Reminiscent of the British response following Waruhiu's assassination, it seems that it had now become 'very necessary' to 'destroy life' in the North Eastern Region after all, unlike the pre-independence pronouncements of less than six months before.[103]

However, with local forces thoroughly committed, this could only be done with the active participation of British forces, which Kenyatta requested on 2 April. This request went far beyond the 'technical and logistic support' provided by British troops to the Kenya Army, and had not formed part of the earlier agreement. Moreover, British troops were, at that very moment, being held in readiness for possible operations in Zanzibar. British officials were well aware, however, that Kenyatta 'may even demand it as an additional price for military facilities which we are in the process of negotiating'.[104]

Within a week of Kenyatta's request, political pressure on him had apparently diminished, allowing Britain to agree in principle, provided that Kenya made a 'specific request' as to the exact nature of the requirements for BLFK.[105] By May, the Kenya government had tabled such a plan. Given British diplomatic sensitivity to the reaction of Somalia, across the border, the scope of assistance was later refined. British troops would act only as a reserve, in support of the Kenya Army, and not in an offensive or 'spearhead' role, and certainly not on Somali soil. Unlike their role during the Mau Mau Emergency, RAF Shackletons would provide reconnaissance only. Also, Britain made a commitment to deliver more Ferret armoured cars to the Kenya forces 'soon'.

In return for this assistance, the Kenya government was expected to 'abandon the more repressive and unpalatable features of the operation (e.g. Evacuation [*sic*] from Isiolo area and polluting wells) and agree to sincere negotiations with Somali Government thereafter'.[106] Britain also hoped that by agreeing to provide this assistance it might enlist Kenyatta's endorsement of British operations against rebel tribesmen in the Radfan area of Southern Arabia. Kenya's request for troop-lifting helicopters would, however, be rejected.[107]

With the defence agreement as good as secure, and the stability of Kenya's frontiers reasonably assured, Britain still had work to do to safeguard Kenyatta's position at the head of it all. On 14 July, Kenyatta was assaulted during his visit to London to attend a meeting of Commonwealth Prime Ministers, causing considerable irritation and embarrassment to the British government.[108] Although perhaps a little negligent in their own back yard, so to speak, British ministers could not afford to risk allowing a far more serious, possibly fatal attack on Kenyatta in his home country.

In line with earlier commitments, by the time Kenya had become a Republic on 12 December 1964, Britain had already set about training a Kenyan Special Force Unit.[109] As an SAS officer explained to Labour's Secretary of State for Defence, Denis Healey:

> The aim of the Special Force Unit is to provide a bodyguard for the President and to act as a counter revolutionary force. SAS observations are that both these requirements, because of the political situation in the country and what could develop in the next few years, are necessary if stability and continuity of government is to be assured. Because the armed forces are not trusted, and there are efforts to infiltrate them by people trained in communist countries, this Special Force Unit is to be recruited from the Kenya Police Force.[110]

The rationale underpinning such decisions had received early impetus, and was soon vindicated. Towards the end of 1964, Kenya's Special Branch, 'with the enthusiastic assistance of British and American intelligence' warned Kenyatta of a possible communist-backed *coup d'état*.[111] On 4 April 1965, Kenya's Attorney General, Charles Njonjo, warned MacDonald of reports that Odinga and his associates might attempt to seize power that month. Kenyatta hoped that Britain would send some Royal Navy ships to the area under the guise of a routine exercise. Ironically, if the need were to arise, Kenya's President would also ask for the intervention of British troops from Aden![112] While the despatch of an empty commando carrier to Mombasa was facilitated quickly, before agreeing that troops could be sent Britain required assurances from Kenyatta that 'Kenyan forces of suspect loyalty' would be kept away from Nairobi, and that British forces would not be required in a primary offensive role. 'Our troops cannot "reconquer" Kenya for President Kenyatta, nor should they become involved in protracted operations against rebels.'[113]

Having done the utmost to ensure that international opinion might remain as favourable as possible in the event of renewed British military intervention, Britain also made some rather more secretive arrangements. The brief for the SAS team was that they would be authorised, without prior reference, to intervene 'in collaboration with their GSU friends' to protect Kenyatta and certain key ministers against assassination.[114] While the assassination of Odinga's chief adviser, the radical Asian, Pio Gama Pinto, and the seizure of a cache of arms from Odinga's headquarters minimised the immediate risk of a *coup* taking place, Britain realised that plans for intervention would have to be refined for the mid- to long-term.[115] Ironically, internal dissent in Kenya had provided Britain with legitimate cause for future military intervention, negating earlier plans for the introduction of troops to assist in the evacuation of British citizens and subjects, and those of 'certain other Commonwealth countries'.[116]

Britain was also finally beginning to learn the oft-neglected internal security maxim that 'prevention is better than cure'. This notion had already underpinned the provision of British finance to the Kenya government and Kenya Land Bank for the purchase of European farms for resettlement by Africans.[117] By satisfying some Africans' 'land hunger' to a certain extent and helping to stabilise Kenya's economy, at least the causes of unrest would be reduced. Barbara Castle, the Labour government's Minister for Overseas Development, was certainly alive to this necessity. By the end of 1964, the Kenya government had proposed an extension of the 'Million Acres Scheme', but not with the sub-division of European-owned land into smaller plots. Rather, these farms would be sold as going concerns. This, it was thought, would help to stabilise Kenya's economy and by extension would, of course, enhance Anglo-Kenyan trading relations. In order to finance the new land settlement scheme, Britain would have to grant a further £30 million in aid to Kenya, incrementally by 1970.

While the increasingly dissatisfied European expatriates looked for British assistance to help them to leave Kenya, Britain was more concerned by the possible economic upheaval which might ensue if aid were not forthcoming. As Castle, who admittedly had never been a friend of the settlers, put it:

> Moreover, the continued presence of so many British settlers in Kenya is an embarrassment to us. Scattered in the countryside they constitute a serious potential security risk which could develop into another Stanleyville situation. Their presence already inhibits our freedom in conducting our relations with Kenya and if things threaten to go seriously wrong with Kenya they would be hostages to fortune. [...] Unless a new scheme is announced to follow on after the present million acre scheme has finished I believe there will be a risk of a serious political situation arising with grave consequences for the Kenya economy.[118]

In the summer of 1963, Britain had already begun to assess the likelihood of hostile competition for influence in developing countries. The Foreign Office Information Research Department (IRD) had circulated a paper on the scope, nature, and objectives of communist economic and technical aid overseas. In 1964, Kenya was known to have accepted $62.5 million in aid ($18.1m. from China, and $44.4m. from the USSR), but had drawn $1.5 million only.[119] To counteract the possible effectiveness of this aid with regard to the extent of influence that it might buy for the communist bloc, Britain's future policy would be to continue to support Kenyatta and the other 'moderates' in the event that he should cease, for whatever reason, to be President. On 14 April 1965, Kenyatta had again demonstrated the right credentials, when he rejected a shipment of Soviet arms apparently bound for Odinga. In a sense, the latter proved to be more of an asset to the British government than it would have liked to admit. The old policy of 'divide and rule' continued to retain some, albeit new-fangled, relevance.[120]

Having outlined the extent of financial and military support that Britain was prepared to offer the Kenyatta regime it remains to consider the manner in which the former suzerain aimed to ensure that 'hostile influences' might be dissipated. As we have seen, Britain was not only prepared to intervene militarily and to provide support for Kenya's armed forces and police in order to minimise direct communist interference. Financial constraints had forced Britain into a situation in which far more subtle tactics would be required.[121] As the Cabinet Counter-Subversion Committee's recommendations reveal, Britain would continue,

> but with great discretion and flexibility, our factual and overt information services and contacts; improve BBC reception if we can; and pursue the IRD's covert programmes; and find ways of training and influencing Kenyan journalists; [...] go as far as we can, in considering the Stamp Mission Report, towards helping the Kenya Government's land settlement programme, which will be vital to the Government's future; [...] be as flexible as possible in maintaining expatriates in Government service, whether as executives or advisers; [...] avoid embarrassing Kenya by introducing "cold war" issues; [...] show relaxation and understanding in [the] face of occasional outbreaks of African nationalist feeling; and discourage the element of unhealthy sensationalism in the interest shown by the British press in Kenyan affairs[!][122]

British ministers and security advisers had long been well aware that a great deal of influence in maintaining independent Kenya's internal stability would be gained by training Kenyan military officers in Britain. In September 1965, the Counter-Subversion Committee began to consider the importance of the role of service attachés and defence advisers in carrying out 'counter subversion work with foreign armies': 'this might have an effect on the allocation of posts and particularly on the selection and training of individual Attaches [*sic*]'.[123] Clearly, these appointments had to be filled by the right types of individual, 'suitably qualified Officers who will also require detailed political guidelines'. While precise evidence of the 'scope and nature' of the activities of British military attachés in Kenya remains scarce, their 'objectives' were all too clear.

At the level of overt intervention, in 1971, yet another attempted *coup* was put down with the assistance of British troops.[124] Kenya continued to send members of its armed forces for training in Britain, and to receive British military personnel in 'training and advisory' roles, albeit in gradually decreasing numbers, at least until 1976.[125] By then, British involvement in independent Kenya had diminished, with the baton being taken up by

Britain's senior partner in the fight for the preservation of western global interests, the United States. That Britain had laid the foundations for this must surely be beyond dispute.

Kenyatta had naturally played his own part in securing his political position, by first dismantling the *majimbo* state and then forming the Republic at the end of 1964.[126] Next, the post of KANU Vice President was abolished, precipitating Odinga's resignation from the government, and his formation of the Kenya People's Union (KPU). With Odinga's faction effectively neutralised following the 1966 'little general election', thereby heralding the 'dominant party state', Kenyatta's fiefdom was politically secure.[127] In January 1965, following Kenyatta's second amnesty offer to the remaining KLFA guerrillas, which was largely ignored, the police began a major offensive against the leaders in the forests, and killed them all.[128] There could have been 'no more ironical' beginnings to the history of the administration of independent Kenya.

Conclusion

Throughout colonial Kenya's history, Britain's wider interests and global competition had dictated, as with most states, that its administrative and political structures should be secured by the build up of security forces and the occasional resort to arms. The greater the threat to the state, as with the 'Mau Mau revolution', the more massive the force employed. With the political climate apparently moderated by Kenyatta's rehabilitation, and the circumstances ripe for the withdrawal of formal British administration, Britain did all in its power to bolster Kenya's independence. By arming the Kenyatta state Britain ensured that future threats to Kenya's stability could be dealt with by largely 'political' means. The iron fist of the government's legitimate monopoly of the use of force was nonetheless wrapped firmly within the velvet glove of effective one-party democracy. President Moi was hardly the first exponent of *nyayoism*. Kenyatta had British footsteps to follow.

The next chapter will examine one of the key motives that underpinned Britain's political and security policy in Kenya from the ending of the Emergency to beyond independence: the hitherto largely neglected defence aspects of decolonisation. This contributes to a more complete picture of British decolonisation in Kenya, and surely must have implications for our understanding of Britain's transfers of power to its colonies elsewhere.

Notes

1. CO 822/1348, 'Extract from "Kenya Calling" [Kenya government Public Relations Department Newsletter]', 25 July 1959; Darwin, *Britain and*

Decolonisation, pp. 244-69, 'British Decolonization since 1945', pp. 202-5; Holland, *European Decolonization*, pp. 241-2; Lapping, *End of Empire*, p. 435.

2. Alistair Horne, *Macmillan 1957-1986* (New York: Viking, 1989), pp. 174-6; Richard Lamb, *The Macmillan Years 1957-1963: The Emerging Truth* (London: John Murray, 1995), pp. 60, 223-4, 237-40, 241-2, 244; Maloba, *Mau Mau and Kenya*, pp. 155-6 John Turner, *Macmillan* (London: Longman, 1994), p. 187-8.

3. Bennett, *Kenya: A Political History*, pp. 144, 147; Murphy 'Lennox-Boyd at the Colonial Office', p. 6.

4. Murphy, *Party Politics*, p. 179.

5. CO 822/1230, Baring to Lennox-Boyd, 28 Sept. 1959.

6. Ibid., telegram 225, Webber (Colonial Office) to Griffith-Jones (Nairobi), 16 Sept. 1959.

7. Ibid., telegram 934, Griffith-Jones to Webber, 17 Sept. 1959.

8. Ibid.

9. CO 822/1819, 'Future Policy in East Africa: Memorandum by the Secretary of State for the Colonies', n.d. (c. Jan. 1959); Darwin, *Britain and Decolonisation*, pp. 244-69, 'British Decolonization since 1945', pp. 202-5; Holland, *European Decolonization*, pp. 241-2; Lapping, *End of Empire*, p. 435.; Murphy 'Lennox-Boyd at the Colonial Office', p. 6.

10. CO 822/1861, Lennox-Boyd to Baring, 26 March 1959, cited in Murphy 'Lennox-Boyd at the Colonial Office', p. 6.

11. CO 822/1230, transcript of speech by Renison to Legislative Council, 10 Nov. 1959.

12. CO 822/2091, Colonial Office minute by Hull, 31 Dec. 1959.

13. CAB 134/1202, CA (56) 18 'Powers of Colonial Governors to Preserve Order. Note by the Lord President of the Council', 16 May 1956.

14. CAB 134/1201, CA (56) 33rd Conclusions, 23 July 1956, CAB 134/1202, CA (56) 21, 'Powers of Colonial Governors to Preserve Order', memo. by Lennox-Boyd, 31 May 1956. Lennox-Boyd had earlier experience of the problems referred to by Salisbury. In July 1955 the Governor of Cyprus, Sir Robert Armitage, had pressed the Colonial Secretary to allow him to declare a State of Emergency in order to deal with the Greek-Cypriot EOKA (*Ethniki Organosis Kuprion Agoniston* - National Organisation of Cypriot Fighters) insurgents. But this might prejudice forthcoming negotiations with the Greek and Turkish governments over the future of the island, as well as being seen to be a prejudicial act in itself. The London negotiations and subsequent talks broke down over a combination of issues, including self-determination for the island, *Enosis* (union with Greece), and the complexities surrounding Britain's relationship with Turkey in the Baghdad Pact. Only following the replacement of Armitage by Field Marshall Sir John Harding, the Chief of the Imperial General Staff, with experience of

counter-insurgency in Malaya and Kenya, and the clear lack of either ability or desire of the police to restore order did the British Cabinet accept that a State of Emergency should be declared, as occurred on 26 Nov. 1955, David M. Anderson, 'Policing and communal conflict: the Cyprus Emergency, 1954-60', in Anderson and Killingray, *Policing and Decolonisation*, pp. 187-98, Murphy, *Alan Lennox-Boyd*, pp. 114-23.

15. CAB 134/1556, CPC (57) 38, 'Powers of Colonial Governors to Preserve Order', memo. by Lennox-Boyd, 20 Dec. 1957.

16. CAB 134/1558, CPC (59) 5, 'Security Powers of Colonial Governors', memo. by Lennox-Boyd, 9 June 1959.

17. Ibid., CPC (59) 2nd Meeting, 18 June 1959.

18. Ibid., CPC (59) 3rd Meeting, 1 July 1959.

19. Edgerton, *Mau Mau*, pp. 198-9; *Report of the Committee on Emergency Detention Camps: Special Supplement to the Kenya Gazette of 1st September 1959*, (R.D. Fairn, Chairman), Aug. 1959. The 'Fairn Committee' was appointed by Macmillan in the wake of the Hola murders.

20. CO 822/1230, telegram 1054, Renison to W.B.L. Monson (Colonial Office), 26 Oct. 1959.

21. CAB 134/1558, CPC (59) 5th Meeting, 5 Nov. 1959. See also: CAB 128/33, CC (59) 57th Meeting, Item 2, 'Kenya', 10 Nov. 1959.

22. CAB 134/1558, CPC (59) 19, 'Kenya: Proposed Act of Grace', memo. by Macleod, 3 Nov. 1959.

23. Ibid.

24. CAB 133/151, AT (GH) 18, 'Prime Minister's Visit to Africa January 1960: Jomo Kenyatta', brief by the Colonial Office, 31 Dec. 1959, fo. 2, para. 4.

25. For details, see: CO 968/693, CO 968/694, CO 968/695, and CO 968/696.

26. Murphy, *Party Politics*, p. 181.

27. CAB 128/34, CC (60) 1st Conclusions, 4 Jan. 1960.

28. Ibid., CC (60) 2nd Conclusions, 18 Jan. 1960.

29. Ibid., CC (60) 11th Conclusions, 22 Feb. 1960.

30. CO 968/696, Gorell Barnes to Baring, 25 March 1959. See also: CO 822/1819, fo. 77.

31. Ibid.

32. DEFE 7/1014, Gorell Barnes to A.D. Peck (Treasury), 11 May 1959.

33. Harold Macmillan, *Pointing the Way, 1959-61* (London: Macmillan, 1972), p. 132.

34. David Goldsworthy, *Tom Mboya: The Man Kenya Wanted to Forget* (Nairobi, London: Heinemann, 1982), pp. 135-9; Kyle, *Politics of Independence*, p. 108.

35. Edgerton, *Mau Mau*, p. 214.

36. CAB 134/1560, CPC (61) 12th Meeting, 'Kenya', 16 Nov. 1961.

37. CO 822/2024, SC (60) 18, 'Civil Disobedience', memo. by the ISWC, 12 May 1960.

38. Bennett, *Kenya: A Political History*, p. 148.

39. Ibid., p. 152; Murphy, 'Lennox-Boyd at the Colonial Office', p. 7.

40. CAB 134/1353, minutes of the Africa (Official) Committee, AF (59) 3rd Meeting, 'The Next Ten Years in Africa: East Africa', 28 Jan. 1959, AF (59) 5, 'Prospects for the African Territories for Which the Colonial Office is Responsible', memo. by the Colonial Office, (c. 6-9) Jan. 1959, fos. 2, 4-6, paras. 4, 6-8.

41. Edgerton, *Mau Mau*, p. 207; Harold Macmillan, *At the End of the Day, 1961-63* (London: Macmillan, 1973), pp. 286-94.

42. Edgerton, *Mau Mau*, p. 207.

43. DEFE 5/105, COS (60) 232, 'Exercise KERRY BLUE', 24 Aug. 1960.

44. CO 822/2024, SC (60) 18, 'Civil Disobedience', 12 May 1960.

45. Ibid., 'Extract from Minutes of the Security Council Advisory to the Governor', 31 May 1960.

46. Edgerton, *Mau Mau*, pp. 215-6; Füredi, *Mau Mau War*, pp. 161, 175, 176, 177, 179-80, 182-6, 187, 190-1, 192-3, 198-9, 200; Kanogo, *Squatters and the Roots of Mau Mau*, pp. 6, 148-9, 164-9, 171-3, 174; Odinga, *Not Yet Uhuru*, p. 221.

47. Füredi, *Mau Mau War*, loc. cit.; Kanogo, *Squatters and the Roots of Mau Mau*, loc. cit.

48. Füredi, *Mau Mau War*, p. 193: 'The movement of landless Kikuyu did not initiate any violent actions, much less did it engage in subversion. Large numbers of Kikuyu were oathed, but the KLFA had no perspective of armed struggle or "civil war" as suggested in government propaganda. During the course of events a number of loyal headmen and newly established African landowners were assaulted but these acts were not part of any systematic campaign. [...] To ascertain the reasons for the arrest of nearly one thousand Kikuyu for KLFA activities in 1962, the Daily Crime and Incident Reports of the Kenya Police were consulted for that year. Of these reports only one, occurring on 15 September, deals with an incident which could be interpreted as the use of force against authority ...'

49. Edgerton, *Mau Mau*, p. 209.

50. CO 822/2024, telegram 107, Renison to Macleod. 1 Feb. 1961, telegram CAPCOS 3, C-in-C, HQ British Forces Arabian Peninsula, to Admiral of the Fleet Earl Mountbatten of Burma, the Chief of the Defence Staff (CDS), 4 Feb. 1961, telegrams 982/OPS, Force Nairobi to War Office (MO 4), 'OP PROPHESY Sitrep 1', 13 Feb. 1961, 229/OPS, 'Sitrep 2', 20 Feb. 1961, 468/OPS, 'Sitrep 3', 27 Feb. 1961, 704/OPS, 'Sitrep 4', 3 March

1961, 'Minutes of 2nd Meeting of the Security Council Advisory to the Governor' 2 Feb. 1961. 'The Security Council advised that ... the Secretary to the Cabinet should replace the Minister without Portfolio as Chairman of the Economic Priorities Committee', thereby removing the possibility of African political interference with the post.

51. DEFE 5/110, COS (61) 26, 'Major Exercises 1961/62', 27 Jan. 1961, COS (61) 39, 'Major Exercises 1961/62', 6 Feb. 1961.

52. CAB 134/1358, AF (61) 9, 'Political Situation in East and Central Africa', note by the secretaries to the Africa (Official) Committee, 7 April 1961, with attached JIC (61) 23 (Final), 'Background to the Political Situation in British Territories in East and Central Africa', report by the JIC, 23 March 1961.

53. CO 822/2114, KIC/K/7 (14) 'The Kenya Land Freedom Army', Appreciation by the KIC, 21 July 1961, and attachment to KIC/K/7 (14), 'A Note on the Kenya Land Freedom Army', July 1961.

54. Ibid., 'A Note on the Kenya Land Freedom Army', July 1961, fo. 4.

55. Ibid., CM (61) 559, 'The Kenya Land Freedom Army', memo. by A.C.C. Swann (Minister for Defence, Nairobi), 28 July 1961.

56. Kyle, 'End of Empire', p. 13; CAB 134/1560, CPC (61) 10th Meeting, Item 2, 'Kenyatta', 19 July 1961; CAB 128/35 (II), CC (61) 44th Meeting, Item 5, 'Kenya: Jomo Kenyatta', 27 July 1961.

57. Edgerton, *Mau Mau*, p. 211.

58. CO 822/2114, CM (61) 559, 'The Kenya Land Freedom Army', 28 July 1961.

59. Apparently, in late 1958, Special Branch had appealed to Baring for Kenyatta's release. Some (unspecified) Special Branch officers shared Grogan's view that 'Kenya's politics would be in turmoil as long as Kenyatta remained a martyr in prison'. There is even some evidence which suggests that some of these 'police intelligence officers' did their utmost to ensure that Kenyatta would be convicted at Kapenguria 'because his imprisonment would make him an irresistible symbol for Africans; after his release he could be relied on as a "safe" leader from the British point of view'. It seems that Baring rejected the request, claiming that Kenyatta 'could never be set free'. See: Edgerton, *Mau Mau*, p. 211.

60. RHL, MSS Afr s 2159, Manby papers, 'The Links between Kikuyu Subversion and KANU', report by Manby, 18 Oct. 1962, box 2, file 3, fo. 126, paras. 10-1 (emphasis added). Apparently, Odinga fulfilled 'the main KLFA criteria for a non-Kikuyu' because they believed that he supported many of their aims, particularly the expulsion of all Europeans, and appeared ready to 'concede to the Kikuyu the dominant place in a future Kenya', ibid., fo. 124, para. 3.

61. CO 822/2114, 'Subversive Tendencies Among the Kikuyu: A Review of the Period 1st Feb. - 22nd Sept. 1962', Office of the Director of Intelligence (Manby), 27 Sept. 1962, CMM (62) 258, 'Kenya Land Freedom Army', memo. by Swann, 28 Sept. 1962.

62. CAB 134/1561, CPC (62) 4th Meeting, Item 4, 'Kenya', 16 Feb. 1962; CAB 128/36 (I), CC (62) 20th Meeting, Item 4, 'Kenya', 8 March 1962, CC (62) 22nd Meeting, Item 4, 'Kenya', 20 March 1962, CC (62) 25th Meeting, Item 7, 'Kenya', 30 March 1962, CC (62) 26th Meeting, Item 4, 'Kenya: Constitutional Conference', 5 April 1962; Bennett, *Kenya: A Political History*, p. 157.

63. Kyle, *Politics of Independence*, pp. 169-71.

64. DEF 13/297, SOSCRO No. 80, Tel. 1a, Sandys to Macmillan, Earl of Home (Foreign Secretary), Thorneycroft, and Lord Lansdowne (Minister of State, Colonial Office), 7 March 1963.

65. CAB 134/1561, CPC (62) 9, 'Kenya Constitutional Conference: Future of the Northern Frontier District', joint memo. by Lord Home (Foreign Secretary) and Maudling, 26 Feb. 1962, CPC (62) 5th Meeting, Item 1, 'Kenya: Future of the Northern Frontier District', 2 March 1962, CPC (62) 7th Meeting, Item 3, 'Kenya: Future of the Northern Frontier District', 5 April 1962.

66. DEFE 13/297, OCS 357/8/3/63, 'Operational Co-ordinating Section brief for Week-End 9/10 March 1963: Kenya (Northern Frontier District)', OCS 357/22/3/63, 'Operational Co-ordinating Section brief for Week-End 23/24 March 1963: Somali and Kenya Northern Frontier District.'

67. Ibid., 'Internal Security in Kenya', minute by Mountbatten for Thorneycroft' 14 Feb. 1963.

68. Edgerton, *Mau Mau*, p. 214.

69. CO 822/2114, 'Extracts from the Minutes of the 44th Meeting of the Kenya Council of Ministers: 472. The KLFA', 4 Oct. 1962; Immediate, Secret Telegram 714, Renison to Sandys, 24 Oct. 1962.

70. PREM 11/4328, brief by Thorneycroft, for Macmillan, 7 March 1963.

71. CO 822/3053, 'Extract from East African Defence Committee Minutes of 25th Meeting', 9 May 1963.

72. Ibid., telegram 338, MacDonald to Sandys, 8 June 1963; Edgerton, *Mau Mau*, p. 227.

73. CAB 128/37, CC (63) 41st Conclusions, 24 June 1963; Kyle, 'End of Empire', pp. 24-6.

74. CO 822/1813, EAC (57) 6 (Final), 'Defence, Police, and Internal Security', paper for the conference of East African governors, n.d. (c. Sept.-Oct. 1957), fo. 2.

75. CAB 134/1560, CPC (61) 1st Meeting, Item 2, 'Colonial Problems, 1961', 5 Jan. 1961, fo. 6, para. 2.

76. CO 822/3053, CMM (63) 36, 'Law and Order Report No. 7', memo. by Swann, 19 Jan. 1963; Füredi, *Mau Mau War*, pp. 188-9.

77. CAB 128/38 (I), CM (63) 7th Meeting, 'Kenya: Land Settlement', 21 Nov. 1963; CAB 129/115, CP (63) 18, 'The Future of European Farming Land in Kenya', memo. by Sandys, 19 Nov. 1963, and Annex thereto, 'An Appreciation by the Director of Intelligence on the Security Situation in the Nyandarua District of the Central Region with Particular Reference to Land Settlement', Special Branch HQ, Nairobi, 28 Oct. 1963.

78. PREM 11/4328, 'Kenya', brief by Burke Trend for R.A.B. Butler (First Secretary of State), 14 Oct. 1963.

79. Ibid.; CAB 128/37, CC (63) 58th Meeting, Item 2, 'Kenya', 3 Oct. 1963; CC (63) 59th Meeting, Item 1, 'Kenya', 8 Oct. 1963, CC (63) 60th Meeting, Item 3, 'Kenya', 15 Oct. 1963; Kyle, 'End of Empire', pp. 26-7. See also: CAB 130/192, Cabinet *ad hoc* Committee, 'Kenya', 17 Oct. 1963; CAB 148/15, Cabinet Defence and Oversea Policy Committee, DOP (63) 1st Meeting, Item 1, 'Kenya', 18 Oct. 1963; and CAB 128/38 (I), CM (63) 1st Meeting, Item 5, 'Kenya', 22 Oct. 1963.

80. Füredi, *Mau Mau War*, pp. 188-9; Maloba, *Mau Mau and Kenya*, pp. 164-6.

81. CAB 133/215, KIC (63) 2, 'Kenya Independence Conference, 1963: Amendments to be made to the Present Constitution for Independence', Annex K, 'The Police Force', 25 Sept. 1963; Odinga, *Not Yet Uhuru*, pp. 238-40.

82. Kyle, *Politics of Independence*, p. 179.

83. PREM 11/4328, 'Kenya', brief, 14 Oct. 1963.

84. CAB 148/15, DOP (63) 1st Meeting, Item 1, 18 Oct. 1963.

85. Ibid.; CO 822/3054, 'OPERATIONAL IMMEDIATE, UK EYES ONLY, Telegram COSMID 99, Exclusive', Mountbatten (CDS) to Harington, 18 Oct. 1963.

86. CAB 128/37, CC (63) 60th Conclusions, 15 Oct. 1963. See also: CO 822/3289.

87. CO 822/3053, telegram 575, Griffith-Jones to Webber, 11 Oct. 1963.

88. Ibid. (Stage 1: the period up to independence. Stage 2: the period between independence and the departure of 24 Brigade.) Reinforcement plans had been in existence for several years, of course, and were reviewed again in March 1963 during the possible furore over the Regional Boundary Commission's findings: PREM 11/4328, Thorneycroft to Macmillan, 7 March 1963. See also: DEFE 13/297, 'Evacuation Plans - Kenya', minute by D.S.S. O'Connor (VCDS), 14 Oct. 1963.

89. CO 822/3055, telegram 946, MacDonald (Governor of Kenya) to Sandys (Secretary of State, Colonial and Commonwealth Relations Office), 6 Dec. 1963.

90. Ibid.

91. CO 822/3053, telegram 721, Griffith-Jones to Sandys, 24 Oct. 1963; MacDonald, *Titans and Others*, p. 266.

92. PREM 11/4889, Thorneycroft to Douglas-Home, 19 Dec. 1963.

93. For brief references to the January 1964 mutiny, see: Blaxland, *The Regiments Depart*, pp. 416-8; Darby, *British Defence Policy East of Suez*, p. 238; Edgerton, *Mau Mau*, pp. 223-4; Gertzel *et al* (eds.), *Government and Politics in Kenya*, (Nairobi: EAPH, 1969), pp. 562-3; W.F. Gutteridge, *The Military in African Politics* (London: Metheun, 1969), pp. 24-40, 126-40; Leys, *Underdevelopment in Kenya*, pp. 238-9; Kyle, *Politics of Independence*, p. 198; James Lunt, *Imperial Sunset: Frontier Soldiering in the 20th Century* (London: Macdonald, 1981), pp. 242-3; William R. Ochieng', 'Structural and Political Changes', in Ogot and Ochieng', *Decolonization and Independence in Kenya*, p. 93; Throup, 'Crime, politics and the police', p. 154.

94. Edgerton, *Mau Mau*, pp. 221-2, 223.

95. PREM 11/4889, 'East Africa Situation Report No. 20 - Prepared by the Defence Operations Staff - Situation up to 0600Z 24th January, 1964', 'East Africa Situation Report No. 21 - [...] - Situation up to 0600Z 25th January, 1964'; CAB 148/1, DO (64) 3rd Meeting, 'East Africa', 23 Jan. 1964. See also: CAB 128/38 (II), CM (64) 6th Meeting, Item 2, 'Foreign Affairs', 23 Jan. 1964.

96. PREM 11/4889, 'East Africa Situation Report No. 22 - [...] - Situation up to 2000Z 25th January, 1964', 'East Africa Situation Report No. 23 - [...] - Situation up to 2000Z 26th January, 1964'; CAB 148/1, DO (64) 4th Meeting, Item 1, 'East Africa', 28 Jan. 1964.

97. PREM 11/4889, telegram 246, Sir Geoffrey de Freitas (British High Commissioner, Kenya) to Sandys, 29 Jan. 1964; Kyle, *Politics of Independence*, p. 198. For Kenyatta's statement on the Kenya Army mutiny, in which no reference is made to assistance from British troops, see *Kenya News Agency Handout No. 127*, reprinted in: Gertzel *et al* (eds.), *Government and Politics in Kenya*, pp. 562-3.

98. Edgerton, *Mau Mau*, p. 224.

99. CAB 148/4, DO (O) (64) 1st Meeting, 'East Africa', 29 Jan. 1964.

100. CAB 148/1, DO (64) 9, 'The Policy Implications of Developments in East Africa', note by the Chairman of the Defence and Oversea Policy (Official) Committee', 4 Feb. 1964. See also: CAB 128/38 (II), CM (64) 7th Meeting, Item 2, 'East Africa', 28 Jan. 1964.

101. CAB 148/1, DO (64) 9, 'The Policy Implications of Developments in East Africa', 4 Feb. 1964, fo. 2, para. 9. See also: ibid., DO (64) 6th Meeting, Item 3, 'East Africa', 5 Feb. 1964; CAB 148/4, DO (O) (64) 3, 'Draft Report on Policy Implications of Developments in East Africa', 31 Jan. 1964 ('British information activities should be organised on a scale

sufficient to overcome any local prejudice against our renewed involvement in East African affairs and to enlist popular support for our policies'); CAB 148/4, DO (O) (64) 2nd Meeting, 'East Africa', 3 Feb. 1964 ('It was to our advantage to maintain the present moderate leaders in power and to provide them with all possible military and governmental support'); CAB 148/1, DO (64) 10th Meeting, Item 3, 'East Africa', 26 Feb. 1964.

102. Kyle, *Politics of Independence*, pp. 156-8, 170-1, 178, 183-4, 190, 198.

103. Edgerton, *Mau Mau*, pp. 218, 223.

104. PREM 11/4889, telegram 661, de Freitas to Sandys, 2 April 1964, brief by P. Rogers (Colonial Office) for Douglas-Home, 2 April 1964, telegram 696, de Freitas to Sandys, 8 April 1964; CAB 148/1, DO (64) 17th Meeting, Item 4, 'Kenya', 8 April 1964.

105. DEFE 13/333, telegram COSMID 117, Mountbatten to Harington, 7 April 1964.

106. PREM 11/4889, telegram 996, de Freitas to Sandys, 29 May 1964. See also CAB 148/6, DO (O) (64) 43, 'Commonwealth Prime Ministers' Meeting - Brief on "The Main Defence Issues"', memo. by the MoD, 12 June 1964, fo. 4, para. 13.

107. CAB 148/1, DO (64) 25th Meeting, Item 3, 'Kenya', 3 June 1964, DO (64) 48, 'Air Support for Kenya Forces', memo. by Sandys, 1 June 1964. Documentary evidence of the full extent of active British participation in Kenya's North Eastern Region is difficult to come by. From the few secondary sources which discuss the subject, it is possible to deduce that some form of direct British military involvement took place their at least until near the end of 1964. See: Anthony Clayton, *Frontiersmen: Warfare in Africa since 1950* (London: UCL Press, 1999), pp. 110-1; Gertzel *et al* (eds.), *Government and Politics in Kenya*, pp. 572-3; Page, *KAR*, pp. 236-7.

108. CAB 128/38 (II), CM (64) 38th Meeting, Item 5, 'Public Order', 16 July 1964.

109. Ken Connor, *Ghost Force: The Secret History of the SAS* (London: Weidenfeld & Nicolson, 1998), pp. 106-7; Tony Geraghty, *Who Dares Wins: The Story of the SAS 1950-1980* (London: Fontana, 1981 [1980]), p. 122.

110. DEFE 25/121, Maj. J.D. Slim (22 SAS, Hereford) to Denis Healey (Defence Secretary), 1 Feb. 1965. For an explanation of the role of the GSU (from which the Special Force Unit was recruited) given on 13 July 1965, by Kenya's Assistant Minister for Internal Security and Defence, Argwings-Kodhek, see: Gertzel *et al* (eds.), *Government and Politics in Kenya*, p. 559. See also: Throup, 'Crime, politics and the police', p. 154.

111. Edgerton, *Mau Mau*, p. 227.

112. DEFE 25/121, telegram 591, MacDonald (High Commissioner, Kenya) to A. Bottomley (Secretary of State, Commonwealth Relations Office), 5 April 1965.

113. Ibid., 'Defence and Oversea Policy Committee - Kenya - (To be raised orally by Commonwealth Secretary)', unattributed brief for Healey, n.d. (c. April 1965).

114. Ibid., telegram 620, MacDonald to Bottomley, 9 April 1965.

115. CAB 148/18, OPD (65) 21st Meeting, Item 7, 'Kenya', 12 April 1965; Bloch and Fitzgerald, *British Intelligence and Covert Action*, pp. 154-5. For details of the scope of the planned operation, see: DEFE 5/158, COS 78/65, 'Military Assistance to Kenya', 13 April 1965; DEFE 5/159, COS 100/65, 'British Military Assistance to Kenya', 26 May 1965; DEFE 25/121, 'Annex A to COS 100/65', 26 May 1965; Edgerton, *Mau Mau*, p. 227; Odinga, *Not Yet Uhuru*, pp. 292-3.

116. CAB 148/4, DO (O) (64) 17th Meeting, Item 4, 'Planning for the Introduction of British Forces into Certain Territories', 29 July 1964; CAB 148/7, DO (O) (64) 60, 'Planning for the Introduction of British Forces into Certain Territories', note by the MoD, 15 July 1964.

117. CAB 148/2, DO (64) 73, 'European Farms in Kenya', memo. by Sandys, 29 July 1964; CAB 128/36, CC (62) 44th Meeting, Item 6, 'Kenya', 5 July 1962.

118. CAB 134/1659, DVO (64) 4, 'Kenya Land Settlement', note by Castle, 4 Dec. 1964.

119. CAB 134/2544, SV (65) 11, 'Communist Economic and Technical Aid to Developing Countries - Survey of Activities in 1964', memo. for the Cabinet Counter-Subversion Committee by the Foreign Office Information Research Department, 28 June 1965. See also: ibid., SV (65) 1st Meeting, Item 1, 'Reports on the Activities of Working Groups', Item 3, 'The Implications of Sino-Soviet Penetration in Black Africa', 17 Feb. 1965, SV (65) 6, 'Foreign Office Military Training Schemes', memo. by FO, IRD, 30 April 1965, SV (65) 3, 'Reports on the Activities of Working Groups', SV (65) 2nd Meeting, Item 4, 'Unattributable Propaganda Activities (Scale and Priorities up to March 1967)', 26 May 1965, SV (65) 3rd Meeting, 'Africa - Country Studies', 11 Aug. 1965, SV (65) 4th Meeting, Item 3, 'The Counter-Subversion Role of Service Attaches and Defence Advisers', Item 5, 'Counter-Subversion Fund Allotments for 1966/7', Item 7 'Advice on Police Matters to Commonwealth and Foreign Governments', 8 Oct. 1965.

120. CAB 134/2544, RJ 5545/235, 'The Implications of Sino-Soviet Penetration in Black Africa (SV (65) 1 - 19 January, 1965) Kenya', memo. for the Cabinet Counter-Subversion Committee, by the CRO (East Africa Political Department), July 1965; Bloch and Fitzgerald, *British Intelligence and Covert Action*, pp. 154-5.

121. DEFE 4/148, COS (62) 61st Meeting, Confidential Annex ('UK Eyes Only'), Item 3, 'Military Requirements for Counter Subversion', 4 Oct. 1962.

122. CAB 134/2544, RJ 5545/235, 'The Implications of Sino-Soviet Penetration in Black Africa (SV (65) 1-19 January, 1965) Kenya'. See also: ibid., SV (65) 12 (2nd Revise), 'Africa - Country Studies', note by J.S.H. Shattock, Secretary to the Counter-Subversion Committee, 31 Aug. 1965.

123. Ibid., SV (65) 13, 'The Counter-Subversion Role of Service Attaches and Defence Advisers', note by the secretaries, 6 Sept. 1965. Besides Britain's 'defence advisers' stationed in Kenya, their counterparts in the following Commonwealth countries were also important 'from Counter Subversion point of view': Ceylon (Sri Lanka); Cyprus; Ghana; India; Malawi; Nigeria; Pakistan; Rhodesia; Sierra Leone; Tanzania; Uganda; and Zambia. See: ibid., 'Appendix 4'.

124. Edgerton, *Mau Mau*, p. 228.

125. Anthony Clayton, 'The Military Relations between Great Britain and Commonwealth Countries, with particular reference to the African Commonwealth Nations', in Morris-Jones and Fischer (eds.), *Decolonisation and After*, pp. 222-3.

126. By declaring Kenya a Republic, and thereby replacing the Queen as Head of State, Kenyatta also took over the Governor-General's considerable residual powers over appointments to public service commissions and, crucially, to the central and regional police service commissions. For an overview of the constitutional deal which led to such powers being retained after independence, see: CO 822/3256.

127. Cherry Gertzel, *The Politics of Independent Kenya* (Evanston: Northwestern University Press, 1970), passim.; Kyle, *Politics of Independence*, pp. 198-201.

128. Edgerton, *Mau Mau*, p. 223.

CHAPTER SEVEN

Defence and Decolonisation, 1959-65

Introduction

If the few, scant references to colonial and newly-independent Kenya in the existing secondary literature on post-war British defence and foreign policy were taken at face value, it would be easy to conclude that Britain's post-Suez experiment with Army and RAF bases on Kenyan soil was ill-conceived and practically doomed from the start.[1] The same can be said of the almost complete absence of analysis of defence-related issues from works on British decolonisation in East Africa. Even the most recent published study of the transfer of power in Kenya, which draws on an extensive range of primary sources, includes only a few passing references to British defence policy and just two pages devoted to 'military considerations'.[2] As the previous chapters have shown, this hardly does justice to Kenya's role in British overseas defence planning.

The aim of this chapter is to show that, as Kenya began its relatively rapid progress to independence from 1959, Britain's strategic interests were far from compromised. This is not to say that there were not difficulties, but simply that constitutional advance in Kenya did not proceed in isolation from Britain's efforts to secure its military requirements. Indeed, British decolonisation and defence policy in Kenya were far more intricately connected than has hitherto been acknowledged, if only as evidenced by the post-independence defence agreement and Britain's continued involvement in the defence and internal security of its former colony well beyond December 1963.

As will be seen in the first section of this chapter, it is possible to trace the relative importance to Britain of securing defence interests vis-à-vis constitutional advance in Kenya from at least as early as January 1959. Moving on, the next section will show how, despite the apparently accelerated pace of the transfer of power from April 1959 onwards, British ministers, officials, and service chiefs adapted their military 'wish list' to accommodate the 'fast moving tide of African nationalism'. By doing so, they facilitated the succession and longevity of a 'moderate' and 'responsible' African government that remained largely friendly to the west. (Chapter Six has demonstrated the lengths to which Britain went in order to establish and maintain this government in power.) This successor regime, in turn, granted Britain 'defence facilities' which made it unnecessary to station a permanent garrison of British troops in Kenya anyway. By examining Britain's close involvement in defence matters in Kenya from independence until 1965, the last section will show that with regard to overseas defence policy, far from having to 'scram from Africa', Britain enjoyed a large degree of continuity. This was even maintained by the first Wilson administration and to a certain extent by successive British governments.

The 'Chequers Timetable' and British Strategy

Recent scholarship has added to contemporary accounts and subsequent publications by participants in furthering our understanding of the background to, and decisions taken during, the Conference of East African Governors at Chequers, in January 1959.[3] Such studies necessarily, if somewhat dismissively, consider the 'Chequers decisions' in the broad context of political development in East Africa as a whole. For example, it seems that Britain's approach of 'gradualness' towards constitutional advance in East Africa generally, and particularly the 'multi-racial' policy in Kenya, began to collapse following the appointment of Kenya's former Chief Secretary, Sir Richard Turnbull, to the governorship of Tanganyika in June 1958.[4] Blundell, for one, heard rumours that Turnbull was 'forcing the pace'.[5] However, it does not necessarily follow that Britain, in adapting its political outlook in East Africa, abandoned all strategic interests in the region.

Certainly, Turnbull was a liberal and, undoubtedly drawing on his experience in Kenya, was opposed to violence, from whatever source, and even made it clear to Tanganyika's nationalist leader, Julius Nyerere, that he was not committed to 'multi-racialism'. Besides, Turnbull had quickly become aware that Nyerere was basically a 'moderate' (that most preferred type of African nationalist), and that TANU was a united and widely popular nationalist party. More important, in Turnbull's view, given that political conditions in Tanganyika were as favourable as they were ever likely to be, any failure by Britain to make substantive concessions to African nationalism in the United Nations Trust Territory could well have instigated an internal security crisis. Tanganyika's security forces, the police in particular, were simply too weak to deal with an Emergency situation.[6]

In Kenya, too, 'gradualness' began to be undermined by the Africans' decision to walk out of Legislative Council, and to boycott the legislature thereafter, following a speech by Baring on 4 November 1958, which they interpreted as a firm rejection of their demands for a constitutional conference.[7] The political *impasse* in Kenya, and the potential for major security problems in Tanganyika, prompted Lennox-Boyd to make arrangements to call the East African governors to the now notorious conference at Chequers. As the Permanent Under-Secretary in the Colonial Office, Sir John Macpherson, put it to the governors and the British Resident, Zanzibar: 'Recent correspondence' with Baring and Turnbull on the political problems in their respective territories 'is leading us to [the] view that we shall have to decide very quickly now whether to maintain the policy of gradualness in East Africa or whether to take the line of least resistance in face of mounting pressures'.[8]

Little need be added here to existing accounts of the Chequers conference in terms of the abortive 'timetable' for the independence of the East African territories. Suffice it to reiterate at this stage that the conference concluded that Tanganyika would be the first British East African territory to gain independence, but not before 1970, with Kenya and Uganda's transfers of power 'pencilled in for a date about 1975 ...'[9] It seems from subsequent accounts that, irrespective of the detailed deliberations at Chequers, within weeks, if not days of the conclusion of the conference, its policy decisions had to be reversed.

At Chequers, Baring and Crawford had protested against the prospect of Britain making news of the 'timetable' public. However, no sooner had the conference ended than upon his return to Kenya concerns over the African boycott of Legislative Council prompted Baring to press Lennox-Boyd for a public statement on British policy for the territory.[10] The veneer of 'multi-racialism' in particular, and of political progress in general, would be severely tarnished if the Africans continued to fail to participate in the process.[11]

TANU's overwhelming election victory of February 1959, and the collapse of the 'multi-racial' alternative, the United Tanganyika Party (UTP), was followed on 17 March by the Tabora Conference threat of 'positive action' if it were not granted 'responsible government' by the end of the year. Turnbull's consequent fear that if Nyerere failed to gain a promise of further constitutional advance he would be unseated from TANU's leadership by 'an extremist', led in the first instance to the governor's announcement that he would replace Tanganyika's Executive Council (ExCo) with a Council of Ministers. Although seven of the places would be held by officials, the five 'unofficial' positions would comprise of three elected Africans, one European, and an Asian.[12] While Turnbull subsequently recommended that in the near future the ratio of officials to unofficials should be reversed, the matter was left largely unattended until Macleod took office in October 1959.[13]

With regard to Kenya, on the other hand, as we have seen in the previous chapter, Baring's pleas and Blundell's formation of the NKG, which apparently kept prospects for 'multi-racialism' alive, along with the impetus added by the Hola murders, led to Lennox-Boyd's April 1959 announcement of a future constitutional conference, albeit with no references to an eventual

African majority government.[14] There appears to be a fairly broad consensus (supported by greater or lesser degrees of detailed evidence) that, from this moment onwards, the devolution of power in Kenya, as with Tanganyika and Uganda, amounted only to a more or less complicated series of political manoeuvrings.

However, by concentrating on the abortive Chequers constitutional timetable and the subsequent political horse-trading and rapid policy reversal brought about by events 'in Africa', previous studies have largely ignored, if they have not dismissed, the continuity in the defence and security aspects of British decolonisation in East Africa in general, and in Kenya in particular. Given the analysis of the internal security aspects of decolonisation in Kenya in the previous two chapters, it seems prudent to re-examine the Chequers conference with regard to Britain's strategic 'requirements'. It will then be possible to discern the essential continuity in British defence policy in Kenya in so far as it related to constitutional advance. Britain's hopes of maintaining responsibility for the administration of Kenya 'for a generation' were indeed dashed by nationalist tactics and, as demonstrated in the last chapter, fears of civil war.[15] As will be seen, however, divisions within Kenyan African nationalism and genuine fears for Kenya's frontier security and the possibility of externally sponsored internal subversion helped to ensure that British strategic interests in East Africa would remain largely unfettered until well beyond independence.

It is significant that in first broaching the subject of a conference on future policy with the East African governors, Macpherson explained:

> Our present view in the Colonial Office is that both the interests of the inhabitants and our own strategic requirements point to the ... [line of least resistance] ... course, if it is at all practicable, and that we should consider making it clear beyond doubt that we intend to retain control for a considerable period - something of the order of perhaps 15 or 20 years though whether this period should be specifically stated would be one of the matters for discussion. We would, of course, continue step by step political development but we should concentrate in this period on educational and economic development and on building up local civil services so as to demonstrate to Africans that we had every intention of bringing them to the stage when HM Government could with reasonable confidence hand over to them and the other communities much of the responsibility now resting with us.[16]

The purpose of the conference could not have been made more clear. Two of the participants at Chequers, Blundell, and Baring's former ADC, Charles Douglas-Home, allude to the serious consideration given to defence and security issues. Referring to the 'timetable', Blundell explains that this 'overall pattern was generally agreed by the British Government and certain steps were taken to enable the British to adhere to it'.[17] Blundell confirms that the policy of administration and financing of EALFO by the local governments, portrayed as a precursor to the assumption of control by the eventual successor regimes, was reversed 'after' Chequers (see Chapter Six) 'in order that full responsibility could be maintained during a period which must inevitably involve moments of political tension'.[18]

From Douglas-Home's account, it is clear that there was general agreement at Chequers as to policy priorities:

> The Governors agreed that the three main British interests involved in Kenya were the military bases essential for British global strategy, the need to ensure that the area remained economically friendly to the west, and the need to secure the area as a stable home for those people of Asian and European stock who over the years had been encouraged to settle there by successive British governments [...] "On the assumption that there can be no question of even an independent Kenya, let alone an independent East Africa, under local European political control - an assumption which even Kenya Europeans now seem tacitly to make - it is so long as HMG retain ultimate control that these three interests can be secured for certain and it is not practical for HMG to maintain ultimate control unless that means defence, external relations and law and order," concluded one of the working papers.[19]

The 'timetable' was arrived at because the governors realised that Britain would be unable to maintain such control indefinitely. As subsequent events and scholarship suggest, a principal condition for Britain securing its strategic interests, by retaining political control of Kenya, was soon rendered doubtful.

However, as is often the case with retrospective accounts, especially by participants, the 'devil' is not so much 'in the detail', as in what such accounts omit. Clearly, whether abortive or otherwise, Britain's attempts at Chequers to fudge an acceptable formula for the management of nationalist politics in East Africa, were undertaken with at least one eye very firmly on strategic interests. As early as April 1957, when planning to station British troops in Kenya was well under way, War Office officials had been aware that 'security of tenure and the operational commitment is subject to change' and it was accordingly 'proposed, in the interest of economy, that the brigade would be established by stages'.[20] This recognition that strategic interests might become hostage to political fortune had crystallised by the time of the Chequers conference, as had contingency plans for such an eventuality. These went far beyond provisional timetables for constitutional advance.

A fortnight before the Chequers conference, the Africa (Official) Committee (A[O]C) met in the Cabinet Office to make arrangements for co-ordinating its study of likely British interests and general developments in Africa over the next ten years. 'The study had been generated by a view that

Africa was likely to be the next object of Soviet attack and influence in various forms, and that it was, therefore, timely for the interests of the United Kingdom to be clarified, in consultation with the United States, and for the means of defending these interests in the next ten years to be decided upon.'[21] It should be noted in passing that the A(O)C planned to clarify British policy before consultations began with the Americans: 'it was important that we should not give the impression of allowing these to determine unduly our future policy towards our own colonial territories'.[22] More important, the A(O)C stressed that, primarily, British policy towards its colonies generally would be to ensure that, in the event of independence, successor governments would remain stable and maintain 'a pro-Western outlook'. At worst, 'neutrality' would be acceptable.[23]

Significantly, the A(O)C considered that 'in East Africa, in particular, where there was as yet no reasonably educated middle class, withdrawal would lead to administrative chaos and a dangerous vacuum which would open the way to anti-Western influences ...'[24] Also, it thought that in East Africa the European population relative to the Africans was too small for a 'multi-racial form of Government' to be maintained 'over a long period'. Britain should therefore be seen to be continuing with administrative, educational, political and socio-economic development in East Africa, with a view to making adequate preparations for eventual independence: 'If we could demonstrate that this was our aim, the period before control was relinquished and during which anti-Western infiltration could be prevented would be likely to be longer, with the result that the final outcome would be more in accord with our general political interests than would otherwise have been the case.'[25]

Turning to Britain's strategic interests, the A(O)C felt that in the event of a great many independent countries in tropical Africa emerging with a 'neutralist' geopolitical stance, 'defence rights' and access to military 'facilities' might well be curtailed. 'The question therefore arose of how essential it was that these rights and facilities should be preserved.'[26] Moreover, any notion that Kenya did not figure prominently in British 'global strategy' can be dismissed by a further reading of the A(O)C's assessment. As C.W. Wright from the MoD made clear, Britain's defence interests in Africa

> principally comprised the stationing of the strategic reserve in Kenya and the possession of over-flying and staging rights in certain territories. The need to retain the strategic reserve in Kenya depended wholly, and that of over-flying and staging rights partly, on the extent to which the United Kingdom would in the long term be prepared to safeguard its oil supplies in the Persian Gulf by the use of force; this was currently under consideration at a high level.[27]

In Wright's opinion, British oil interests could be safeguarded if they retained control of Aden, although this was an 'extremely expensive' option. Certainly, the emphasis in planning would have to be on the long term, but 'for the foreseeable future the United Kingdom would continue to be prepared to use force, in the last resort, in defence of its oil interests in the Persian Gulf.' This was supported by the MoD's paper contribution to the A(O)C's proceedings, which added, importantly: 'For the present, therefore, we should assume that if, during the next ten years, we continue to have strategic requirements for reinforcing the Middle East or Far East by air, we shall continue to need overflying and staging rights across Africa.'[28] In summing up this aspect of its discussion, the A(O)C concluded that a 'pro-Western Africa' would be the best means of securing Britain's 'defence requirements'.

An important benchmark was then tabled. This has vital significance for our understanding of Britain's approach not only to its defence interests in Kenya, but more importantly the often frenetic and sometimes desperate political bargaining that preceded independence:

> But in aiming at this ideal we might in the event lose the opportunity of securing the least satisfactory solution that was acceptable from a defence point of view. It was for consideration, therefore, region by region, whether it would not be wiser to adopt in the first place political aims which would ensure that our minimum strategic requirements were met, rather than risk losing all by aiming too high.[29]

It appears that, irrespective of the abortive Chequers 'timetable', the British already had a clear idea of how they would proceed politically in East Africa in the face of difficulties arising with regard to securing their defence requirements and, more importantly, what those minimum requirements would be.

In a review of the Chequers conference proceedings of 24 to 25 January, Lennox-Boyd outlined the governors' and his conclusions. Unsurprisingly, 'British interests' were at the top of the list. Significantly, and in apparent contradiction of the A(O)C's assessment, Lennox-Boyd explained that Britain's 'positive defence interest' comprised of

> the need for over-flying and staging rights and the use of ports and, for the time being at any rate, the need to station in East Africa the forward reserve for use in Southern Arabia and the Persian Gulf. The former need is of considerable importance though not necessarily vital. The latter need is vital so long as HM Government are prepared to use force to protect their [oil] interests ... and so long as there is no alternative method of effectively protecting those interests (e.g. a kind of "sixth fleet" defence policy).[30]

Britain's 'negative defence and economic interest' entailed ensuring that 'the area is as friendly to the West as possible and, at the very least, is benevolently neutral. Failure to secure this interest, even after the positive defence interest was not no longer [*sic*] important, would seriously prejudice British prestige and influence.'[31] Ensuring the security of the immigrant minorities in East Africa was next, thus last, on the list. However, regardless of relative priorities, Lennox-Boyd and the governors concurred with the view that all such interests could be secured '*for certain*' so long as Britain retained control of defence and external relations, law and order, the legal system and 'the internal security side of the work of the Provincial Administrations'.[32]

Of course, the political uncertainties that had necessitated the Chequers conference had a considerable bearing upon how all this might be achieved.[33] Given what we now know about the ultimate achievement of political independence in Britain's East African territories, it would be futile to analyse Lennox-Boyd's assessment of the 'four possibilities' for constitutional development that Britain could pursue. Suffice it here to again mention the 'timetable' and the Secretary of State's recommendation that Britain should adhere to the policy of 'gradualness'.

However, for the purpose of clarifying the lengths that Britain was already prepared to go to in order to secure its strategic interests, several points are noteworthy. Firstly, one of the three political 'possibilities' rejected at Chequers was that of allowing the East African territories 'to develop normally towards full self-government'. This was effectively a euphemistic substitute for abandoning the other possibilities, including ideas of staying in Kenya indefinitely (while the other territories became 'fully self-governing'), maintaining control of Mombasa and the coastal strip only (a kind of 'sovereign base areas' strategy), or developing all the territories together under a federal umbrella.[34] Secondly, while the actual pattern of constitutional advance in East Africa resembled most closely the former possibility, it is particularly significant that Lennox-Boyd suggested that, in the event of Britain choosing to pursue that political option, it would 'rely on defence agreements for the securing of any interests which might still be vital to HM Government'.[35] Given that the political stakes in East Africa were raised soon after Chequers, Britain's strategic 'bottom line' should be borne in mind when considering the relationship between constitutional development and the rise and fall of defence-related construction projects in Kenya.

Clearly, British political and strategic deliberations at Chequers were far more significant than has hitherto been acknowledged. Perhaps most significant of all were Lennox-Boyd's precautionary recommendations.

Kenya's revenues were already suffering because of the decline in global commodity prices, and it would cease to draw Emergency aid and loan assistance at the end of the year. In line with earlier thinking, Lennox-Boyd therefore suggested that Britain should be seen to be 'prepared to come to some extent to the assistance of the territorial governments to prevent the slowing down of educational and other programmes through financial stringency'. The all too convenient solution to this was for Britain to take over the cost of 'the East African defence forces ...'

We saw in Chapter Six how, in practice, this suggestion was aligned closely with Britain's 'vital interests'.[36] This had certainly been the intention at Chequers, rather than after. As Lennox-Boyd put it:

> In making the specific suggestion that the cost of the defence forces should be taken over I have naturally had regard to the possibility of devising a method by which HM Government might retain for a considerable, of [*sic*] not indefinite, period some control in the area. The question will not assume any urgency until one or more of the territories attain internal self-government, but it may be as well to give preliminary consideration to the matter now. [...] A further advantage attaching to this arrangement is that the evolution from internal self-government to full self-government may not be so rapid as might otherwise be the case if the successor Governments, who would doubtless wish to have control over their own defence forces, were faced with the prospect of finding a considerable sum of money from territorial resources to pay for them.[37]

As will be seen below, Britain did not adhere to a policy of 'gradualness' when it came to this latter proposal.

Following Chequers, the British government awaited further inter-departmental consultation, and settled for a likely decision in March on how to proceed politically in East Africa.[38] In February, however, government officials had already begun to consider the possibility of reversion of EALFO back to War Office control, well before completion of the political compromises that culminated in Lennox-Boyd's April Commons statement.[39] Their conclusions make interesting reading in the light of our knowledge of subsequent events. At that time, it seems, Britain's control of EALF was ensured under the governors' administrative auspices through EALFO, so any transfer of responsibility was deemed to be unnecessary provided that a Colonial Office representative were appointed to that body. It was, however, financially and politically 'essential' that Britain should assume 100 per cent of the costs of EALFO, rather than the current 80 per cent, in line with earlier considerations.[40] Of course, as we saw in Chapter Six, within a month these comfortable assumptions had to be revised when a more rapid withdrawal of administrative responsibility seemed likely.[41]

Irrespective of this, as can be seen clearly above, the defence-related internal security groundwork was, perhaps fortunately for Britain, already in place, at least conceptually, to cater for such eventualities. It was time for Britain to begin to aim its sights lower than had hitherto seemed desirable. As will be shown below, while Britain's 'political objectives' in Kenya perforce had to change soon after Chequers, *strategic objectives* were retained rather than abandoned, subject to some far from novel modifications to the means of attaining them.

British Defence and the 'Fortress Colony', 1959-63

As the previous chapter has shown, with the stakes in Kenya so high from early 1959 onwards, the British government was not satisfied with relying simply on legal devices and political concessions to attempt to maintain control. Within days of news of the Hola murders, the Colonial Office had begun to unravel the British policy on the control and financing of colonial armed forces, as Lennox-Boyd had suggested at the January Chequers conference. Further arrangements proposed by Lennox-Boyd at Chequers were already in place, 'whereby a report, agreed by Local Intelligence Committees, should be submitted at six-monthly intervals on the state of security in locally raised colonial forces'.[42] There were apparently many 'military and administrative advantages' in the War Office taking back control of EALF, and any funds thereby released would be presented as additional resources to be used for agricultural and educational development. The measure was announced at the January 1960 Lancaster House conference, along with the pledge of a loan of £5 million for land development. On the one hand these 'sweeteners' were intended to help Britain 'to "sell" the policy of gradualness to those who would have us out of East Africa within the next few years'. On the other hand, removing EALF from 'local [African] political control' would 'restore to us one political counter which we need' and enable Britain, so it was thought, to apply 'a brake' to rapid political advance. By avoiding a 'premature withdrawal of our authority' Britain hoped to be able to leave behind a political structure that would 'safeguard our vital interests'.[43] Principal among these interests, of course, was the British Army's base at Kahawa and the RAF installations in Nairobi and elsewhere in Kenya.

In the political arena, following Lennox-Boyd's April 1959 Commons statement, the Africans had returned to Legislative Council, only to boycott the opening of the constitutional conference in January 1960. This was because Kenyatta's associate, Peter Mbiyu Koinange, was refused entry to the proceedings.[44] With this difficulty overcome by the compromise of allowing Koinange to enter Lancaster House, but not the inner chamber, the conference proceeded.[45] The conclusion of the Lancaster House conference, which was seen widely as a victory for the Africans, led to a 'slump' in the Nairobi stock market and property dealings, reflecting not only European but also international uncertainty.[46] Among other things, this prompted the British government to take financial steps to ensure that members of the Oversea Civil Service did not resign precipitately, and to consider measures to assist East African building societies.[47]

By the time of the July 1960 Congo 'crisis', Britain had resumed direct control of EALF, and Kenya's various political parties were preparing for elections the following year. Demands for Kenyatta's release had been forestalled, at least temporarily, by Renison's 'leader to darkness and death' speech and the publication of the Corfield Report which, unsurprisingly, confirmed the findings of the 1953 Kapenguria trial. While racial barriers to access to education and land had been removed, at least in principle, it was the Kenyatta issue which kept KANU, by its own volition, from government, even after winning the February 1961 election with 67.4 per cent of the vote.[48] Clearly, the legitimacy of Britain's political project in Kenya was thereby brought into question, at least until Kenyatta's release in August 1961, if not until June 1963.

Naturally, all of this activity, or lack of it, led to deliberations behind the scenes in London, especially with regard to defence. In early 1960, as a result of the deepening Middle East air barrier and the earlier assumptions which had led to the seemingly abortive 'Next Ten Years in Africa' study, the Chiefs of Staff began to lay the groundwork for a study of British military strategy until 1970 in 'circumstances short of global war'.[49] In line with usual practice, given the wide-ranging financial and political implications of the study, the Chiefs of Staff incorporated the views of the three services and related government departments. The study therefore underwent several revisions before its initial presentation to ministers. This was not least because the political situation in Cyprus and Malta had enhanced the importance of the 'east of Suez' role, and gave rise to another upgrade of Kenya's strategic significance.[50] One squadron of a British tank regiment had already been shipped to Aden in February 1960; the rest moved to Kenya later that year.

One of the principal assumptions underlying the review and upgrade of Britain's 'east of Suez' strategy was that continued restrictions on the rapid movement of troops and military hardware brought about by the 'barrier' necessitated strengthening military installations overseas and stationing sufficient reserves in the area.[51] The upgrade in the 'east of Suez' role and its implications for determining the necessary levels of conventional forces had been greatly assisted by the appointment of Harold Watkinson as Sandys' successor as Minister of Defence. Watkinson shared the view of the Chiefs of Staff that the greatest threat to Britain's defence interests would arise in the 'east of Suez' area, and that nuclear capability, although still essential generally, was effectively an irrelevance in such circumstances.[52] The problem was that there was only so much of the fiscal pie to go around. As Darby explains:

> In 1960 ... 49 per cent of total defence expenditure went on paying the forces and looking after them. Add to this the cost of the deterrent, variously estimated at between 10 and 20 per cent, and with the best will in the world and regardless of how much nibbling was done around the edges of the nuclear component, the development of conventional capability was inevitably a piece-meal affair.[53]

Certainly, when the Cabinet Defence Committee first met to discuss the issue, in July 1960, Macmillan felt that the complexity of the 'strategic, political and financial' issues raised in the various memoranda submitted for the meeting necessitated further study and reflection before decisions could be taken.[54] Events in Africa, the Congo 'crisis' in particular, may well have had a bearing on this.

Whatever the case, the committee next discussed the 'circumstances short of global war' strategy in October. Macmillan summarised the views put forward by the Chiefs of Staff on the force levels needed to meet their perception of Britain's maximum requirements in the 'east of Suez' area, inevitably necessitating increased expenditure;[55] 'but our balance of payments position made it essential to look rather for reductions'.[56] Macmillan continued:

> It was desirable therefore to consider ... the nature of our interests in the Far East and in the Middle East and the best method of preparing ourselves to forestall or to meet foreseeable threats to these interests, within the limits of our capacity to sustain the resultant level of overseas expenditure. Never before in peacetime had we attempted to maintain such large forces overseas as we now had in Europe, Africa and Asia. It was doubtful whether we could continue to carry this burden in addition to the programmes of economic aid without which our military effort might well be useless.[57]

Much of the discussion thereafter centred on the political and strategic commitments in each area generally, moving on to detailed consideration of Malaya and Singapore, and Cyprus, Gibraltar and Malta, for example. Reductions in expenditure could be found in the first instance by depending on less sophisticated air-to-ground missiles for base defence. A great deal pivoted on the possibility of reductions in the numbers of personnel stationed in a particular territory. For example, if the Cyprus garrison were reduced by one battalion (from four and a third), 'it could still provide a satisfactory military force, although it would be less well balanced than a normally organised brigade group'.

When it came to consideration of East Africa and the Arabian Peninsula, because of 'direct commitments in Africa' and the need to safeguard Britain's air-staging capability in the region, the Chiefs of Staff had recommended the retention in Kenya of a 'long-term army garrison at its present level'. In Macmillan's opinion, Britain's strategic interests in the Arabian Peninsula and the Persian Gulf made it essential that the Aden base should be retained, 'at least until 1966, and probably for longer ...' However, 'in view of the uncertain political future of Kenya, it was thought desirable that projected expenditure on works services there should be closely examined'.[58]

Nevertheless, unlike Cyprus and Libya, where the army contingents would be reduced, the Defence Committee agreed, much as they had in the case of Gibraltar and Malta, that the Kenya garrison should remain at its current strength, in this case three battalions.[59] Despite his remarks to the Defence Committee, Macmillan does not appear to have rejected the possibility of staying on in Kenya. Indeed, in referring earlier to Britain's need to protect Kuwait, Macmillan explained: 'We should need limited ground forces, suitable for police type operations, with great mobility and air transportability. [...] For these purposes retention of the Kenya base and Aden seem essential.'[60]

Given the above reference to political uncertainty regarding Kenya's future, it is notable that in Aden there was also a fervent nationalist movement vying with moderate elements for political influence.[61] While the British political plan for Aden, which was supported by the moderates, envisaged internal self-government in January 1963, the nationalists wanted Britain out of Aden 'as quickly as possible, and to unite Colony, Protectorate and a "reformed" Yemen with the UAR'.[62] In late 1960, in terms of determining the most likely area where security of tenure for British forces could be ensured, it must have been difficult to choose between the African and the Arab solutions. 'Nevertheless, from ... [the British] ... point of view Aden was considered to be the safest of the Colonial territories in the [Middle East] theatre.'[63] As will be seen below, some 18 months later, events in the Arabian Peninsula would raise questions about this assumption, and again bring Kenya to potentially greater strategic prominence.

In the meantime, with elections due in Kenya in February 1961, officials on the ground had more immediate concerns. At the end of October 1960, Renison paid a visit to J.N.A. Armitage-Smith, Private Secretary to the Minister of State, Lord Perth, in London. Following on from issues raised at a recent meeting of the EADC, they discussed 'a number of matters affecting KAR'. These included a back-dated pay rise for all Africans, in line with similar increases proposed for civilians, undoubtedly intended to keep both in service. There was also the matter of increasing the number of commissioned African officers, which was 'a task of higher priority' than expanding the size of KAR battalions except, perhaps, in Uganda.[64] Since 1949, KAR battalions had been reduced in size by one rifle company, and were reduced in number following the April. 1955 Templer Report. This had to be reversed if they were to remain effective. Expansion of the number of Africans in the Officer Corps could not be undertaken rapidly because quality would suffer, so the earlier that this could begin, the better.[65] It had also become clear that Tanganyika had decided to end its contributions to the upkeep of the Royal East African Navy (REAN). With Kenya and Uganda refusing to make up the shortfall, and given the need to maintain ground forces at full strength, the question remained regarding the 'pleasant extravagance of a local navy' as to 'whether it is worth while keeping the REAN in being'.[66]

Clearly, the East African governments were concerned that their ability to be seen to be developing their respective territories, from both the financial and 'African advancement' perspectives, would be impaired by defence and security-related budgetary anomalies. There was also the matter of maintaining security in a potentially volatile political climate, which could not be considered in isolation from Britain's defensive commitments in the area. More will be said about all of this later. For the time being, suffice it to note the stage at which Renison and his colleagues stressed the importance of the local defence and security implications of political developments.

Back in London, Kenya's forthcoming general election also began to have an impact on the ongoing deliberations over Britain's global strategy. Mboya had come under pressure from both colleagues and rivals because KANU's draft election manifesto was 'not radical enough over land', and decided to make it so, adding to the nationalist pressure on Britain. The manifesto would now include a passage which, on one view, set 'red lights ... flashing in the Defence Ministry':[67]

> KANU like many of the other new nations and consistent with our policy of non-alignment with either the East or West military power blocks [*sic*], will not allow any form of foreign military base(s) [*sic*] to be established in Kenya. Kenya must not be a pawn in the struggles of the East and West nor do we want to see Kenya transformed into a battleground in the event of an East/West military conflict. We are certain that our people would not approve of Kenya being used by NATO or the British in any localised conflicts between NATO or British forces and any part of Africa, Asia or the Middle East. KANU condemns the fact that British [*sic*] chose to ignore African protestations at the time when they started to establish the Kahawa British military base. KANU will press for the immediate closing down of the base.[68]

This certainly put brakes on Britain's planning for its projected global strategy requirements.[69] With £5 million expenditure still outstanding for the completion of military construction projects in Kenya, Watkinson urged Macleod to investigate whether Britain's minimum requirement of five years security of tenure still seemed feasible. 'In the meantime, I should be most reluctant to see any further commitments entered into for new works services.'[70]

Given the current financial climate, Watkinson's concerns were understandable enough. Nevertheless, the Colonial Office did have a contingency plan to help it to buy some time. Labour MP John Stonehouse had tabled a written Parliamentary Question as to the costs and likely future of Britain's military installations in Kenya. In the event that this might lead to concerns being raised regarding the KANU election manifesto, the Colonial Office had prepared a supplementary written answer which was transmitted to Renison for prior approval: 'it is proposed to say that HMG are willing to consider the future of bases in Kenya with the Government of Kenya at an appropriate time'.[71] However, the problem with this suggestion, at least from Renison's perspective, was that while the manifesto might not be KANU's 'last word on this subject', the proposed reply

> would not (repeat not) be helpful and might have [the] opposite [of the] desired effect by antagonising the party or seeming to attempt to drive [a] wedge among them at the time of acknowledged differences of opinion within the party. [...] Impossible to forecast how KANU will view such matters if and when they achieve power as much depends on personalities.[72]

Of course, Britain could not be seen to be attempting to divide the KANU politicians in public. As will be seen later, such tactics were reserved for behind the closed doors of constitutional conferences.

The confusion over the likely attitude of KANU to Britain's defence requirements in the event of winning the February 1961 election, left Macleod unable to provide Watkinson with a definitive answer to his query.[73]

> As you know, the East African Governors will be discussing defence matter [*sic*] with the chiefs of staff [*sic*] during the informal conference I am having with them next month. I hope that that Conference [*sic*] will enable us (against the background of defence and other considerations) to clear our minds on the right way to move politically in the foreseeable future.[74]

Much depended on the prospects for an East African Federation, which Macleod hoped to establish in late 1962 or early 1963: 'a Federal Government, which would no doubt be responsible for defence, might take a less extreme attitude than KANU now does'.[75]

However, Macleod warned that even a federal government might refuse to allow Britain to use its military 'facilities' for 'the conduct of "colonial" operations'. Nevertheless, Macleod still held high hopes that, even in the event of failure to achieve a federation, 'it is not impossible' that the government of an independent Kenya 'will recognise a number of strong reasons for seeking a close understanding on defence matters with us'.[76] He saw 'little prospect' of British troops being allowed to remain in Kenya 'primarily for UK purposes', although he thought 'we should be able to count on the use of our existing facilities until the end of 1965'.

Again, because KANU's post-election attitude could not be determined at that stage, Macleod hoped that the final decision on new works services could be deferred until early in the following summer. If Watkinson were unable to postpone his final decision, Macleod was 'particularly anxious to avoid' any 'overt action' being taken in the 'immediate future'. Britain could not be seen to be caving in to Mboya's pressure, lest KANU's Secretary-General sought to apply more of the same, and militant elements in Kenya's population decided to follow suit, if in a far less sophisticated manner. 'On the other hand, I am not suggesting that we should openly take the uncompromising line that whatever Mr Mboya says we intend to hang on to the base. This would make the situation much more difficult than it now is.'[77]

Watkinson agreed with Macleod's uncertain, if far from optimistic, assessment, and that the final decision on how to proceed should be deferred until after talks with the East African governors.[78] He also initiated an examination of which of the construction programmes in Kenya could be deferred for either three months or eight months, as well as preparing a draft paper for submission to the Defence Committee in which he recommended postponement until 1 April 1961, when the Kenya election result and its implications would be clearer.[79]

Naturally, all of the above issues came under scrutiny at the Colonial Office conference with the East African governors, held in London between 4 and 9 January 1961.[80] One of the key decisions taken during the conference related to Nyerere's recent offer to postpone Tanganyika's independence in lieu of preparations for Kenya and Uganda to join in forming a federation.[81] Given the importance of achieving a federation to British policy generally, and defence interests in particular, Macleod devised yet another, albeit ultimately abortive, timetable. Tanganyika would be granted internal self-government in mid-May. Nyerere would then be encouraged to convene a federation conference that August with the (yet to be appointed) Chief Ministers of Kenya and Uganda, with the initiative being seen to come from him rather than Britain. According to Kyle, in order to lessen concerns in the MoD, in any future references to British defence requirements the term 'facilities' would be substituted for 'base'.[82]

Despite his earlier objections to making the fact public, Renison felt that defence negotiations should be left until as near to Kenya's independence as possible: 'To attempt to discuss it just after an election vote on a manifesto which specifically stated that the bases should be removed would not be a worthwhile operation.'[83] By continuing to pay for KAR until independence, and by being seen to be prepared to do so for longer, the British also hoped that they might even gain agreement to the retention of their troops in Kenya as a *quid pro quo*.[84] Significantly, with regard to overflying and staging rights, the conference concluded that more progress could in all probability be made through an informal defence agreement rather than a formal treaty which would have more serious political implications for Kenya's nationalist leadership.[85] It is noteworthy that KADU was thought to be more likely to be amenable to Britain's defence aims, although less capable of governing the country.[86]

Following Macleod's post-conference submission to Watkinson, eyebrows began to be raised in the rest of Whitehall because even though a positive outcome to the defence conundrum did not seem impossible, there were still likely to be 'restrictions on our freedom of action after Kenya achieves independence'.[87] If, for reasons of political sensitivity, British troops in Kenya could not be deployed elsewhere in Africa or the Arabian Peninsula and Persian Gulf, what was the point of keeping them there? As a somewhat perplexed Treasury official put it to the MoD: 'Is there thus some risk of our being forced into a Malayan type of situation where the troops cannot be used for their primary purpose but are used instead partly for some form of internal security role and partly to bolster up the economy of the territory.'[88]

Given the uncertainty over Kenya's political future, the simple fact was that Britain might well find itself able to use RAF Eastleigh and the Templer Barracks to conduct operations in Kuwait, for example, even if the rest of Africa were, by agreement, to end up out of bounds.[89] KANU's refusal to form a government, while prolonging all the political uncertainty, also left Britain's defence planners none the wiser. Nevertheless, the MoD decided to hedge its bets and to proceed in a piecemeal fashion according to the CPC's 'best estimate', whereby 'it was possible ... that we might be able to retain military bases [*not* 'facilities'] in Kenya for six to seven years'.[90] The MoD reached a significant conclusion, which was later approved by ministers, and is particularly noteworthy if Britain's African strategic bottom line is borne in mind: 'The technical facilities planned for Eastleigh and Embakasi were essential for the planned squadron deployment and to meet the staging requirements for long range transport aircraft and no reduction could be made unless some reduction in task were accepted by the Chiefs of Staff.'[91]

After a summer of continued uncertainty, exacerbated by hostile public comments from not only Mboya, but from Nyerere as well, and contributing to some rather rattled nerves in the Treasury, Macmillan decided to intercede in an apparent attempt to resolve the situation once and for all.[92] In a directive to Watkinson, Macmillan explained:

> In the light of discussions which I have recently held with Ministers directly concerned we can now re-define the political assumptions on which our defence policy and strategy should be based. We cannot be sure that all the developments predicated in ... this paper will materialise-especially since some of them depend on future constitutional developments in the Commonwealth or on the decisions of other Governments. But I am satisfied that we shall make the best use of our limited resources if we re-cast our policies and plans for the medium and longer term on the basis of the assumptions set out ...[93]

Crucial among these assumptions was that Britain would not be able to rely on using its 'military bases or facilities' in any independent country for purposes which were not 'in full accord with the policies and views of the Governments and peoples of those countries'. Britain believed that until 1970 it could rely on having 'unrestricted use' of 'facilities' in Aden, Adu Atoll, Bahrain, Gibraltar, Malta, and the Seychelles. However, the British could 'expect to suffer restrictions on our freedom to use for military purposes facilities in' Cyprus, Greater Malaysia, Kenya, and Libya. The assumption remained that this could well be different during a global war, 'and in some circumstances on a once-for-all basis for limited war'. Yet, even securing staging and overflying rights 'for purposes with which the Government concerned' was not sympathetic might well prove increasingly difficult. While Britain had 'an obligation' to assist any Commonwealth country in the event of external aggression, Macmillan stressed that this did not constitute sufficient grounds for retaining troops on an emergent nation's soil: 'We should encourage dependent territories to take a greater share of responsibility for their internal security.'[94]

Given what we now know about Britain's strategic bottom line with regard to Africa generally, and Kenya in particular, and especially in the light of the need to exact economies in overseas defence expenditure, Macmillan's directive was not the radical departure that it appears to be at first sight. Certainly, when it came to the Prime Minister's outline of Britain's strategic objectives in the Middle East, while admittedly at the bottom of the list (after preserving the countries of the area from communist influence), retaining air staging facilities in Kenya 'if possible' remained. 'Future plans should be framed on the assumption that Kenya will not be available as a military base after 1963, when it is expected to attain independence.'[95] Accordingly, the

Chiefs of Staff would soon begin to examine plans for redeploying troops from Kenya to Aden.[96] Britain would, however, hope to retain training and leave camp facilities.[97] It is quite clear that with regard to defence aims, British policy in Kenya thereafter would be to 'adopt in the first place political aims which would ensure that our minimum strategic requirements were met, rather than risk losing all by aiming too high', as had been envisaged two years earlier by the A(O)C.[98]

By January 1962, as a result of the Defence Committee's decisions, the Air Ministry and the War Office had already imposed a 'standstill' on some defence-related construction projects. One example, a hardened aircraft hangar, serves to demonstrate the curious significance that such schemes had taken on.[99] In response to the information that the hangar was to be dismantled, Renison explained that it was 'very desirable that [the] hangar should not be demolished before the Lancaster House conference since such action might be presumed to imply a decision to withdraw troops and might affect attitudes at the conference'.[100] The standstill also created difficulties in terms of commitments to local contractors and their employees. Moreover, news of the moratorium, irrespective of the fact itself, would demonstrate clearly that the colonial power was uncertain of the likely duration of its tenure at the pinnacle of Kenya politics. The last thing Britain wanted was to be seen to be 'retreating'.[101] This might in turn have a grave effect on the already serious levels of capital outflow from the colony as well as further undermining inward investment.[102]

On the eve of the February 1962 constitutional conference, the CPC conducted an examination of a recent A(O)C report on Kenya's finances.[103] Macmillan's Private Secretary, Michael Cary, submitted a far from optimistic assessment:

> Already in fact bankrupt but with worse to come, wholly lacking in political, cultural, social and economic cohesion, threatened with internal tribal strife and external attack from the north but lacking both funds and forces to maintain adequate security services, an independent Kenya represents the least hopeful prospect of all the Colonial territories to which we have given or contemplated giving independence. Nevertheless, the consequences of withholding independence seem likely, both in the short and in the long term, to be even more menacing to our interests ...[104]

As far as British interests were concerned, the security of tenure of British troops at Kahawa had by now been seriously brought into question. Earlier, it had been surmised that in the likely event of the government of an independent Kenya requiring military aid from Britain, this should be limited to just enough to cover internal security requirements, leaving little choice in the matter. It was even considered essential that the African ministers should be apprised of the 'good government' practice of restricting military expenditure, which would serve the same purpose.

Although Mboya, for one, had consistently stated that there could be no place for foreign military bases on sovereign Kenya's soil, even tabling several Private Member's Motions in Legislative Council to that effect, the British hoped that a 'responsible' African government would recognise the benefits of British troops in terms of external defence requirements.[105] British policy at the February 1962 constitutional conference had been to attempt to promote 'a split' within KANU, between the 'extreme wing' represented by Kenyatta and Odinga, and the 'essentially national' Mboya and his supporters. With 'national' now a euphemism for 'moderate', the then Secretary of State for Colonial Affairs, Reginald Maudling, had hoped that the Mboya faction would then enter into a 'moderate coalition' with KADU. The perceived 'essentially tribal' stance of Kenyatta and Odinga might this time be used to Britain's advantage.[106] Certainly, as a category, relatively 'moderate' nationalists like Mboya figured more closely in Britain's calculations for the transfer of power than communist-backed 'extremists' like Odinga who, as we have seen in the previous chapter, also held the dubious honour of being acceptable to the KLFA.[107]

Towards the end of 1961, British fears of 'another outbreak of Mau Mau' had added impetus to efforts to secure a constitutional solution to Kenya's internal problems. These included the decision to allow Kenyatta to stand for election to the legislature as a precursor to the February 1962 constitutional conference.[108] However, with Tanganyikan independence imminent, and that of Uganda expected the following year, the wholesale expansion of the three territories' KAR battalions and acceleration of the Africanisation of the Officer Corps proposed earlier by the governors and local military authorities, although viewed 'with great sympathy' in Whitehall, could not be approved on financial grounds, unless corresponding savings were made elsewhere. In other words, unless the territories paid for the expansion themselves.[109]

While the British government accepted, on political grounds, that it had been slow to address the problem of training local officers, the situation was complicated by Britain's long-term defence aims in the region, including hopes for a federation. With the political climate uncertain, and internal security in Kenya ever fragile, memories of the former Belgian Congo had not yet faded. The withdrawal of British officers, it seemed, 'would reduce the local forces to an armed rabble'. 'We might be faced with a difficult choice between the involvement of British officers in internal affairs and the acceptance of serious disorder if the local forces were left to operate without British commanders or other support.'[110] A major difficulty for Britain at the time was uncertainty over the levels of British forces, if any, that would be retained in Kenya after independence.[111]

Given this ongoing political uncertainty, Britain still had to devise a means of ensuring that members of its armed forces would continue to be involved after independence in the 'executive and command' functions of the Kenyan military. The solution turned out to be simple enough: Britain would pay for the retention of expatriate personnel. As the CRO explained in a note for the Africa Committee:

> Only by doing so can we ensure that they will be retained, thus making a real contribution to the preservation of stability in the area and at the same time barring the way to penetration by hostile influences into this most sensitive sector of activity. We should also help to ensure the continuity of British methods, equipment etc. and thus of our power to exert influence, and should gain a measure of good will by giving aid in a desired and acceptable form.[112]

As it turned out, as if to vindicate Britain's new-found faith in his apparently new-found moderate credentials, Mboya would soon take the lead in fulfilling his government's side of Britain's hoped for defence bargain, despite his public pronouncements to the contrary.[113]

In late July 1962, Mboya and Gichuru, then ministers for labour and finance, respectively, along with Bruce McKenzie, the minister for land settlement and alleged MI6 agent, held discussions with General Sir Richard Hull (CIGS) and General Goodwin (GOC, East Africa) over 'the question of Kenya's armed forces after independence'.[114] In line with their pronouncements against foreign military bases, the two African ministers hoped to reach an agreement whereby Britain would assist Kenya in developing its own army, navy, and air force. 'They realised that Kenya could not hope to have enough in defence to look after itself, and clearly hoped to have a Defence Agreement with us. It was clear that they would need United Kingdom help in training, and it was possible that they might ask for British units to stay on.'[115] While the latter proposition remained uncertain, the Chief of the Defence Staff, Lord Mountbatten, initiated the reversal of the disbanding of the REAN, requesting that it be reconstituted into a smaller Kenyan force. This would demonstrate Britain's *bona fides* and, by doing so, would remove the necessity for Kenya ministers to look elsewhere to satisfy their defence requirements. Equally, Britain would retain a stake in Kenya's naval defence, perhaps smoothing the way for continued use of dockyard refit and refuelling facilities. All Kenyan military forces would, of course, come under the direction of a 'central MoD administration'. Even the reduction of British 'influence' following the probable replacement of British officers with their locally recruited counterparts after independence, although preferable to that by 'personnel from what we should regard as undesirable sources', could be addressed: 'and as regards achieving the desired result, it would often be possible to work through a training mission even when secondment had ceased to be acceptable'.[116]

In the meantime, while the Chiefs of Staff were busily planning to redeploy forces from Kenya to Aden, Britain had to contend with the potential crisis represented by Yemeni raids into Aden.[117] The Governor of Aden, Sir Charles Johnston, enjoyed authority without prior reference to London for 'counter battery and retaliatory action' against such incursions. Measures were also being considered 'to promote the favourable climate of opinion in Aden necessary to ensure the long term security of the Aden base', including proposals for a merger of Aden Colony with the Federation of South Arabia, and the rather belated appointment of a 'senior British Arabist'.[118] Yet Britain was ill prepared for the 27 September 1962 Yemen revolution, as well as its implications.[119]

Earlier British hopes of establishing legally entrenched principles for the retention of 'sovereign base areas' in Aden before the colony joined in a federation were diminished by fears of antagonising Adeni public opinion in the potentially volatile circumstances created by the Yemen *coup*.[120] While the Yemen revolution was expected to remain a primarily internal affair, at least for the first month or so, serious consideration had to be given to the prospects for overt British military action to defend Aden's frontiers, as well as counter-subversion measures.[121] 'It is conceivable that political developments in the Arabian Peninsula may make it difficult for us to rely on continuing use of our defence facilities in Aden after 1967.'[122] This again raised questions over Britain's handling of constitutional advance in Kenya with regard to strategic requirements. If security of tenure could not be expected in Aden all that long after withdrawal from Kenya, and while there still remained a faint hope of staying on in East Africa, upgrading facilities in the former could well end up being a case of throwing 'good money after bad'. Why risk increasing turbulence in the Middle East when a friendly Kenya could still be amenable to a British military presence?

Britain was equally, if not more, afraid of the possible implications of the Yemen situation for Kuwait. In the event of operations being conducted to deter or expel Iraq from Kuwait, 1,300 troops would have to be flown quickly to Aden. This made it imperative that accommodation intended for the redeployment from Kenya, although cheaper and reduced in standard, should be completed as soon as possible.[123] As might have been expected, given the general climate of financial stringency, and especially in the light of concerns over the Yemen and Aden, any further expenditure had to be justified. Because Britain had managed successfully to postpone until independence any substantive defence negotiations with Kenya government ministers, it still remained uncertain whether attitudes to the British base would soften under the afterglow of having achieved full sovereignty. After all, by the time Britain had withdrawn from formal administration of the colony, then surely any question of imperialist aims or domination would become anachronistic?

In late 1962, the Parliamentary Under-Secretary in the Colonial Office, Nigel Fisher, certainly felt that the dire prospects for Kenya's economy of withdrawing British troops could be used as a lever in negotiations.[124] Some Treasury officials even questioned the levels of political sensitivity that Britain ascribed to prospective defence negotiations: 'I should think it unwise for Kenya Ministers to be given any idea that we are open to suggestions from them as to the number of troops we should keep there.'[125] It followed that it appeared to be equally unwise to commit funds to Aden when it could still prove to be the case that British troops might well remain in Kenya. Naturally, the Treasury was more than prepared to consider such ideas.[126]

Britain had delayed holding detailed defence negotiations with Kenya ministers until the last moment in the hope of forestalling a rash and unfavourable decision. However, in a sense, by doing so Britain was hoist by its own petard. The delay in holding the negotiations would always lead to a correspondingly late agreement, making it impossible to foresee whether or not an independent Kenya would be amenable to the retention of British troops after all. While there were still some officials in Whitehall who felt that unfavourable pronouncements on Britain's military bases in Kenya by KANU ministers amounted to little more than political posturing, driven by the requirement to be seen to be more nationalistic than their rivals, the consequences of ignoring such statements could well have proven to be far more damaging to Britain's defence interests. The likelihood that even if British troops remained in Kenya after independence there would be 'severe restrictions' placed on their use left Britain with little option other than to adhere to the spirit of Macmillan's 1961 directive.[127] Why risk losing all by aiming too high?

This decision was vindicated in November 1962, when Kenyatta, then President of KANU, congratulated the Permanent Representative of the Saudi-Arabian Delegation to the UN on his recent demand for the removal of British military bases in Kenya and Aden. It thereby finally became a practical certainty that it would be politically impossible to retain large numbers of British troops for more than a very limited period, no matter who, ultimately, was to rule Kenya.[128] Britain thus had to proceed with the fateful plan for upgrading Aden, as well as ensuring that Kenya's military would be able to fulfil at least its internal security role.[129] It should be stressed, though, that this did not spell the end of Britain's strategic interests in Kenya, nor the achievement of its minimum defence aims, which would be facilitated by some far from novel means.

'Stage 4': Arming the Kenyatta State, and Maintaining British 'Influence', 1963-5

By January 1963, the likelihood of the withdrawal of British troops from Kenya, and probable restrictions on their use after independence, forced British ministers to concede that Kenya's military had to be built up vigorously. 'Unless, therefore, we are prepared to risk a Congo-type situation in Kenya from mid-1964 onwards we must act quickly to expand 70 Brigade.'[130] Britain would have to continue to plan for the phased withdrawal of its forces, making any proposed arrangements to expand and, more importantly, to train Kenya's forces thereafter, all the more vital. As Thorneycroft explained to Nigel Fisher at the Colonial Office:

> We certainly could not take the risk of cancelling or stretching out these [withdrawal] plans against the possibility that Kenya Ministers might at some future date welcome military help. [...] That is not to say that we should refrain from negotiating ... for the retention for as long as may be of air staging, overflying, training and communications facilities and so on and for assistance, including seconded personnel, in the training of Kenya Defence Forces. With regard to the latter, in view of the especial importance of EASTLEIGH [*sic*], the Air Ministry are working out proposals for the training of a small Kenyan air force as an inducement to Kenya to grant us these facilities.[131]

Despite the imposition by the Treasury of a temporary standstill on construction projects in Aden, Thorneycroft's caution had been justified by London's reluctance to second-guess KANU's ultimate outlook on the stationing of British troops in Kenya.[132] In the run up to the June 1963 elections, both KANU, in its manifesto, and KADU, orally, had made statements to the following effect: 'In accordance with the principles of non-alignment we shall not permit the existence of foreign military bases on our soil.'[133] Following the June 1963 election, Britain therefore wasted little time in trying to keep KANU 'on side'. The Sandys-Mboya communiqué of 20 June 1963 dispelled any notion that Britain would retain a permanent military base in Kenya, with troop withdrawals planned to be completed by December 1964.[134] In a stroke Sandys had unravelled years of painstaking military planning and expenditure. 'Thus finally perished the doomed post-Suez project of basing Britain's Middle East reserves on Kenyan soil.'[135] Despite Kyle's dismissive remark, it should be stressed that Britain already had contingency plans for withdrawal from Kenya and, as we have seen, was well prepared to accept a very modest strategic settlement. Britain's public acceptance of KANU's demands for closure of the Kahawa base suggests that it seemed expedient to remove one of the main African 'extremist' objections to the independence settlement: the diminution of sovereignty represented by a British military base in Kenya. Far better than to risk undermining Kenyatta's legitimacy as nationalist leader by providing his rivals with quite literally concrete political capital. KANU ministers might therefore also be amenable to Britain's requests for staging and overflying rights, especially now that it was incumbent on the latter to expand Kenya's military.[136]

As it turned out, this astute act of political *legerdemain* paid off, and did not prove to be the end, nor even the swansong of Britain's military involvement in Kenya. Britain was determined to ensure that any promise of financial and logistic support in expanding Kenya's armed forces would be attached to a reciprocal promise of the military 'concessions' mentioned above. Even during the September/October 1963 'Independence Conference', Britain therefore agreed to its commitment to Kenya taking the form of 'proposals in principle only'.[137] Of course, the delay implied by all this would, in the event of agreement, add to the longevity of the duration of British military training teams in Kenya, thus continuing access to military 'facilities'.[138]

The impetus added to the defence negotiations by Britain's involvement in suppressing the January 1964 Kenya Rifles mutiny ensured that it did not take long for this hope to be realised.[139] On 12 March 1964, following a recent visit to East Africa, Sandys informed the Cabinet that the Kenya government was 'anxious to strengthen their armed forces and to improve their arrangements for maintaining internal security'.[140] He had reached 'broad agreement' that Britain would help to train the Kenya army and air force, and would transfer 'certain items of equipment and accommodation to the Kenya forces'. In exchange, the Kenya government would grant overflying and staging rights to British military aircraft, and naval facilities at Mombasa. 'They had also agreed that British units might visit Kenya at intervals for military training and exercises.'[141]

The icing on the cake, however, had come in a telegram from the then British High Commissioner, Sir Geoffrey de Freitas, dated 10 March 1964, in which he outlined the contents of a recent letter from Kenyatta: 'I shall be grateful if the British Government will agree to retain in Kenya after 12th December 1964 sufficient British Army and Royal Air Force personnel to carry [out] these duties in Kenya which are beyond the present capability of Kenya Armed Forces.'[142] Following the January mutiny, it had already been agreed that, under the guise of maintaining internal stability, British troops could operate 'back and forth on the mainland ... as the military situation requires'.[143] Barring the difficulty of tying the defence negotiations to the land settlement question, the matter of some £45-7 million of financial aid 'over the next few years', and Kenyan concerns over the all too convenient delays in forming the Kenya Navy, Britain had gained practically all that it wanted.[144] While Kenya would never attain the kind of defensive 'pole position' that had been ascribed alternately to, say, Aden, Cyprus, Egypt, Libya, Malaya, or Singapore, it would remain an important 'fall back' option and would help to maintain a significant degree of British influence in a sensitive region of the world. As the CRO East Africa Political Department put it in July 1965, with regard to the need to minimise communist penetration in Kenya: 'We enjoy military facilities which have proved useful already and some of which cannot yet be replaced from elsewhere.'[145] Under the terms of the 1964 Anglo-Kenyan Defence Agreement, British troops in Kenya would, if required, assist in 'dealing with internal disturbances', while Britain also agreed to 'cancel the eight interest free loans (totalling £6.05 million) made to the Kenya Government during the period September 1954 to March 1960'! *Quid pro quo* or *status quo*?

In the previous chapter it has been shown that even the new British Labour government supported its Conservative predecessor's initiatives when it came to assisting in the maintenance of independent Kenya's internal security and, more important, was equally committed to keeping Kenyatta or a 'moderate' successor in power. Labour also had to follow in the footsteps of the previous administration in attempting to apply economies to defence expenditure, while at the same time remaining equally reluctant to reduce Britain's worldwide commitments, at least until the financial crises of 1966-7.[146] This was especially the case because the new party of government had inherited an £800 million balance of payments deficit, as well as the ongoing deployment of some 390-400,000 military personnel overseas, around 54,000 of whom were engaged against the 'Indonesian Confrontation' in Southeast Asia.[147]

The newly-elected Labour government was aided initially in this task by the decision taken earlier in the year by the Douglas-Home government to establish in May 1964 a defence and oversea policy 'Long Term Study Group' (LTSG), in an effort to rationalise defence commitments with expenditure; in itself a logical extension of Macmillan's initiatives of 1960-1 and the amalgamation of the defence and oversea policy committees in October 1963.[148] With the help of the new Defence Secretary, Denis Healey, Prime Minister Harold Wilson soon demonstrated that he was in fact an 'east of Suez man', with savings in defence expenditure found by scuttling US proposals for a multi-lateral nuclear deterrent (MLF) in favour of the less expensive British alternative, the Atlantic Nuclear Force (ANF), and the eventual cancellation of several very costly military aviation development projects, in favour of buying US aircraft 'off the shelf'.[149]

While all this was eventually to prove to be futile, given Britain's ultimate withdrawal of a large part of its military forces from east of Suez, ironically, it seems that Britain's defence and internal security links with Kenya survived long after the evacuation from Aden.[150] The LTSG had been set up with a view to 'breaking the pattern of seeking "automatically to justify the *status quo*"'. However, there was disagreement between the Board of Trade and the Treasury, and the Foreign Office over how in future to protect Britain's overseas interests: the former favoured commercial and diplomatic means, while the latter could not conceive of abandoning a British military presence. With Foreign Office officials Michael Palliser and Sir John Nicholls, the Deputy Under-Secretary, dominating the proceedings and writing the LTSG report, it is not surprising that the latter view prevailed. The report recognised that hitherto Britain had maintained global commitments and '"an influence disproportionate to" its economic strength'. Yet, as Dockrill observes, the question arose whether Britain, by contracting some of its overseas interests in order to reduce the costs of maintaining them, would find the consequent reduction in 'power and influence' so great 'as to endanger her economic and political independence'.[151] There was also the matter of whether withdrawal from east of Suez would in fact produce any savings, not to mention what the US attitude would be. Significantly, the report was completed just days before Labour's election victory, and the condensed version (for Cabinet perusal) concluded that 'there will never be an ideal moment for decisions to be taken, but unless they are taken in the very near future, the carrying out of policy will be seriously prejudiced'.[152]

Of course, one of the main assumptions underlying the LTSG study, that Britain could not expect to retain its military bases in Aden and Singapore for another ten years, had to be shelved because of immediate financial difficulties. The Wilson government had accepted that in the long-term withdrawal would take place, and that it should be an ordered affair. In the short term, however, Britain would remain east of Suez, and savings were made in the fields of nuclear deterrence and military aviation projects. There was 'considerable support' within Wilson's immediate coterie 'for the view that our first priority should be the maintenance' of the east of Suez role.[153] With the reduced commitment in Kenya negotiated by the Conservative government, it follows that it was unnecessary to make any drastic changes there. This was especially the case given that, in the long term, besides the commitment to Europe through NATO, and the nuclear deterrent, Britain's interests in the Middle East were seen as paramount.[154] Kenya could still prove to be very useful if things 'went wrong' in Aden and/or the Gulf, and the LTSG was certainly aware of the importance to Britain of retaining military facilities there.[155] In 1965, although Britain was allowed passage through the Suez Canal, the southern air route via Libya, Sudan, and Kenya was closed by the recently changed Sudan government. 'But our use of the ... route may well be restored to a substantial degree and it must be our aim to keep the maximum options open.'[156] Without the Defence Agreement with

Kenya, even this unlikely outcome would have been practically impossible.

Conclusion

In many respects it could be argued that any consideration of Kenya in terms of Britain's 'east of Suez role' after December 1963 is largely academic, if not irrelevant. Yet, the former colony's effective invisibility from previous studies of British defence policy presents an ironic departure from current interpretations of the transfer of power. In a sense, Britain's staggered military withdrawal from Kenya served as a model for the ultimate abandonment of east of Suez. Of course, Britain did not maintain military facilities, even on a small scale, in all of the territories where it formerly held political influence. Libya is one good example. However, Britain's strategic bottom line in Kenya, whereby minimal 'defence rights' were retained, in exchange for financial, internal security, and military assistance, whether overt or secret, has proved to be far more successful than the pre-1968 Foreign Office model, if it can be called that, and belies earlier failures to take seriously Kenya's place in British defence policy. Equally, Britain's achievement in keeping Kenya pro-Western will not have been lost on its principal ally. Mombasa Harbour, which in the late 1970s was dredged by the US to enable the berthing of aircraft carriers from the Sixth Fleet, at the cost of some $50 million, has proven to be a far safer haven than Aden. Even if Kenya's significance to British defence strategy did indeed diminish from the early 1970s onwards, that significance during the twenty years after the Second World War, no matter how periodic, has surely warranted more detailed consideration than previous scholarship would suggest. Moreover, one suspects that, available documentation allowing, detailed analysis of Anglo-Kenyan defence and foreign relations, and British assistance in maintaining Kenya's internal security over the ten years or so from 1965, would produce more than a few surprises.

Notes

1. For example, the documentary readers edited by Goldsworthy, Hyam, and Kent (see Chapters One and Two), and Devereux's *British Defence Policy*, include occasional references to Kenya's passing significance in British strategic thinking during the post-war, pre-Suez period in relation to the Middle East. Although Darby's pioneering *British Defence Policy East of Suez* necessarily refers to the establishment and demise of Britain's post-Suez strategic project in Kenya, like earlier studies, his reliance on contemporary secondary sources, interviews, and official publications, does little more to enhance our knowledge and understanding than many of the subsequent studies which naïvely cite Darby, and accept the inevitable, and factually

incorrect, failure of British defence policy as the colony gained independence under the extreme pressures of African nationalism. For other studies which refer to Kenya in a post-war British defence context, see: Correlli Barnett, *Britain and Her Army 1509-1970* (London: Allen Lane/Penguin, 1970), p. 481; Blaxland, *The Regiments Depart*, pp. 411-9; Robert Holland, *The Pursuit of Greatness: Britain and the World Role, 1900-1970* (London: Fontana, 1991), pp. 293, 300; Low and Lonsdale, 'Introduction: Towards the New Order', pp. 3-7; Elizabeth Monroe, *Britain's Moment in the Middle East 1914-1956* (London: Chatto & Windus, 1964), pp. 157-8, 214; Jeffrey Pickering, *Britain's Withdrawal from East of Suez: The Politics of Retrenchment* (London: Macmillan, 1998), pp. 4, 117, 121, 122.

2. Kyle, *Politics of Independence*, pp. 122-3, 183-4.

3. Blundell, *So Rough a Wind*, pp. 261-2; Douglas-Home, *Evelyn Baring*, pp. 282-4; Edgerton, *Mau Mau*, p. 202; John Iliffe, *A Modern History of Tanganyika* (Cambridge: Cambridge University Press, 1979), pp. 563-5; Kyle, *Politics of Independence*, pp. 89-90; Murphy, *Lennox-Boyd*, p. 224; Shepherd, *Iain Macleod*, p. 161.

4. Iliffe, *Tanganyika*, p. 563.

5. Blundell, *So Rough a Wind*, p. 261.

6. Ibid.; Iliffe, *Tanganyika*, pp. 563-4.

7. Kyle, *Politics of Independence*, p. 88.

8. CO 822/1819, telegram 'Personal No. 5', Sir John Macpherson to Baring, repeated to Tanganyika (12), Uganda ('Personal No. 2), and Zanzibar (5), 9 Jan. 1959.

9. Douglas-Home, *Evelyn Baring*, p. 283.

10. Ibid.; Murphy, *Lennox-Boyd*, p. 224.

11. Murphy, 'Lennox-Boyd at the Colonial Office', p. 6.

12. Iliffe, *Tanganyika*, p. 564; Murphy, *Lennox-Boyd*, p. 224, 228-232; Rodger Yeager, *Tanzania: An African Experiment* (London: Dartmouth, 1989), p. 24.

13. Murphy, 'Lennox-Boyd at the Colonial Office', pp. 4, 7.

14. Murphy, *Lennox-Boyd*, pp. 224-5, 'Lennox-Boyd at the Colonial Office', pp. 5-6.

15. Murphy, 'Lennox-Boyd at the Colonial Office', p. 5.

16. CO 822/1819, telegram 'Personal No. 5', Sir John Macpherson to Baring, repeated to Tanganyika (12), Uganda ('Personal No. 2), and Zanzibar (5), 9 Jan. 1959.

17. Blundell, *So Rough a Wind*, p. 262.

18. Ibid.

19. Douglas-Home, *Evelyn Baring*, p. 283, n. 6.

20. CO 968/693, 'Stationing Part of the Strategic Reserve in Kenya', summary of a meeting held in the War Office, 5 April 1957.

21. CAB 134/1353, AF (59) 1st Meeting, 'The Next Ten Years in Africa', 14 Jan. 1959, fo. 1, AF (59) 6th, Item 1, 'The Next Ten Years in Africa: International Influences', 2 March 1959, fo. 2, para. 1.

22. Ibid. In the end, and perhaps reflecting Britain's difficulties in formulating policy from March onwards, discussions did not begin with the US until after the 1959 UK general election. A 'suitably adjusted version' of the paper had been given to the Americans that summer. See: ibid., AF (59) 14th Meeting, Item 1, 'Africa: The Next Ten Years: Talks with the Americans', 15 Oct. 1959.

23. CAB 134/1353, AF (59) 1st Meeting, 14 Jan. 1959, fo. 2.

24. Ibid., fo. 3.

25. Ibid.

26. Ibid., AF (59) 1st, 14 Jan. 1959, fo. 3. See also: ibid., AF (59) 1, 'The Future in Tropical Africa: Defence', note by the MoD, 7 Jan. 1959, fo. 2: 'A territory is of concern to the Defence Departments either (a) because there is a political commitment to defend it (and this may mean either "external defence" or "internal security"), (b) because, if it falls into the wrong hands, this would constitute a threat to the security of vital UK interests in neighbouring territories, or (c) because the use of the territory or its air space is necessary for the discharge of defence commitments elsewhere.'

27. Ibid., AF (59) 1st, 14 Jan. 1959, fo. 3, ibid., AF (59) 5, 'Prospects for the African Territories for Which the Colonial Office is Responsible', memo. by the Colonial Office, (c. 6-9) Jan. 1959, fo. 1, para. 2: 'Since ... [May 1957] ... the strategic importance of East Africa has, if anything, increased.'

28. Ibid., AF (59) 1, 'The Future in Tropical Africa: Defence', 7 Jan. 1959, fo. 4.

29. Ibid., AF (59) 1st, 14 Jan. 1959, fo. 4.

30. CO 822/1819, 'Future Policy in East Africa', draft memo. by Lennox-Boyd, n.d. (c. 26 Jan. 1959), fo. 1. See also: CAB 134/1354, AF (59) 23, 'Draft Paper for Submission to the Colonial Policy Committee: Future Policy in East Africa', memo. by Lennox-Boyd, 4 March 1959; and the final version, printed for the Colonial Policy Committee, CAB 134/1558, CPC (59) 2, 'Future Policy in East Africa', 10 April 1959.

31. CO 822/1819, 'Future Policy in East Africa', fo. 1.

32. Ibid., fo. 2.

33. Ibid., fos. 2-10.

34. Ibid., fo. 12.

35. Ibid.

36. Ibid., fos. 10-1.

37. Ibid., fos. 11-2, 12-3.

38. CAB 134/1353, AF (59) 3rd, Item 2, 'The Next Ten Years in Africa: East Africa', 28 Jan. 1959, fo. 5.

39. CO 822/1819, 'Future Administration and Financing of the East African Land Forces: Note of a Meeting in Mr Carstairs's room on Friday, February 13th, 1959.'

40. Ibid., fo. 4.

41. It is noteworthy, and perhaps also indicative of a kind of 'bailiwick mentality' that, in the current political climate in Africa generally, the Foreign Office considered the prospects of retaining control of East Africa and stationing the strategic reserve in Kenya to be incompatible: 'If our primary strategic interest in Kenya is as a base for our strategic reserve, this reserve must retain its mobility. The disorders provoked by the application of the policy recommended by the Colonial Office could involve the reserve [in] local tactical commitments and thus vitiate its primary function.' See: CAB 134/1354, AF (59) 22, 'Comments on the Colonial Office memorandum (AF (59) 5) on "Prospects for the African Territories for which the Colonial Office is Responsible"', note by the Foreign Office, 26 Feb. 1959, fo.1, para. 2.

42. CO 968/588, EADC (59) 7, 'Security of East African Forces', memo. by the chairman of the East Africa Regional Intelligence Committee, 20 March 1059. 'We do not consider that the effectiveness of any of the East African forces was impaired by political or any other subversion during the period under review.' For the detailed assessment, see: ibid., 'Annexure to EADC (59) 7 (Draft) Security of East African Forces Period 1st July - 31st December 1958', memo. by the East Africa Regional Intelligence Committee, 7 March 1959, attached 'Draft Report on the Security of the East African Forces during the Period 1st July - 31st December 1958', 7 March 1959, EARIC/FINAL/59/3, 'The Influence in East Africa of recent Events in the Horn of Africa: Appreciation by the East Africa Regional Intelligence Committee', 7 March 1959, and EADC (59) 1, 'East Africa Defence Committee Periodical Report to the Colonial Office on External Subversive Influences', memo. by Hutt, 13 Feb. 1959. It is noteworthy that Britain's inability to anticipate the 1964 East African mutinies was considered by MI5 to be one of its major intelligence failures, or 'hotspots': Tom Bower, *The Perfect English Spy: Sir Dick White and the Secret war 1935-90* (London: Heinemann, 1995), p. 342. For the 1963 Colonial Office review of security within the British and Kenyan armies, see: CO 822/3288.

43. CAB 134/1358, AF (61) 3 (Final), 'Economic Consequences of Political Development in East and Central Africa', report by the Africa (Official) Committee, 12 July 1961, fo. 5, para. 7. From 1 July 1960, the three East African territories saved around £3 million per year as a result of the War Office resumption of financial control of EALF: 'Kenya benefits to the extent of about £1.5 millions and Tanganyika and Uganda to the extent of about £700,000 each.' See also: CO 968/696, 'Report by Colonial

Office/War Office Working party on Army Organisation in east Africa', Sept. 1959, fo. 1; and Percox, 'Internal Security', pp. 105-6.

44. Bennett, *Kenya: A Political History*, p. 147.

45. For details, see: ibid., 146-50; Kyle, *Politics of Independence*, pp. 102-6; and Shepherd, *Iain Macleod*, pp. 175-86.

46. Bennett, *Kenya: A Political History*, p. 149; Macmillan, *Pointing the Way*, p. 165.

47. CAB 128/34, CC (60) 44th Meeting, Item 7, 'Oversea Civil Service', 27 July 1960, CC (60) 46th, Item 1, 'Oversea Civil Service', 26 July 1960, CC (60) 52nd Meeting, Item 2, 'East African Building Societies', 6 Oct. 1960, CC (60) 55th Meeting, Item 5, 'East African Building Societies', 25 Oct. 1960.

48. Bennett, *Kenya: A Political History*, pp. 151-5. Before the completion of polling for the 1961 election, the British Cabinet decided, on Renison's advice, to keep Kenyatta under restriction because his release would prejudice 'political development and possibly security': CAB 128/35 (I), CC (61) 9th Meeting, Item 6, 'Kenya: Jomo Kenyatta', 21 Feb. 1961.

49. DEFE 5/99, COS (60) 20, 'Outline for a Joint Study on the Tasks and Force Requirements of the Three Services for Limited War', note by the Secretaries to the Chiefs of Staff Committee, 27 Jan. 1960.

50. DEFE 5/101, COS (60) 93, 'The Strategic Importance of Malta', 11 April 1960; DEFE 5/104, COS (60) 175, 'Military Strategy for Circumstances Short of Global War - 1960-1970: A Joint Study - Part III: Broad Force and Logistic Requirements', 24 June 1960; DEFE 5/105, COS (60) 200, 'Military Strategy for Circumstances Short of Global War - 1960-70: A Joint Study', 5 July 1960, COS (60) 208, 'Military Strategy for Circumstances Short of Global War - 1960-70: A Joint Study: Effects on Force Levels and Deployment', 26 July 1960. See also: Darby, *British Defence Policy East of Suez*, pp. 163-4.

51. Darby, *British Defence Policy East of Suez*, pp. 163-5.

52. Ibid., pp. 171-3.

53. Ibid., p. 172.

54. CAB 131/23, D (60) 8th Meeting, 'Future Work of the Committee', 27 July 1960.

55. CAB 131/24, D (60) 48, 'Military Strategy for Circumstances Short of Global War', note by Macmillan, 10 Oct. 1960.

56. CAB 131/23, D (60) 10th Meeting, Item 1, 'Military Strategy for Circumstances Short of Global War, 1960-70', 17 Oct. 1960. For an overview of the Tory government's balance of payments problems, see: Andrew Boxer, *The Conservative Governments 1951-1964*, (Harlow: Addison, Wesley, Longman, 1996), pp. 4, 6, 17, 23-37, 95-7, 101; Dilwyn Porter, 'Downhill all the way: thirteen Tory years 1951-64', in R. Coopey *et al* (eds.), *The Wilson Governments 1964-1970* (London: Pinter, 1993), pp. 10-28; John

Turner, *Macmillan* (Harlow: Longman, 1994), pp. 119, 129, 241, 243, 245-6, 251.

57. CAB 131/23, D (60) 10th, 'Military Strategy for Circumstances Short of Global War', 17 Oct. 1960.

58. Ibid.

59. CAB 131/24, D (60) 51, 'Military Strategy for Circumstances Short of Global War, 1960-70', note by the Cabinet Secretary, Norman Brook, 17 Oct. 1960.

60. Ibid., D (60) 48, 'Military Strategy for Circumstances Short of Global War', 10 Oct. 1960, fo. 2.

61. M.A. Fitzsimons, *Empire by Treaty: Britain and the Middle East in the Twentieth Century* (London: Benn, 1965), pp. 220-1.

62. CAB 131/24, D (60) 53, 'Constitutional Development in Aden', memo. by Macleod, 27 Oct. 1960.

63. CAB 131/27, D (62) 8th Meeting, Item 1, 'Redeployment in the Middle East', 16 May 1962, D (62) 26, 'Deployment of Forces in the Middle East Command', memo. by Watkinson, 11 May 1962.

64. CO 968/723, minute by J.N.A. Armitage-Smith, 1 Nov. 1960.

65. CO 822/2886, 'Future of the King's African Rifles', note by Maj.-Gen. R.E. Goodwin (GOC, East Africa), 31 Dec. 1960,

66. CO 968/723, minute by J.N.A. Armitage-Smith, 1 Nov. 1960.

67. Kyle, *Politics of Independence*, p. 122.

68. CO 822/2892, 'Extract from KANU Manifesto: "Foreign Military Bases"', n.d. (c. Nov.-Dec. 1960); also part-cited in Kyle, *Politics of Independence*, p. 122.

69. CAB 131/23, D (60) 12th Meeting, Item 7, 'Review of Action Taken on the Committee's Decisions of 16th and 17th October', 7 Dec. 1960.

70. CO 822/2892, Watkinson to Macleod, 6 Dec. 1960. For an overview of Britain's overseas defence expenditure reviews from 1960-4, see: DEFE 7/1490, 1698-9, 1780-1, 1931-7, 2091, 2155, and 2319, and T 225/2434-40, and 2455-6.

71. CO 822/2892, telegram 237, Webber to Renison, 12 Dec. 1960.

72. Ibid., telegram 1128, Renison to Webber, 13 Dec. 1960, hand-written minute by Kitcatt, 13 Jan. 1960, commenting on Renison's telegram: 'One of the difficulties in this situation is that decisions about expenditure have to be made now [*sic*] based on the assessment of the future of the military facilities after independence; another is one of the primary functions of the base is to provide support, not in East Africa itself, but in the Persian Gulf. However, it is probably as well that future difficulties have come into the open now rather than at the stage of independence when much nugatory expenditure might already have been incurred.'

73. Ibid., Macleod to Watkinson, 16 Dec. 1960; Kyle, *Politics of Independence*, p. 123.

74. CO 822/2892, Macleod to Watkinson, 13 Dec. 1960.

75. Ibid. For further discussion of the desirability of an East African Federation, from the British defence point of view, see also: CAB 134/1560, CPC (61) 1st Meeting, Item 2, 'Colonial Problems, 1961', 5 Jan. 1961, CPC (61) 1, 'Colonial Problems in 1961', memo. by Macleod, 3 Jan. 1961.

76. CO 822/2892, Macleod to Watkinson, 13 Dec. 1960.

77. Ibid.

78. Ibid., Watkinson to Macleod, 23 Dec. 1960.

79. Ibid., Hobkirk (MoD) to Kitcatt (CO), 21 Dec. 1960, telegram 246, Macleod to Renison, 22 Dec. 1960, 11/018/02, Hobkirk to Kitcatt, 4 Jan. 1961, 'Kenya: Service Building Programme', draft brief (for Cabinet Defence Committee), by Hobkirk, 4 Jan. 1961.

80. CO 822/2886, EAC (61) 3, 'East African Conference: Defence Interests, Security of Tenure of United Kingdom's Military Bases in Kenya', paper by the Colonial Office, Dec. 1960, 'Future of the King's African Rifles', note by Goodwin, 31 Dec. 1960, Annex to JP (60) 103 (Final), 'Future Strategic Importance of East Africa: Brief for the Chiefs of Staff Meeting with the Governors of the East African Territories', EAC (61) MINUTES 2, 'Report of Proceedings: Defence and Internal Security', n.d. (c. Jan. 1961), EAC (61) 18 (Revise), 'East African Conference, 1961: Summary of Principal Conclusions', n.d. (c. Jan. 1961).

81. For a contemporary account of the political background and manoeuvring regarding an East African Federation , see: A.J. Hughes, *East Africa: The Search for Unity* (Harmondsworth: Penguin, 1963), passim., esp. pp. 213-68.

82. Kyle, *Politics of Independence*, p. 123.

83. CO 822/2886, EAC (61) MINUTES 2, 'Report of Proceedings: Defence and Internal Security', n.d. (c. Jan. 1961), EAC (61) 18 (Revise), 'East African Conference, 1961: Summary of Principal Conclusions', n.d. (c. Jan. 1961),.

84. Ibid., EAC (61) MINUTES 2, 'Report of Proceedings', n.d. (c. Jan. 1961), fo. 2, para. 4 (e). See also: Kyle, *Politics of Independence*, pp. 123, 227, n. 41.

85. CO 822/2892, Macleod to Watkinson, 12 Jan. 1961.

86. Ibid.

87. Ibid., Peck (Treasury) to C.E.F. Gough (MoD), 19 Jan. 1961.

88. Ibid. For Britain's defence agreement with Malaya, see: David Hawkins, *The Defence of Malaysia and Singapore: from AMDA to ANZUK* (London: RUSI, 1972).

89. CO 822/2892, Gough to Peck, 26 Jan. 1961, 2-DM 593/01, Peck to Gough, 27 Jan. 1961, Carstairs (CO) to Peck, 10 April 1961.

90. Ibid., MISC/M (61) 27, 'Services Building programme: Kenya - Record of a Meeting held in the Ministry of Defence ... Monday, 13 March 1961.'

91. Ibid.; CAB 131/25, D (61) 7th Meeting, Item 2, 'Kenya Building Programme', 17 May 1961, D (61) 25, 'Kenya Building Programme', memo. by Watkinson, 4 May 1961.

92. Ibid., Peck to Gough, 11 July 1961, Peck to Wright, 18 July 1961, Wright to Peck, 19 July 1961, telegram 243, Griffith-Jones to Webber, 23 July 1961, John Orme (Air Ministry) to E. Melville (CO) 3 Nov. 1961.

93. CAB 131/26, D (61) 65, 'Defence Policy', note by the Cabinet Secretary, Norman Brook, 23 Oct. 1961.

94. Ibid., para. 7.

95. Ibid., para. 12.

96. DEFE 4/142, COS (62) 9th Meeting, Item 6, 'Defence Facilities in Aden', 6 Feb. 1962; DEFE 4/143, COS (62) 15th Meeting, Item 3, 'Administrative Implications of the Redeployment of Forces from Kenya to Aden', 28 Feb. 1962; DEFE 4/144, COS (62) 26th Meeting, Item 2, 'Implications of the Redeployment of Forces from Kenya to Aden', 10 April 1962, COS (62) 32nd Meeting, Item 2, 'Redeployment of Forces from Kenya to Aden and Increased Strength of Bahrain Garrison', 3 May 1962; DEFE 4/145, COS (62) 33rd Meeting, Item 3, 'Psychological Operations in the Middle East', Item 4, 'Television Service in Aden', 8 May 1962, COS (62) 34th Meeting, Item 1, 'Redeployment of Forces from Kenya to Aden and Implications of Increasing Strength of Bahrain Garrison' 10 May 1962, COS (62) 41st Meeting, Item 2, 'Retention of Defence Facilities in Aden', 19 June 1962; T 225/2210, 118/Arabia/132, H.H. Hobbs (War Office) to Peck, 18 April 1962; CAB 131/27, D (62) 30, 'The Services Building Programme in the Middle East Command', memo. by Watkinson, 1 June 1962.

97. CAB 131/25, D (61) 17th Meeting, Item 2, 'Oversea Defence Expenditure', 6 Dec. 1961, fo. 4, para. 5.

98. CAB 134/1353, AF (59) 1st Meeting, 14 Jan. 1959, fo. 4.

99. CO 822/2892,, E.F.C. Stanford (AM) to Webber, 15 Nov. 1961, S 5702/S9, T.H. Shearer (AM) to Webber, 8 Dec. 1961, telegram 17, Monson to Renison, 11 Jan. 1962.

100. Ibid., telegram 20, Renison to Monson, 14 Feb. 1962.

101. Ibid., Macleod to Harold Watkinson (Minister of Defence), 16 Dec. 1960, Hobkirk (MoD) to P.J. Kitcatt (Colonial Office), 21 Dec. 1960, telegram 1177, Griffith-Jones (Acting Governor, Kenya) to Macleod, 29 Dec. 1960, 'Kenya: Service Building Programme', draft brief, 4 Jan. 1961, Renison to Monson, 14 Feb. 1962.

102. Ibid., Macleod to Watkinson, 12 Jan. 1961.

103. CAB 134/1357, AF (61) 10th Meeting, 'Financial Implications of Constitutional Development in Kenya', 8 Dec. 1961, AF (61) 11th Meeting, Item 2, 'Financial Implications of Constitutional Development in Kenya', 21 Dec. 1961; CAB 134/1358, AF (61) 29, 'Financial Implications of Prospective Constitutional Development in Kenya', note by Burke Trend, 5 Dec. 1961, AF (61) 32, 'Financial Implications of Constitutional Development in Kenya', memo. by the Colonial Office, 19 Dec. 1961, AF (61) 32 Addendum, 'Financial Implications of Constitutional Development in Kenya', 20 Dec. 1961, AF (61) 33, 'Financial Implications of Prospective Constitutional Development in Kenya', note by the MoD, 19 Dec. 1961; CAB 134/1359, AF (62) 1st Meeting, 'Financial Implications of Constitutional Development in Kenya', 16 Jan. 1962, AF (62) 2nd Meeting, Item 1, 'Financial Implications of Constitutional Development in Kenya', 25 Jan. 1962, AF (62) 5 (Final), 'Financial Implications of Constitutional Development in Kenya', report by Burke Trend, 30 Jan. 1962; CAB 134/1561, CPC (62) 3rd Meeting, Item 2, 'Kenya', 2 Feb. 1962, CPC (62) 3, 'Kenya Constitutional Conference', memo. by Maudling, 30 Jan. 1962.

104. PREM 11/3856, 'Secret Brief for Prime Minister', by M. Cary, 1 Feb. 1962, fo. 7; also cited in part in Kyle, 'End of Empire', pp. 15-6, and *Politics of Independence*, pp. 143-4.

105. Ibid., Leg Co N/314/VII/42, 'Notice of Motion Tabled on 8th June 1961 by The Hon T.J. Mboya (Member for Nairobi East)', telegram 210, Griffith-Jones to Webber, 10 July 1961, telegram 343, Webber to Griffith-Jones, 13 July 1961, telegram 936, Maudling to Profumo, 5 January 1962. For the immediate British response to such a motion which they had been unable to curtail by filibustering, see Griffith-Jones to Webber, 1 December 1961: 'Mboya's motion on British bases was debated in the Legislative Council yesterday, and after amendment by Government, was passed in the following terms without opposition:- "That this Council, whilst recognising the feelings of certain sections of the public regarding foreign military bases, undertakes that the question of the future of British bases in Kenya will be the subject of negotiations between the Kenya Colony Government and the Government of the United Kingdom, at the time of transition to independence, and that, meanwhile Government will initiate discussions with HMG regarding a solution compatible with the true interests of a sovereign Kenya."'

106. CAB 134/1561, CPC (62) 3, 'Kenya Constitutional Conference', memo. by Maudling, 30 Jan. 1962, fos. 3-4, para. 7; CAB 128/36 (I), CC (62) 12th Meeting, Item 5, 'Kenya', 8 Feb. 1962; Kyle, 'End of Empire', p. 9, and *Politics of Independence*, pp. 143-4; Maudling, *Memoirs*, pp. 92-6.

107. Maloba, *Mau Mau and Kenya*, p. 156; Louis and Robinson, 'The Imperialism of Decolonization', passim.

108. CAB 134/1560, CPC (61) 12th Meeting, 'Kenya', 16 Nov. 1961, CPC (61) 30, 'Kenya', memo. by Maudling, 14 Nov. 1961; CAB 128/35 (II), CC (61) 63rd Meeting, Item 5, 'Kenya', 16 Nov. 1961.

109. CO 968/723, 80050 APA, 'African Officers in the KAR', memo. by Gen. R.E. Goodwin, GOC, East Africa, 27 Sept. 1961, C of M (61) 165, 'Plan for Training Officers for 4th KAR', memo prepared by the Minister for Security and External Relations, Uganda, 30 Sept. 1960, minute by J.N.A. Armitage-Smith (Private Secretary to Minister of State), 1 Nov. 1960, 'Extra Expenditure on KAR in 1961-2 and 1962-3', unattributed Colonial Office draft memo., 24 Oct. 1961, 2583/61, Renison to Maudling, 8 Nov. 1961, 'African Officers', minute by Profumo for Watkinson, 6 Jan. 1962, 0165/4163 (SD 2 b) DEF 78/6/012, Lt.-Col. W.M.L. Adler (CO, Defence Department) to Maj. C.D.B. Troughton (War Office), 4 June 1962, DO/81350 APA, Brig. S.C. Chambers (HQ, EAC) to Brig. W.G.F. Jackson (WO), DO/0165/4101 (SD2b), Troughton to Adler, 31 July 1962.

110. CAB 134/1560, CPC (61) 12th, 'Kenya', 16 Nov. 1961.

111. CAB 134/1358, AF (61) 33, 'Financial Implications of Prospective Constitutional Development in Kenya', note by the Ministry of Defence, 19 Dec. 1961.

112. CAB 134/1359, AF (62) 27, 'Proposal for Military Technical Assistance in East Africa', note by the Commonwealth Relations Office, 17 April 1962, AF (62) 6th Meeting, Item 2, 'Proposal for Military Technical Assistance in East Africa', 3 May 1962. See also: ibid., AF (62) 26 (Final), 'British Policy in Southern and Eastern Africa', note by the Secretary to the Africa (Official) Committee, 18 May 1962, fos. 19-20, paras. 53-8, fo. 23, para. 59 (g).

113. Tom Mboya, *Freedom and After* (London: Andre Deutsch, 1963), p. 236-7.

114. McKenzie, Kenya's former agriculture minister (1959-1961), had an interesting past, to say the least. Apparently a long-standing friend of SAS and Capricorn Africa Society founder, David Stirling, McKenzie recommended to the Kenyatta government that it should appoint Stirling 'to negotiate with the British government a scheme for training Kenya's special forces, including the paramilitary General Service Unit'. As a result of his alleged contacts with, if not membership of MI6, he was apparently also able to inform Kenyatta in advance of a Soviet arms shipment, supposedly bound for Odinga. He also had dealings with Amin in Uganda: Bloch and Fitzgerald, *British Intelligence and Covert Action*, pp. 43, 153-57, 168. Following Sir Dick White's reorganisation of MI6 in early 1966, McKenzie asked the new controller for Africa, John Taylor, for assistance in establishing a Kenyan foreign intelligence service, 'a request which was accepted with

alacrity': Bower, *The Perfect English Spy*, pp. 349-50. See also: Austen Morgan, *Harold Wilson* (London: Pluto Press, 1992), p. 515.

115. DEFE 32/7, 'Minutes of a Chiefs of Staff (Informal) Meeting held on Tuesday, 7th August, 1962'.

116. CAB 134/2276, OC (O) (62) 5th Meeting, Item 1, 'Secondment of British Personnel to the Armed Forces of Newly Independent Countries', 28 Sept. 1962, OC (O) (62) 14, 'Subsidisation of Cost of British Personnel Serving with the Armed Forces of Certain Commonwealth Countries', memo. by the CRO, 13 Sept. 1962, OC (O) (62) 6th Meeting, Item 1, 'Subsidised Secondment of British Servicemen to Commonwealth Countries', 19 Oct. 1962. For the importance attached to training African military officers in Britain, see: CAB 148/46, OPD (O) (A) (65) 3, 'Africa South of the Sahara', note by the FO and the CRO, 11 Feb. 1965, para. 32: 'These courses of training provide us with a valuable opportunity to influence potentially key military leaders in the new Commonwealth countries in Africa.'

117. DEFE 4/146, COS (62) 47th Meeting, Item 4, 'Authorities for Counter-Battery and Retaliatory Action against the Yemen', 19 July 1962.

118. Ibid., COS (62) 48th Meeting, Item 3, 'Information Services in Aden', 24 July 1962, COS (62) 50th Meeting, Item 3, 'Defence Facilities in Aden', 31 July 1962, COS (62) 52nd Meeting, Item 1, 'Retention of Sovereign Base Areas in Aden', 7 Aug. 1962; CAB 128/36, CC (62) 52nd Meeting, Item 1, 'Aden', 11 Aug. 1962; DEFE 4/147, COS (62) 53rd Meeting, Item 5, 'Retention of Defence Facilities in Aden', 21 Aug. 1962, COS (62) 57th Meeting, 'Retention of Defence Facilities in Aden', 20 Sept. 1962, COS (62) 58th Meeting, Item 4, 'Retention of Defence Facilities in Aden', 25 Sept. 1962.

119. Balfour-Paul, *The end of empire in the Middle East*, p. 78; Fitzsimons, *Empire by Treaty*, p. 216; Lapping, *End of Empire*, p. 287.

120. DEFE 4/147, COS (62) 60th Meeting, Item 8, 'Retention of Defence Facilities in Aden', 2 Oct. 1962.

121. DEFE 4/148, COS (62) 62nd Meeting, Confidential Annex ('UK Eyes Only'), Item 5, 'Situation in the Yemen', 9 Oct. 1962, COS (62) 64th Meeting, Item 1, 'Retention of Defence Facilities in Aden', Item 2, 'Information Services in Aden', 16 Oct. 1962, COS (62) 66th Meeting, Item 4, 'Measures Necessitated by the Situation in the Yemen', Item 5, 'Little Aden Oil Refinery', 23 Oct. 1962; DEFE 4/149, COS (62) 70th Meeting, Item 2, 'Measures Necessitated by the Situation in the Yemen', 8 Nov. 1962, COS (62) 75th, Item 2, 'The Yemen', Item 3, 'Air Defence in Aden', Item 10, 'Sovereign Base Areas in Aden', 27 Nov. 1962.

122. DEFE 4/148, COS (62) 68th Meeting, Confidential Annex, Annex to Minute 8, 'Methods of Meeting Middle East Defence Commitments in the Event of Loss of Defence Facilities in Aden', 30 Oct. 1962.

123. T 225/2210, 118/Arabia/140 (WA2(a)), R.W. Barrow (WO) to P.H.F. Dodd (Treasury), 12 Oct. 1962, 11/018/02, J.A. Millson (MOD) to Dodd, 30 Oct. 1962. For Britain's increasing concern over Kuwait's security from Iraq as Kenya drew closer to independence, see: CAB 148/15, DOP (63) 1st Meeting, Item 3, 'Middle East Command forces', 13 Nov. 1963, and DO (63) 5, 'Middle East Command Forces', note by the Chairman of the DOP (O) C, 8 Nov. 1963.

124. DEFE 13/297, Fisher to Thorneycroft, 27 Nov. 1962.

125. Ibid., John Boyd Carpenter (Chief Secretary, Treasury) to Fisher, 28 Dec. 1962.

126. T 225/2211, Treasury minute, 'Kenya Forces After Independence: Mr Nigel Fisher's Letter of 28th November [*sic*]', 19 Dec. 1962.

127. DEFE 13/297, Thorneycroft to Fisher, 11 Jan. 1963, 'British Troops in Kenya' unattributed brief for Profumo, n.d. (c. Feb.-March 1963); PREM 11/4328, minute by Thorneycroft for Macmillan, 7 March 1963.

128. CO 822/2892, un-numbered telegram, Kenya (Public Relations Department) to Webber, 14 Nov. 1962, hand-written minute by Hull (CO), n.d. (c. 15 Nov. 1962): 'It is clear ... if the position was at all doubtful before, that the recent Kenya proposals that we might retain some military facilities in exchange for building up the Kenya Army amount at best to a dollar pro quo [*sic*].'

129. DEFE 4/150, COS (62) 76th Meeting, Item 1, 'The Implications of the Yemeni Revolt', 4 Dec. 1962, COS (62) 77th Meeting, Item 1, 'Television Service in Aden', 6 Dec. 1962, COS (62) 79th Meeting, Item 3, 'Western Aden Protectorate Security Report', 11 Dec. 1962, COS (62) 82nd Meeting, Item 2, 'The Situation in the Yemen', 20 Dec. 1962; DEFE 13/297, Thorneycroft to Fisher, 11 Jan. 1963; T 225/2211, 118/Arabia/20 (WA2(A)), Batho (WO) to Dodd (T), 29 Jan. 11963, 'Kenya/Aden', Treasury minute by Dodd, 31 Jan. 1963.

130. DEFE 13/297, Thorneycroft to Fisher, 11 Jan. 1963.

131. Ibid. See also: CAB 134/2278, OC (O) (63) 27, 'Expansion of Kenya Military Forces', note by the Colonial Office, 26 July 1963.

132. T 225/2211, Sir R.H. Scott (MoD) to R.W.B. Clarke (T), 19 April 1963, 'Service Building in the Middle East and Far East: Sir R Scott's letter of 19th April', Treasury minute by Peck for Sir R. Harris and Clarke, 24 April 1963: 'I agree with Mr Peck that we should be throwing away a valuable instrument of leverage vis-a-vis [*sic*] the Service Department's if we were now to accede to Sir Robert Scott's request [to lift the ban on works in Aden]', appended minute by Harris, 26 April 1963.

133. Ibid., Sir Hilton Poynton (CO) to Clarke, 21 May 1963.

134. Kyle, *Politics of Independence*, p. 183.

135. Ibid.

136. DEFE 13/297, 'Military Implications of a Phased Withdrawal of British Forces from Kenya during 1964', brief by Mountbatten for Thorneycroft, 28 Aug. 1963.

137. CAB 134/2277, CC (O) (63) 13th Meeting, Item 1, 30 July 1963; CAB 134/2278, OC (O) (63) 27, 'Expansion of Kenya Military Forces', note by the Colonial Office, 26 July 1963.

138. DEFE 13/297, 'Military Implications of a phased Withdrawal of British Forces from Kenya During 1964', minute by Mountbatten for Thorneycroft, 28 Aug. 1963.

139. PREM 11/4889, telegram 246, de Freitas to Sandys, 29 Jan. 1964.

140. CAB 128/38 (II), CM (64) 18th Meeting, Item 3, 'East Africa', 12 March 1964. See also: CAB 148/1, DO (64) 13th Meeting, Item 1, 'East Africa', 11 March 1964, DO (64) 15th Meeting, Item 2, 'East Africa: Kenya Discussions', 18 March, 1964; and CAB 148/2, DO (64) 19, 'East Africa - Defence Arrangements', memo. by Sandys, 9 March 1964.

141. CAB 128/38 (II), CM (64) 18th Meeting, Item 3, 'East Africa', 12 March 1964.

142. CAB 148/2, telegram 511, de Freitas to Sandys, 10 March 1964.

143. CAB 148/4, DO (O) (64) 4, 'British Defence Obligations in the Commonwealth', memo. by the CRO, 10 Feb. 1964, fo. 146, para. 38.

144. For details of the defence negotiations see, for example: PREM 11/4889, 'East Africa - Kenya Discussions', brief by Burke Trend, 17 March 1964, 'Memorandum of Intention and Understanding Regarding Certain Financial and Defence Matters of Mutual Interest to the British and Kenya Governments (As approved by British Ministers)', n.d. (c. April 1964). See also: CAB 134/2279, OC (O) (64) 4th Meeting, 'East Africa: Defence and Financial Negotiations', 21 Feb. 1964, OC (O) (64) 2, 'East Africa: Defence and Financial Negotiations', memo. by the CRO, 20 Feb. 1964; CAB 148/1, DO (64) 10th Meeting, Item 3, 'East Africa', 26 Feb. 1964, DO (64) 16, 'East Africa - Defence Arrangements', memo. by Sandys, 24 Feb. 1964; CAB 148/4, DO (O) (64) 6th Meeting, 'Kenya - Defence and Financial Discussions', 13 March 1964, DO (O) (64) 8th Meeting, 'Kenya - Defence and Financial Discussions', 7 April 1964; CAB 148/2, DO (O) (64) 13, 'Kenya: Defence and Financial Discussions', memo. by the CRO, 12 March 1964, DO (64) 19, 'East Africa - Defence Arrangements', memo. by Sandys, 9 March 1964, DO (64) 21, 'East Africa: Kenya Discussions', note by the Chairman of the Defence and Oversea Policy (Official) Committee, 16 March 1964; CAB 148/5, DO (O) (64) 20, 'The Defence and Financial Discussions with Kenya in Nairobi, March 1964', Report by the Leader of

the British Delegation', 3 April 1964; CAB 148/7, DO (O) (64) 61, 'Formation of the Kenya Navy', joint memo. by the CRO and the MoD, 27 July 1964, DO (O) (64) 61, 'Copy of letter from the Prime Minister of Kenya to the Commonwealth Secretary dated 14th July - FORMATION OF THE KENYA NAVY [*sic*]', 27 July 1964; and Page, *KAR*, pp. 264-8; PREM 11/4889, 'Formation of the Kenya Navy', brief by Burke Trend for Douglas-Home, 29 July 1964.

145. CAB 134/2544, RJ 5545/235, 'The Implications of Sino-Soviet Penetration in Black Africa (SV (65) 1 - 19 Jan. 1965', paper by the CRO, July 1965, fo. 126.

146. Carver, *Tightrope Walking*, pp. 70-5; Dan Keohane, *Labour Party Defence Policy since 1945* (Leicester, London: Leicester University Press, 1993), p. 21; Ovendale (ed.), *British Defence Policy since 1945*, p. 8; Pickering, *Britain's Withdrawal from East of Suez*, pp. 135-49, 150-76; Clive Ponting, *Breach of Promise: Labour in Power 1964-1970* (London: Hamish Hamilton, 1989), pp. 102-6, 107-19; Chris Wrigley, 'Now you see it, now you don't: Harold Wilson and Labour's foreign policy 1964-70', pp. 123-35, in R. Coopey *et al* (eds.), *The Wilson Governments*.

147. R. Coopey *et al*, 'Introduction: The Wilson Years', p. 3, Lewis Johnman, 'The Conservative Party in Opposition, 1964-70', p. 184, Nicholas Woodward, 'Labour's economic performance, 1964-70', pp. 72-8, 80, 98, in R. Coopey *et al* (eds.), *The Wilson Governments*; Saki Dockrill, 'Britain's Power and Influence: Dealing with Three Roles and the Wilson Government's Debate at Chequers in November 1964', draft, seen by courtesy of Dr Dockrill, p. 1; A. Morgan, *Harold Wilson*, pp. 242-56; Ben Pimlott, *Harold Wilson* (London: Harper Collins, 1992), p. 350; Ponting, *Breach of Promise*, pp. 61-3.

148. Dockrill, 'Britain's Power and Influence', pp. 2-3.

149. Ponting, *Breach of Promise*, pp. 85-101; Denis Healey, *Time of My Life* (New York: Norton, 1990), pp. 249-325.

150. Space precludes further consideration of the 'east of Suez decision'. For debate and details, see, for example: Sir Ewen Broadbent, *The Military and Government: from Macmillan to Heseltine* (London: Macmillan, 1988), pp. 28-39; Peter Catterall (ed.), 'The East of Suez Decision', *Contemporary Record*, 7/3 (Winter 1993), pp. 612-53; Darby, *British Defence Policy East of Suez*, pp. 283-326, 'East of Suez Reassessed', in John Baylis (ed.), *British Defence Policy in a Changing World* (London: Croom Helm, 1977), pp. 52-65; David Greenwood, 'Defence and national Priorities since 1945', in Baylis (ed.), *British Defence Policy in a Changing World*, pp. 198-205; Michael Howard 'Britain's Strategic Problem East of Suez', *International Affairs*, 42/2 (April 1966), pp. 179-83; Elizabeth Monroe, 'British Bases in the Middle East: Assets or Liabilities?', *International Affairs*, 42/1 (1966), pp. 24-34; Peter Nailor, 'Denis Healey and

Rational Decision-Making in Defence', in Beckett and Gooch (eds.), *Politicians and Defence*, pp. 154-77; Pickering, *Britain's Withdrawal from East of Suez*, pp. 150-76; D.C. Watt, 'The Decision to Withdraw from the Gulf', *Political Quarterly*, 39 (1968), pp. 310-21.

151. Dockrill, 'Britain's Power and Influence', pp. 3-6.

152. CAB 130/213, MISC 17/2, 'British Interests and Commitments Overseas', 18 Nov. 1964, cited in ibid., p. 7.

153. Dockrill, 'Britain's Power and Influence', p. 9.

154. CAB 128/39, CC (64) 11th Meeting, Item 5, 'Defence and Oversea Policy', 26 Nov. 1964; CAB 148/7, DO (O) (64) 77, 'Introduction and Terms of Reference' [for LTSG report], 12 Oct. 1964, fo. 14, para. 28 (iv).

155. CAB 148/8, DO (O) (S) (64) 10, 'British Defence Obligations in the Commonwealth', memo. by the CRO for the LTSG, 4 Aug. 1964.

156. CAB 129/120, C (65) 49, 'The Middle East', memo. by M. Stewart (Foreign Secretary), 24 March 1965.

CONCLUSION

British Defence and Colonial Internal Security Policy in East Africa, 1945-65

This book has examined a hitherto largely neglected aspect of British decolonisation in Kenya. By considering Kenya's vacillating place in Britain's overseas defence strategy and related internal security issues in the context of the first twenty years of the Cold War, it has demonstrated the large degree of continuity in British policy. Clearly, given this broad perspective, defence and security issues beyond the confines of the Mau Mau Emergency were far more significant to Britain than has hitherto been acknowledged.

As the Second World War drew to an end, and Cold War preparations began, British officials in East Africa began to assess their readiness to cope with the possible threat to internal security posed by the imminent mass demobilisation of African soldiers and an expected upsurge in anti-colonial nationalism. The East African governors found their intelligence systems to be woefully inadequate. They also had considerable restrictions placed upon their ability to fulfil the manpower requirements deemed necessary to maintain control in the event of a State of Emergency, as a result of financial and manpower limits imposed in London. As the Cold War took hold, the situation was exacerbated by uncertainty in London over the precise nature of future defence policy in the Middle East, and the broad question of colonial defence and security throughout the British Empire. The prognosis for internal security in Kenya was not helped, either, by the considerable levels of political and socio-economic hardship, thus disaffection, among the colony's majority African population.

Nevertheless, the Kenya government took serious steps in planning and preparing for the possibility of a serious breakdown in 'public security'. The Kenya Police did all in its power to 'nip' a potential security crisis 'in the bud'. Yet, if anything, the major problem for Kenya's security planners during the early stages of the Cold War was the multitude of potential threats that they had to assess. Ironically, in the absence of meaningful or sufficient political and socio-economic improvements, government repression, even at the level of a handful of pre-emptive arrests, served only to increase the likelihood of the insurgency that they were designed to prevent. Between 1945 and 1952, Kenya might not in fact have been in the throes of an armed insurrection, but the declaration of the State of Emergency and the concomitant increase in repressive measures soon brought this about.

As government repression led to the onset of the Emergency it was designed to forestall, so the level and sophistication of that repression had to be increased. Clearly, despite the piecemeal political reforms and selectively targeted socio-economic developments introduced during the 1952-6 period, British counter-insurgency was not designed to pave the way for the transfer of power to anti-colonial nationalists. British prerogatives were, primarily, to regain control. By the end of 1956, it appeared that this had largely been achieved. This was perhaps a fortunate coincidence for a Britain which had so very recently fallen foul not only of the stubborn Egyptian nationalist, Colonel Nasser, but also of diplomatic and economic pressures applied from that most unlikely of quarters, Washington.

Britain's decision to 'permanently' station elements of the UK Strategic Reserve in Kenya, taken shortly after the Mau Mau and Suez conflicts, confirms that the reforms introduced during the previous four years were designed to ensure British control of the colony. The Lyttelton Constitution and Swynnerton Plan in no way constituted a precursor to the planned transfer of power to an African majority government. Indeed, British defence chiefs and officials concerned themselves mainly with the day-to-day mundanities associated with moving troops to Kenya, while their colleagues in the Colonial Office did their utmost to silence the increasingly vocal and, it must have seemed, irrational African nationalists. Britain's strategic project in Kenya did not seem doomed from the start to those involved at the time. Besides, with Mau Mau apparently defeated, the imposition of the Lennox-Boyd Constitution surely demonstrated that political development in Kenya was proceeding in an orderly, if not break-neck fashion. While the nationalists adhered to the ethereal Colonial Office timetable for further constitutional advance, little regard had to be paid to African political sensibilities.

Yet, just as the numerous problems associated with stationing British troops in Kenya seemed to have been ironed out, British defence strategists were compelled once more to take account of African political considerations. With the Africans' boycott of Legislative Council of January 1959 serving to undermine the veneer of political stability in Kenya, so too was the legitimacy of Britain's nominal developmental strategy brought into question. Only then did Britain begin to contemplate seriously its strategic options in Kenya with regard to the Africans' refusal to legitimise the process further with their participation. As Britain's political legitimacy in Kenya was brought increasingly into question, the grounds for retaining its military bases there became all the more difficult to justify. Yet, three years of painstaking military planning and implementation would not be cast aside lightly.

Every effort was therefore made by Britain to be seen to make concessions to legitimate African nationalist aspirations, and thereby hoped that Kenya would remain stable enough for Britain to be able to 'guide' future political developments at its leisure. This seemed the best means of safeguarding existing economic interests and prolonging the post-Suez regional defence strategy. However, ever-increasing socio-economic hardship among Africans provided fertile ground for the nationalists, if they were radical enough, and those who did not care for politics, especially among the Kikuyu, reverted to their traditional secretive practices. Rising crime and militancy on a par with levels seen before the Mau Mau Emergency and scarce resources ensured that the fiction of 'normality' in Kenyan society could only be perpetuated while the African nationalists continued to legitimise Britain's political dalliance. Once African participation was withdrawn, Britain was compelled to meet the nationalists halfway if it were to avoid a repeat of Mau Mau and the dangerous prospect of an irreversible loss of control.

With the principle of the constitutional conference established in January 1960, Britain still had more work to do in order to bring the KANU nationalists on board. Again, it was perhaps fortunate, if not totally unexpected in all quarters, that Kenyatta's release provided the appropriate calming influence. The political climate in Kenya was thereby moderated to a considerable extent, and many colonial officials' nerves were correspondingly settled by his rehabilitation. Thus, with the circumstances apparently ripe for the withdrawal of formal administration, Britain did all in its power to bolster Kenyatta's position in readiness for independence. By arming the Kenyatta state Britain ensured that future threats to Kenya's stability could be dealt with by largely 'political' means.

As the last chapter in this book makes clear, one of the key motives underpinning Britain's political and internal security policies in Kenya from early 1957 to beyond independence was its defence interests. Hitherto, it could be argued that British defence policy in Kenya, especially with regard to the 'east of Suez role' after December 1963, does not warrant detailed academic attention. Yet, as this book has shown, the former colony remained, if not in the forefront, then certainly not absent from British defence planner's thinking. Kenya may not have remained a large military installation, at least not for Britain, but the staggered military withdrawal, it could be argued, was at least representative of an orderly and mutually beneficial model. Britain no longer needed a base.

This is confirmed by the very fact that Britain did not maintain military facilities, even on a small scale, in all of the territories where it formerly held political control. However, it should be stressed that Britain did retain albeit minimal 'defence rights' in Kenya, in exchange for financial, internal security, and military assistance, designed to maintain the country's stability. The defence and security aspects of that particular decolonisation were therefore a resounding success, at least from the Cold War perspective.

While Kenya's strategic significance to Britain did indeed diminish from the early 1970s onwards, the former colony remained largely pro-Western, if not benevolently neutral, throughout the Cold War. Although Kenya has been sullied by massive levels of political corruption, and far too many of its citizens still suffer from 'land hunger' and remain in abject poverty, in comparative African terms the country represents a rare post-independence success story.

Bibliography

Unpublished Primary Sources

Public Record Office, Kew

CABINET PAPERS

CAB 128 Cabinet Minutes, 1945-.
CAB 129 Memoranda, 1945-.
CAB 130 *Ad Hoc* Committees.
CAB 131 Defence Committee.
CAB 133 Overseas Conferences Reports to Cabinet.
CAB 134 Cabinet Committees.
CAB 148 Defence and Overseas Policy Committee, 1963-.
CAB 158 Joint Intelligence Committee Memoranda, 1947-.
CAB 159 Joint Intelligence Committee Minutes, 1947-.

COLONIAL OFFICE

CO 822 East Africa Department Original Correspondence.
CO 967 Secretary of State's Private Office Papers.
CO 968 Defence Department Original Correspondence.

DEFENCE PAPERS

DEFE 4 Chiefs of Staff Committee Minutes.
DEFE 5 Memoranda.
DEFE 6 Joint Planning Staff and Defence Planning Staff Reports.
DEFE 7 Defence Registered Files.
DEFE 11 Chiefs of Staff Committee Registered Files.
DEFE 13 Minister/Secretary of State's Private Office Papers.
DEFE 25 Chief of Defence Staff Registered Files.
DEFE 32 Chiefs of Staff Committee Secretary's Standard Files.

PRIME MINISTER'S OFFICE

PREM 8 Correspondence and Papers, 1945-51.
PREM 11 Correspondence and Papers, 1951-64.

TREASURY PAPERS

T 220 Imperial and Foreign Division.
T 225 Defence Policy and Material Division.

WAR OFFICE

WO 216 Chief(s) of the Imperial General Staff Unregistered Papers.
WO 236 General Sir George Erskine Papers.
WO 276 East Africa Command.

Imperial War Museum, Lambeth, London

75/134/1, 4	General Sir George Erskine.

National Army Museum, Chelsea, London

ARC 8908-144-1, 5, 14, 18, 19	Lord Harding of Petherton.
ARC 7410-29, 8011-132, 8301-6	Sir Gerald Templer.

Rhodes House Library, Oxford

MSS Afr s 746	Sir Michael Blundell.
MSS Afr s 1574	Lord Howick (Evelyn Baring), interview, 19 Nov. 1969.
MSS Afr s 1580	General Sir William R.N. Hinde.
MSS Afr s 1694	Sir John Whyatt.
MSS Afr s 1784 (20)	M.K. Akker.
MSS Afr s 1784 (21)	R.C. Catling.
MSS Afr s 1784 (24)	M.C. Manby.
MSS Afr s 2159	M.C. Manby.
MSS Brit Emp s 486	Sir Arthur E. Young.

Published Primary Sources

Cmnd. 1030, *Historical Survey of the Origins and Growth of Mau Mau*, (London: HMSO, 1960).

Hansard, House of Commons Debates.

Report of the Committee on Emergency Detention Camps, Special Supplement to the Kenya Gazette of 1 September 1959, (R.D. Fairn, Chairman), August 1959.

The Colonial Office List (London: HMSO, 1959-65).

The Times.

Published Secondary Sources

Adekson, J. 'Bayo, 'Ethnicity and army recruitment in colonial plural societies', *Ethnic and Racial Studies*, 2/2 (1979), pp. 151-65.

Aggett, W.J.P., *The Bloody Eleventh: History of the Devonshire Regiment. Vol. 3: 1915-1969* (Exeter: Devonshire & Dorset Regiment, 1995).

Aldrich, Richard J., *The Hidden Hand: Britain, America and Cold War Secret Intelligence* (London: John Murray, 2001).

Aldrich, Richard J., and Michael F. Hopkins (eds.), *Intelligence, Defence and Diplomacy: British Policy in the Post-War World* (Ilford: Frank Cass, 1994).

Allen, Charles, *The Savage Wars of Peace: Soldiers' Voices 1945-1989* (London: Michael Joseph, 1990.

Anderson, David M., and David Killingray (eds.), *Policing and Decolonisation: Politics, Nationalism and the Police, 1917-65* (Manchester: Manchester University Press, 1992).

______. *Policing the Empire: Government, Authority and Control, 1830-1940* (Manchester: Manchester University Press, 1992).
Balfour-Paul, Glen, *The End of Empire in the Middle East: Britain's Relinquishment of Power in Her Last Three Arab Dependencies* (Cambridge: Cambridge University Press, 1991).
Barnett, Correlli, *The Lost Victory: British Dreams, British Realities 1945-1950* (London: Pan, 1996 [1995]).
______. *Britain and Her Army 1509-1970: A Military, Political and Social Survey* (London: Allen Lane, 1970).
Bartlett, C.J., *The Long Retreat: A Short History of British Defence Policy 1945-70* (London: Macmillan, 1972).
Baxter, John, *State Security, Privacy and Information* (Hemel Hempstead: Harvester Wheatsheaf, 1990).
Baylis, J. (ed.), *British Defence Policy in a Changing World* (London: Croom Helm, 1977).
Beckett, Ian, and John Gooch (eds.), *Politicians and Defence: Studies in the Formulation of British Defence Policy, 1845-1970* (Manchester: Manchester University Press, 1981).
Bennett, George, *Kenya. A Political History: The Colonial Period* (London: Oxford University Press, 1963).
Bennett, George, and Carl G. Rosberg, *The Kenyatta Election: Kenya 1960-1961* (London: Oxford University Press, 1961).
Berman, Bruce, and John Lonsdale, *Unhappy Valley: Conflict in Kenya and Africa* Book One: State and Class (London: James Currey, 1992).
______. *Unhappy Valley: Conflict in Kenya and Africa* Book Two: Violence and Ethnicity (London: James Currey, 1992).
Berman, Bruce, *Control and Crisis in Colonial Kenya: The Dialectic of Domination* (London: James Currey, 1990).
Blaxland, Gregory, *The Regiments Depart: A History of the British Army, 1945-1970* (London: William Kimber, 1971).
______. *The Farewell Years: The Final Historical Records of the Buffs, Royal East Kent Regiment, 1948-1967* (Canterbury: Queen's Own Buffs Office, 1967).
Bloch, Jonathan, and Patrick Fitzgerald, *British Intelligence and Covert Action: Africa, Middle East and Europe since 1945* (Dingle, London: Brandon, Junction, 1983).
Blundell, Sir Michael, *So Rough a Wind: the Kenya Memoirs of Sir Michael Blundell* (London: Weidenfeld & Nicolson, 1964).
Bower, Thomas M., *The Perfect English Spy: Sir Dick White and the Secret War, 1935-90* (London: Heinemann, 1995).
Boxer, Andrew, *The Conservative Governments 1951-1964* (Harlow: Addison Wesley Longman, 1996).
Broadbent, Sir Ewen, *The Military and Government: From Macmillan to Heseltine* (London: Macmillan, 1988).
Bullock, Alan, *Ernest Bevin: Foreign Secretary, 1945-51* (Oxford: Oxford University Press, 1985 [1983]).
Bunyan, Tony, *The History and Practice of the Political Police in Britain* (London: Quartet, 1978 [1976]).
Butler, David, and Anne Sloman, *British Political Facts 1900-1975* (London:

Macmillan, 1975 [1963]).
Butler, R.A.B., Lord, *The Art of the Possible: The Memoirs of Lord Butler* (London: Hamish Hamilton, 1971).
Campbell, Guy, *The Charging Buffalo: A History of the Kenya Regiment* (London: Leo Cooper, 1986).
Carruthers, Susan L., *Winning Hearts and Minds: British Governments, the Mass Media and Colonial Counter-Insurgency, 1944-60* (London: Leicester University Press, 1995).
Carver, Michael, *Tightrope Walking: British Defence Policy since 1945* (London: Hutchinson, 1992).
______. *War Since 1945* (London: Ashfield Press, 1990).
______. *Out of Step: The Memoirs of Lord Carver* (London: Hutchinson, 1989).
Catterall, Peter (ed.), 'The East of Suez Decision', *Contemporary Record*, 7/3 (1993), pp. 612-53.
Chamberlain, M.E., *The Scramble for Africa* (London: Longman. 1980 [1974]).
Clayton, Anthony, *Frontiersmen: Warfare in Africa since 1950* (London: University College London Press, 1999).
______. *Counter-Insurgency in Kenya: A Study of Military Operations Against Mau Mau* (Nairobi: Transafrica, 1976).
Clayton, Anthony, and David Killingray, *Khaki and Blue: Military and Police in British Colonial Africa* (Athens, Ohio: Ohio University Center for International Studies, 1989).
Cloake, John, *Templer, Tiger of Malaya: The Life of Field Marshall Sir Gerald Templer* (London: Harrap, 1985).
Clough, Marshall S., *Mau Mau Memoirs: History Memory and Politics* (Boulder, CO, London: Lynne Rienner, 1998).
Connor, Ken, *Ghost Force: The Secret History of the SAS* (London: Weidenfeld & Nicolson, 1998).
Coopey, R., S. Fielding, and N. Tiratsoo (eds.), *The Wilson Governments 1964-1970* (London: Pinter, 1993).
Crocker, Chester A., 'Military Dependence: the Colonial Legacy in Africa', *Journal of Modern African Studies*, 12/2 (1974), pp. 265-86.
Croker, G.W., 'Mau Mau', *Journal of the Royal United Services Institute*, 100 (Feb.-Nov. 1955).
Darby, Phillip, *British Defence Policy East of Suez 1947-1968* (London: Oxford UP, 1973).
Darwin, John, *The End of the British Empire: The Historical Debate* (Oxford: Blackwell, 1991).
______. *Britain and Decolonisation: The Retreat from Empire in the Post-War World* (Basingstoke: Macmillan, 1988).
Devereux, David R., *The Formulation of British Defence Policy Towards the Middle East, 1948-56* (New York: St. Martin's Press, 1990).
Dewar, Michael, *Brush Fire Wars: Minor Campaigns of the British Army Since 1945* (London: Hale, 1984).
Dockrill, M., and J.W. Young (eds.), *British Foreign Policy 1945-56* (London: Macmillan, 1989).
Douglas-Home, Charles, *Evelyn Baring: The Last Proconsul* (London: Collins, 1978).

Edgerton, Robert B., *Mau Mau: An African Crucible* (London: I.B. Tauris, 1990).

Emsley, Clive, *The English Police: A Political and Social History* (Hemel Hempstead: Harvester Wheatsheaf, 1991).

Fitzsimons, M.A., *Empire by Treaty: Britain and the Middle East in the Twentieth Century* (London: Benn, 1965).

Foran, W. Robert, *The Kenya Police, 1887-1960* (London: Robert Hale, 1962).

Füredi, Frank, *Colonial Wars and the Politics of Third World Nationalism* (London: I.B. Tauris, 1994).

______. 'Creating a Breathing Space: The Political management of Colonial Emergencies', *Journal of Imperial and Commonwealth History*, 21/3 (1993), pp. 89-106.

______. 'Britain's Colonial Wars: Playing the Ethnic Card', *Journal of Commonwealth and Comparative Politics*, 28 (1990), pp. 70-89.

______. *The Mau Mau War in Perspective* (London: James Currey, 1989).

Gann, L.H., and P. Duignan (eds.), *Colonialism in Africa, 1870-1960*, Vol.2: *The History and Politics of Colonialism, 1914-1960* (Cambridge: Cambridge University Press, 1970).

Geraghty, Tony, *Who Dares Wins: The Story of the SAS 1950-1980* (London: Fontana, 1981 [1980]).

Gertzel, Cherry, *The Politics of Independent Kenya, 1963-1968* (Nairobi: EAPH, 1971).

Gertzel, Cherry, Maure Goldschmidt, and Donald Rothchild (eds.), *Government and Politics in Kenya* (Nairobi: EAPH, 1969).

Gifford, Prosser, and Wm. Roger Louis (eds.), *Decolonization and African Independence: The Transfers of Power, 1960-1980* (New Haven CT: Yale University Press, 1988).

______. *The Transfer of Power in Africa: Decolonization 1940-1960* (New Haven CT: Yale University Press, 1982).

Gilbert, Martin, *'Never Despair': Winston S. Churchill 1945-1965* (London: Heinemann, 1988).

Goldsworthy, David (ed.), *The Conservative Government and the End of Empire 1951-1957* Three Volumes (London: HMSO, 1994).

______. *Tom Mboya: The Man Kenya Wanted to Forget* (Nairobi: Heinemann, 1982).

______. *Colonial Issues in British Politics, 1945-1961: From 'Colonial Development' to 'Wind of Change'* (Oxford: Clarendon Press, 1971).

Gorst, Anthony, Lewis Johnman, and W. Scott Lucas (eds.), *Contemporary British History, 1931-1961: Politics and the Limits of Policy* (London: Pinter, 1991).

Gupta, P.S., *Imperialism and the British Labour Movement, 1914-1964* (London: Macmillan, 1975).

Gutteridge, William F., *The Military in African Politics* (London: Methuen, 1969).

Hallows, Ian S., *Regiments and Corps of the British Army* (London: Cassell, 1994 [1991]).

Harbeson, John W., 'Land Reform and Politics in Kenya, 1954-70', *Journal of Modern African Studies*, 9/2 (1971), pp. 231-52.

Haswell, Jock, *British Military Intelligence* (London: Weidenfeld & Nicolson, 1973).

Hargreaves, J.D., *Decolonization in Africa* (London: Longman, 1988).

Hatch, John, *A History of Postwar Africa* (New York: Praeger, 1970 [1965]).

Hawkins, David, *The Defence of Malaysia and Singapore: from AMDA to ANZUK* (London: RUSI, 1972).

Healey, Denis., *Time of My Life* (London: Joseph, 1989).

Heather, Randall W., 'Intelligence and Counter-Insurgency in Kenya, 1952-56', *Intelligence and National Security*, 5/3 (July 1990), pp. 57-83.

Holland, R.F., *The Pursuit of Greatness: Britain and the World Role, 1900-1970* (London: Fontana, 1991).

______. *European Decolonization 1918-1981: An Introductory Survey* (London: Macmillan, 1985).

Holland, R.F., and G. Rizvi (eds.), *Perspectives on Imperialism and Decolonisation: Essays in Honour of A.F. Madden* (London: Frank Cass, 1984).

Horne, Alistair, *Macmillan 1957-1986* (New York: Viking, 1989).

______. *Macmillan 1894-1956* (London: Macmillan, 1988).

Howard, Michael, 'Britain's Strategic Problem East of Suez', *International Affairs*, 42/2 (1966), pp. 179-83.

Hughes, A.J., *East Africa: The Search for Unity* (Harmondsworth: Penguin, 1963).

Hyam, Ronald (ed.), *The Labour Government and the End of Empire 1945-1951* Four Volumes (London: HMSO, 1992).

Iliffe, John, *A Modern History of Tanganyika* (Cambridge: Cambridge University Press, 1979).

James, Lawrence, *Imperial Rearguard: Wars of Empire, 1919-1985* (London: Brassey's, 1988).

Jeffery, Keith, 'Intelligence and Counter-Insurgency Operations: Some Reflections on the British Experience', *Intelligence and National Security*, 2/1 (1987), pp. 118-149.

Jeffery, Keith, and Peter Hennessy, *States of Emergency: British Governments and Strikebreaking since 1919* (London: Routledge & Kegan Paul, 1983).

Judd, Denis, *Empire: The British Imperial Experience from 1765 to the Present* (London: Harper Collins, 1996).

Kanogo, Tabitha, *Squatters and the Roots of Mau Mau 1905-63* (London: James Currey, 1987).

Kariuki, J.M., *Mau Mau Detainee* (Harmondsworth: Penguin, 1964 [1963]).

Keesing's Contemporary Archives.

Kent, John (ed.), *Egypt and the Defence of the Middle East* Three Volumes (London: The Stationary Office, 1998).

______. *British Imperial Strategy and the Origins of the Cold War 1944-49* # (Leicester, London, New York: Leicester University Press, 1993).

Keohane, D., *Labour Party Defence Policy since 1945* (London: Leicester University Press, 1993).

Killingray, David, and David Omissi (eds.), *Guardians of Empire: The Armed Forces of the Colonial Powers c.1700-1964* (Manchester, New York: Manchester University Press, 1999).

Killingray, David, and Richard Rathbone (eds.), *Africa and the Second World*

War (New York: St. Martins Press, 1986).

Killingray, David, 'The Maintenance of Law and Order in British Colonial Africa', *African Affairs*, 85 (1986), pp. 411-37.

______. 'The Idea of a British Imperial African Army', *Journal of African History*, 20/3 (1979), pp. 421-36.

Kirk-Greene, Anthony, *On Crown Service: A History of HM Colonial and Overseas Civil Services, 1837-1997* (London: I.B. Tauris, 1999).

Kitching, Gavin, *Class and Economic Change in Kenya: The Making of an African Petite-Bourgeoisie 1905-1970* (New Haven and London: Yale University Press, 1980).

Kitson, Frank, *Bunch of Five* (London: Faber & Faber, 1977).

______. *Low Intensity Operations: Subversion, Insurgency and Peacekeeping* (London: Faber & Faber, 1971).

______. *Gangs and Counter-Gangs* (London: Barrie & Rockliff, 1960).

Kyle, Keith, *The Politics of the Independence of Kenya* (London: Macmillan, 1999).

______. *Suez* (New York: St. Martin's Press, 1991).

Lamb, Richard, *The Macmillan Years 1957-1963: The Emerging Truth* (London: John Murray, 1995).

______. *The Failure of the Eden Government* (London: Sidgwick & Jackson, 1987).

Lapping, Brian, *End of Empire* (London: Granada, 1985).

Laqueur, Walter, *Guerrilla: A Historical and Critical Study* London: Weidenfeld & Nicolson, 1977).

Lee, Air Chief Marshall Sir David, *Flight from the Middle East: A History of the Royal Air Force in the Arabian Peninsula and Adjacent Territories 1945-1972* (London: HMSO, 1980).

Leys, Colin, *Underdevelopment in Kenya: The Political Economy of Neo-Colonialism* (London: Heinemann, 1976 [1975]).

Liang, Hsi-Huey, *The Rise of Modern Police and the European State System from Metternich to the Second World War* (Cambridge: Cambridge University Press, 1992).

Lonsdale, John, 'Mau Maus of the Mind: Making Mau Mau and Remaking Kenya', *Journal of African History*, 31 (1990), pp. 393-421.

Louis, Wm. Roger, and Ronald Robinson, 'The Imperialism of Decolonization', *Journal of Imperial and Commonwealth History*, 22/3 (1994), pp. 462-513.

Louis, Wm. Roger, and Roger Owen (eds.), *Suez 1956: The Crisis and its Consequences* (Oxford, Clarendon Press, 1991 [1989]).

Low, D.A., *Eclipse of Empire* (Cambridge: Cambridge University Press, 1991).

Low, D.A., and Alison Smith (eds.), *History of East Africa* Vol. III (Oxford: Clarendon Press, 1976).

Lunt, James, *Imperial Sunset: Frontier Soldiering in the 20th Century* (London: Macdonald, 1981).

Lustgarten, Laurence, and Ian Leigh, *In from the Cold: National Security and Parliamentary Democracy* (Oxford: Clarendon Press, 1994).

MacDonald, Malcolm, *Titans and Others* (London: Collins, 1972).

MacKenzie, J.M., *The Partition of Africa 1880-1900* (London, New York: Methuen, 1983).

Macmillan, Harold, *At the End of the Day, 1961-63* (London: Macmillan, 1973).
______. *Pointing the Way, 1959-61* (London: Macmillan, 1972).
______. *Riding the Storm, 1956-59* (London: Macmillan, 1971).
______. *Tides of Fortune, 1945-55* (London: Macmillan, 1969).
Maloba, Wunyabari O., *Mau Mau and Kenya: An Analysis of a Peasant Revolt* (Oxford: James Currey, 1998 [1993]).
Mansfield, Peter, *A History of the Middle East* (London: Viking, 1991).
Maudling, Reginald, *Memoirs* (London: Sidgwick & Jackson, 1979).
Mboya, Tom, *Freedom and After* (London: Andre Deutsch, 1963).
Messenger, Charles (ed.), *Reader's Guide to Military History* (Chicago, London: Fitzroy Dearborn, 2001).
Mockaitis, Thomas R., *British Counterinsurgency, 1919-1960* (London: Macmillan, 1990).
______. 'The Origins of British Counter-Insurgency', *Small Wars and Insurgencies*, 1/3 (1990), pp. 209-225.
Monroe, Elizabeth, 'British Bases in the Middle East: Assets or Liabilities?', *International Affairs*, 42/1 (1966), pp. 24-34.
______. *Britain's Moment in the Middle East, 1914-1956* (London: Chatto & Windus, 1963).
Morgan, A., *Harold Wilson* (London: Pluto, 1992).
Morris-Jones, W.H., and Georges Fischer (eds.), *Decolonisation and After: The British and French Experience* (London: Frank Cass, 1980).
Murphy, Philip, *Alan Lennox-Boyd: A Biography* (London: I.B. Tauris, 1999).
______. *Party Politics and Decolonization: The Conservative Party and British Colonial Policy in Tropical Africa, 1951-1964* (Oxford: Clarendon Press, 1995).
Murray-Brown, Jeremy, *Kenyatta* (London: Allen & Unwin, 1979).
Newsinger, John, 'Revolt and Repression in Kenya: The Mau Mau Rebellion, 1952-1960', *Science and Society*, 45/2 (Summer 1981), pp. 159-85.
Odinga, Oginga, *Not Yet Uhuru: the autobiography of Oginga Odinga* (London, Ibadan, Nairobi: Heinemann, 1969 [1967]).
Ogot, B.A., and W.R. Ochieng' (eds.), *Decolonization and Independence in Kenya 1940-93* (London: James Currey, 1995).
Omosule, Monone 'Kiama kia Muingi: Kikuyu Reaction to Land Consolidation in Kenya, 1955-1959', *Transafrican Journal of History*, 4/1-2 (1974), pp. 115-34.
Ovendale, Ritchie, 'Macmillan and the Wind of Change in Africa, 1957-60', *Historical Journal*, 38/2 (1995), pp. 455-77.
______. (ed.), *British Defence Policy Since 1945* (Manchester: Manchester University Press, 1994).
Page, Malcolm, *KAR: A History of the King's African Rifles and East African Forces* (London: Leo Cooper, 1998).
Paget, Julian, *Counter-Insurgency Operations: Techniques of Guerrilla Warfare* (New York: Walker & Co., 1967).
Percox, David A., 'Internal Security and Decolonization in Kenya, 1956-63' *Journal of Imperial and Commonwealth History*, 29/1 (Jan. 2001), pp. 92-116.
______. 'British Counter-Insurgency in Kenya, 1952-56: Extension of

Internal Security Policy or Prelude to Decolonisation?', *Small Wars and Insurgencies*, 9/3 (1998), pp. 46-101.

Pickering, Jeffrey, *Britain's Withdrawal from East of Suez: The Politics of Retrenchment* (London: Macmillan, 1998).

Pimlott, B., *Harold Wilson* (London: Harper Collins, 1993 [1992]).

Ponting, C., *Breach of Promise: Labour in Power 1964-1970* (London: Hamilton, 1989).

Popplewell, Richard, '"Lacking Intelligence": Some Reflections on Recent Approaches to British Counter-insurgency, 1900-1960', *Intelligence and National Security*, 10/2 (1995), pp. 336-352.

Porter, A.N., and A.J. Stockwell (eds.), *British Imperial Policy and Decolonization, 1938-64* Two Volumes (London: Macmillan, 1989, 1987).

Porter, Bernard, *Plots and Paranoia: A History of Political Espionage in Britain 1790-1988* (London: Unwin Hyman, 1989).

______. *The Lion's Share: A Short History of British Imperialism, 1850-1970* (London, New York: Longman, 1975).

Pratt, Cranford, *The Critical Phase in Tanzania 1945-1968* (Cambridge: Cambridge University Press, 1976).

Ramsden, John, *The Winds of Change: Macmillan to Heath, 1957-1975* (Harlow: Longman, 1996).

Reynolds, David, *Britannia Overruled: British Policy and World Power in the Twentieth Century* (Harlow: Longman, 1991).

Rosberg, Carl G., and John Nottingham, *The Myth of "Mau Mau": Nationalism in Kenya* (New York: Praeger, 1966).

Sampson, Anthony, *Macmillan: A Study in Ambiguity* (London: Allen Lane, 1967).

Sanders, David, *Losing an Empire, Finding a Role: British Foreign Policy since 1945* (London: Macmillan, 1990).

Scott, L.V., *Conscription and the Attlee Governments: The Politics and Policy of National Service, 1945-1951* (Oxford: Clarendon Press, 1993).

Shepherd, Robert, *Iain Macleod* (London: Hutchinson, 1994).

Tamarkin, M., 'Mau Mau in Nakuru', *Kenya Historical Review*, 5/2 (1977), pp. 225-41.

Thorpe, D.R., *Alec Douglas-Home* (London: Sinclair-Stevenson, 1996).

Throup, David W., *Economic and Social Origins of Mau Mau 1945-53* (London: Currey, 1987).

Thurlow, Richard, *The Secret State: British Internal Security in the Twentieth Century* (Oxford: Blackwell, 1994).

Thurston, Anne, *Sources for Colonial Studies in the Public Record Office: Records of the Colonial Office, Dominions Office, Commonwealth Relations Office and Commonwealth Office* (London: HMSO, 1995).

______. *Smallholder Agriculture in Kenya: The Official Mind and the Swynnerton Plan* (Cambridge: Cambridge University Press, 1987).

Tignor, Robert L., *Capitalism and Nationalism at the End of Empire: State and Business in Decolonizing Egypt, Nigeria, and Kenya, 1945-1963* (Princeton NJ: Princeton University Press, 1998).

Towle, Philip Anthony, *Pilots and Rebels: The Use of Aircraft in Unconventional Warfare, 1918-1988* (London: Brassey's, 1989).

Townshend, Charles, *Making the Peace: Public Order and Public Security in Modern Britain* (Oxford: Oxford University Press, 1993).

______. *Britain's Civil Wars: Counterinsurgency in the Twentieth Century* (London: Faber, 1986).

Trench, Charles Chenevix, *Men Who Ruled Kenya: The Kenya Administration, 1892-1963* (London: Radcliffe, 1993).

Turner, J., *Macmillan* (London: Longman, 1994).

Verrier, Anthony, *An Army for the Sixties: A Study in National Policy, Contract and Obligation* (London: Secker & Warburg, 1966).

Watt, D.C., 'The Decision to Withdraw from the Gulf', *Political Quarterly*, 39 (1968), pp. 311-18.

West, Nigel, *A Matter of Trust: MI5 1945-72* (London: Weidenfeld & Nicolson, 1982).

Widner, Jennifer, *The Rise of a Party-State in Kenya: From Harambee! to Nyayo!* (Berkeley, Los Angeles CA: University of California Press, 1992).

Wilson, Keith M. (ed.), *Imperialism and Nationalism in the Middle East: The Anglo-Egyptian Experience 1992-1982* (London: Mansell, 1983).

Wright, Peter, with Paul Greengrass, *Spycatcher* (Richmond, Victoria: Heinemann Australia, 1987).

Yeager , Rodger, *Tanzania: An African Experiment* (London: Dartmouth, 1989).

Young, John W. (ed.), *The Foreign Policy of Churchill's Peacetime Administration 1951-1955* (Leicester: Leicester University Press, 1988).

Young, Kenneth, *Sir Alec Douglas-Home* (London: Dent, 1970).

Unpublished Secondary Sources

Dockrill, Saki, 'Britain's Power and Influence: Dealing with Three Roles and the Wilson Government's Defence Debate at Chequers in November 1964', draft, courtesy of Dr Dockrill, November 1999.

Heather, R.W., 'Counterinsurgency and intelligence in Kenya: 1952-6', PhD thesis, University of Cambridge, 1994.

Kyle, Keith, 'The End of Empire in Kenya', University of London, Institute of Commonwealth Studies Postgraduate Seminar Paper, courtesy of the ICS, 14 March 1996.

Morrison, H., '"Quis custodiet ipsos custodes?": The problems of policing in Anglophone Africa during the transfer of power', PhD thesis, University of Aberdeen, 1995.

Murphy, Philip, '"Holding Back the Tides"? Alan Lennox-Boyd at the Colonial Office, 1954-59', University of London, Institute of Commonwealth Studies Postgraduate Seminar Paper, courtesy of the ICS, 28 March 1996.

______. 'Tory Reactions to Rapid Decolonization in East and Central Africa', University of London, Institute of Commonwealth Studies Postgraduate Seminar Paper, courtesy of the ICS, 21 October 1993.

Percox, David A., 'The British Campaign in Kenya, 1952-1956: The Development of Counter-Insurgency Policy', MA, Lancaster, 1996.

INDEX